JOANNA LILLIS is a Kazakhstan-based journalist reporting on Central Asia whose work has featured in outlets including *The Economist*, the *Guardian* and the *Independent*, the *Eurasianet* website, and *Foreign Policy* and *POLITICO* magazines. Prior to settling in Kazakhstan in 2005, she lived in Russia and Uzbekistan between 1995 and 2005, and worked for BBC Monitoring, the BBC World Service's global media tracking service. While completing a BA in Modern Languages at the University of Leeds, she studied Russian in the Soviet republics of Belorussia and Ukraine before the collapse of the USSR, and she has an MA in Translation and Interpreting from the University of Bradford.

'This is the essential book about an increasingly important, but highly secretive, country. With a keen eye and sharp analysis, Joanna Lillis goes beyond the "post-Soviet" clichés to explore the depths of Kazakhstan's politics, history and money.'

Peter Pomerantsev, author of *Nothing is True
and Everything is Possible: Adventures in Modern Russia*

'Astute, refreshing and revelatory.'

Peter Frankopan, *The Spectator*

DARK SHADOWS

Inside the Secret World of Kazakhstan

JOANNA LILLIS

BLOOMSBURY ACADEMIC
LONDON · NEW YORK · OXFORD · NEW DELHI · SYDNEY

BLOOMSBURY ACADEMIC
Bloomsbury Publishing Plc
50 Bedford Square, London, WC1B 3DP, UK
1385 Broadway, New York, NY 10018, USA
29 Earlsfort Terrace, Dublin 2, Ireland

BLOOMSBURY, BLOOMSBURY ACADEMIC and the Diana
logo are trademarks of Bloomsbury Publishing Plc

First published in Great Britain 2018
This edition published 2022

Cover design by Nam Cho
Cover illustration: Akorda presidential palace, Nur-Sultan, Kazakhstan.

A catalogue record for this book is available from the British Library.

A catalog record for this book is available from the Library of Congress.

ISBN: PB: 978-0-7556-2669-4
          ePDF: 978-0-7556-2671-7
          ebook: 978-0-7556-2670-0

Printed and bound in Great Britain

To find out more about our authors and books visit www.
bloomsbury.com and sign up for our newsletters.

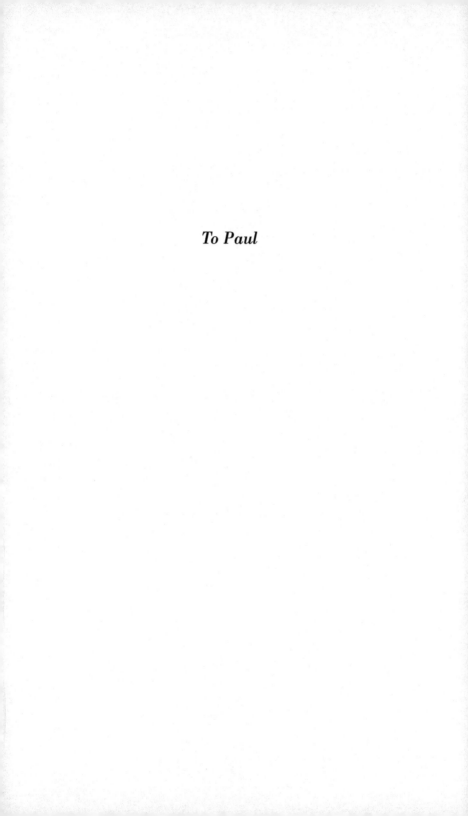

To Paul

Contents

III. Stories from the Steppe

Жамандықты кім көрмейді? Үмітін үзбек – қайратсыздық. Дүниеде ешнәрседе баян жоқ екені рас, жамандық та қайдан баяндап қалады дейсің? Қары қалың қатты қыстың артынан көгі қалың, көлі мол жақсы жаз келмеуші ме еді?

АБАЙ ҚҰНАНБАЙҰЛЫ

Who has not encountered misfortune? To lose hope is spineless. Truly, nothing in the world is immutable. How can you say that misfortune lasts forever? Is not a harsh winter with thick snow followed by a good summer with thick grass and bountiful lakes?

KAZAKH POET ABAY KUNANBAYULY

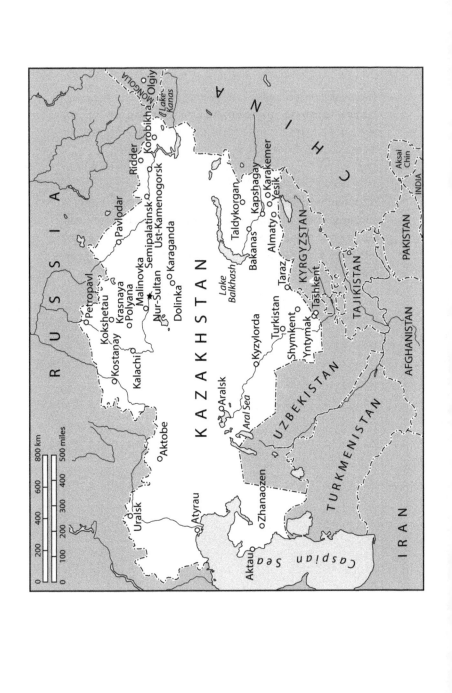

Kazakhstan historical timeline

1465 Kazakh Khanate founded

1584 Cossacks build military settlement at site that is now Uralsk/Oral

1613 Official foundation of Yaitskiy Gorodok (Uralsk/Oral) marks Russian expansion into present-day Republic of Kazakhstan

1718 Foundation of Semipalatinsk (Semey)

1720 Foundation of Ust-Kamenogorsk (Oskemen)

1720s Dzungar raids lead to '*aktaban shubyryndy*' ('barefooted flight'), an exodus of Kazakhs, which motivates tribes to seek alliances with Russia

1731 Kishi Zhuz khan swears oath of allegiance to Russia

1740 Orta Zhuz khan swears oath of allegiance to Russia

1742 Uly Zhuz khan swears oath of allegiance to Russia

1773 Pugachev Rebellion starts in Yaitsk (Uralsk/Oral)

1820s Russians abolish khan rule over Kishi Zhuz and Orta Zhuz and assume direct control

1841 Kazakh Khanate revived under Kenesary Khan, during uprising against Russian rule

1847 Death in battle of Kenesary Khan marks end of Kazakh Khanate

1854 Foundation of Fort Vernyy (Almaty)

1864 Conquest of Chimkent (Shymkent) and Turkestan (Turkistan) seals Russian control over territory that is now Republic of Kazakhstan; remaining Kazakh tribes are then subsumed into Russian Empire

1916 World War I anti-conscription uprising in Central Asia

1917 Russian Revolution

1917–20 Civil war in parts of Kazakhstan; *Alash Orda* movement set up in abortive bid to win Kazakh autonomy; bid for Central Asian self-determination by Turkestan (Kokand) Autonomy crushed

1920 Kirgiz Autonomous Soviet Socialist Republic formed in Kazakhstan

1925 Republic renamed Kazakh Autonomous Soviet Socialist Republic

1927 Collectivisation of agriculture begins

1930–33 *Asharshylyk* (famine) in Kazakhstan

1930 Turksib railway completed, linking Central Asia to Russia via Kazakhstan

1931 Karlag prison camp opens as Gulag system rolled out in Kazakhstan

1936 Kazakh Soviet Socialist Republic formed

1937–38 Height of Stalin's Terror, which decimates Kazakh intelligentsia

1940 President Nursultan Nazarbayev born in Shamalgan

1940s Deportations to Kazakhstan of peoples from other parts of USSR

1949 Soviet Union conducts first successful nuclear weapons test at Semipalatinsk

1950s Virgin Lands agricultural programme begins in northern Kazakhstan

1959 Karlag prison camp closed down

1960 Dinmukhamed Kunayev appointed first secretary of Communist Party of Kazakhstan's Central Committee

1960s Aral Sea starts shrinking owing to diversion of waters for agricultural use

1984 Nazarbayev appointed chairman of Kazakhstan's Council of Ministers

1986 *Zheltoksan* (December) protests following Kunayev's dismissal

1989 Nazarbayev appointed first secretary of Communist Party of Kazakhstan's Central Committee

Last nuclear explosion at Semipalatinsk test ground; moratorium takes effect

1990 Nazarbayev becomes Kazakh president through rubber-stamp vote in Kazakhstan's Supreme Soviet (parliament)

1991 Kazakhstan gains independence after USSR's collapse

Nazarbayev wins presidential election with 99 per cent of vote

Semipalatinsk nuclear test ground closed down

Attempt to mark Cossack celebration in Uralsk increases separatist tensions

1994 Parliament votes to move capital from Almaty to Akmola

1995 Nazarbayev dissolves parliament to rule by decree

Nazarbayev's term of office extended until 2000 through referendum

1997 Capital moves from Almaty to Akmola

1998 Akmola renamed Astana and officially unveiled as capital

Constitution amended, extending presidential term and removing upper age limit

1999 Nazarbayev re-elected with 81 per cent of vote

Nazarbayev's Otan party wins majority in parliamentary election; four other parties and movements win seats

Russian separatist plot foiled in Ust-Kamenogorsk

2000 *Respublika* newspaper founded

2001 Kazakhgate 'oil contracts for kickbacks' corruption scandal breaks
Democratic Choice of Kazakhstan (DVK) reform movement founded

2002 DVK co-founders Mukhtar Ablyazov and Galymzhan Zhakiyanov jailed on corruption charges
Respublika newspaper targeted with decapitated dog and firebombed

2003 Ablyazov pardoned and released from prison
Journalist Sergey Duvanov jailed on charges of raping a minor
Middleman James Giffen arrested in USA in Kazakhgate investigation

2004 Nazarbayev's Otan party wins majority in parliamentary elections; three other pro-government parties enter parliament; opposition wins single seat
Ablyazov's business partner Yerzhan Tatishev killed on hunting trip; death ruled an accident

2005 Court orders disbandment of DVK
Opposition politician Zamanbek Nurkadilov found shot dead; death ruled a suicide
Nazarbayev re-elected with 91 per cent of vote

2006 Opposition leader Altynbek Sarsenbayev shot dead; family condemns murder trial as political cover-up
150 children infected with HIV in hospitals in Shymkent through corruption and negligence

2007 Parliament approves 'president for life' constitutional amendment allowing Nazarbayev to run for an unlimited number of terms
Nazarbayev's Nur Otan party wins all elected seats in parliamentary election
Disappearance of two bankers leads to downfall of Rakhat Aliyev, who is divorced by Dariga Nazarbayeva, the president's daughter, and declared wanted by Kazakhstan
Kazakh, US and Swiss governments agree that Kazakhstan will give $84 million in Kazakhgate bribery proceeds to charity

2008 Aliyev sentenced *in absentia* to 40 years in prison in Kazakhstan on charges including abduction, embezzlement and coup plotting

2009 Ablyazov leaves Kazakhstan for UK
Human rights campaigner Yevgeniy Zhovtis jailed over fatal traffic accident

2010 Kazakhstan chairs Organisation for Security and Cooperation in Europe (OSCE)

Nazarbayev granted title *Yelbasy* (Leader of the Nation), with extra privileges

Kazakhgate corruption case ends with middleman James Giffen pleading guilty to one tax misdemeanour in USA

2011 Nazarbayev re-elected with 96 per cent of vote

Fifteen civilians shot dead in clashes between striking oil workers and security forces in Zhanaozen

2012 Nazarbayev's Nur Otan party wins majority in parliamentary elections; two other pro-government parties win seats

Ablyazov flees UK after being sentenced to jail for contempt of court

Media crackdown: 36 independent outlets closed, including *Respublika* newspaper

2013 Ablyazov detained in France

2014 Protests in Almaty over currency devaluation

Eurasian Economic Union founding treaty signed

Sarsenbayev murder retrial finds Aliyev contracted his killing

Aliyev gives himself up to Austrian authorities to face trial on charges of murdering two bankers

2015 Aliyev found hanged in Austrian prison cell; death ruled a suicide

Nazarbayev re-elected with 98 per cent of vote

More independent media outlets closed, including *Adam bol* and *Adam*

2016 Nazarbayev's Nur Otan party wins majority in parliamentary elections; two other pro-government parties win seats

Land protests around Kazakhstan; businessman Tokhtar Tuleshov and civil society campaigners Maks Bokayev and Talgat Ayan jailed

Ablyazov released after winning legal battle in France against extradition to Russia

2017 Ablyazov sentenced *in absentia* to 20 years in prison in Kazakhstan on corruption charges; he re-forms DVK opposition movement

2018 Court bans DVK; crackdown on supporters begins

2019 Nazarbayev resigns as president to occupy Leader of the Nation role; Qasym-Jomart Toqayev assumes presidency

Astana renamed Nur-Sultan

2020 Eleven people killed in ethnic violence during attacks on Dungan villages in south-eastern Kazakhstan

2021 Nur Otan party wins majority in Kazakhstan's first parliamentary elections featuring no opposition parties on the ballot; two other pro-government parties win seats

2022 Violent unrest in Kazakhstan heralds end of Nazarbayev era

Note on transliteration and names

For transliteration from Russian, I have used the BGN/PCGN (United States Board on Geographic Names/Permanent Committee on Geographical Names for British official use) system, but I have simplified transliteration of the Cyrillic letter 'ё' to 'yo' (except in the names Gorbachev and Pugachev, since most historical sources render them using 'e'). For transliteration from the Kazakh Cyrillic alphabet, I have deviated from the BGN/PCGN system to use a simplified method that does not use the letter 'q' or apply diacritics, in the interests of ease for non-Kazakh-speaking readers. Deviations from my system include rendering names of organisations as they spell themselves at the time of writing in Latin script (Kairat football club, rather than Kayrat, for example); rendering names as people are known professionally by a certain spelling (Qasym-Jomart Toqayev rather than Kasym-Zhomart Tokayev and Erlan Idrissov, rather than Yerlan Idrisov, for example); and in the rendering of the word for 'village', which I have transliterated as *aul* (the Russian form) rather than '*auyl*' (the Kazakh), since the former is more commonly found in English-language sources. In quotes from English-language sources, I have retained the transliteration used in the original source. I have not used the new Latin alphabet for the Kazakh language, approved in 2018 and modified in 2021, and due to come into force fully in Kazakhstan by 2031.

I have sometimes referred to interviewees using first names or polite forms of address rather than surnames: patronymics in the Russian style, which Kazakhs still widely use, or Kazakh terms of address for respected figures.

Many places in Kazakhstan have two names: a Kazakh name and a Russian one. I have tended to use Kazakh names, except in cases where the place has not been officially renamed since independence, such as Ust-Kamenogorsk; or in cases where the Kazakh may cause confusion, such as the town of Aral near the Aral Sea, which I refer to by its Russian name, Aralsk, to distinguish it from the sea. In some cases, I use the pre-independence Russian name when writing about events that took place in tsarist or Soviet times (Alma-Ata for the city that is now Almaty, for example).

Introduction

Kazakhstan first clicked into my consciousness on 3 August 1988, at a football match in Minsk, the capital of a place that no longer exists: Soviet Belorussia. As Dinamo Minsk kicked off, I wondered where the other team was from – 'Kairat' sounded strange, certainly not Russian. It turned out Kairat were from an exotic-sounding city called Alma-Ata, 4,500 kilometres away in Central Asia, in a place called Kazakhstan on the eastern fringe of the USSR – about as far as you could go across the country before hitting China, in fact. I was a Russian-language student on my first visit to the Soviet Union, and the sight of this team from Kazakhstan – which thrashed Dinamo Minsk 3–0 – brought home to me just what a vast country this was. Minsk, with its brutalist architecture and food queues, had come as a culture shock – what on earth might far-off Alma-Ata be like?

It would be another 13 years before I actually set foot in Kazakhstan, a decade after the collapse of the USSR, when it was an independent state which had emerged blinking from a post-Soviet depression and stumbled into an oil boom. Between 2001 and 2005 my travels in Kazakhstan took me all over the country, and in 2005 I moved there to work as a journalist. Reporting on Kazakhstan seemed to me important, partly because it often seemed to take a back seat in international media coverage of Central Asia. Journalists appeared to consider it the least sexy of the 'Stans', the five countries of post-Soviet Central Asia: less eccentric than Turkmenistan, less dictatorial than Uzbekistan, less exotic than Tajikistan, less turbulent than Kyrgyzstan. It often came through to the West in clichés, through broad-brush images of a brash oil-rich nation run by a zany autocrat basking in a cult of personality. And a lot of people in Britain, where I come from, had not heard of it at all.

Kazakhstan was nuanced, its stories often difficult to tease out – but there are countless stories to be told. Over the last twenty years I have had encounters with people the length and breadth of this vast and beautiful country, which have mostly been extraordinary and inspiring, sometimes depressing and often pleasingly quirky: from principled politicians to crusading journalists, from strutting oligarchs to striking oilmen, from survivors of famine to victims of nuclear testing.

This is a book about Kazakhstan – the people who live there, and the stories that they have so generously shared with me over the years.

It was the study of the Russian language that took me to the USSR in the first place, in the late 1980s.

I started learning Russian in 1984, when the Soviet Union was in the grip of a period of decline known as the 'Era of Stagnation', ruled by the last in a succession of doddering leaders who presided over that dispiriting age: Konstantin Chernenko, whose death in 1985 ushered in a time of dramatic transformation that ultimately led to the collapse of the USSR.

I chose to study Russian more by accident than design – because I liked languages and it was offered at my local sixth-form college as a course from scratch to A level in two years – but I had no particular yearning to visit the stagnating USSR, and the idea that this choice would later lead me to spend half my life in the former Soviet Union and take me to live in Kazakhstan in the twenty-first century would have seemed preposterous: to all of us then the USSR seemed like a colossus that would last forever.

The Cold War between the West and the 'Evil Empire' (in the demonising epithet coined by Ronald Reagan) was in full swing, but around the time I started learning Russian the Soviet Union began to feature on British TV screens as a place where people just like ourselves lived. I was entranced by *Comrades*, a series of BBC fly-on-the-wall documentaries that went behind the Iron Curtain to look at how ordinary Soviets lived – from a schoolteacher to an underground jazz musician – and revealed that there was far more to the USSR than communists, dissidents and food queues.

In 1985 Chernenko died, and the reformer Mikhail Gorbachev came to power and set in motion some drastic policy changes that unintentionally paved the way for the fall of the Soviet Union: glasnost (openness, to political debate) and perestroika (restructuring, of the creaking economy), which unleashed a new wave of Western interest in the USSR. Exciting things seemed to be happening there, and after I finished my A levels I chose a degree course – Modern Languages at the University of Leeds, specialising in Russian and French – that would take me behind the Iron Curtain to see the 'Evil Empire' with my own eyes.

My first visit to the USSR was in 1988, to attend a Russian-language summer school in Minsk. The town was no beauty – razed in World War II, it had been rebuilt as a Soviet city par excellence, a monument to socialist realism that, to my eyes (seeing the Soviet Union for the first time), appeared drab and soulless as much as monumental and impressive. Yet coming into contact with Soviet people for the first time was exciting, and in spring 1989 I returned to the USSR for three months to study Russian at the university in Kiev (nowadays Kyiv), the capital of Soviet Ukraine, which had hit the headlines three years earlier when the Chernobyl nuclear power station had exploded nearby. Kiev was a city of golden cupolas offsetting the grey Soviet tower blocks, and beaches lining the Dnieper River where we swam and sunbathed, heedless of the dangers from radiation exposure. In Gidropark ('Hydropark', where we used to go for swimming and kebabs) loudspeakers were broadcasting the proceedings of the Congress of People's Deputies, a new Soviet parliament just created by Gorbachev. I paid little heed to the droning of the long speeches crackling through the loudspeakers, but had I listened harder I would have heard the Kazakh poet Mukhtar Shakhanov, whom I interviewed in Kazakhstan twenty-seven years later, railing against a political crackdown on Kazakh 'nationalists' following anti-Soviet riots in Alma-Ata three years earlier.

With glasnost in full swing, we foreign students lived alongside our Soviet counterparts in the same dorms, and we could discuss whatever we liked – though we suspected there were informers in our midst. Most of the time we just hung around, drinking vodka (if we could get it – Gorbachev had introduced measures dubbed 'dry law' to root out alcoholism, and it was not easy to procure), but sometimes we talked of serious matters: whether perestroika would work, how far glasnost could go (the Soviet students got irate if any foreign students tested its limits by making disparaging remarks about Lenin, which was still a complete no-no) and whether the war in Afghanistan – from which the last Soviet troops had just been pulled out – had been a mistake, a conversation that was sparked by the horrific sight of a young man on a trolleybus in Kiev who had had both his legs blown off.

When I returned to Leeds to finish my degree, I was hooked on the exhilaration of experiencing this different world behind the Iron Curtain at a time of momentous change, and I decided to return after my graduation in 1991 – little knowing that by that time the Soviet Union would be disintegrating into the dustbin of history.

In 1992 I moved to Moscow, by now in independent Russia, to teach English at a university. It was a turbulent year and often bleak, as Russians wrestled with the aftershocks of the USSR's collapse. These were the years of 'shock therapy' – the blitzkrieg replacement of communism with capitalism that pitched millions into destitution – and the sight of babushkas flogging their meagre possessions on Moscow's pavements for the price of a loaf of bread has always stayed with me. I lived in a student dorm, on a 'posh' floor reserved for teachers, which for some reason I shared with some Bangladeshi traders who used to bring home wads of roubles in plastic bags every evening until armed robbers burst in one day and stole their money at gunpoint. Life in Moscow was edgy, and I hung around with my students and my Bangladeshi neighbours, and occasionally – when I could get the money together to buy overpriced drinks (I earned the same salary as the Russian lecturers, which was a pittance) – with the expats who frequented Moscow's wild pubs, where customers danced on the bar and guns were occasionally fired. Shortly before Boris Yeltsin shelled the Russian parliament to resolve a political stand-off, I left Russia to do an MA in Translation and Interpreting in the UK. I was keen on a career as a UN interpreter, but then I realised I had no desire to live in the places where this would be possible – New York, Geneva, Paris. They seemed too sedate after the rollercoaster of 1990s Russia, so I went back to Moscow. I returned in 1995, first working in a menial job at the British embassy (as 'social secretary' to the ambassador, organising his receptions and dinners) then joining BBC

Monitoring's Moscow bureau. I lived through the rest of Yeltsin's reckless rule of a Russia in dramatic flux, leaving just after Vladimir Putin came to power in 2000.

By 2001, drawn to Central Asia, I was working for BBC Monitoring at its bureau in Uzbekistan. This was the land of the fabled turquoise-domed Silk Road cities of Samarkand, Bukhara and Khiva, which were mind-blowingly beautiful places. It was also an unreconstructed dicta-torship, run by the tyrannical Islam Karimov, with violent excesses that sounded like something out of a medieval emirate: in one case which became notorious while I lived there, two dissidents were killed through immersion in hot water – effectively boiled alive. Politics in Moscow in the 1990s had been stormy and exciting – here, in a country completely lacking opposition parties and political debate, it was soporific on the surface and deadly beneath. Russia had been growing more authoritarian over the years that I lived there – but Uzbekistan was a real police state. Green-uniformed officers lined Mustaqillik, a broad avenue behind which I lived in a Soviet tower block, and the road closed twice a day so that Karimov could zoom between his residence and his office, AK-47-toting guards hanging out of the windows of the cavalcade of black jeeps that accompanied him.

Uzbekistan came as a culture shock: it seemed somehow more impenetrable than Russia because so much went on unseen, below the surface. There was also a linguistic shock: I had harboured the blasé certainty that speaking Russian would get me all over the Soviet Union (it did, and mostly still does), but as I found out when I first visited Khiva, there were places where the colonial language was either being forgotten or had not penetrated very far in the first place. (Nowadays, there are even more such places.) At first, I tended to view the world of Uzbekistan through a Russian prism, but life there suggested I should tilt the angle of my globe and look from a different perspective: that of the people who lived there.

Then, a month after I arrived in Uzbekistan, the world was turned upside down. I was sitting in a rented flat in Bukhara when the landlord came running round to tell me to turn the TV on: New York was under attack. I switched on Uzbek TV – but it was so heavily censored that it could not react to the news that was gripping the rest of the world, so while channels around the globe began breathless live reporting on the crisis, screens in Uzbekistan continued to show the balls pinging back and forth in a local tennis competition. We switched to Russian TV to watch the planes crashing into the Twin Towers, not suspecting that this would bring war to Uzbekistan's doorstep. The drama of 9/11 briefly put Central Asia in the global spotlight as the US burst into Russia's former sphere of influence, invading Afghanistan to pursue Osama bin Laden and toppling the Taliban in the process. The US opened airbases in Uzbekistan and Kyrgyzstan, and Craig Murray, the British ambassador in Tashkent, scandalised his own government when he publicly attacked it for cosying up to serial human rights abuser Uzbekistan. Alongside his younger Uzbek lover, with whom he had shacked up in his official residence, he also became renowned for hosting wild embassy parties that were a far cry from the usual stuffy diplomatic receptions.[1]

I left Uzbekistan in March 2005, two months before the regime gunned down hundreds of protesters in the city of Andijan, when my secondment to Tashkent with BBC Monitoring finished. I had a permanent job in their headquarters in Reading, but neither the work nor the idea of moving back to Britain after a decade in the former Soviet Union grabbed me. So I took the plunge and moved to Kazakhstan.

I paid my first visit to Kazakhstan in 2001, landing in Almaty in the middle of a thick December blizzard. I wanted to skate at the alpine fir-fringed Medeu ice rink – which I had heard about in Moscow, where I used to skate on winter afternoons along the frozen alleys at Gorky Park – but the blizzard was so severe that Medeu was closed. Nevertheless, Almaty was alluringly atmospheric. Snowflakes swirled around the golden crown atop the Hotel Kazakhstan, once the city's tallest building but now being dwarfed by new skyscrapers, and settled upon the golden cupola of the wedding-cake Russian church in Panfilov Park, where the trees drooped ethereally with thick layers of snow. Old Soviet trams juddered along, jostling for space with the flashy jeeps that had just started to crowd onto the streets, and the communist-era tower blocks were interspersed with little wooden houses that were a throwback to an earlier tsarist colonial past.

Almaty was no longer the capital of Kazakhstan, which had shifted a thousand kilometres north a few years earlier, but it did not seem to care: it was a jaunty, self-confident city, busy rebranding itself as the business and entertainment hub of Central Asia.

Astana, by contrast, seemed a sleepy place for a capital city when I stepped off a train two years after that first visit to Almaty, drawn there by the celebrations of its fifth anniversary as Kazakhstan's capital (I would later return for the tenth, fifteenth and twentieth anniversaries, too). On the right side of the Yesil River it looked like a provincial Soviet backwater (which indeed it had been until recently), with low-rise blocks of flats, unremarkable restaurants with surly service and limited menus and a run-down park in which the main attraction was a boy offering rides on a resigned-looking donkey. On the left bank, where dachas had stood until not long before, Nursultan Nazarbayev, the president who had been leader of Kazakhstan since Soviet times, was busy building his new city: the lollipop-shaped Bayterek Tower, opened less than a year before, loomed up in the middle of nowhere, and between the new ministries that were springing up were large empty spaces which are nowadays crowded with glitzy edifices. Astana, nowadays called Nur-Sultan, had already sparked plenty of headlines in the Western media about the space-age city rising out of the steppe at the whim of a Central Asian despot – but, hubristic though both its concept and design certainly were, the truth was clearly more complex: Astana was about the reinvention of a nation, and I watched, fascinated, over the years that followed as this old Soviet city was rapidly reinvented as a futuristic capital, at a breathtaking pace.

Over the next few years I would visit other places in Kazakhstan that offered tantalising glimpses of a land both blighted and beautiful, with a history both intriguing and troubled. I rattled through the western desert on a 900-kilometre train journey from Karakalpakstan in north-western Uzbekistan to Aktau, powerhouse of Kazakhstan's oil boom, and swam in the warm waters of the Caspian Sea. I travelled to Ust-Kamenogorsk, a gritty industrial city near the border with Siberia where most of the people were Russians, and to Semipalatinsk, a laid-back town in the north-east whose monuments are redolent with the history of Kazakhstan, and which had also given its name to a nuclear testing ground that wreaked havoc on the health of the people living around it. I stayed in a hamlet called Belaya Uba on the fir-fringed slopes of the majestic Altay Mountains in the east, and marvelled at the startling rock formations jutting out of Lake Burabay in the north. I saw camels galumphing across the western steppe lands, and horsemen galloping across the northern plains.

On a crisp February morning in 2006, six months after I moved to Kazakhstan to live, I watched the leaders of the country's political opposition carry aloft a flower-strewn coffin along Shevchenko Street in front of the neoclassical Academy of Sciences. An opposition leader had been shot dead, execution-style, his body left on a path in the mountains outside Almaty. The killing of Altynbek Sarsenbayev was shocking and horrifying, and it served as a gruesome reminder to me of the evil undercurrents rippling under the surface of Kazakhstan's political life.

Two months previously, I had reported on a presidential election which Nazarbayev won with a crushing landslide – and while it was a rigged one-horse race of the type favoured by Central Asia's autocrats, I had been struck by how vibrant the political debate seemed after Uzbekistan's stifling political silence. In Kazakhstan's presidential election in 2005 there were opposition candidates running, and it seemed incredible to me that on election day voters on the streets of Almaty would openly admit to voting for them. The political opposition existed in a state of constant pressure and intimidation, sometimes violent – but it existed. Yet although no one knew it at the time, that election was the last in which any opposition tried to challenge Nazarbayev, because over the years that followed it was hounded out of existence. For me, reporting on the presidential election in 2005 was engaging, because although Nazarbayev was a shoo-in, there were political battles being hard fought; but reporting on his last re-election a decade later in 2015 was dispiriting, because a vote that offered the people of Kazakhstan all the trappings of an election without the one essential ingredient – an actual political choice – seemed to me an insult to their intelligence. There was, by contrast, plenty of political drama when Nazarbayev stepped down as president in 2019. Reporting on Nazarbayev's handover to his handpicked successor, Qasym-Jomart Toqayev, and the often creative and sometimes absurd protests that followed as young people found their political voice while trying to seize this once-in-a-generation opportunity to push for change was inspiring – even if hopes that this would be a seminal moment for reform were not borne out. It was the end of an era for Kazakhstan – although not quite the start of the post-Nazarbayev age as the elder statesman still loomed over the political scene. Violent unrest that appeared to herald the end of the Nazarbayev era convulsed Kazakhstan in January 2022 as this paperback went to press, and is covered in a brief afterword.

'The Making of a Potentate', the first part of this book, charts this creeping authoritarianism that I observed in Kazakhstan over the course of his rule, and looks at what happened after he stepped down. It examines the towering figure of Nazarbayev and the cult of personality he has fostered around himself, and reveals the lengths – often extreme, sometimes farcical and absurd – to which the government goes in order to crush dissent. It charts the rise and fall of some colourful characters who have stormed over Kazakhstan's political scene, like Rakhat Aliyev, Nazarbayev's son-in-law who – quite literally – got away with murder before he ended up hanging from the bars of a prison cell in Vienna, and Mukhtar Ablyazov, a flamboyant tycoon and Nazarbayev foe who recounted his rollercoaster life to me in a plush skyscraper in the City of London after he fled Kazakhstan.

This section also looks at why many ordinary people in Kazakhstan admire and even revere their autocratic first president. Yet not everyone buys into the Nazarbayev dream, and reporting in 2011 from the riot-torn town of Zhanaozen, where striking oil workers had been shot dead by the security forces, was a chilling reminder of this.

There are stories here of political dissidents and courageous human rights campaigners who have crossed the regime and suffered the consequences, and crusading journalists who go to extraordinary lengths to get their stories out. I was reminded of this on a dark night in 2011 when I visited a semi-clandestine printing operation in Almaty that was a modern-day version of samizdat, a trick used by Soviet dissidents to bypass the censors, and on the afternoon in 2015 when I dropped in on a journalist who was on hunger strike in a futile attempt to stop the authorities from muzzling her magazine.

The government runs a formidable spin machine to generate positive coverage of Kazakhstan in the Western media, and supports the publication of hagiographic biographies of Nazarbayev, so telling these tales seemed an important counterweight to the starry-eyed PR.

Some of these stories may be dispiriting, perhaps – but they are also uplifting, because they reveal the indomitable spirit of so many people in Kazakhstan who are willing to risk being crushed by the bulldozer of repression to stand up for their rights and principles.

One afternoon in 2011 I met a man in a café in the unremarkable Almaty district of Tastak, who told me how his brother had been sentenced to death in Kazakhstan a quarter of a century earlier. At that time this man's brother was vilified as a traitor to the Soviet Union – but now he is celebrated as a hero of modern-day Kazakhstan. What led to his death was a protest which came to be known as 'Zheltoksan' ('December'), which erupted in midwinter 1986 into unrest on the streets of Alma-Ata and other towns that was brutally quelled by Soviet security forces in the middle of Gorbachev's political thaw.

This felt to me like the echo chamber of history, because the protest was sparked by grievances harboured by Kazakhs about being treated as second-class citizens in their own land, and these decades-old resentments reverberate today in Kazakhstan, where passionate debates rage over language, ethnicity and identity. Kazakhstan's twentieth-century history was traumatic, particularly the years during which Stalin ruled the Soviet Union, when the Kazakh population was decimated and their traditional way of life was wiped out. These traumas have left scars on the national psyche that will probably never heal.

Part Two of this book, 'Identity Crisis', explores the harrowing history that turned Kazakhstan into a melting pot of peoples, and Kazakhs into a minority in their own land. This history is told through the voices of the people who lived through it: the feisty nonagenarian who recounted how she survived famine and a forced march to China when she was six years old; the bright-eyed old Chechen lady who was branded a traitor by Stalin at the age of three months and deported as punishment to Central Asia; the elegant septuagenarian whose family was torn asunder as it faced the firing squad and the Gulag during the purges of the 1930s. There are few survivors of these tragedies left, so it seemed important to record their stories for posterity – and interviewing these redoubtable women was also extremely rewarding. I also interviewed Kazakhs in rural corners of

China and Mongolia whose families were cast abroad by the turbulence of Kazakhstan's twentieth-century history, and spoke to two bright and talented young women who have answered the Kazakh government's clarion call to come 'home' to Kazakhstan, and are thus contributing to this country undergoing another momentous transformation of its ethnic and linguistic landscape. Later, I interviewed Kazakhs from China who had tragic tales to tell about their own incarceration or the imprisonment of their relatives in the infamous 're-education camps' in Xinjiang in which the Chinese government was locking up ethnic minorities, and some of these harrowing stories form the basis of a new chapter in this latest edition of Dark Shadows.

One dazzlingly sunny winter afternoon in 2015 I stepped far back into history – half a millennium, onto a fifteenth-century battlefield in south-eastern Kazakhstan. This was a film set where the ancient history of the Kazakhs was being reimagined by a director with a passion for rebuffing Russian colonial interpretations. History is written by the victors, which in Kazakhstan's case meant the Russians and the Soviets, but now reinterpreting the past – both recent and distant – is in fashion as Kazakhstan grapples with questions of identity in the present. I started learning Kazakh when I moved to Almaty because it seemed to me impossible to understand Kazakhstan without understanding Kazakh, and while my knowledge of it has never reached the level of fluency of my Russian, the language has helped me see different dimensions in these debates.

One freezing morning in 2015 I drove along a lonely road that kept vanishing under snowdrifts to a hamlet called Kalachi in the icy expanses of northern Kazakhstan, where the villagers were suffering from a baffling affliction: they kept falling asleep for days and no one could work out why. The clue lay in emissions emanating from an abandoned Soviet uranium mine nearby, in a derelict landscape that had once hummed with life but was now a ghost town, filled with spectral ruins. This story captured the imagination of the world's media for its quirkiness, but to me it was also a living example of how Kazakhstan's Soviet past so often comes back to haunt it. I was reminded of this on other occasions, too: bumping in a jeep across a desert that had once been a sea, its waters sucked out by reckless Soviet planners; travelling across the silvery snowbound north-eastern steppe to a village called Znamenka, where the people told hair-raising tales of mushroom clouds exploding on the horizon in their childhood. In nearby Semipalatinsk, I visited a young woman left severely disabled by nuclear tests that had ceased before she was even born, and admired the courage of the loving mother who had dedicated every day of the previous quarter of a century to looking after her.

Part Three of this book, 'Stories from the Steppe', tells the human tales of people in Kazakhstan who are left grappling every day with the momentous consequences of the USSR's use of their country as a giant guinea pig for its industrial, atomic and agricultural experiments. I was left humbled by their courage and resilience in the face of a lifetime of adversity created by a faceless state that no longer exists.

This section also contains encounters that illustrate the sheer variety of lives that people are living across the enormous country that is Kazakhstan. There are the Russian Old Believers harbouring 500-year-old grievances in an out-of-the-way corner of the north-east, and the oddball atheist in a small town on the Russian border who has suffered prison and forced psychiatric treatment for his refusal to back down in a clash of principles with the state. There are also inspirational tales of people throwing their energies into labours of love, from the nuclear physicist-turned-ostrich farmer tending his brood of gangling bipeds, to the government minister-turned-viticulturist reinventing a dilapidated Soviet collective farm as a boutique winery.

These snapshots will, I hope, conjure up a picture of Kazakhstan in all its diversity, as a vibrant, living, breathing place, full of extraordinary people living extraordinary lives.

I

THE MAKING OF
A POTENTATE

CHAPTER 1

Arise, Kazakhstan

Astana, 2008

Kazakhstan's capital is in festive mood. The lustrous surface of a giant pyramid twinkles turquoise and yellow, reflecting the Kazakh flag as it flutters patriotically in the breeze. A gleaming obelisk thrusts into the bright blue sky, and beside it a horde of gold-clad warriors is feting the nation's leader. As Kazakhstan's president departs with a regal wave, the warriors drop to their knees and bow their heads in respect. It looks like a scene from a historical drama – but this is how Nursultan Nazarbayev likes to be glorified in the modern day.

'We love this holiday, we love this city, and we love Nazarbayev,' gushes Sara Gabdiyaliyeva, who is shepherding her family out of this pageant and off for a day of festivities in Astana, the brash capital city that is the president's brainchild, whose name simply means 'capital'. Today is Astana Day, when this glitzy town of idiosyncratic architecture celebrates its anniversary – but this year is a special occasion. On 6 July 2008 Astana is marking a decade since it was unveiled as Kazakhstan's capital at a stroke of Nazarbayev's pen. In fact, the whole country is also joining in the celebrations, because it has been declared a national holiday. It also just happens to be Nazarbayev's birthday.

The golden warriors are part of a spectacle to open a new monument called *Kazak Yeli* (Kazakh Nation), the latest architectural embellishment to adorn Astana, whose construction was ordained by the president after independence – a brand-new capital for a brand-new country. Erected alongside that ostentatious glass pyramid that is one of Astana's many offbeat landmarks, the obelisk rises 91 metres into the sky – symbolising

Kazakhstan gaining independence from the collapsing Soviet Union in 1991 – and is topped by a golden *samruk*, a phoenix-like mythical bird that, legend has it, lays the golden egg that starts a new cycle of life. Nowadays, a familiar face peers out from the side of the soaring column: Nazarbayev, whose image is carved into a bas-relief featuring him taking his presidential oath. The message is crystal clear: *l'état, c'est moi.*

Former steelworker and communist boss Nursultan Nazarbayev had been Kazakhstan's president since it gained independence in 1991 as the USSR shattered around it. He stood for his last re-election in 2015 and won with an eye-popping 98 per cent of the vote, marked a quarter of a century in power in 2016, then left his nation reeling by tendering his surprise resignation as president in 2019 – though he would be bowing out of office but not out of power. By then, Nazarbayev had been at the helm of his homeland for three decades: he became leader of Soviet-ruled Kazakhstan in 1989, and was propelled from there into the presidency of a sovereign state at independence. By the time of his resignation in 2019, a whole generation had grown up never knowing another president but Nazarbayev, a man with a big personality that he has stamped on the nation. Ruthless despot to his detractors, visionary leader to his acolytes, Nazarbayev leaves few in Kazakhstan indifferent. For his fans, he presided over years of political stability and petrodollar-fuelled prosperity, and forged a coherent nation state out of a melting pot of peoples inherited from the USSR. For his critics, he created a repressive get-rich-quick kleptocracy that looked set to endure beyond his rule, clinging on to power by rigging elections, crushing dissent and nourishing a creeping – and creepy – cult of personality that only gained momentum after he stepped down to occupy an elder statesman role.

Nazarbayev was born on 6 July 1940 into Stalin's Soviet Union, in a rural community in the village of Shamalgan on the south-eastern fringe of the USSR. He was the 'son, grandson and great-grandson of herders', he said in his autobiography, harking back to a past that had just disappeared by the time of his birth: the ancient nomadic lifestyle of the Kazakhs, which was wiped out by the Soviets.[1] Nazarbayev's father worked on a collective farm, where, according to his official biography, the future president, the eldest son of four children, helped out with the herding and haymaking when he was not at school, where he was an outstanding student.[2]

At the age of eighteen, Nazarbayev escaped the rural backwaters of Kazakhstan, first for a stint at technical college in Ukraine, then for a baptism by fire into the world of work. He became a blast furnace operator at the Karaganda Metallurgical Plant, a steelworks in the town of Temirtau in the industrial heartland of central Kazakhstan a thousand kilometres north of his birthplace. It was a tough job, but the ideal place for an ambitious young man to forge a political career: workers (along with peasants) were the ideological bulwark of the Soviet state, and in the factories of the USSR they were ideally placed to take up jobs as Communist Party functionaries – the way to get ahead in life. 'I was an ambitious young man and party membership was the route to advancement,' Nazarbayev once recalled. To further his ambition he would have become a Buddhist if necessary, 'but as it was I became a member of the Communist Party – and a good one'.[3]

In the 1960s, Nazarbayev combined his job in the steelworks with studying for a metallurgical engineering degree and working his way up the ranks of the Komsomol, the Communist Party's youth wing, before leaving manual work behind to embrace a political career as a full-time apparatchik. Personable and politically savvy, Nazarbayev leapfrogged up the ranks: by 1984 he was chairman of the Council of Ministers of the Kazakh Soviet Socialist Republic (the prime minister of Soviet Kazakhstan's government, which had limited autonomy to administer the republic). From there, he ascended to the top job in his homeland: appointed in 1989 by the last Soviet leader, Mikhail Gorbachev, as first secretary of Kazakhstan's Communist Party, then sliding smoothly into the role of Kazakhstan's president when that new title was introduced in 1990.

Nazarbayev's political star was still rising: the village-born ex-steelworker was tipped for a high-flying career in Moscow, but fate intervened to grant him a more precious prize: the USSR's collapse in 1991 propelled him into the presidency of an independent Kazakhstan.

'We found ourselves in unique conditions: a single body of the Soviet economy burst open and we ended up like a shard of a broken plate.'[4] The comparison Nazarbayev later reached for reflects the shock many apparatchiks, as well as ordinary people, felt when the monolith of the USSR suddenly shattered into 15 countries after ruling Russia and its former tsarist colonies for seventy years. For the party bosses turned presidents, inheriting a nation state was a heady experience that opened up myriad opportunities – but it was also a poisoned chalice.

Like other countries emerging blinking from the rubble of the USSR, Kazakhstan woke up to independence to find itself going broke: the Moscow-controlled command economy was falling apart; factories and farms were grinding to a halt; jobs were disappearing; and an emboldened and impoverished population – used to living in a communist state that provided at least the basics to get by – was taking to the streets to protest. The first five years of independence were grim: the economy shrank by 9 per cent a year on average, hitting its nadir in 1994 when it slumped by 13 per cent and inflation hit a whopping 1,547 per cent.[5]

As he wrestled with the nosediving economy, Kazakhstan's new president was also grappling with a national security dilemma: how to shape a nation state out of a land that sceptics doubted was viable as a country at all. Many Soviet republics had emerged from the melting pot of the USSR with large ethnic minorities – but Kazakhstan was the only one where the people whose name the country bore were outnumbered by other groups combined. Waves of immigration under the Russian Empire and the Soviet Union, including the forced deportations of entire peoples from other parts of the USSR to Kazakhstan under Stalin, had combined with demographic disasters that had decimated the indigenous population – notably a devastating famine in the 1930s – to push Kazakhs into a minority in their new country. Among its 125 or so ethnic groups lived a large, restive Russian minority left feeling angry and dispossessed by the collapse of their Soviet motherland, some harbouring dreams of splintering off to join Russia, so the demographic challenge raised the spectre of disintegration for the fragile new Kazakhstan. 'We tumbled about and worked to ensure survival,' Nazarbayev said of the tempestuous 1990s. Defying bleaker expectations, Kazakhstan 'became a state'.[6] His stewardship of the country during these tough times won international plaudits from an early stage: in 1991 James Baker, the US Secretary of State, reportedly praised Nazarbayev privately 'as an intelligent, careful leader who appreciates the depth of the Soviet crisis and the need for urgent but thoughtful change'.[7]

One lifesaver was oil. Kazakhstan was sitting on massive reserves, which would become key to getting the new country on its feet. Foreign energy companies were eager to flash their cash in this emerging market – and Kazakhstan was keen to suck it in. After bust came boom: investment poured in, and petrodollars began powering the economy into double-digit growth. It hit 14 per cent in 2000, and over the next decade the economy expanded by an average of 9 per cent a year.[8]

Oil has been a blessing for Kazakhstan in many ways, creating a feel-good factor that kept Nazarbayev's popularity ratings sky-high for years. Yet it can be a curse too. 'Black gold' has played a role in spawning the massive graft that blights Kazakhstan, typified in the 'Kazakhgate' scandal in which Nazarbayev was personally fingered by US prosecutors investigating kickbacks shelled out for oil contracts in Kazakhstan during the 1990s.[9] The disputed assets stashed in Swiss bank accounts in the names of Kazakh officials were eventually donated to charity.[10]

Oil is a lubricant for the wheels of the economy, but it can also be a distraction. Addicted to easy money, the government has taken its eye off the ball in developing other industries – which is fine while prices are riding high, but painful when they nosedive, as they did in 2014. A recession rippling out of Russia – a country with which Kazakhstan is locked in the tightest of political and economic clenches – combined with tumbling oil prices to put an end to the boom times, and by 2016 growth had plunged to its lowest level since 1998: 1 per cent. It subsequently picked up, until the coronavirus pandemic struck in 2020, when a drastic plunge in global oil prices combined with other pandemic-induced economic shockwaves to drive Kazakhstan into its first recession for over two decades. The drying-up of the petrodollars served as a reminder that oil was the key to unlocking Nazarbayev's social contract with his people, by which they broadly acquiesced to his iron-fisted rule in exchange for him delivering social stability and rising living standards – a pact that was wearing thin by the time Kazakhstan celebrated its thirtieth anniversary of independence in 2021, with the boom times now well in the past.

And iron-fisted his rule certainly was. Although Kazakhstan professes to be a democracy, Nazarbayev transformed himself into a potentate with a stranglehold on power in a country where the political opposition had been hounded out of existence and a docile parliament would rubber-stamp his every whim. Small wonder that by the end of his presidency he was winning elections with nearly 100 per cent of the vote.

Akmaral Aldongarova is the same age as Kazakhstan. She was born in 1991, the year Kazakhstan emerged into independence out of the debris of the USSR. A Nazarbayev supporter, she was happy to cast her ballot for the septuagenarian leader in 2011, when she and her country turned twenty, in the first presidential election in which she was old enough to vote. 'I voted for our president, of course,' said Akmaral, dainty-featured and almond-eyed with a cascade of dark hair and a friendly smile. 'I looked at his track record and what he's done for the country.'

She was a young professional living in Almaty, the Soviet-era capital of Kazakhstan and nowadays its commercial hub, a city cosier and less raffish than the new capital a thousand kilometres north, which at this time was called Astana but would later be rechristened 'Nur-Sultan' after Nazarbayev. On a warm spring afternoon in 2014, Akmaral was sitting on the terrace of a trendy café where customers in oversized sunglasses and designer T-shirts were cooling down over mocktails and lattes as expensive jeeps whooshed past alongside. Beyond the urban sprawl, the silvery skyscrapers of the financial district sparkled against the snow-capped Tian Shan Mountains in a dazzling reminder that Almaty is the wealthiest city in Central Asia.

Akmaral came from a generation of Kazakhs who had never had it so good – as Nazarbayev never tired of reminding them. Over the previous century, her forefathers had lived through revolution, war and famine, but hers was a generation that aspired to shopping in modish boutiques, sipping mojitos in cocktail bars and jaunting off on foreign holidays to Dubai and Turkey – a lifestyle her parents, who grew up in the drabber days of communism, could never have imagined. Her great-great-grandparents were from a generation that lived through the revolution that swept away Russian colonial rule and the civil war that installed the communists as Kazakhstan's new overlords. Her great-grandparents were from a generation that lived through famine and the destruction of the Kazakhs' nomadic way of life, and a world war that killed millions of their Soviet compatriots. Her grandparents were from a generation born into the tail-end of Stalin's Terror that exterminated the Kazakh intelligentsia and many more besides. Her parents grew up in the 1970s and 1980s, as the USSR turned into a dysfunctional machine ruled by doddering leaders, and came of age in the mayhem of the collapse of communism that propelled Kazakhstan into independence.

The 23-year-old was a member of what could be dubbed the Nazarbayev Generation: she and her peers had lived their entire lives in a period of peace, rising prosperity and political stability under the rule of one man in a country where 40 per cent of the population had been born since he came to power.[11] 'I don't know another president apart from him. I don't know what would happen if there was someone else,' she said contemplatively. 'We've been progressing very well all this time, thank God.'

In those days, after a quarter of a century under the political one-man show that was Nazarbayev's rule, this was an opinion heard across the generations. Charismatic but with a steely edge, Nazarbayev was genuinely popular among many of his compatriots, who prized the values he recited as his mantra for building the nation of Kazakhstan: political stability, economic prosperity and ethnic harmony among the diverse peoples who form the population of 19 million (over half born since independence by 2021[12]) in this vast country – the ninth-largest in the world, with borders stretching from Russia in the north to China in the east.

But was it Nazarbayev's track record that was the source of his popularity – or was it something altogether more sinister: the power of propaganda? 'You all know that I have categorically put a stop to all praise directed at me and proposals to especially glorify me personally,' Nazarbayev explained in 2010. 'As ruling president, I have when it comes to this issue always opposed vanity such as the imprinting of my images on banknotes and all kinds of titles. I have always tried to be above all kinds of praise and eulogies and I will continue to uphold this position.'[13] But was the president, as his enemies sniped, the subject of a pernicious cult of personality that was brainwashing the public mind?

Nazarbayev sat regally on a pedestal, looming over the Park of the First President in Almaty on a gloomy midwinter day. As snow drifted down from a ponderous grey sky and billowed around this hulking statue, Bakhyt Akimov was raving about his president. 'I consider Nursultan Abishevich to be our father,' said the 33-year-old banker, using the president's patronymic, 'son of Abish', as a term of respect. 'I believe he should keep on leading our country and propelling us forwards.' It was 16 December 2016, a special occasion: Kazakhstan was marking not only Independence Day but also twenty-five years as a sovereign state with the 76-year-old president at the helm. This made Nazarbayev one of the world's longest-ruling leaders, and the elder statesman of the former Soviet Union: he had lived through every Soviet leader bar the first, Lenin, and was at the time the only ruler of an ex-Soviet country who had been in power since before the USSR collapsed. The ageing president once declared that Kazakhstan's public servants should retire after twenty-five years to make way for fresh blood[14] – but the long-ruling septuagenarian exempted himself from this rule. This was a source of frustration to critics, but a relief to fans who could not imagine their country without Nazarbayev at the helm. 'You can see for yourself how the country's developing. We live well now. We love our president. It's all thanks to him,' said Aselya Iskitbayeva, a cheerful young housewife pushing a pram through the park. 'I don't even know what will happen after him. It would be better for him to stay in power for a long time.'

That gargantuan granite Nazarbayev gazing down – sharp-eyed, strong-featured and statesmanlike – on the snowy scene in December 2016 was an unmissable reminder of how hard it was in Kazakhstan to escape the overweening presence of the president, who still cut a trim and dapper figure in his late 70s. Even after his retirement from the presidency, his smiling face topped with thinning silver hair bore down from giant billboards across the land; his slogans adorned buildings, bridges and roadsides; and whenever you paid for something, there he was: his handprint graced the banknotes, and his face appeared there in 2021. Nazarbayev has been immortalised on the silver screen (most recently in a fawning eight-part documentary by US film-maker Oliver Stone in 2021), as well as on stage and in song, most memorably when eighty boys named Nursultan once sang him a birthday eulogy. In print, he has starred in the usual hagiographic biographies, but also as a dashing fairy-tale hero charging about scoring diplomatic successes on the international stage. That sounds like strange fodder to pique children's interest in their president, but he was still winning hearts and minds among the very young. 'Kazakhstan is the best country in the world – thank you to our President Nazarbayev,' chirped a ten-year-old girl named Aruzhan in sing-song style, as her mother, standing not far from the statue of the man her daughter was effusively praising, smiled and nodded approval.

Nazarbayev fans can climb Nursultan Peak, after his first name (a combination of the words 'nur', 'ray', and 'sultan', 'king'), which was bestowed on his capital city after his resignation. They can celebrate First President's Day, a national holiday in his honour every 1 December, and learn all about him at a museum in his former school in Shamalgan, where a white-haired old lady who used to be his teacher would proudly point out kooky highlights among the Nazarbayev memorabilia: a painting of a dream his grandmother once had of him riding a white horse in the sky, a portrait of the president painstakingly fashioned out of grains of rice.

After landing at Nursultan Nazarbayev International Airport, visitors to the capital that is now called Nur-Sultan (that clumsy hyphen has never been explained) can go and visit a golden statue of Nazarbayev standing tall in military regalia, or one of him seated regally, overseeing his domain with a smile. In the city, there is a Nazarbayev University and a Museum of the First President, which is one of his special titles; the other is *Yelbasy*, 'Leader of the Nation'. With these titles comes a litany of personal privileges that he began exercising to the full after his resignation: the right to intervene in policy-making and the appointment of all key officials after retirement; the right to chair the Security Council (and thus control the military and security forces) for life; lifetime immunity from prosecution; no-questions-asked guarantees for him and his family over property and assets; and an exemption from insults to his 'honour and dignity', for which critics can be slung in jail for three years (and defacing his image carries a prison term of up to five years). As well as his official titles, Nazarbayev went by other, unofficial titles: sometimes he was '*Papa*' to ordinary people (either affectionately or sarcastically), and it was an open secret that his nickname in the corridors of power in the capital was '*Nul Odin*': 'Zero One' – first among equals.

With its quirky constructions in resplendent gold and lustrous glass, Nazarbayev's capital is a love-it-or-hate-it kind of place: fun and flamboyant to fans, a statement of bold modernity; tawdry and tasteless to critics, the epitome of 'dictator chic'.

The city may look like an exorbitant vanity project built to stroke a vainglorious leader's ego, but for Nazarbayev it was much more than that: it was a nation-building endeavour to stamp a new identity on the new Kazakhstan. At its heart – not far from Akorda, the wedding-cake presidential palace (which takes its name from an ancient nomadic kingdom to which the Kazakhs trace distant roots), and the glass pyramid that flashes neon at night – stands the lollipop-shaped Bayterek Tower, a golden globe atop a white column, symbolising an egg laid by the mythical *samruk* bird atop the 'tree of life'. Tradition holds that visitors whizz up into the egg to an observation deck to press their hands inside a gilded handprint of Nazarbayev's and make a wish as they behold the swaggering space-age cityscape below. The symbolism is unmistakable: Nazarbayev, the leader who made his people's dreams come true.

Nazarbayev always credited himself with delivering to his people a land of opportunity – all they had to do was reach out and grab it. 'If you have the desire and the aspiration, you can do anything in Kazakhstan,' said Akmaral, whose salary as a manager at a state company funded an aspirational lifestyle: driving her own car, buying the latest fashions, socialising in Almaty's buzzing nightspots and holidaying abroad.

Akmaral was a member of a nascent middle class that was (broadly, and with many reservations) happy with its lot. Such people do not have it easy – nepotism is rife, and jobs are hard to come by without the right connections; salaries are not high compared to the cost of living, and many people are maxed out on credit – but life, for all its challenges, seems to be getting better: they see a way to get ahead. There are people like this all over the country, not only in flashy Astana and wealthy Almaty, but out in the provinces too, where a new consumer culture has sprung up to cater for those with money to spend, if not to burn: from the slick oil cities of the western deserts to the gritty industrial heartlands of the east; from the laid-back leafy cities along the northern border with Siberia to the sparky towns of the Central Asia-facing south. The people of Kazakhstan 'have never lived as they live now', said Nazarbayev in 2016.[15] In other words, they have never had it so good.

That is certainly true for the super-rich elite, the oligarchs and Nazarbayev relatives and cronies who have made billions out of the petrodollar bonanza. They embody the showy face of a country powered by the oil that has greased the wheels of the economy – and the palms of the corrupt.

At the other end of the spectrum lies a dispossessed underclass left behind by the boom times, whose numbers have swelled as growth has faltered in recent years: the doctors and teachers struggling by on miserly salaries; the oil workers toiling in grim conditions whose labour fuels prosperity for the rest of Kazakhstan; the villagers living in dilapidated housing with no running water; the low-paid looking on as venal officials enrich themselves with bribes; the parents raising children infected with HIV because of corruption in the healthcare system; the victims of Soviet nuclear testing struggling by on benefits belying Nazarbayev's boasts about how rich Kazakhstan is. By his own admission, plenty of his compatriots have failed to cash in on the good times: in 2013, he said there were 1.5 million people in petrodollar-flush Kazakhstan – 9 per cent of the population – living on less than the minimum wage.[16] At the time the average monthly salary was $900,[17] but by 2021 it had actually fallen by a third in dollar terms to stand at just $600, because Kazakhstan's currency had lost so much value over the years.[18]

For the 'haves', Kazakhstan is a land of opportunity – but the 'have-nots' have struggled to buy into the Nazarbayev dream. 'No one's dying from hunger, but this is a rural area, salaries are low [...] and pensions are tiny,' griped an old man standing outside his dilapidated house on a potholed track in a village called Badam in southern Kazakhstan, as Nazarbayev was up in gaudy Astana fretting about that rich–poor divide. 'To be honest, people are dissatisfied with the current leadership, but they're afraid to say so.'

They have reason to be – as those who have crossed the regime and suffered the consequences can attest. For Kazakhstan has one smiling face that it likes to project to the world: an economically dynamic, socially stable, go-getting country ruled for three decades by a man the spin doctors portray as a popular and visionary president who had the grace and foresight to step down to play the role of elder statesman, steering his country into the post-Nazarbayev future. But it has always had another countenance that it shows to critics who step out of line at home: a dictatorial state where dissenting views are crushed, the media is muzzled, peaceful protesters are arrested or gunned down, and political foes can end up at best in jail or exile, at worst dead.

CHAPTER 2

A Family Affair

Taldykorgan, 2006

In a crowded courtroom on a baking late summer's day in the town of Taldykorgan in south-eastern Kazakhstan, the judge is pronouncing the verdict in a murder trial. The ten men in the dock are accused of slaughtering an opposition leader, 43-year-old former regime insider Altynbek Sarsenbayev, in an execution-style assassination which has left the country reeling. Kazakhstan is known for repressing opposition leaders – but not for shooting them in the back of the head in cold blood.

The mood is tense. Sarsenbayev's family do not believe the version unfolding in the judge's summing-up as the trial draws to an end in September 2006: that an obscure parliamentary official ordered the killing out of personal animosity, and a gang of renegade security officers carried out the deed. The real story, they believe, is even murkier: they suspect a plot with tentacles reaching deep into the president's family.

Guilty verdicts are delivered, long jail sentences handed down – but for Rustam Ibragimov, the ex-police officer accused of carrying out the contract killing, the judge orders the death penalty. Mayhem erupts as his mother is carried sobbing and screaming from the courtroom. Case closed, justice has been done – or has it?

Minister-turned-opposition leader Altynbek Sarsenbayev was found face down in the blood-spattered snow with a bullet in the back of his head in the Tian Shan Mountains outside Almaty in February 2006. Alongside lay the bodies of his aides Baurzhan Baybosyn and Vasiliy Zhuravlyov, hands bound behind their backs, torsos covered by branches, legs askew across the mountain path. Sarsenbayev's grisly end sent shock waves through the opposition, to which he had not long before pledged his fealty.

'We have to rebel against this politics of fear, creeping terror and now political extermination,' exhorted Serikbolsyn Abdildin, one of the shocked opposition leaders who gathered at the grand neoclassical headquarters of Kazakhstan's Academy of Sciences in Almaty a few days later to pay their respects before the funeral.[1] Distress, outrage and fury rippled through the crowd of mourners, aghast at a killing that bore the hallmarks of a gruesome political execution. The powers that be were allowing 'terror' to reign, railed Sergey Duvanov, a journalist all too familiar with the consequences of crossing the regime: a few years earlier he had served a jail term on charges of raping a minor, a conviction that was widely condemned as a reprisal for his outspoken reporting. 'People are being killed for their views,' Duvanov continued, choking back his emotions to address the hushed crowd. 'Everyone's afraid to say who's behind it, but I'm not afraid: Mr 91 Per Cent!'

Nazarbayev had recently stormed to victory in his latest re-election, with a 91 per cent landslide in December 2005 which his entourage depicted as a ringing endorsement from his adoring people – but these mourners had their own messages for the triumphant president. 'No to the regime's bloody "democracy", read one banner fluttering above their heads. 'No to dictatorship and murderers,' beseeched a second. 'Let's save our country from executioners,' implored a third. 'They want to scare us; they want to stop us from speaking out, but they won't achieve their aim,' pledged Bolat Abilov, a political ally of Sarsenbayev.

The funeral cortège then drove into the foothills of the Tian Shan to lay the murdered politician to rest in Kensay cemetery, resting place of Kazakhstan's great and good, with expansive views stretching up to the snow-capped peaks and down over the smog-draped skyscrapers of Sarsenbayev's home town.

The opposition had had a bumpy ride in Kazakhstan's fifteen years of independence under Nazarbayev, who cut his political teeth in the one-party state of the USSR and was certainly no diehard democrat. Like many post-Soviet leaders, he embraced Western-style multi-party democracy in name, but hardly in spirit: he harboured deep suspicions of anything that smacked of opposition to his rule, a position that had only hardened with time.

After independence, a semblance of multi-party democracy briefly prevailed: parliament contained a smattering of opposition, and genuine challengers ran in presidential elections – albeit in one-horse races in which Nazarbayev trounced his rivals. When the first real challenge to his rule emerged, Nazarbayev nailed his colours to the mast. In 1998, Akezhan Kazhegeldin, a former prime minister, declared his intention of contesting the 1999 presidential election, publicly protesting at reforms he decried as a smokescreen for Nazarbayev's plans to 'institute a dictatorship' and stay in power for life.[2] Disqualified from standing, Kazhegeldin was effectively run out of Kazakhstan: he fled into exile (a well-cushioned one, in London) to escape criminal charges of corruption and possessing weapons. He was later convicted *in absentia* – a pattern that would become familiar to ex-allies who dared challenge the president.

Sarsenbayev was no rabble-rousing Nazarbayev adversary: the affable, balding, bespectacled intellectual was a loyal member of the president's team for over a decade before joining the opposition in 2003, a defection he couched in his usual mild manner. 'Democratisation is already knocking at our door, and the question is from which side the door will be opened,' he said laconically,[3] shortly before resigning as ambassador to Russia and joining Ak Zhol, an opposition party with a liberal agenda, as a co-leader. Sarsenbayev's family would later claim that intermediaries dangled mind-boggling sums to entice him back into Nazarbayev's fold – a million dollars just before the killing[4] – but Sarsenbayev stuck to his principles and declined. He briefly returned to government as minister of information in 2004, but Astana's experiment in inclusive politics ended in an embarrassing fiasco: Sarsenbayev resigned from the cabinet in protest at an election that all but shut the opposition out of parliament: Ak Zhol was the only opposition force to get in, winning just one seat, which it boycotted over vote-rigging claims.

Even as an administration insider, Sarsenbayev was close to reformist circles. He was associated with a progressive movement called Democratic Choice of Kazakhstan (known as DVK) which brought political turmoil in 2001, as doves within the administration pushed for liberalisation and hawks pushed back to maintain the authoritarian status quo. During that stand-off, Sarsenbayev made some powerful enemies: he was among a group of reformers who presented Nazarbayev with shocking evidence that the president was the target of a sinister palace coup – plotted from within the ranks of his own family.[5]

'After autumn 2001, Altynbek said: "They will not forgive, because Rakhat and Dariga were literally half a step away from power; they only had to take power into their hands."'[6] That was how Saltanat Atusheva, Sarsenbayev's widow, characterised the grudge she believed two of the most powerful people in the land harboured against her husband: Dariga Nazarbayeva, the president's politician-cum-media magnate daughter, and her husband Rakhat Aliyev, who had held a series of plum positions in Nazarbayev's administration and controlled a sprawling business empire. The president's son-in-law, a Machiavellian figure in his late 40s with steely eyes and a cold smile, was notorious for his voracious appetite for business and ruthless attitude to rivals. His wife Dariga – matronly and manicured, with bouffant hair and shiny eyeshadow – was an MP with her own political party, and controlled an influential stable of media outlets (which Sarsenbayev had lobbied to prevent her from amassing).

When the reformers went to warn Nazarbayev of an impending coup plot, it was Aliyev they fingered, backed by a dossier of evidence. They had counted on bringing Aliyev down, but misjudged the clout of their omnipotent target and the indulgence Nazarbayev would show his relatives. Aliyev sailed through the storm, albeit not unsullied: Nazarbayev pushed him out of Astana's corridors of power (where he had variously held powerful positions in the security service, the tax police and Nazarbayev's personal protection squad) and dispatched him to Vienna as ambassador to ride out the storm. After that, Sarsenbayev 'started to fear for his life', his widow said.[7]

'Irrespective of who stands behind this crime and who is the executor, who is the organiser and who is the contractor of these murders, they will all stand before a court and receive the most severe punishment.'[8] This was Nazarbayev's personal pledge, in the face of the furore following Sarsenbayev's murder, that justice would be done – no matter how high the tentacles of the assassination plot reached.

The first arrests confirmed the suspicions of the distraught family that they reached high indeed. Five officers from a crack unit under the command of the National Security Committee, the security service (successor to the Soviet KGB), were detained on suspicion of performing the contract killing. The news that elite troops from the security service (nowadays known as the KNB) where Aliyev had once been deputy chief were available as hired killers came as a shock, and caused a senior head to roll. KNB chief Nartay Dutbayev resigned over the involvement of renegade officers in 'this appalling murder'.[9] The hired killer was quickly tracked down: Rustam Ibragimov, a former police officer whom investigators accused of murdering Sarsenbayev for a payment of $60,000.

But what could the motive be? The killing had the ring of a 'deep state' conspiracy, a plot by shadowy forces operating within the political or security establishment for their own nefarious aims – but the explanation was more prosaic.

Next up for arrest was Yerzhan Utembayev, an unassuming parliamentary bureaucrat fingered as the contractor of the killing – with the most humdrum of motives: Utembayev had ordered the murder after his career took a nosedive following derogatory insinuations Sarsenbayev had made about his drinking habits, said Baurzhan Mukhamedzhanov, the interior minister.[10] Case closed. But many smelt a rat. Had the timid bureaucrat really ordered Sarsenbayev slaughtered as payback for suggesting he was too fond of a drink, in an article published in the press over two years earlier? Where had Utembayev got the money to hire a contract killer? He had taken out a loan to pay for the murder, the minister explained, to an outburst of sarcastic laughter from sceptical reporters attending his briefing.

Despite a slew of confessions pouring forth from the arrested men, confusion reigned. Sarsenbayev's relatives were convinced someone was lurking in the shadows behind Utembayev, Ibragimov and his crew of renegade intelligence operatives – and the name of Rakhat Aliyev, a known foe of Sarsenbayev, kept cropping up.

With a veil of suspicion hanging over him, Aliyev issued a spirited denial of complicity – 'a malicious lie'[11] – while his wife published a hysterically worded statement titled 'Déjà Vu' containing a claim more damning against the ruling family than anything that had gone before: Nazarbayev had received intelligence that one of his relatives had ordered the killing: either her own husband, or Timur Kulibayev, her sister Dinara's billionaire businessman husband, or Kayrat Satybaldy, the president's nephew.[12] Her revelations caused a storm of confusion and muddied the waters even further – but all Sarsenbayev's family wanted was the truth.

Ten people stood in the dock when the murder trial opened in June 2006: Utembayev, Ibragimov, the five renegade KNB officers, and three accomplices who had allegedly been part of Sarsenbayev's death squad.

From day one, Sarsenbayev's family were sceptical: the trial resembled 'a theatre of the absurd, where everyone's playing their role, as judge, as prosecutors, as the accused', the victim's brother Ryspek Sarsenbay said wrathfully as it got under way (he has dropped the Russian-style -ev ending from his surname).[13] Utembayev and Ibragimov had recanted confessions made, they claimed, under duress, and the prosecution's case rested on a grovelling confession written by Utembayev to Nazarbayev after his arrest, where he detailed how animosity had eaten away at him until he resolved to have Sarsenbayev killed to avenge his besmirched honour.[14] 'I wanted to seek him out and have a man-to-man chat, but I was dissuaded,' he elucidated. Then Sarsenbayev had cut him dead in a restaurant, and 'it all came flooding back to me, and I asked Rustam to smash his face in'.[15] That instruction metamorphosed into an order to kill Sarsenbayev, through a series of hazy events that 'defies logic and understanding', Utembayev explained. The motive was, by his own admission, 'ridiculous'.

The trial dragged on until Ibragimov made a sensational about-turn: he changed his testimony, and the idea of a 'deep state' political plot was back on the agenda. The killings, Ibragimov now claimed, were the prelude to a conspiracy to topple Nazarbayev, concocted by two of the president's closest confidants: Dutbayev, the security chief who had resigned over the murders, and Nurtay Abykayev, the Senate speaker and Utembayev's boss, who had been shifted out of the public eye with a posting to Moscow as ambassador after his underling's arrest.

But Ibragimov's fresh testimony led nowhere. The judge threw out a motion to summon the two political heavyweights to testify, and moved with lightning speed to conclude the trial, prompting Sarsenbayev's family to declare a boycott. The proceedings had 'unfortunately not discovered on whose conscience lies the blood'[16] of the murdered trio, his brother Ryspek said shortly before the court delivered its verdict: all defendants guilty as charged. Utembayev had contracted Ibragimov to murder Sarsenbayev as vengeance for revealing his drinking problem, and rogue KNB operatives had formed a death squad which had kidnapped Sarsenbayev and his aides and delivered them to Ibragimov, who murdered them.

Utembayev was jailed for twenty years; the others got from three to twenty years. For Ibragimov, the man who had pulled the trigger, the judge handed down the death penalty, as his mother was dragged screaming and sobbing from the court.

A year after Sarsenbayev's murder, two Almaty bankers went missing. Their relatives were frantic – and a familiar name kept cropping up: Rakhat Aliyev. Nurbank executives Zholdas Timraliyev and Aybar Khasenov had last been seen heading to a meeting with Aliyev, and rumours were rife that they had recently been held prisoner in a sauna complex and tortured in a mafia-style operation to put the screws on them over business dealings with Aliyev. That was what Timraliyev's wife Armangul Kapasheva was claiming, to none other than the president himself. She wrote to Nazarbayev urging him to act over her husband's disappearance; Aliyev, who owned Nurbank, airily dismissed allegations of involvement as 'open slander'.[17] The police took his side: Kapasheva's claims were nonsense – the bankers were involved in financial machinations and they had gone on the run to avoid arrest.

Within days, Aliyev was on the move again. A few years earlier, Nazarbayev had dispatched Aliyev to Vienna as ambassador, after evidence of coup-plotting had hit the president's desk. Aliyev had later returned to Astana, but within days of the latest scandal Nazarbayev sent his errant, scandal-ridden son-in-law back to Austria to resume his previous ambassadorial role. A life of luxury as a diplomat in Vienna did not look like much of a punishment – but it would not last long. The 'Rakhatgate' saga was about to begin.

Three months after the bankers were reported missing, police burst into the home of Aliyev's father looking for them: investigators had finally started posing the question their wives had been asking for months: could Aliyev, ensconced in the embassy in Vienna, hold the key to the mystery of their disappearance?

Events moved fast: Aliyev suddenly found himself accused of abducting the bankers, and of a litany of financial crimes too. Sacked and stripped of diplomatic immunity, he was briefly arrested by Austrian police at Kazakhstan's request before being released to begin a long battle against extradition. Aliyev had finally tested his father-in-law's indulgence once too often, and soon he was cast out of the ruling family. In June 2007 he learnt – via a fax left at the gate of his Vienna mansion in the dead of night, he claimed – that Dariga Nazarbayeva had divorced him.

Suddenly locked out of the corridors of power, Aliyev assumed the role of political victim. 'My only crime is that I expressed an opinion which deviates slightly from the president's opinion,' he sighed. 'This is what President Nazarbayev does to potential opponents and opposition politicians when they even just think of challenging him.'[18] Aliyev was honing his technique of painting himself as a wronged reformer, which would peak with the publication of his memoirs under the catchy title *The Godfather-in-Law* in 2009. Those at the sharp end of his ruthless practices found this image of regime insider-turned-dissident democrat hard to swallow. 'If he'd long disagreed politically with Nazarbayev, why didn't he say so?'[19] wondered Kapasheva, the wife of one of the bankers, who were still missing.

What had happened to her husband? Six months later, a court delivered its findings, and the fears she had been voicing since day one were corroborated: Timraliyev and Khasenov had been abducted from Nurbank's glitzy headquarters by Aliyev, handcuffed, dressed in overalls, driven to an out-of-town farm, beaten and tortured, then driven away never to be seen again.

Aliyev was not in the dock to hear himself declared guilty on charges of running an organised crime ring, abduction, theft and extortion, and sentenced to twenty years in jail. The term was purely theoretical: he was tried *in absentia* after (predictably) winning a battle against extradition to Kazakhstan on the grounds that its skewed justice system would not give him a fair trial.

The missing bankers' families, tormented by the mystery about their fates, were scathing in their verdict on whether the trial had delivered justice. 'We are not one iota closer today to our main aim: discovering the whereabouts of Zholdas Timraliyev and Aybar Khasenov,' lamented Timraliyev's mother. 'What happened to them?' wondered his wife desperately. 'Are they alive?'[20]

Abduction and extortion were merely the tip of Aliyev's iceberg. He had, it transpired, also been the mastermind of a plot to topple Nazarbayev – just as Sarsenbayev had warned back in 2001. The version that unfolded in court as another trial *in absentia* got under way was a convoluted James Bond-style conspiracy involving radioactive isotopes, poison-shooting devices and a horde of militant fighters trained in Egypt and Israel.

Using a multi-tentacled crime syndicate created to pursue his iniquitous goals under the Orwellian name 'Top Secret Directorate', Aliyev – from his lair in Vienna – had been on the verge of overthrowing Nazarbayev when the KNB spotted the plot in 2007, the court heard. Acting in collusion with former security chief Alnur Musayev, Aliyev had, prosecutors alleged, infiltrated conspirators into the highest echelons of power to ferret out state secrets for foreign intelligence; engaged in extortion to acquire financial muscle; used the stable of media outlets run by his wife Dariga Nazarbayeva to manipulate public opinion; and applied 'forcible pressure on the political and business elites' to do his bidding. Fellow conspirators had been recruited through a combination of threats, blackmail and cash incentives to entice them 'to carry out any orders, up to the physical removal of unwanted people.'[21] Like Sarsenbayev, perhaps, wondered grieving relatives, still agonising two years on over the circumstances of his death.

These stunning claims raised awkward questions about how Aliyev and his 'Top Secret Directorate' had pursued their malevolent goals, unnoticed and with impunity, for eleven years. 'They are saying "yes, Aliev is a criminal", and they are correct in making this assessment of him,' remarked opposition politician Asylbek Kozhakhmetov – but where was the debate about 'how these people so easily came to power, made careers, committed crimes and abuse without facing punishment'?[22] Aliyev was the product of the system that had bred him, suggested Gulzhan Yergaliyeva, a prominent journalist who had crossed Aliyev (and blamed him for once ordering an attack on her family that had left her husband with permanent injuries). 'I don't believe the threat has disappeared in Kazakhstan along with Rakhat Aliyev,' she said: the 'dark forces' that prevailed when he appeared invincible were 'the logical accompanying force of the political regime that rules today in Kazakhstan.'[23]

Aliyev and Musayev were convicted of attempting to seize power, divulging state secrets, running a crime syndicate, theft and possession of firearms, embezzlement and abuse of power, and Musayev was also found guilty of treason. Tried *in absentia* since they were in Vienna, the two were sentenced to twenty years in jail, in addition to the twenty years from Aliyev's previous trial – all moot, since he was not in Kazakhstan to serve them.

From Vienna, Aliyev pooh-poohed the 'absurd accusations' and slammed Kazakhstan's 'puppet justice system' which 'only rubber-stamps decisions which pass down from the presidential administration.[24] The matter of his guilt or innocence aside, his remarks that Kazakhstan's justice system was marching to political orders had the ring of truth.

Then the bodies started turning up.

The first corpse to be dug up was that of Anastasiya Novikova, a TV presenter exhumed from a secret grave in southern Kazakhstan in 2008 amid frenzied media speculation that she was Aliyev's lover and the mother of his love child. According to her family, the 24-year-old, an attractive blonde who was the wife of Aliyev's cousin Daniyar Esten, had disappeared four years earlier. Her corpse, showing signs of multiple fractures, had been spirited into Kazakhstan on an aircraft from Lebanon, where she had evidently met a violent death, investigators said. Unfortunately, Novikova's husband, a former diplomat at Kazakhstan's embassy in Austria, was unavailable to shed light on the circumstances of his wife's death: he had died in a car crash in Vienna in 2005.

Novikova's brother told Kazakhstan's tabloids that she had been having an affair with a highly placed married man, and the newspapers printed emails she had reportedly sent, revealing remarkable similarities between the life of her lover and that of Aliyev: from his date of birth to the timing of his son's wedding. There were whisperings of a secret love child, Luiza, born the year before Novikova's death.

Aliyev reacted with outrage to hints of his involvement in yet another death: 'When your spin doctors start using a tragedy in our family – the death of my cousin Daniyar and his wife Nastya – for their PR purposes, it surpasses all imaginable borders of immorality,' he huffed in an open letter to Nazarbayev complaining of dirty tricks extending 'beyond the boundaries of good and evil'.[25] There was a simple explanation: Novikova had committed suicide by throwing herself out of a window in Lebanon, and he had arranged the return of her body to Kazakhstan – all perfectly legal. Novikova briefly became a cause célèbre and a tool in Astana's campaign to bring Aliyev home to face justice, but the case soon disappeared from the headlines and was never pursued in court, leaving the circumstances of the young woman's death a mystery to this day.

The next two corpses turned up three years later, stuffed into lime-filled barrels in a mountain gorge outside Almaty, showing signs of torture and suffocation: Zholdas Timraliyev and Aybar Khasenov, the bankers who had gone missing four years earlier. Aliyev had never faced a murder charge, but evidence 'irrefutably proving' he had killed the men was now in the bag, prosecutors said – and if Astana could not get him extradited over fair trial concerns, it would take the case to the European courts.

By now, Aliyev had become Rakhat Shoraz, after marrying an Austrian national originally from Kazakhstan and taking her surname, and was living in style in Malta; he had retreated there after surviving an attempt on his life in Vienna, or so he claimed. His multi-million-dollar assets in Kazakhstan had been seized, while his stake at Nurbank, whose executives he stood accused of murdering, had made a tidy fortune for his ex-wife and son. Dariga Nazarbayeva and their son Nurali Aliyev, a banker, had suddenly been declared major stakeholders in Nurbank – previously owned by Aliyev – immediately after his fall from grace, and later sold their controlling stake.[26] The price was undisclosed, but the profits must have helped them bump up their wealth, which stood at a combined $800 million by 2012, according to a rich list compiled by *Forbes Kazakhstan*.[27]

Dariga Nazarbayeva had survived the scandal of her husband's involvement in coup-plotting and the trail of corpses following in his wake, although her political wings had been clipped. In 2006, Nazarbayev forced his daughter to disband her political party, Asar (All Together), which merged with his ruling party, and in 2007 she was squeezed out of parliament – but the fallout did no lasting damage to her political career. In 2012 she staged a comeback as an MP; in 2015 she was parachuted into the cabinet as deputy prime minister; in 2016 she became a senator; then in 2021 she became an MP again. Mutterings persisted that she could yet succeed her father as president when the time came, though in 2016 Nazarbayev appeared to rule out a dynastic succession – heedful, no doubt, of his chequered family history.[28] When he stepped down in 2019, he did not anoint his daughter as his successor, though tongues kept wagging about the possibility of her still taking the reins of power at some point.

It was not only the families of the murdered bankers who were clamouring for justice: Sarsenbayev's family had been saying since 2006 that the murder trial that had taken place before Aliyev's downfall had failed to deliver justice. Eight years on, they would have their day in court again.

Rustam Ibragimov, the convicted killer, was no longer on death row: Kazakhstan had a moratorium on the death penalty, so his sentence had been commuted to life imprisonment. From his cell, Ibragimov did another U-turn: he still admitted killing Sarsenbayev, but not on the orders of Utembayev, Dutbayev or Abykayev, as he had previously claimed – the contractor of the killing was Rakhat Aliyev, whom the family had long suspected of complicity. The original trial had been botched: it was time for a retrial.

'I wrote in my [new] statement that the real contractor of Altynbek Sarsenbayev's murder was not Utembayev, but Alnur Musayev and Rakhat Aliyev,' Ibragimov, casually clad in a baseball cap, testified at the retrial in 2014, standing in the dock beside a balaclava-wearing, gun-toting guard. Musayev produced a pistol 'and told me to eliminate Sarsenbayev', he continued calmly, only the constant flickering of his eyes betraying his nerves. 'I said I couldn't do that, and he told me to think about my family.'[29] Aliyev and Musayev – who vehemently denied the latest claims – had set Utembayev up to take the rap for the murder and manipulate the ensuing chaos to topple Nazarbayev and seize power, Ibragimov testified.

The first investigation was exposed as faulty, the first trial as a bungled miscarriage of justice – as Sarsenbayev's family had said all along. The court accepted Ibragimov's new confession, and Utembayev, the man convicted of contracting the killing, soon walked free: his sentence was slashed from twenty to thirteen years on a lesser charge of accessory to murder, and he was paroled. No one was tried for perjury, despite the original proceedings being peppered with false testimony.

Justice had been done, trumpeted the authorities again – and they had an international endorsement to prove it. The findings of the FBI, invited in to boost the credibility of the second investigation after the first was revealed as at best a fiasco and at worst a cover-up, were 'consistent' with those of Kazakh investigators.[30]

For Sarsenbayev's relatives, though, the retrial was another travesty of justice. 'The court was really not interested in establishing the true picture of the tragedy,' said Marzhan Aspandiyarova, his sister-in-law, and the slew of unanswered questions confirmed 'our suspicions and suppositions that the upper echelons of power are implicated in this crime.'[31] The retrial, fulminated opposition leader Tolegen Zhukeyev, was 'a tragi-farce playing out on Kazakhstan's stage of the theatre of the absurd.'[32] Fifteen years later, the sense of not knowing the truth about Sarsenbayev's murder still tortured the family, and his brother, deeming the crime 'political terrorism', was still pointing the finger at the very top. Ryspek Sarsenbay had always said that Aliyev had a motive to take revenge on the opposition leader, who had 'destroyed [his] plans for a coup d'etat' in 2001 by reporting them to Nazarbayev. But he found it impossible to believe that Nazarbayev could have been ignorant of any murder plot right up until the re-trial eight years after the killing. As a 'political opponent' fighting to place democratic leaders in power, Sarsenbayev presented 'a threat to what [Nazarbayev] valued most', his brother said in 2021: 'his wealth and power'. Ultimately, 'the crime was committed by the state'.[33]

As for the missing bankers' families, they were pinning their hopes for justice on the Austrian courts, and suddenly after all these years it began to look as if they might get it. The net had been closing in on Aliyev since the bankers' bodies were produced in 2011, and Austria (acting on its legal duty to investigate after refusing Aliyev's extradition) had opened a murder case. In June 2014, his options narrowing and evidence piling up against him, Aliyev flew to Vienna from Malta and gave himself up for arrest – to clear his name, he said, since he was totally innocent.

In 2015, he was due to stand trial in Vienna for the bankers' murders, alongside Musayev and another alleged accomplice, Vadim Koshlyak – but Aliyev never made it into the dock. In February 2015, he was found hanged in his prison cell from a noose fashioned out of bandages. His death was declared a suicide, though he left behind him no note and lingering suspicions of foul play.

The trial went ahead without the star defendant, amid a storm of controversy over allegations that the KNB had tried to abduct the suspects and exert pressure on Austrian MPs.[34] After three months of hearings, the two Aliyev associates walked free, both acquitted of the murder of the two bankers. Koshlyak was convicted of their abduction and given a jail sentence of two years, mostly suspended, and released on time already served. Nobody has ever been convicted of the murders of Zholdas Timraliyev and Aybar Khasenov.

Rakhat Aliyev never stood in any dock to face justice for any of the litany of crimes of which he was accused, including the killings of the two bankers and the political assassination of Altynbek Sarsenbayev and his two aides. But with his death, the long-running Rakhatgate saga was well and truly over.

CHAPTER 3

Don't Mess With the Boss

London, 2009

A suave Kazakh oligarch sits in a swish boardroom in a skyscraper overlooking the twinkling lights of the City of London on a balmy autumn evening. In rapid-fire sentences, Mukhtar Ablyazov is protesting his innocence of accusations levelled at him from Kazakhstan that he has pilfered billions of dollars from a bank he owned until the government seized it from him. 'The underlying cause is very simple – it's political,' he blurts out, with the urgency of a high-powered businessman driving through a packed agenda without a minute to spare. As the source of his troubles, he is pointing the finger at the very top: Nazarbayev, who he claims has grabbed his bank and sent him fleeing Kazakhstan in fear of arrest.

Ablyazov is gearing up for the legal battle of a lifetime: a high-stakes case in the High Court of England and Wales, on which his fortune and his reputation hinge. The billionaire is bullish: he promises to clear his name of damning charges that he defrauded his bank of billions of dollars through a series of complex machinations involving offshore accounts, shell companies and fake loans in what – if true – amounts to one of the world's biggest ever financial swindles.

Ablyazov is down but not out – and the comeback kid has bounced back from worse before. From riding high as a millionaire businessman and government minister in the 1990s, he tumbled into political disgrace and swapped a life of luxury for a Kazakh jail cell, only to emerge to rebuild his business empire, his fortune and his lavish lifestyle. Now the rollercoaster ride that is the life of this flamboyant tycoon is about to start up again – and there are plenty more dramatic twists and turns to come.

Sitting in October 2009 in his office in the plush Tower 42 skyscraper in the City flanked by three PR gurus, Ablyazov – short and spruce, with a smooth manner and an infectious smile that he flashes wryly to win sympathy as he recounts his trials and tribulations – is adamant that he did not rob his own bank blind before hotfooting it off to London. 'The question arises as to why I set up the bank and turned it into a leading one in order to steal some sum in such a banal manner,' he says, with an elegant shrug of his expensively besuited shoulders.

Ablyazov is talking about BTA Bank, hitherto hailed as a flagship in Kazakhstan's petrodollar-buoyant financial sector and now a basket case on the brink of collapse. On one side of the conflict stands the combative 46-year-old, who fled Kazakhstan in February 2009, fearing arrest, days before the government forcibly nationalised his bank in what the tycoon slams as an illegal asset grab. On the other side stand the government and the new management it has installed, a measure the authorities say was necessary to prevent BTA from going into financial meltdown and taking half of Kazakhstan's banking sector down with it.

The crux of the tug of war over the bank is not so much the question of BTA's financial position – undeniably dire at this point – but something else entirely, Ablyazov says. 'At the bottom of this lies the desire of Nazarbayev to seize the bank. He thinks that a person who has political ambitions shouldn't control such a huge financial institution; he should be dependent. He couldn't manage to get me under his control.'[1]

Sophisticated conman or persecuted political dissident – which is the true face of Mukhtar Ablyazov?

Ablyazov had always had a nose for business. A nuclear physics graduate from a prestigious Moscow university, he abandoned his postgraduate studies when the Soviet Union collapsed to throw himself into the exhilarating entrepreneurial opportunities opening up with the fall of communism. Wheeling and dealing in the heady new capitalist economy suited him: he made money importing faxes and photocopiers, before forming his own company, Astana Holdings, which diversified from producing salt, pasta and sugar (he was a rival of Rakhat Aliyev, who started out in the sugar trade) into the lucrative financial sector.

The self-made millionaire soon attracted the attention of Nazarbayev, on the lookout for young go-getters to join his team to build the new Kazakhstan, and in 1998 he propelled the businessman into the cabinet as minister for energy, industry and trade. The first decade of independence had been kind to Ablyazov – but as 2001 drew to a close, his days as a powerful establishment player were numbered. The charismatic entrepreneur was about to risk a political gamble that would see him cross swords with Nazarbayev and end with him languishing in a prison cell in northern Kazakhstan.

In late 2001, as Kazakhstan geared up for its tenth anniversary of independence, some movers and shakers were getting frustrated. A decade after the USSR's collapse, they believed it was time Kazakhstan shed the old Soviet legacy by embracing sweeping political and economic reforms. 'We suggested conducting democratic reforms to Nazarbayev, because it was already obvious that the country was retreating very quickly into authoritarianism, and that a clan state was taking shape in which people loyal to Nazarbayev were appointed not because of their professional skills but because of personal loyalty,' Ablyazov recalled seventeen years later.[2] Some of the reformers harboured an idealistic desire to democratise a political system increasingly monopolised by Nazarbayev, while others (like Ablyazov) were also intent on ushering in accountability to allow their businesses to thrive. 'Can you live without air?' he asked rhetorically at the time. 'No. And business also suffocates without democracy. Because two things are most important in it: capital and people. If state officials can come to you at any moment and take away your money, goods, property – that's frightening. But what's more frightening is when your staff lose their initiative, resourcefulness, energy and self-confidence, because at any moment they can, without being guilty of anything, end up guilty before the law. In Kazakhstan, the state is stronger than any business group and than business as a whole, and that's why we need democracy. And not tomorrow, but today.'[3]

Prescient words, as it turned out. The founders of Democratic Choice of Kazakhstan (DVK) hoped to nudge Nazarbayev towards political liberalisation and economic transparency, but ended up inadvertently throwing down the gauntlet to a president accustomed to untrammelled rule.

The list of powerful establishment players who joined DVK in November 2001 was impressive: from the government, deputy prime minister Oraz Zhandosov, labour minister Alikhan Baymenov and several deputy ministers; and from parliament, senators like Zauresh Battalova and MPs from both ends of the political spectrum – from pro-business liberal Bolat Abilov to communist Serikbolsyn Abdildin. From the cohort of officials running Kazakhstan's large provinces there was Galymzhan Zhakiyanov, governor of Pavlodar Region; and from the business community there were top entrepreneurs like Ablyazov, his business partner Yerzhan Tatishev, banker Nurzhan Subkhanberdin and automobile magnate Nurlan Smagulov.

DVK's calls for political reform were hardly radical: more powers to parliament to check Nazarbayev's rule; the screws loosened on the media; and regional governors elected by the people instead of appointed by the president, making them accountable to those they were serving instead of the man at the top. 'Democratic reforms in Kazakhstan have come to a halt,' DVK said in its founding statement.[4] The reformers were urging Nazarbayev to loosen his vice-like grip and shift Kazakhstan onto a more liberal trajectory – and for that they incurred his wrath.

First the government tried the carrot: you're either with us or against us, so quit DVK and return to the fold. Some complied, but others refused. It was time for the stick.

Dubbed 'plotters' by Qasym-Jomart Toqayev, the prime minister (the man who would be catapulted into the presidency when Nazarbayev stepped down nearly two decades later), senior officials like Zhandosov, Baymenov and Zhakiyanov were summarily fired. Instead of engaging with the reform movement nudging for change from within, Astana had chosen to interpret it as a threat – though Nazarbayev's spokesman insisted the president shared DVK's political and economic goals. Soon Toqayev was hinting at dark forces at play: the security forces had recently foiled two assassination plots against Nazarbayev, he revealed out of the blue, and 'I would venture to assure you that the terrorists are not that far away from us.'[5]

Two months after the creation of DVK, Nazarbayev 'warned me that if I didn't renounce my convictions and renounce Democratic Choice of Kazakhstan […] I'd be jailed and my business taken away', Ablyazov later recalled. 'He said your fate and that of Galymzhan Zhakiyanov will be under my personal control. Now', he concluded with a humourless laugh, 'I see that it was under his personal control.'[6]

In March 2002, Ablyazov was suddenly arrested as part of a three-year-old corruption probe in which he had previously been questioned but never charged. Zhakiyanov leapt to Ablyazov's defence, pointing to a 'political motivation' – but he was next up for arrest himself, on corruption charges that had been filed against him immediately after he had joined DVK.

Zhakiyanov's detention took a dramatic turn: tipped off about a raid to snatch him at an Almaty hotel, he holed up in the French embassy to seek protection. The embarrassing diplomatic stand-off was resolved when the government signed a deal with the French, German and British ambassadors pledging to ensure Zhakiyanov's safety and place him under house arrest. Zhakiyanov left the embassy – and was bundled onto a plane to northern Kazakhstan and thrown into jail. 'The arrests came years after the alleged crimes were committed, but only months after Ablyazov and Zhakiyanov founded an opposition political movement,' noted the US government drily.[7] In July 2002, the two were convicted in separate trials. Ablyazov was jailed for six years, Zhakiyanov for seven.

Ablyazov did not languish long behind bars. According to a letter later published in the press, he sent Nazarbayev a heartfelt *mea culpa* begging for a pardon, regretting that he had 'out of my stupidity permitted myself to get dragged into totally pointless political battles' that had 'undermined your trust, dealing a blow to the country's image and to you personally' and urging the president to 'forgive me as one of your disciples who has made a mistake'.[8] Ablyazov said later that this letter was a fake, published in the media to discredit him, but he did acknowledge doing a deal as a 'manoeuvre' to get out of jail.[9] Ten months into his six-year sentence, he walked free, while Zhakiyanov stayed in prison, refusing to ask for a pardon for crimes he said he had never committed, and after his release bowed out of politics. After Ablyazov was freed, he made a public pledge to quit politics that was a quid pro quo for his freedom, renouncing DVK and loftily accusing it of offering 'few constructive ideas'.[10]

Ablyazov's friends in the business community had vouched for him to the president – and when he broke his promise to steer clear of politics and fled Kazakhstan in 2009, Nazarbayev's wrath would fall on their heads. 'You swore to me in writing, on oath, that he would serve the motherland,' the president railed ominously at Kazakhstan's top entrepreneurs in 2010. 'He has now spat in the face of all his friends. [...] All of you are going to answer for it.'[11] Six weeks later, Mukhtar Dzhakishev, an Ablyazov associate who was widely respected as an upstanding member of the business community, was jailed for fourteen years in a contentious trial involving allegations of corruption in the nuclear industry of which he had been in charge. This, said opposition leader Bolat Abilov, was plainly a 'reprisal' over the Ablyazov case.[12]

After his early release in 2003, the comeback kid bounced back. Ablyazov picked up his entrepreneurial interests, basing himself in Russia (and surviving an assassination attempt in 2004, he said, though he was sketchy on the details) until returning to Kazakhstan to head BTA Bank – at Nazarbayev's behest, according to his 2009 interview in the City of London: Nazarbayev wanted to keep him close to keep an eye on him, and use Ablyazov's return 'to demonstrate his wisdom as the father of the nation who could find compromises with his former opponents'.

Ablyazov became CEO of BTA Bank, to which he was no stranger: he had bought a majority stake in 1998, but concealed this behind his business associate Yerzhan Tatishev when he was jailed. In another twist to the tale, Tatishev was shot dead in 2004 in a wolf-hunting accident in circumstances US diplomats described as 'close to incomprehensible', given his 'renown as a hunter'.[13] In 2017, Muratkhan Tokmadi, a businessman and alleged criminal kingpin who had recently been jailed on corruption charges, made the dramatic claim that he had shot Tatishev on Ablyazov's orders in exchange for a debt write-off, and subsequently bribed investigators $20,000 to call it an accident.[14] Ablyazov dismissed the claim as a 'fairy tale' and said he had never even heard of, let alone met, the alleged contract killer.[15] However, in 2018, a Kazakh court sentenced him *in absentia* to life in jail over the killing,[16] while Tokmadi – after a dramatic jail break and rapid recapture – was jailed for ten and a half years. The dead man's family hailed that conviction as a triumph of justice, fourteen years after Kazakhstan's legal system had permitted the murder to be covered up using corruption and connections.[17]

Before Ablyazov's return, he said Nazarbayev dropped 'a threatening hint' that 'I should be politically loyal' – but did he really harbour political ambitions, as the president suspected? 'I have a desire to change the country,' he said cautiously in London in 2009. 'That's perceived as political ambitions.' Did he break his pledge to stay out of politics? 'Nazarbayev knew that I also support – well, in his opinion, let's say – political parties, that I held consultations with them. That was true,' he hedged. There were persistent rumours that Ablyazov was bankrolling a successor to the DVK movement called Alga! (Forward!), which had been operating in Kazakhstan under its leader Vladimir Kozlov on the fringes of the law since the government had refused to register it as an official party. 'You know, I can't say that I finance it,' said Ablyazov evasively. 'But I will say there was a period when I supported the party in various ways. Support doesn't have to be financial.' The government also believed he was financing media outlets, such as the newspaper *Respublika*, which pulled no punches in its criticism of the government. Was that true? 'It's an independent newspaper,' with which he had 'friendly relations, partnership relations, ideological relations' – but no, he definitely did not fund it, Ablyazov said. He was, however, lying about not channelling funds to the opposition and the press: years later, in 2016, Ablyazov admitted that he had always been financing 'the opposition, dissident media outlets'.[18] In fact, he said he had started channelling funds to opposition forces back in 1997 and never stopped.[19]

Ablyazov touted his political asylum in the UK as proof that he was a victim of persecution in Kazakhstan. 'I'd just got tired of living in a country where there is no law, where the power is one person, where one day everything can be taken away, someone can be put in prison, can be killed,' he explained airily when pressed on his political ambitions. 'The authorities have shown this, and in this sense I had the desire to change the country – to change the country so that it would become a normal European[-style] state with the same civilised law.'

For now, though, Ablyazov was focused on the battle to clear his name of the multi-billion-dollar fraud charges, of which he claimed total innocence.

Three years after this interview in the City of London, Ablyazov was on the run again – escaping not a Kazakh arrest warrant but the long arm of the English law.

As the complex legal drama played out between the bank and the banking magnate in the High Court, one of the biggest wrangles was over

Ablyazov's assets: how much was he worth? Billions, said BTA's lawyers, much of it stolen from the bank and held in assets concealed behind a murky web of offshore companies – over a thousand of them – and proxy owners. Ablyazov argued that fudging ownership of assets was all part of doing business in Kazakhstan for political reasons (and one judge duly noted the 'chilling picture' his legal team painted of a country that appeared to have 'much in common with Ancient Rome'[20]) but insisted he had complied with court rulings ordering full disclosure. In 2012, after three years of legal wrangling in a case that was at one point costing Ablyazov at least £1.5 million a month, a High Court judge's patience snapped: he ordered the businessman slung behind bars on contempt of court charges for concealing his assets in a 'deliberate and brazen' deception.[21]

Ablyazov was not in court to hear himself sentenced to 22 months in prison, and he was not going to serve them either. He fled the UK, the billionaire who had once flown by private jet and zoomed about in armoured cars reportedly opting for more modest transport to cross the Channel to France: he went by coach, using 'a passport that he failed to deliver up', a BTA lawyer claimed.[22] Ablyazov was in possession of a Central African Republic diplomatic passport issued in his capacity as adviser to the CAR president, his lawyer later explained, in the assumed name of Marat Ayan for security reasons.[23]

This convoluted CAR link later caused difficulties for Ablyazov's wife, Alma Shalabayeva, and the couple's six-year-old daughter. One night in 2013, Italian security forces descended on a villa in Rome where they were living (located with the help of private investigators). Ablyazov had been in Rome visiting them a few days before.[24] He had slipped away before the raid took place, but his wife and daughter were detained and bundled – accompanied by Kazakh diplomats – onto a plane to Almaty, where Shalabayeva was accused of document fraud: prosecutors suspected her CAR passport in the name of Alma Ayan was forged. The case caused a political storm over claims that democratic Italy had colluded with autocratic Kazakhstan to kidnap a woman and child living there legally: Italy's interior minister faced a no-confidence vote in parliament, his chief of staff resigned, and later Kazakhstan quietly allowed Shalabayeva and her daughter to return to Italy.[25]

Ablyazov later denied fleeing arrest, saying he left Britain because his life was in danger and the police could not guarantee his safety – and it was true that he had received a warning from the London Metropolitan Police about a politically motivated threat to his security a year earlier. But his flight sounded the legal death knell for his court battle: his disappearance awarded BTA a de facto, if not de jure, victory at the High Court, where a judge debarred him from continuing to fight the case since he had gone to ground – a ruling BTA triumphantly hailed as 'a ringing endorsement' of its claims. 'Mr Ablyazov has been unconscionable in his refusal to abide by the orders of the court,' the judge stated. 'It is difficult to imagine a party to commercial litigation who has acted with more cynicism, opportunism and deviousness towards court orders than Mr Ablyazov.'[26] (The litigant was unmoved by the damning characterisation. He 'didn't give a damn' about that 'absurd and shameful' ruling, he said later. 'I believe it was the judge who showed opportunism and cynicism when making that ruling.'[27])

Theresa May, then the UK's Home Secretary, tried to revoke his asylum, prompting Ablyazov to urge her to 'recognise that you and your courts are being manipulated by a kleptocratic dictator.'[28] His asylum automatically expired in 2016.

High Court orders granted BTA Bank the right to recover $4.8 billion from Ablyazov to recoup losses that the bank believed actually ran to at least $6 billion and possibly as much as $10 billion. The list of assets attributed to Ablyazov was mind-bogglingly long, including anything from swish properties in the UK and Kazakhstan to passenger jets, from luxury Moscow property construction projects to stakes in Central Asian mineral deposits (though Ablyazov disputed ownership of much of what was up for seizure, making the asset recovery process a tortuous one that was still ongoing a decade after it began.[29]). There were UK homes worth over £40 million – including a Surrey country estate and a mansion on The Bishops Avenue in London, a street so chic it is nicknamed Billionaires' Row – and an ostentatious mansion in Almaty decorated in faux Louis XIV style complete with gilded mirrors, ornate chandeliers and white cherubs.[30] That was one of 20 houses seized in Kazakhstan, along with 3 aeroplanes, 106 cars and stakes in 22 companies.

BTA's multi-million-pound litigation, encompassing 11 different trials in the UK, more than 200 court hearings and nearly 500 lawyers fighting the bank's corner had scored a victory, but only by default, since Ablyazov was merely debarred. However, one High Court ruling issued in 2013 in a related case was damning: 'There can be only one explanation for the fact that the very large sums of money which were advanced [by BTA] were immediately transferred to companies owned or controlled by Mr. Ablyazov, namely, that the original loans were part of a dishonest scheme whereby Mr. Ablyazov sought to misappropriate monies which belonged to the bank.'[31] Ablyazov, one of BTA's lawyers once said, was 'the spider at the centre of the web' in 'one of the largest corporate frauds the world has ever seen'.[32]

But where was the fugitive oligarch?

He was holed up in a sumptuous villa on the oligarchs' playground of the French Riviera, where commandos captured him in a dramatic swoop in 2013.

Ablyazov's arrest was suitably theatrical for a man whose life story resembles a far-fetched film plot. Private detectives hired by BTA Bank followed his glamorous blonde Ukrainian lawyer Olena Tyshchenko from the steps of the High Court to an assignation with Ablyazov on the French Riviera, where they tracked him down to his swanky lair in the village of Mouans-Sartoux near Cannes. Ablyazov's lawyer, the ex-wife of his business partner Sergey Tyshchenko, featured in salacious British press reports speculating that their relationship was more than a purely legal one,[33] after BTA's spin doctors had briefed journalists that their sleuths – one bikini-clad, to blend in – had snapped the two of them in a clinch and photographed Ablyazov making a bed in his boxers. Russian media added spice by suggesting that the lawyer's jealous ex had helped entrap the pair by bugging her Riviera home and recording her Skype conversations with Ablyazov.[34]

Olena Tyshchenko also later landed behind bars for a spell: she was arrested in Moscow on charges of laundering some of the Ablyazov millions, but released without charge. In an improbable twist, she was then appointed anti-corruption tsarina in her home country, Ukraine, to track millions of dollars spirited away by the overthrown president Viktor Yanukovych. She resigned in 2015 amid a furore over her failure to declare ownership of millions of dollars' worth of assets she held abroad.

*

Ablyazov's future looked bleak: he had swapped a mansion on the French Riviera for a jail cell in Paris, from where he launched a mammoth extradition battle that his supporters depicted apocalyptically as a fight for his very survival.

Ablyazov was wanted on corruption charges by Russia and Ukraine as well as Kazakhstan, which had no extradition treaty with France and dim prospects of extraditing him from Europe, given his claims of political persecution. Ablyazov's legal team alleged that Russia and Ukraine were acting as Astana's proxies in its political pursuit of Ablyazov, and that he risked being sent onwards to Kazakhstan by either of these countries, which would be a violation of his human rights. At first things did not go his way: in 2014, a court gave the green light to his extradition, and Ablyazov then lost an appeal – but the fight was not over yet. Once again, Ablyazov was down but not out.

In 2015, the high-profile case landed on the desk of Manuel Valls, the French prime minister, who had to weigh up the argument: was Ablyazov a slippery conman evading justice, or a persecuted political dissident whose extradition might jeopardise his safety – or even his life? The French PM gave the go-ahead for Ablyazov's extradition to Russia, leaving his lawyer Peter Sahlas declaring himself 'shocked that France, which is supposed to be the land of human rights, is thus validating the Russian judicial and penitentiary system'.[35]

Ablyazov had one last throw of the dice left: the Conseil d'État, France's highest court for administrative justice. The magnate's fate balanced on a knife edge: would he walk out of jail to a life of freedom in Europe, or be bundled onto a plane, to be thrown behind bars in Russia or dispatched onwards to Kazakhstan, allegedly at risk of losing not only his liberty but also his life?

In December 2016, a jubilant Ablyazov walked free. Kazakhstan had 'pressured' Russia and Ukraine to issue arrest warrants for him, the Conseil d'État ruled, and 'all circumstances in this case show clearly that [Ablyazov's] extradition to Russia was sought for a political purpose; therefore, such extradition could not be lawfully granted'.[36]

Three months after his release in France, where he later gained asylum, Ablyazov was put on trial in Kazakhstan *in absentia* on charges of embezzlement and money laundering, with the prosecution alleging that he had robbed BTA Bank of $7.5 billion through an entangled network of dodgy offshore accounts, shell companies and falsified loans. In 2017, he was sentenced to twenty years in jail that he will never have to serve, provided he never steps into any jurisdiction that might extradite him to Kazakhstan.

Unbowed by his three and a half years in a French jail cell, Ablyazov came out guns blazing. He pledged to remake his fortune, sue for compensation and asset recovery – and overthrow his arch-enemy Nazarbayev. This he set about doing by re-forming (from his comfortable exile) the DVK political opposition movement, to achieve his goal of 'regime change and the establishment of a democratic state' in Kazakhstan.[37] This reignited the feud with Kazakhstan's powers that be, which banned the group as extremist and set about hunting down and arresting supporters, while Ablyazov set about fomenting dissent and calling for street protests.[38] Ablyazov had, he claimed after his release in 2016, already bankrolled one revolution that had toppled the president in neighbouring Kyrgyzstan in 2005, a sort of practice run for Kazakhstan, and Nazarbayev, he prophesied incorrectly, could be overthrown within a 'maximum' of three years. 'He's old, he's been in power for twenty-six years, everyone's fed up,' claimed the bullish Ablyazov as he bounced back again. People in Kazakhstan, he said with pharisaic sanguinity, 'are tired of lies, corruption and poverty'.[39]

CHAPTER 4

Fault Lines in the Feel-Good Factor

Zhanaozen, 2011/2016

The town out in the far west of Kazakhstan, a couple of hours' drive inland from the Caspian Sea, looks like a war zone. The streets are lined with the charred shells of buildings and the burnt-out carcases of cars. A scorched propaganda poster of a smiling Nazarbayev hangs peeling from a wall. The hospital is crammed with gunshot victims – but these survivors are the lucky ones: others lie dead in the town morgue. The police station cellars are packed with detainees, some of whom later say they were beaten, throttled, suffocated and threatened with rape.

This is Zhanaozen, a dust-blown town out in the oilfields that power Kazakhstan's economy. A few days earlier, on 16 December 2011, like the rest of the country, it had been gearing up to celebrate Independence Day, with pomp and ceremony and adulation lavished on the Leader of the Nation, whose face stares out of that charred poster with its cheery slogan: 'Congratulations on the Independence Holiday!' The festivities were to be extra special for the twentieth anniversary of independence – but in Zhanaozen the party did not exactly go with a swing.

On the big day, the president was 2,500 kilometres away from the heartlands of Kazakhstan's oil industry in his glitzy capital, opening the latest folly to adorn ostentatious Astana: a whimsical replica of the Arc de Triomphe in cream and beige, built 'as a sign of our labour, our successes, as a sign of our transition into the future', as he put it.

'We are all gathered here today to celebrate a great holiday together: the twentieth anniversary of our country's independence,' Nazarbayev declaimed. 'Long live Kazakhstan! Long live Independence! Long live the unity of the Kazakhstanis!'[1]

Out west, this feel-good speech failed to touch the hearts of the oil workers living in forlorn Zhanaozen (pronounced nasally 'Zhangaozen', like 'singing'), whose drab streets could not contrast more starkly with shiny Astana. Zhanaozen erupted in riots, police opened fire on the crowds, and Nazarbayev's grand celebrations were wrecked. By an unfortunate historical coincidence, it was twenty-five years to the day since the last time a demonstration had been violently quelled in Kazakhstan, when Soviet security forces had quashed the *Zheltoksan* ('December') protest that is nowadays celebrated as the harbinger of independence.

Nazarbayev later claimed he had no idea trouble was brewing in Zhanaozen – but tensions had been simmering for months before they boiled over into the worst social unrest to hit Kazakhstan for a quarter of a century.

In May 2011, thousands of oil workers had downed tools in a dispute over pay and conditions, beginning a strike no one suspected would spiral into fatal violence. Grievances had been festering not for months but for years, and were not purely related to the immediate demands. 'The workers weren't happy with salaries and with living and working conditions,' Samat (a pseudonym), a thirty-something oil worker who was one of the strikers, explained long after the dust had settled. 'We have the status of an oil town, but it doesn't look like an oil town, does it? It's like a village. There are no amenities.' The oil workers had long been disgruntled. Their labour had propelled Kazakhstan's oil boom – but where were the benefits for them? They laboured in tough conditions and lived in a town that lay atop Kazakhstan's hydrocarbon wealth but boasted little to show for it. The oil workers felt inadequately rewarded for their contribution, tired of watching the petrodollars seeping into vanity projects in Astana (like that Arc de Triomphe), or enriching Nazarbayev's cronies, or disappearing into the pockets of venal local officials.

When the workers downed tools, the companies dug their heels in. OzenMunayGaz, the state-owned oil company at the heart of the dispute, pointed out that salaries were already above the national average, and that it had raised wages six times in three years.[2] By July, with thousands of workers still out on strike, oil production dipping and profits taking a hit, the companies decided to force the strikers' hands. They went to court, had the stoppages declared illegal and delivered an ultimatum: go back to work or face the chop. When many strikers refused to return to the oilfields, the companies delivered on their promise and fired over 2,000 staff.

The dismissed oil workers began squatting on the main square to protest at their treatment and demand reinstatement, declaring hunger strikes to draw attention to their plight. As the baking summer progressed, the political temperature in Zhanaozen heated up against a drumbeat of intimidation.[3] 'There was browbeating,' recalled Samat. 'We were told to go back to work, not to strike. Everyone was being intimidated, but we kept striking because there were no results. The authorities didn't want to talk to us, to reach an agreement, to negotiate, to take any measures. And the court immediately declared our strike illegal. It's in international conventions, isn't it? In any state, the right to strike exists.' Roza Tuletayeva, an oil worker who became a prominent figure in the dispute because of her eloquence in putting the strikers' case, also noted an official reluctance to engage with the disgruntled staff as a factor behind mounting tensions: 'At that time, there was no dialogue between the government and the workers.'

Samat and Roza were sharing their memories in autumn 2016, ahead of the fifth anniversary of the violence, in separate interviews in Zhanaozen. Samat was speaking after coming off his shift in the industrial part of town, where a cheery sign beside the road greeted oil workers with the message 'Thank You for Your Labour!', and Roza, a 51-year-old with striking features and a colourful, geometric-patterned headscarf, was talking in a café in Zhanaozen. Both had ended up being fingered as ringleaders of the violence in 2011 and put on trial, and Roza was sent to prison – but the first person to be jailed was the strikers' lawyer. Three months into the industrial dispute, Natalya Sokolova was sent to prison for six years for 'inciting social discord', an unmistakable warning to anyone considering offering the strikers legal advice (her sentence was later commuted and she was released early).[4]

That summer, two mysterious murders ramped up the tension. Zhaksylyk Turbayev, an oil worker and trade union activist, was beaten to death at his place of work, and Zhansaule Karabalayeva, the eighteen-year-old daughter of a striker, disappeared and was found stabbed to death. Investigators said these murders were unrelated to the industrial action, but the strikers – nervous, angry and embattled – were not so sure.

When Independence Day came round on 16 December, the strikers were still squatting on Yntymak Square (the name, ironically, means 'accord'). To their outrage, the *akimat* (town hall) decided to organise a party on the square, with a stage for musicians, Kazakh yurts selling snacks and souvenirs, and a *yolka* (Christmas tree) to get Zhanaozen into a festive mood for the forthcoming New Year holiday. 'What kind of a celebration is that, when we'd been striking for seven months, when children were going hungry, when we'd seen no salary or money or help for seven months?' asked Samat, still bristling five years later. The party, he believed, was intended 'firstly to provoke us, secondly to make us leave'.

The celebrations kicked off in Zhanaozen as elsewhere in Kazakhstan – but they did not last long. Protesters started interrupting the festivities, before storming the stage, hurling the PA systems blaring out cheerful music to the floor, overturning the festive *yolka* and tearing down the yurts. Amidst the chaos, the police opened fire. 'I was standing on the square and the shooting started, and after that a bullet hit me, from a Kalashnikov,' striker Nurlibek Nurgaliyev recalled in 2016, touching his face at the painful memory. 'It hit me in the chin, and got stuck in the back of my jaw. They couldn't get it out.' Doctors eventually managed to extract the bullet, but Nurlibek suffered permanent damage to his facial tendons and still speaks with a slight slur.

Before long a full-blown riot was raging through the town. An early target was the OzenMunayGaz headquarters, before protesters turned their ire on the *akimat*, the symbol of power, storming it and setting it alight. The angry mob rampaged through the town, overturning and torching cars and ransacking buildings and setting them alight in an orgy of violence that caused damage running to at least $13 million.[5] The unrest spread to the nearby town of Shetpe, where there were more clashes. Security forces kept firing on the restive crowds, and by the end of the day 15 people lay in the morgue: 14 shot dead in Zhanaozen, one in Shetpe.

Who gave the order to use live fire on the unarmed protesters? The government insisted no command was issued; the police claimed that they had only opened fire after armed demonstrators had begun shooting. Those who had been hit by bullets had never been placed in the cross hairs, said the police; they had simply been struck by ricocheting bullets. The strikers said this was an outright lie. 'They said we fired shots, but there was no video evidence of that,' said Samat bluntly. 'We had no weapons. It was the police who fired shots.' Roza also strongly denied that claim. 'I always had the labour code in one hand and the constitution in the other,' she said quietly. 'They were my weapons.' Zhanaozen's police chief pledged to produce exonerating video proving demonstrators fired at his officers from sawn-off shotguns and pistols, but he never delivered.[6] Another video that surfaced told a different story: posted online by a resident, it showed riot police advancing on unarmed protesters, some of whom were hurling rocks, then shooting them in the back as they fled. As one demonstrator lay prone and another hopped away injured, officers descended on a third and set about beating him with truncheons.[7]

'Everyone's terrified,' said Guldan Agiyeva, choking back a sob. 'People are afraid of the riot police. They have weapons and we have nothing.' She was sitting by the hospital bed of her son, just out of the operating theatre, one of seventy-five gunshot victims lying in Zhanaozen's hospital, according to medical staff (official figures later released cited a lower civilian injury toll of sixty-four people wounded by firearms; thirty-five members of the security forces also sustained injuries).[8] Those figures suggested that there had been a lot of bullets ricocheting around the town, given that some of the bullets must have missed the demonstrators since the police claimed that they had not been aiming at them. No one admitted to taking part in the riot – not surprisingly, since the wards were swarming with police taking statements from the wounded and plain-clothes KNB agents. Bekmurat Turashev, an oil worker who said he had not been on strike or protesting, lay groaning on an intravenous drip after being shot in the stomach, hand and back. What happened? 'I haven't got a clue. I was just passing and people were running at me. There was shooting.' Others offered similar explanations for their injuries. 'I just stepped out of my house to smoke and I got shot in the lung,' said Toktan Bergaliyev. 'I was going to the mosque to pray and suddenly I was shot,' said Beknur Amantayev.

The government, eager to demonstrate transparency to the world, had granted journalists access to the closed-off town, still under a state of emergency four days after the violence, but I was accompanied by a minder, a young female *akimat* official whom I had given the slip in the maze of hospital corridors. Most of the casualties had gunshot wounds, but others claimed police brutality. 'The riot police did it,' whispered a young man with two black eyes. 'They caught me there on the square and beat me up there,' said another, displaying bruises on his head, back and arms. One man lay unconscious, hooked up to a life support machine, beaten to a pulp. The police had brought him in without explanation, a nurse murmured. By this time, my minder was banging furiously on a door at the end of the corridor which the medics had locked to give a journalist an unimpeded glimpse of the violence inflicted on the townspeople by the security forces, who were still roaming the streets outside clad in riot gear and toting AK-47s.

Nazarbayev soon jetted into the troubled town and demonstrated that he had not lost his famous popular touch. 'I've been with the people for twenty years,' he told the townspeople. 'I know this industry, I know all the difficulties, and we, the state, are going to do everything to make life better. [...] Understand this: I don't want our country to live through such a nightmare again.'⁹

Millions of dollars would be poured into the depressed town – a *monogorod*, a town dependent on a single industry – and the dismissed strikers would be found new jobs, Nazarbayev pledged. Complaining that officials had kept him in the dark, he forced the resignation of his son-in-law, billionaire businessman Timur Kulibayev, for bungling the strike in his official capacity overseeing the energy sector. Nazarbayev may have passed the buck, but the unusual spectacle of a member of the ruling family taking the rap suggested he meant business.

Still, someone would have to pay the price for the turmoil, which in Nazarbayev's Kazakhstan could not be down to disaffection. 'We will seek the organisers of the unrest, in whatever corner of the world they are hiding,' he thundered. 'There will be a trial and the guilty will be punished.' He blamed 'provocateurs' who had paid 'hooligans' to riot, behind whom stood 'organised criminal groups' with links abroad which aimed 'to sow discord in our society'.¹⁰

Soon, the authorities named the evil mastermind: Mukhtar Ablyazov, who had allegedly hatched a sinister plot to overthrow Nazarbayev by stoking and bankrolling unrest in a far-flung town 2,500 kilometres from the seat of government in Astana, all from his London lair. Ablyazov dismissed the theory as ludicrous and professed himself 'horrified by the violence'.[11] (Many years later, however, he publicly embraced the tactic of stoking protests to achieve 'regime change' in Kazakhstan.[12])

Five years on, the oil workers scoffed at the idea that Ablyazov had stirred up the turmoil. 'We didn't know Ablyazov and we don't know him,' insisted Nurlibek. 'We learned about Ablyazov from the internet.' Roza gave a derisive hoot at the idea that the strikers were incited from afar. 'Workers are not sheep,' she snapped, with a wave of her hand. 'Why do they have to be told to do something by someone?' 'The government looks for scapegoats,' barked Samat. 'They want to come out of it clean, so they need to blame it on someone, so they pin it all on Ablyazov. Ablyazov has nothing to do with this.'

The authorities could not get their hands on Ablyazov, but soon they started rounding up his alleged co-conspirators. In January 2012, police swooped down on a diverse crowd in Almaty – including political activists, journalists and even a theatre director – who had one common denominator: suspected or real links to Ablyazov, financial or otherwise. Some had visited the strikers in Zhanaozen in a show of solidarity – although so had an Irish MEP, because the strike about which Nazarbayev knew so little had become a socialist cause célèbre: it had even led British rock star Sting to cancel a planned concert in Astana on Nazarbayev's birthday, months before the violence.[13]

The list of those arrested included Vladimir Kozlov, the leader of Alga!, an opposition party Astana suspected Ablyazov of funding (and he later admitted he had been); newspaper editor Igor Vinyavskiy; elderly theatre director Bolat Atabayev; and youth activist and journalist Zhanbolat Mamay. In his last editorial before his detention, Vinyavskiy had declared prophetically that the security services were 'strenuously seeking enemies' to scapegoat for Zhanaozen.[14] Vinyavskiy was held on charges of calling for a forcible seizure of power some two years earlier, in a case supposedly completely unrelated to the Zhanaozen turmoil; after two months, he was suddenly released without charge under amnesty, and he subsequently moved to Poland.[15] Atabayev and Mamay were released without charge after six months behind bars (Atabayev moved abroad and passed away in 2021; Mamay continued to rankle with his political activism and outspoken journalism; his reporting was silenced in 2017, with a conviction on charges of laundering money for Ablyazov, for which his non-custodial sentence included a three-year ban on working as a journalist, but he continued to engage in politics).[16]

Kozlov and two others – Serik Sapargaly, an Alga! party activist, and Akzhanat Aminov, a striker from Zhanaozen – were left facing the rap for being the political ringleaders of the violence; but before their trial, scores of oil workers entered the dock.

The interrogator 'suffocated me with a trash bag, he strangled [me] – when the bag's taken away your eyes pop out and you can't breathe and you start breathing deeply, and when you breathe deeply your head spins'.[17] That is how the police extracted from Roza the confession that she had orchestrated the Zhanaozen violence, according to her testimony at a mass trial of strikers and townspeople that opened in March 2012. There were thirty-seven defendants crammed into the enclosed glass dock in the city of Aktau, a couple of hours' drive from Zhanaozen across the desert, and another twelve on trial in Shetpe, on charges ranging from inciting unrest to arson, looting and assaulting police officers. The atmosphere in the courtroom was charged, as hundreds of relatives observed the proceedings with mutterings of discontent that occasionally erupted into heckling.

Most were angry that the defendants had been singled out as scapegoats for the violence, when the deaths had been caused by the security forces. Some officers had been charged – but there were ten times as many civilians on trial as police. One mother could not understand why her son was being tried for looting a mincer and a frying pan; a man complained that his cousin had tried to warn the authorities that the oil strike was dangerously close to spiralling out of control but had now landed in the dock. 'There's no justice,' complained one mother bitterly. 'The president himself came and said that third forces were to blame. So why are these people being tried?' asked another bewildered woman. (The question of these mysterious 'third forces' was never resolved, but some strikers recalled strangers suddenly appearing in their midst just before the violence erupted.)

Allegations of confessions coerced by torture came thick and fast: defendant Shabdal Utkilov testified to being suffocated with a plastic bag; Maksat Dosmagambetov and Naryn Dzharylgasynov said police had beaten them up and broken their ribs; Yesengeldy Abdrakhmanov claimed interrogators had jumped on his chest; Tanatar Kaliyev complained he was hit around the face with a stool; Kayrat Edilov said he was suffocated six times with a plastic bag; and Parakhat Dyusenbayev – whose father was among those killed in the hail of police bullets and whose sister was also on trial – said interrogators had beaten him up, smashed his head against a wall and threatened to sodomise him with a bottle.[18] 'What has rattled me more than anything is that we, who didn't beat anyone up, are sitting in the cage [the dock in court] and those with bloody hands are sitting in the [court]room,' Dyusenbayev said.[19]

The judge sent these torture allegations back to Zhanaozen for investigation, where law enforcement bodies unsurprisingly dismissed them as lies. The only torture case not ruled a product of the detainees' imagination was that of Bazarbay Kenzhebayev, an oil worker who had died after a fatal beating in a police cell. The perpetrators were never identified, but the head of the detention centre was jailed for five years ('a scapegoat for all those who tortured, raped and abused the people of Zhanaozen during those tragic days', remarked human rights campaigner Galym Ageleuov).[20] As for the shootings that had killed fifteen people, five junior police officers were jailed on charges of abuse of office, leaving their embittered relatives pondering why no top brass ever answered for the killings.[21]

All but four of the forty-nine defendants from Zhanaozen and Shetpe were convicted of crimes related to the violence; twenty-one were jailed. The longest term went to Roza Tuletayeva: seven years, later reduced to five on appeal. When the verdicts were passed, the courtroom erupted in uproar, and the judge was forced to retreat to escape a barrage of shoes and plastic bottles hurled by angry relatives that rained down on his head.[22]

The government had pledged to deliver justice to the troubled town – 'nothing will be hidden; nothing will be kept under wraps,' Erlan Idrissov, Kazakhstan's ambassador to Washington, had promised.[23] The authorities would 'prove to the world that Kazakhstan respects the rule of law, believes in an open and transparent system of government, and does not tolerate violence against its citizens'. Yet the government slapped down a request from the United Nations human rights commissioner for an international investigation, and instead Kazakhstan's well-oiled Western PR machine kicked in to spin the turmoil as an unfortunate blip for a country dedicated to democratisation.[24]

On hand to massage the message was former British prime minister Tony Blair, employed on a multi-million-pound consultancy contract for Nazarbayev, which critics attacked as shilling for a dictator but which Blair defended as intended to help improve governance. Blair advised his client to communicate the message (in a speech Nazarbayev was due to give in the UK) that 'these events, tragic though they were, should not obscure the enormous progress that Kazakhstan has made' – a sound bite would come in handy later 'as a quote that can be used in the future setting out the basic case for Kazakhstan'.[25]

The wheels of Kazakhstan's justice system continued to turn: next in the dock were Kozlov, Sapargaly and Aminov. As the leader of Alga!, the successor party to the DVK movement that had so riled Nazarbayev in 2001, Kozlov was a prominent opposition leader and a no-holds-barred critic of the president. He was 2,500 kilometres away at home in Almaty when the unrest erupted in Zhanaozen, though he had visited the strikers during their seven-month industrial action, as Nurlibek remembered: 'We'd met Kozlov on the square, but he didn't tell us to fight, to take up guns, to fire them, he didn't say that. He said to resolve all this by lawful means.'

The prosecution's case was that Kozlov had fomented the unrest in a bid to topple Nazarbayev at the instigation of Ablyazov, who had used his accessories on the ground to channel money to the strikers while Ablyazov-funded media outlets stoked the riots with incendiary material. In the absence of firm proof, the prosecution resorted to circumstantial evidence about Kozlov's contacts with Ablyazov, including bugged conversations over Skype in which they discussed capitalising on the oil workers' disaffection, and evidence from 'expert witnesses' about the dissolute nature of Kozlov's character: a 'bohemian personality', one testified solemnly.[26]

Kozlov's co-defendants escaped with suspended sentences, but the opposition leader was jailed for seven and a half years, to a chorus of condemnation from human rights campaigners ('silencing an outspoken opponent and muzzling the Alga! party, one of Kazakhstan's few alternative political voices', said Human Rights Watch[27]) and a languid expression of 'concern' from the US embassy over 'the apparent use of the criminal system to silence opposition voices'.[28] Shortly afterwards, Alga! was closed down by court order on the grounds that it was 'extremist'.

Were lessons learnt from the whole fiasco? The shuttering of independent trade unions in the years since the violence, the jailing of trade union leaders on spurious charges in the years that followed amid periodic outbreaks of industrial unrest in the oilfields of Zhanaozen and elsewhere, and expressions of concern from the International Labour Organisation (which has called on Kazakhstan to amend restrictive trade union laws) suggest perhaps not.[29]

'This is the first time I've been here since 2011,' said Roza quietly, walking in the gathering dusk to Yntymak Square on a balmy autumn evening in 2016 as the fifth anniversary of the violence approached. 'I didn't understand a thing,' she mused, still dazed when recalling the moment bullets started flying through the air on Independence Day 2011. 'I wanted to hide behind that wall, but it was pointless. The bullets were coming in all directions.'

Now, children were whizzing around on chairoplanes and leaping about on a bouncy castle, as a woman with a blue-bonneted baby snapped a selfie in front of a giant 'I Love Zhanaozen' sign. The town had been spruced up: the once drab blocks of flats lining the main street were painted bright shades of blue, orange, green and pink, and new schools and sports facilities signalled that the government had taken on board the oil workers' grievances over shabby conditions. Zhanaozen had also acquired its first Western-style shopping centre – albeit nowhere near as flash as the famous mall in Kazakhstan's capital designed in the swooping shape of a khan's tent, which boasts an indoor beach complete with sand brought from the Maldives.

Five years on from the violence, all those imprisoned were out of jail. Kozlov was paroled in 2016 after serving four and a half years. Roza was freed three years into her five-year term, and was taking a philosophical approach to it. 'It's nothing compared to Guantanamo,' she said, putting things in perspective – and clearly guarded about what she should say publicly. 'They didn't keep us inside for our whole lives, they let us out gradually.'

Roza, Samat and Nurlibek all had jobs in a new company created on Nazarbayev's orders especially to employ the couple of thousand oil workers dismissed in 2011, where they deemed the conditions reasonable and the salaries satisfactory. Roza was reluctant to blame the government for the three years of her life spent behind bars. 'Kazakhstan', she said over a pot of tea in a Zhanaozen café, where a TV blared out pop music and people were grabbing an after-work bite, 'is like my mother and father to me. There are things I don't want to say, although inside, perhaps I can say them.' Did that mean she could forgive her country if it wronged her? 'No,' she said firmly. 'Just that it's better not to bring shame on them.' Would she have done things differently, had she known how it would end? 'No,' she said, with a hard sideways look out of sharp eyes. 'Of all the ills that happen in life, you take a little piece of good from that.'

But for Nurlibek, the oil worker who suffered permanent injuries from catching a bullet in the jaw, it still rankled that the strikers bore the brunt of the blame for the deaths caused by the security forces. 'Thirty-seven oil workers were tried. Those thirty-seven oil workers didn't take up arms,' he said bitterly. 'They were the ones who were tortured and beaten up. What conclusion did you draw from that?' His own judgement was stark: 'There's no justice.'

CHAPTER 5

Publish and Be Damned

Almaty, 2011–16

Copies of *Respublika* are flying off the presses, and its reporters are gathering them up and stapling them together. Kazakhstan's most outspoken newspaper must hit the news-stands by morning – and this semi-clandestine printing operation smack in the centre of Almaty will make sure that it does.

Stepping into *Respublika*'s makeshift printing house is like stepping back in time: this is a modern-day version of samizdat, a trick used by dissidents in Soviet times to bypass the censors. 'This is unusual for the twenty-first century,' says Oksana Makushina, *Respublika*'s deputy editor, with a wry chuckle, gesturing at the old-fashioned printing machine spewing out blurry black-and-white copies that will become the newspaper's latest edition.

Loosely translated as 'self-publishing', samizdat involved copying subversive material – books, leaflets, cassettes – to share covertly with like-minded nonconformists in the USSR. The list of prohibited material was long: polemical tracts criticising communism; banned books by blacklisted writers like Boris Pasternak and Aleksandr Solzhenitsyn; and Western music such as rock 'n' roll, deemed too decadent for delicate Soviet ears (bootleg cassettes were called *magnitizdat*, from the word for tape recorder, *magnitofon*). It was all part of a cat-and-mouse game between the Soviet censors and the recalcitrant citizens who refused to accept their diktats – much like the one *Respublika* is now, in March 2011, playing with the government in modern-day Kazakhstan.

*

Respublika was not banned in Kazakhstan – yet. Its journalists had resorted to samizdat not to bypass the censors (who no longer exist) but to circumvent an unofficial prohibition on printing a newspaper that was a thorn in the side of the authorities. 'There's no ban on the publication and distribution of the newspaper, but there is a secret order to all printing houses not to take us,' explained Oksana, a vivacious woman in her forties with a heart-shaped face and a short, sharp haircut. 'We call this technical censorship: all the printing houses refuse to take our paper on for printing, on trumped-up pretexts. We tested it out. If you want to print a literary newspaper with the same print run at approximately the same time, printing houses have the technical capacity. But if you want to print *Respublika* newspaper, the technical capacity isn't there.' To circumvent the unofficial ban, 'we had to create a small printing facility right here in the editorial office' – on Almaty's Gogol Street, where smart boutiques jostle for space with Soviet-era blocks of flats like the one housing *Respublika's* operation – 'so we can always deliver at least a portion of the print run to the readers.'

The clue lay in *Respublika's* punchy content: that night, the front-page story churning off the presses was headlined 'Has Nursultan Divorced Sara?' and contained scurrilous speculation about whether Nazarbayev had split up with his wife to shack up with a younger lover. Not surprisingly, the government reviled *Respublika's* gutsy, often muckraking and not always well-sourced reporting and its hard-hitting personal attacks on Nazarbayev – a no-no for any media wishing to survive. *Respublika*, presidential aide Yermukhamet Yertysbayev had recently fulminated, was full of 'information terrorism against the first president and against our whole country' penned by 'hacks' intent on fomenting revolution in Kazakhstan.[1] Yertysbayev's nickname was 'the president's nightingale', because he was believed to be the voice of Nazarbayev's innermost thoughts.

The government's hostility ran deeper than antipathy towards *Respublika's* reporting: it believed the newspaper to be an attack dog on a leash held by Nazarbayev's arch enemy Mukhtar Ablyazov. Both the oligarch and the journalists vehemently denied this, although years later Ablyazov admitted to bankrolling media outlets hostile to Nazarbayev – not that there is anything illegal in this in Kazakhstan, which professes to espouse freedom of speech.

Official antagonism to *Respublika* had stopped the presses, so its journalists had to be inventive. The printing process would take just forty minutes in a conventional publishing house – here it took three days. Thursday evening was a burst of frantic activity ahead of the middle-of-the-night deadline for the weekly to hit the stands. The printer churned out pages with a deafening din that echoed through the office until the early hours, drowning out the traffic whooshing past on Gogol Street below. The reporters laid the pages out and then dashed down the piles stapling copies together, a laborious process taking well into the night. In the early hours, a driver arrived to deliver the new edition to the news-stands – those agreeing to stock them, because not all would risk selling newspapers antagonistic towards the powers that be. Then the exhausted staff went off home to fall into bed.

Respublika's crusading journalists had survived many a setback in their decade of existence, and samizdat was the least of them. The tale of *Respublika* is a murky one of violence and intimidation, featuring a decapitated dog, a funeral wreath, a firebombing, the suspicious death of a young woman and claims of cyberwarfare.

Respublika ran into trouble soon after its foundation in 2000 by Irina Petrushova, a Russian-born journalist with family connections to Kazakhstan, where her father had been a reporter for the USSR's most famous national newspaper, *Pravda*, in Soviet times. 'We experienced the first pressure on the newspaper in 2002,' Oksana explained during a break from checking the proofs, her matter-of-fact tone belying the shocking words to come. 'That was when the decapitated dog was hung up here; that was when the editorial office was firebombed.' It was a time of political turmoil, with the government facing down the DVK reform movement and warding off the Kazakhgate 'oil contracts for kickbacks' case, which *Respublika* was covering extensively.

The first warning was a macabre gift: Petrushova received a funeral wreath, a chilling message whose interpretation required little imagination. Next came the decapitated dog hung outside the office, a note pinned to its torso: 'There will be no next time.' Then *Respublika* was firebombed – an attack police initially claimed that the newspaper's publisher Muratbek Ketebayev had orchestrated as a publicity stunt. Two men were later jailed, but it was never established who ordered the attack.[2]

Shortly afterwards, the 25-year-old daughter of Lira Bayseitova, a *Respublika* editor who had just returned from interviewing the Swiss prosecutor in Geneva about the Kazakhgate accounts, died in police custody. Leyla Bayseitova had been arrested on possession of heroin charges, police said (though relatives claimed she was not a drug user), and had hung herself with her own jeans. The official version seemed riddled with holes, and human rights campaigners said photographs of her body showed signs consistent with a violent struggle – a head wound, bruising, bashed heels, smashed fingers – but the official verdict of suicide stood.[3]

In 2002, violence and intimidation dogged journalists reporting on Kazakhgate: Sergey Duvanov, a reporter voraciously pursuing the story, ended up in hospital with head injuries after a beating, and was later jailed on charges of raping a teenage girl that media watchdogs around the world decried as a set-up to silence him.[4] That summer, Petrushova, targeted by probes into tax and migration violations that she denounced as trumped up, fled Kazakhstan for Russia.[5]

All that could have sounded the death knell for *Respublika* – but over the next decade the journalists refused to be gagged and the newspaper kept printing its eclectic mix of groundbreaking exposés and salacious muckraking, fending off libel suits, seizures of entire print runs, online censorship, hacker attacks and lawsuits to close it down. The newspaper seemed indefatigable: every time the courts slapped a closure notice on one version, it launched under a different *Respublika*-themed name: *Nasha Respublika* (Our Republic); *Vsya Respublika* (The Whole Republic); *Moya Respublika* (My Republic); *Respublika Delovoye Obozreniye* (Republic Business Review); *Golos Respubliki* (Voice of the Republic); *Ne Ta Respublika* (Not That Republic); *Respublika-2000* (Republic-2000); *Respublika Dubl-2* (Republic Double-2); *Moy Dom Respublika* (My Home Republic).

In Kazakhstan's beleaguered media environment, *Respublika* was an institution that had survived against the odds, slapped down one minute only to pop up the next – and it would survive this samizdat experiment too, returning to more orthodox printing methods when pressure abated. As Oksana asked with frustration as the flimsy, blurry sheets rolled off the presses in defiance of attempts to muzzle *Respublika*: 'It's our point of view that we have a point of view, so why can't we express it?'

But at this point *Respublika* did not have long left to live: the newspaper that refused to die would be slain.

Soon afterwards, the oil workers in Zhanaozen downed tools, setting off a chain of events that would bring the newspaper down. *Respublika* had always been stridently hostile towards the government (and vice versa), but now the authorities would depict it as a sinister propaganda tool wielded by Nazarbayev's foes as part of a plot to topple him.

Respublika had covered the oil strike extensively and reported graphically (and not always accurately) on its fatal culmination, but the authorities decided that the newspaper had not been just covering the industrial action and its violent end – it had been fomenting it: engaging in 'propaganda of a forcible seizure of power and sabotage of state security', according to a lawsuit filed in 2012.[6]

This time, the authorities were determined to end the decade-long game of cat and mouse which had seen new *Respublika*-themed newspapers pop up every time one was closed. The lawsuit targeted thirty-one newspapers, websites and social media accounts, all registered at different addresses and owned by different people, deemed a 'single media outlet' under the *Respublika* brand. For good measure, other lawsuits were filed against several other outspoken newspapers, websites and online TV channels which the government believed Ablyazov was financing as a 'weapon' to 'attack Kazakhstan', in the foreign minister's words.[7]

In late 2012, the courts ordered thirty-six media outlets closed in one fell swoop, prompting human rights campaigners in Kazakhstan to despair that this muzzling of almost all media critical of the government was pushing their country towards 'a dangerous brink, beyond which lies a total rejection of all democratic values and submersion in the darkness of totalitarianism'.[8]

Over two years later, four former *Respublika* reporters were sitting around the table in the tiny kitchen of their new editorial office, glumly drinking tea. The surroundings in June 2015 were different – but the story was wearily familiar. 'They're closing our mouths,' sighed Nazira Darimbet, as the sword of Kazakh justice prepared to strike again.

In the dock this time was Guzyal Baydalinova, who had massive libel damages hanging over her head which threatened to bankrupt her personally and drive out of business a new website which had risen from the ashes of *Respublika*.[9] Guzyal owned the domain name of *Nakanune.kz*, a small news site founded by these ex-*Respublika* journalists, which now stood accused of libelling a bank. The lawsuit hinged on claims published on *Nakanune* of sleaze in Almaty's construction industry involving the city hall, a building company and Kazkommertsbank, owned by Kenes Rakishev, an oligarch close to the government. The source of the allegations was an anonymous letter whose contents the journalists sheepishly admitted they failed to verify before publication.

The exposé failed to make a splash when it was published in 2014, but six months later Kazkommertsbank suddenly took umbrage and sued Guzyal, seeking $130,000 in damages. 'They obviously think I'm Rockefeller's daughter!' she joked, but it was no laughing matter, and her eyes clouded behind her rectangular glasses as she absently tucked a strand of unruly dark hair behind her ear. If found guilty, she faced financial ruin, and the site – one of a smattering of independent outlets still operating since the sweeping media crackdown of 2012 in which *Respublika* had been shuttered – faced closure. Guzyal was wondering what was really at the root of her troubles: an anonymous letter read by a few hundred people, or something darker and deeper? 'The thought springs to mind that it's not just the bank that thought this up [...], that Astana's behind it,' she fretted. 'I don't know who exactly, it's hard to say. Evidently, whoever was bothered by *Respublika* is now bothered by the *Nakanune* project.'

That association with *Respublika* seemed toxic. Some of its former journalists had set up another paper called *Assandi Times* – but in April 2014 this was closed down in a dramatic raid by bailiffs, citing a ruling from a secret court hearing, deeming its existence illegal.[10] Days later, several ex-*Respublika* reporters announced the creation of *Nakanune*, which means 'On The Eve' and was evocatively named after a newspaper published in 1920s Berlin by Russian writers-in-exile fleeing the Bolshevik Revolution.

Compared to *Respublika*, which boasted fifty staff in its heyday, *Nakanune* was a shoestring operation: five journalists working out of a tiny office, publishing a few reports a day, attracting 500 or so hits. Desperate to carve out a tiny niche for reporting, *Nakanune* had adopted a survival mechanism, Oksana acknowledged candidly: 'We have to switch on the self-censorship, to preserve a platform where we can report.' It had only been running a year – now its existence was under threat from the Kazkommertsbank lawsuit. 'I think this was a planned action, and this was just something for them to latch on to,' muttered Nazira darkly.

At the trial a few days later, Kazkommertsbank's lawyer asked Guzyal directly if she was associated with *Respublika*. The question was posed because also named in the lawsuit was a Russia-based news site called *Respublika-kaz.info*, run from abroad by Petrushova, the founder of the original *Respublika* newspaper. *Respublika-kaz.info* had reposted the anonymous letter that had landed Guzyal in court – but it had also been publishing something else: a cache of hacked Kazakh government emails that had just become the subject of a legal battle that the authorities would fight out in courtrooms spanning the globe, as allegations swirled of cyberespionage and covert spyware surveillance of regime opponents.

The trove of hacked government emails surfaced on Kazaword, a WikiLeaks-style website, in late 2014, and *Respublika-kaz.info* started publishing them in early 2015. The government fired back with lawsuits filed in US courts to uncover the identities of the 'John Does' – the unidentified hackers – in a case *Respublika*'s lawyer described as a bid 'to attack whistle-blower activity writ large'.[11]

The hacked emails not only cast the government in an embarrassing light, hinting at unsavoury financial dealings and profligate spending, but they also revealed details of the authorities' tenacious international behind-the-scenes machinations to get their hands on Ablyazov, their public enemy number one, and it was him that Kazakhstan's government fingered in the US courts as 'a prime suspect in, and major beneficiary of, the alleged hacking' – which he denied.[12] *Respublika*, Kazakhstan's lawyers alleged, had wielded the leaked emails 'as part of an ongoing propaganda campaign that portrays Ablyazov and his accomplices as innocent victims of a frame-up orchestrated by the Kazakhstan government'.[13]

The legal ping-pong began: one–nil to the government with a US court injunction preventing publication of the stolen emails, then one–all as *Respublika* was exempted from the ban under the First Amendment. Two–one to *Respublika* when Kazakhstan's lawyers failed to subpoena Petrushova's website and Facebook to disclose confidential user data to expose the hackers' identities; two–all when the government took its legal battle across the world to New Zealand, whose High Court ordered a cloud-storage company to disclose user information to help Kazakhstan reveal the data thieves.[14]

As the government was slugging it out in the international courts, a new battlefront emerged in the cyberwar. 'Please find attached our invoice,' began a message that landed in the inbox of Irina Petrushova's brother in 2015 – but the attachment contained no invoice. A click of the mouse would boot up Trojan malware that would start hoovering up digital information to transmit to the cyber-spies who had sent it – down to switching on webcams remotely to conduct covert video surveillance of targets. Operation Manul had begun: an online dirty tricks campaign targeting Ablyazov associates involved with the 'John Doe' case, according to the findings of the Electronic Frontier Foundation, a US organisation championing digital civil liberties. EFF's research found that Operation Manul (named after a species of wildcat found in Kazakhstan) was a spear-phishing campaign that sent messages containing Kazakhstan-related words to lull recipients into opening Trojan malware. Targets included Irina Petrushova, her brother Alexander Petrushov, Ablyazov's relatives, his lawyer Peter Sahlas, and Bolat Atabayev, the elderly theatre director and Ablyazov associate who had spent six months in jail after the Zhanaozen violence. 'Based on available evidence, we believe this campaign is likely to have been carried out on behalf of the government of Kazakhstan,' the EFF stated.[15] Hacking allegations were not restricted to one side: in 2017, Ukraine sought the extradition of Ablyazov's son-in-law Ilyas Khrapunov for allegedly orchestrating the hacking of a law firm representing BTA Bank, which had filed international lawsuits alleging that Khrapunov helped Ablyazov conceal assets. Khrapunov dismissed the allegations as 'preposterous' and politically motivated.[16]

After two years of costly court battles around the globe, the government's 'John Doe' lawsuit fizzled out in 2017, when the statute of limitations ran out because it could not name a defendant.[17] The saga continued, however: Kazakhstan immediately launched new proceedings in a California court against Muratbek Ketebayev, Petrushova's Poland-based husband, and Khrapunov (who is Geneva-based), accusing them of involvement and suing for damages.[18] In 2017, a judge threw the case out, citing lack of jurisdiction.[19]

By then, the last vestige of *Respublika* – *Respublika-kaz.info* – had given up the ghost. 'We're closing,' announced Petrushova in September

2016, citing 'technical and financial problems' and 'other reasons' which would be clear to anyone acquainted with Kazakhstan's political situation. She thanked readers for their support 'in times that were hardest for us: when *Respublika* was closed by the courts virtually every week, when printing houses refused to print the newspaper and the website was choked by hacker attacks, when our journalists were arrested and our editorial office was firebombed'.[20]

As Guzyal's libel trial drew to an end in June 2015, the journalists sitting around the table in the *Nakanune* office were despondent. 'Lately the authorities have started to react sharply not only to criticism but also to the objective coverage of information,' said Tatyana Panchenko indignantly. 'In our country even being a mirror of events is dangerous.' There was a sense of déjà vu, she said glumly, with a shake of her bobbed head. Referring to her childhood in the totalitarian USSR, she added: 'It's a return to the politics of the past. It's the end of the 1980s.' Oksana, only half-joking, agreed that things seemed to be going from bad to worse: 'I never thought in 2015 I'd be looking back nostalgically at 2001!' As for *Nakanune*'s future, Oksana was uncertain, although she harboured hopes it would survive: 'I want to believe. I have some stocks of optimism left. But not so many.'

'We'll see how the trial goes and how it all turns out,' said a jittery Guzyal. A week later, she was convicted and ordered to pay $100,000 in damages – money she had no hope of raising. But things would soon get far worse: Guzyal would end the year sitting in a prison cell facing a decade behind bars. The endgame was coming.

One morning in December 2015, police swooped on *Nakanune*'s office and the homes of some of its reporters, including Guzyal's, in an operation that looked as if it were targeting a crime ring of tooled-up mafia bosses rather than a few small-time journalists.

Over a year after *Nakanune* had published that anonymous letter and six months after Kazkommertsbank had won its case against Guzyal, police claimed to have unmasked her as a ringleader in a sinister 'conspiracy' to disseminate false information about Kazkommertsbank, using *Nakanune* and *Respublika-kaz.info* as the channels, thereby 'creating the danger of a violation of public order and causing losses to the bank'.[21]

Guzyal was thrown behind bars to await trial for the crime of disseminating false information, which carries a jail sentence of up to ten years. Also detained was freelance journalist Rafael Balgin, who was soon released to go public with claims that he had conspired with Guzyal and Irina Petrushova to help a little-known Kazakh property magnate called Tair Kaldybayev slander Kazkommertsbank on their websites, at a purported cost to the businessman of $5,000–$10,000 per article.

A call from the European Parliament for the government 'to stop harassing independent and opposition journalists' inside Kazakhstan and 'stop the persecution of *Respublika* and its journalists in the courts of the United States' fell on deaf ears.[22] Guzyal was sentenced to eighteen months in jail. Kaldybayev got four and a half years – but he did not survive to serve it.

Sitting in the sunshine on the terrace of an Almaty café days after the verdict, eating pizza and drinking a jug of *mors* (berry juice) in bright sunshine, Guzyal's friends and colleagues Oksana and Tatyana were in a state of shock. The case was of 'Kafkaesque absurdity', bemoaned Tatyana: 'Everyone's been given the signal: if you want to destroy or punish or fine a media outlet you can brazenly file a lawsuit and the court will always take your side. And there's no need for proof. The media will always be guilty.' 'Kazakhstan does all that as if it's in an aquarium and no one sees anything – but an aquarium is transparent and the whole world can see!' exclaimed Oksana. 'It's a dirty tale,' she added in disgust. 'I keep saying: it can't get any worse. And the echo comes back: it can, it can!' She laughed, and then there was a long silence.

Two months later, Kaldybayev was found hanged in his prison cell, shortly before his appeal was to be heard.[23] His death was ruled a suicide (and in a fit of remorse, Kazkommertsbank returned to the family nearly half a million dollars he had paid it in damages).[24] A week later, Guzyal was suddenly released, her conviction standing but her sentence suspended. 'I don't regret working for the independent media. I have never, not once, regretted that,' she said emotionally, as supporters greeted her with hugs and bouquets of flowers.[25]

As for *Nakanune*, the journalists had already shut down the last media outlet launched inside Kazakhstan by *Respublika* reporters. 'There's no point, absolutely no point,' Oksana said resignedly. 'I don't know how to write in Kazakhstan so as not to end up in the dock.'

CHAPTER 6

Trials and Tribulations

Bakanas, 2009

'Prosecutor! Shame on you! Have you got a conscience?' comes an angry shout from the public gallery. In the dock of a tiny courtroom in the small town of Bakanas in south-eastern Kazakhstan stands Yevgeniy Zhovtis, the country's most prominent human rights campaigner, fighting to avoid a conviction that may land him behind bars.

The basic facts of this case are not in dispute. Zhovtis was driving home to Almaty from a fishing trip when his car struck and killed a man on a dark country road and now, in September 2009, he is on trial charged with causing death by dangerous driving. At issue is not those events but the motivation for bringing the activist to trial: Zhovtis denies culpability for the accident and has reached an out-of-court financial settlement with the family of the victim, Kanat Moldabayev, that under Kazakh law means he can avoid prosecution. Yet here he is in the dock in Bakanas, near where the accident occurred on a road passing through Moldabayev's village, Akdala.

Is the campaigner really facing years in jail because of this accident – or is someone seizing a convenient opportunity to silence a principled man who has been relentlessly holding Kazakhstan's flawed human rights record up to scrutiny for years?

For Kazakhstan, image is everything – and its performance was about to come under the international spotlight. Four months after Zhovtis's trial, the country would assume the chairmanship of an international organisation that it had long coveted, and as it basked in the glory of global recognition and respectability the last thing the government needed was a barrage of negative press about human rights abuses. In 2010, Kazakhstan was to chair the Organisation for Security and Cooperation in Europe (OSCE), an international grouping of European countries, post-Soviet states, the USA and Canada. To position Kazakhstan as a player on the global stage, Nazarbayev's administration had lobbied long and hard for the chairmanship, pushing back against concerns about its human rights record in order to win it. While member states agreed that Astana was well placed to promote the OSCE's agenda of political and security cooperation, some wondered how a country with a record of abusing political and civil liberties could seriously be expected to advance the organisation's human rights commitments. The government won the position by pledging sweeping reforms in the interests of liberalisation and promising to uphold the OSCE's democratic values during its year-long chairmanship. It had already broken the first pledge by merely tinkering with a few laws, and Zhovtis would be hovering at the ready to hold the government to its second promise.

His voice carried weight: no opposition firebrand, the 54-year-old Zhovtis was a sober-minded lawyer whose bespectacled, moustachioed face was a familiar sight at the world's top human rights hearings, from the UN and the EU to the OSCE's own forums, pushing back against officials' attempts to whitewash the country's record. The Kazakh government was notorious for shelling out millions to Western lobbying firms to polish its image: from Tony Blair Associates (the consultancy of the British ex-prime minister, now closed) and Portland Communications (employing virtu-oso British spin doctor Alastair Campbell) to BGR Gabara (which later boasted of securing for Kazakhstan 'phenomenal media exposure' during its OSCE chairmanship, and bragged about its bright idea of running an online campaign to counterbalance negative reporting over the Zhanaozen oil strike, involving sock puppets posing as children disappointed by Sting's cancellation of his concert in the Kazakh capital).[1] Their tactics to buff Kazakhstan's image have included placing puff pieces in influential global media, doctoring Wikipedia to remove unflattering truths and 'optimising' Google search engine results to bury bad news.[2]

Zhovtis supported his country's OSCE chairmanship, hoping the limelight would encourage it to live up to its human rights commitments,

but he would have been making waves in order to hold it to its promises –
so his supporters could not help thinking it would be convenient if he
landed behind bars for the duration of Kazakhstan's moment in the sun.

As a lawyer, Zhovtis was no stranger to the vagaries of Kazakhstan's
judicial system, where no more than lip service is paid to the presumption of innocence and the scales of justice are heavily weighted against
the defendant (the acquittal rate is around 1 per cent).[3] This was the
first time Zhovtis had personally found himself on the wrong side of
the dock, and the experience made this lawyer despair of Kazakhstan's
justice system. 'It's a demonstration of strength, a demonstration of the
absence of the rule of law,' he lamented. 'It's all decided at the political
level.' Officials issued heated denials of political motivations – even when
Barack Obama personally urged Nazarbayev to review Zhovtis's case.[4]
    'This is a person who's been defending people's rights for two decades,
but unfortunately […] you haven't been able to defend his rights,' Vera
Tkachenko, Zhovtis's formidable public defender, thundered to the
court. She was referring to his human rights work dating back to before
the fall of the USSR, when Zhovtis was a mining engineer who served
as a lay judge and became involved in trade unionism. After independence, he founded a human rights organisation and retrained as a lawyer.
    The defence was furious that Zhovtis's rights were flouted from the
outset, since he was described in the case materials as a criminal. 'Are
you acquainted with the presumption of innocence?' Zhovtis inquired
caustically of an uncomfortable-looking investigator testifying for the
prosecution. 'Who else committed the crime apart from you?' replied
the bemused officer, to hoots of derisive laughter from the public gallery.
'Respect the court!' barked the judge to dozens of Zhovtis supporters,
trial observers and journalists who had made the nine-hour round trip
by road from Almaty to Bakanas.
    As the trial wound up, the defence requested several days' adjourn-
ment to prepare final arguments to keep Zhovtis out of jail, while the
prosecutor asked for an hour. The judge settled on 40 minutes, sparking
uproar in the public gallery. 'Prosecutor! Shame on you! Have you got
a conscience?' cried journalist Sergey Duvanov, leaping to his feet.
'Tomorrow you'll be on trial and there'll be no one to protect you!'
heckled opposition leader Vladimir Kozlov. Duvanov knew what it

was like to serve time in Kazakhstan's jails, and Kozlov would find out. Duvanov was jailed in 2003 for three and a half years on charges of raping a fourteen-year-old girl, amid a storm of international controversy over suspicions that the case – centring on an incident at Duvanov's dacha where he said he was drugged – was trumped up as retaliation for his exposés of the Kazakhgate bribery scandal.[5] Kozlov's sentence came later, when he was jailed for allegedly fomenting the fatal unrest in Zhanaozen in 2011. Such cases have compounded suspicions that Kazakhstan's courts are sometimes used not to mete out justice but to take revenge on perceived foes of the regime. A few years after Zhovtis's trial, the case of Maksat Usenov, the son of a powerful official, revealed judicial double standards when he was treated far more leniently than Zhovtis. After killing a pedestrian in aggravating circumstances – he was behind the wheel while disqualified for drink-driving, and to make matters worse he also fled the scene of the crime – Usenov was sentenced to just forty-five days in jail, and he went on to reoffend.[6] His case demonstrated that the well-connected can expect leniency, but Zhovtis, on the other hand, was not expecting any for himself.

'I see no point in this trial,' he said, as the judge retired to consider his verdict. 'There's no point in proving or demonstrating anything. There's no law here; there's no justice here; there's only politics.' The trial was a 'political reprisal' by 'Kazakhstan's powers that be, who wanted to set me up over this unfortunate accident'. (Years later, Zhovtis revealed that he was offered his freedom in exchange for toning down his human rights work.[7])

The judge reappeared after fifteen minutes with a sheaf of papers that must have been written in advance, since it took longer to read the ruling than he had supposedly spent writing it. Guilty as charged, he intoned, sentencing Zhovtis to four years in jail as mayhem broke out around him. 'Shame, shame!' shouted supporters, as Kazakhstan's most prominent human rights campaigner was bundled from the courtroom and driven off to prison.

CHAPTER 7

Back to the USSR

Almaty, 2014

Three women are parading up and down Almaty's Republic Square with lacy knickers on their heads. The giggling protesters do not look like a threat to the stability of the Kazakh state – but the authorities think otherwise. As the trio tries to place the lacy underwear on the monument to Kazakhstan's independence, a tall column whose base features their president's gilded handprint, police swoop in to arrest them. 'Why are you afraid of knickers?' shouts Zhanna Baytelova gaily as they frogmarch her to a waiting police van.

The absurd outcome of this absurdist protest in February 2014 is symptomatic of the government's attitude to dissent: it must be crushed, and quickly, lest it get out of hand. There is another reason, too: public protest belies the official narrative of near universal support for Nazarbayev, which the powers that be view as the bedrock of the stability that they vaunt as one of Kazakhstan's national values.

Baytelova is a journalist in her late twenties with a penchant for eye-catching stunts: in 2010, she was jailed for ten days for hurling manure at a courthouse, in a novel type of dirty protest. Her gripe with the court was its refusal to hear a case she wanted to bring against officials for approving Nazarbayev being granted sweeping new powers along with his title of Leader of the Nation.[1] She and her fellow 'pantie protesters' (as the media dubbed them) Yevgeniya Plakhina, like Baytelova a former reporter on the defunct *Respublika* newspaper, and Valeriya Ibrayeva, an artist, were protesting – ostensibly at least, although there was more to it than met the eye – against obscure regulations governing lace imports adopted under Kazakhstan's membership of the Customs Union, a free trade zone with two other post-Soviet countries, Russia and Belarus.

The pernickety new rules stipulating what kind of lace was acceptable amounted to a finicky piece of red tape that had got under people's skin – like the EU's notorious 'straight bananas' – but alarmingly for the government, this was grabbing headlines just as Kazakhstan's alliance with Russia was making news for all the wrong reasons. Amid rumblings of discontent in some quarters, the Customs Union was about to be revamped into a much more ambitious organisation: the Eurasian Economic Union, which alarmists were decrying as a grandiose bid by Russian President Vladimir Putin to revive the Soviet Union by another name, nearly a quarter of a century after the original had collapsed. The timing for Kazakhstan to edge even closer to Russia was not exactly auspicious: Moscow was embroiled in a conflict with another neighbour and one-time ally, Ukraine, which was rattling nerves across the post-Soviet neighbourhood, and soon Russia would become the target of Western sanctions that would combine with plunging oil prices to send its economy into a tailspin – and get the new Eurasian Economic Union off to a very shaky start.

Yet the 'pantie protest' was not really about the union or its obscure rules about lace at all; rather, it was 'a symbol of the absurdity which is taking place in our country', explains Yevgeniya, a vivacious character with a blonde bob and a slash of red lipstick, after she's been arrested, hauled through the courts and fined on hooliganism charges. 'In Russian we have a saying, "giving one's last underpants", which literally means becoming poor,' she says, in a nod to the economic ill winds blowing in from Russia. 'It was a symbolic action.' So it was a joke, of sorts. But the government was not laughing.

The three knicker-wielding protestors were not the only ones out on the streets in Almaty during that chilly February weekend in 2014. Her voice cracking with fury, a young woman was confronting riot police who were pouncing on demonstrators on Republic Square and hurling them onto police buses the day before the 'pantie protest'. 'By what right are you rounding people up? By what right? We have no weapons!' yelled Zhanar Sekerbayeva in the face of an officer holding back the crowd. 'You, son of the Kazakh people! What do you want to do with me, on my own native land? [...] Look me in the eye!' The officer shifted his embarrassed gaze to look anywhere but in her eyes. Some bolder protesters started shouting a slogan that could not fail to ring alarm bells up in Astana: '*shal ket!*' ('old man out!').

This young woman was one of a couple of hundred demonstrators who had marched on Republic Square to protest against an economic malaise gripping Kazakhstan. Days earlier, protesters had stormed the central bank headquarters in Almaty to voice their rage at plunging salaries and spiralling debts after Kazakhstan's currency, the tenge, had lost a fifth of its value in one fell swoop. 'Lies, lies! Why do you deceive us?' they yelled at Kuat Kozhakhmetov, the central bank's deputy chairman, who emerged from his office, looking abashed, to explain why their purchasing power had just fallen so dramatically. Recalling the bitter experience of a previous devaluation in 2009, ordinary people knew they would feel the pinch: jobs lost, purchasing power plummeting as import prices rocketed, home repossessions looming as mortgages became unpayable. One major driving factor behind the tumbling tenge was the crash of the Russian rouble: so intertwined is the Kazakh economy with its neighbour's that when Russia sneezes, Kazakhstan catches a cold. After years riding the oil boom, Kazakhstan's economy was starting to tank – and a few months later global oil prices would slump, piling on the economic woes.

These scenes on Republic Square were a rare show of defiance in a country where protesters risked arrest under draconian laws controlling street demonstrations. Over that weekend in 2014, around three dozen people were snatched off the street by riot police, bundled into police buses and marched into the dock. Most got off with a fine – including the 'pantie protesters' and the woman haranguing the riot police – but one man was jailed for ten days as a salutary lesson to others.[2]

Just what was it that made Kazakhstan's rulers so allergic to the sight of people taking to the streets to express their opinions peacefully, so unwilling to brook public questioning – however mild – of their rule?

Tumultuous events taking place 3,500 kilometres away on the other side of the former Soviet Union offered a clue to the government's fears. In February 2014, Ukraine's president was chased out of office after months of street demonstrations in the kind of scenario that gave post-Soviet autocrats like Nazarbayev nightmares. The official attitude to protest had hardened over years of nervously eyeing revolutions that have toppled authoritarian presidents in countries near and far, starting with the 'coloured revolutions' that unseated leaders around the former USSR in the 2000s: Georgia's 'Rose Revolution' in 2003, then in 2005 both Ukraine's 'Orange Revolution' and, closer to home, the 'Tulip Revolution' next door in Kyrgyzstan. Five years on, in 2010, another uprising in Kyrgyzstan ousted a second president (ten years later, in 2020, another revolution would chase out a third Kyrgyz leader), and shortly afterwards the Arab Spring started toppling entrenched Middle Eastern autocrats like dominoes, sparking overblown chatter about a Central Asian Spring to follow.

Small wonder, then, that officials had for years been hammering home an insistent message to the public: revolution was not a byword for democracy and freedom but for death and destruction, and regime change in other countries had brought nothing but social chaos and economic collapse. His basic instinct for self-preservation aside, Nazarbayev genuinely believed, as indeed did many of his compatriots, that rising living standards were the key to social stability, which he prized above airy-fairy notions of democracy and civil liberties. That was the 'Nazarbayev dream', and the president was convinced he had delivered – but for those not buying into it, protest was not an option.

Under the constitution, Kazakh citizens enjoy the right to peaceful protest, but according to the law on public assembly at the time, they had to obtain prior permission from the local authorities to exercise it, applying ten days ahead – which would certainly take the sting out of any revolutionary spontaneity. The authorities used to grant permission for some demonstrations, grudgingly and in out-of-town locations to keep dissent out of the public eye, but by the time of the 'pantie protest' applications were routinely rejected. Since protesters were required to have permission but the authorities almost never granted it, any protest became a priori illegal, any peaceful protester a criminal. Official paranoia about public protest begged some questions: did the government not believe its own propaganda or official election results indicating that the Leader of the Nation enjoyed 98 per cent support? Did the ruling clique actually think the Nazarbayev system was but a castle built on sand?

This zero-tolerance attitude to public protest has led to farcical scenes over the years, like the headline-grabbing arrest of Gulzhan

Yergaliyeva, a high-profile journalist, for attempting to exercise her right to freedom of assembly in 2015 – right in the middle of a visit to Kazakhstan by a rapporteur dispatched by the United Nations to assess whether citizens were able to exercise their right to free assembly.[3] Maina Kiai reported back to the UN that Kazakhstan offered 'very limited space for the expression of dissenting political views', and that the government's restrictive approach to public assembly 'renders that right meaningless'.[4]

Ryspek Sarsenbay, a journalist and opposition activist, put it more acidly at the time. 'There is no freedom of assembly in Kazakhstan,' he said as a couple of dozen people gathered peacefully on Republic Square during the UN rapporteur's visit to support Yergaliyeva. 'The authorities fear the people, their own citizens. They fear their expressions of protest, of discontent.' Sarsenbay's doleful assessment was drowned out by a uniformed prosecutor issuing repeated warnings through a megaphone to the small crowd to disperse because they were breaking the law.

Heavy-handed reactions creating absurd scenes were the norm rather than the exception: in 2014, for example, Astana police herded screaming children into detention along with their mothers at a small housing protest, then Almaty police arrested a woman for standing alone in a park waving a banner reading 'our children are not criminals' to protest over the detention of those children.[5] In 2018, police stopped and questioned citizens waving balloons during holiday celebrations, after the government's public enemy number one Ablyazov had called on supporters of his banned DVK movement to carry blue balloons as a sign of solidarity.[6] With public protest all but banned, dissenters resorted to satire and symbolism, like the group which marched down an Almaty street in 2008 dressed in sheep's masks, waving posters proclaiming in Latin 'the king's will is the highest law'. They called themselves 'Nur Otar', a riff on Nazarbayev's ruling party, Nur Otan: 'otan' is Kazakh for 'fatherland', 'otar' means a 'herd', as in of sheep. The government failed to appreciate the joke: the ringleader of that sardonic march was jailed for fifteen days.[7]

In May 2014, three months after the absurdist 'pantie protest', satirists were back on Almaty's Republic Square – this time with blue surgical masks strapped across their mouths, which embarrassed-looking police officers vainly tried to persuade them to remove. 'What right do you have?' mumbled one woman in a muffled voice from behind her mask. 'We're not breaking any laws.'

Masked protesters quietly began laying Kazakh flags at the monument to Kazakhstan's independence – but the joyful colours of the turquoise and yellow pennants were tempered by sombre black ribbons attached. This post-modern protest, taking place years before the coronavirus pandemic struck, was a symbolic action to guard against the 'virus' of Russian imperialism spreading into Kazakhstan, with the black ribbons symbolising a loss of sovereignty as the country bound itself into the Eurasian Economic Union – that new alliance with Russia which was being signed into existence on that very day, a thousand kilometres away in Astana. The masks symbolised the lack of a public voice in the making of game-changing political decisions, because the government had rejected calls for a nationwide referendum on whether to join the Russia-led union. The masked protest was designed, said activist Serikzhan Mambetalin, to 'show to the rest of the world that Kazakhs do not support a new form of colonisation by Russia in the form of the Eurasian Union'.

The signing ceremony was meant to be a joyous occasion, consummating years of painstaking negotiations to shape the new alliance, founded by the trio of Russia, Kazakhstan and Belarus, with the door wide open to welcome (or press gang, Putin's critics thought) more countries into the fold; Armenia rushed across the threshold, Kyrgyzstan followed more reluctantly, but no other country was keen. Far from being triumphant, the mood among the three post-Soviet comrades – Nazarbayev, Putin and Alexander Lukashenko of Belarus – was grim as they signed the union treaty in May 2014. It was an inauspicious moment for the creation of the Eurasian Union (as it is commonly called). There was a spectre at the feast as the trio sealed the deal on the ambitious integration project: Ukraine, which was imploding on the other side of the former Soviet Union, with the Kremlin accused of stoking the strife.

None of the gloomy-faced leaders sitting, pens poised, around the oversized table in Astana had forgotten where the roots of Ukraine's turmoil lay: in Kyiv's geopolitical flip-flopping. Should it look east, towards Moscow, or west, towards Europe? Which geopolitical alliance should it join: the European Union, a club of Western-style democracies, or the Eurasian Union, which its founders billed as a benign post-Soviet version of the EU while doomsayers visualised it as a bold Kremlin gambit to reincarnate the USSR by another name? The tumult set in motion by that conundrum had set Putin – with his zero-sum 'with us or against us' attitude to foreign policy – on the warpath and brought revolution and separatist insurgency to Ukraine. No wonder the three founders looked so morose.

Ukraine's deadly turmoil had begun in November 2013, when, egged on by Putin, President Viktor Yanukovych tore up an agreement he was about to sign with the EU and instead signalled an interest in hitching Ukraine to the Eurasian Union, in a geopolitical about-face which brought demonstrators onto the streets in protests that toppled him three months later. The Kremlin reacted to the overthrow of its protégé and the installation of pro-Western leaders with cold fury, and a punitive land grab: it annexed a strategic slice of Ukraine's territory, the Black Sea peninsula of Crimea, then a pro-Russian separatist insurgency erupted in Ukraine's south-eastern borderlands, which Kyiv accused Moscow of fomenting. Western states reacted by slapping sanctions on Russia, sending its economy into a nosedive whose after-effects would ripple out to its neighbours. Geopolitical upsets combined with economic woes to create a perfect storm into which the Eurasian Union was being born.

Even for staunch Russian allies like Kazakhstan and Belarus, hitching their fortunes to an aggressively expansionist Russia was starting to appear foolhardy. The new union was looking less like an economic alliance than a geopolitical vehicle for a bellicose Putin (who is famously nostalgic for the Soviet Union, once dubbing its collapse the 'greatest geopolitical catastrophe' of the twentieth century) to drive Russian expansionism through its former backyard. Putin scathingly brushed off talk that Russia was hell-bent on revisiting its colonial ambitions, and Nazarbayev vowed that Kazakhstan would not cede an 'iota' of sovereignty.[8] But some of his citizens were not convinced, and in Kazakhstan mini-protests over the Eurasian Union and perceived Russian expansionism had been going on for months.

'Yesterday Abkhazia and South Ossetia, today Crimea, tomorrow north Kazakhstan!' read a placard waved at a one-man picket by activist Makhambet Abzhan at the Russian embassy in Kazakhstan's capital in March 2014. Abkhazia and South Ossetia are Russian-backed separatist republics that broke away from Georgia following the collapse of the

USSR, and the poster voiced apprehensions that Russia could be eyeing slices of northern Kazakhstan to snap off, as it had snapped Crimea off Ukraine. The idea of Russia marching in and seizing land sounded crazy to many in Kazakhstan, where Moscow is widely seen as friend not foe. But some were fearful, and a cacophony of bellicose territorial claims on northern Kazakhstan emitted by nationalists in Russia fired up by the annexation of Crimea was adding to their jitters. Abzhan, attired in a bushy fur hat against the frost, was yelling at the police: 'Today, Russia's acted like this by going into Crimea, tomorrow they'll be coming to Petropavlovsk [a city in northern Kazakhstan just sixty kilometres from the Russian border], and what are you going to do? Stand there and disperse us again?' He was arrested and thrown in jail for seven days for protesting without permission.

For a small but vocal minority, the idea of Kazakhstan cementing itself into a tighter embrace with Russia was anathema – which is why some opponents of the Eurasian Union donned surgical masks over their mouths, as symbolic protection against the 'imperial virus' being borne into Kazakhstan from the north. Like the protest itself, the spot in Almaty upon which dissenters chose to converge on the day the union treaty was signed was iconic: the monument to independence on Republic Square, on top of which soars a golden warrior standing erect on the back of a mythological winged snow leopard. This is the Golden Man, an ancient Scythian prince found interred, draped in gold, in a burial mound near Almaty, adopted as a symbol of independent Kazakhstan. 'Dark days are coming our way,' intoned Ryspek Sarsenbay, as he laid his black-beribboned Kazakh flag and a red carnation at this statue heavy with the symbolism of Kazakhstan's national pride. 'We're losing our independence.'

CHAPTER 8

Stop the Presses

Almaty, 2015

Wearing a white armband with 'hunger strike' emblazoned across it in red, Gulzhan Yergaliyeva looks emaciated: on a diet of only water, the sexuagenarian magazine editor has lost nine kilos and weighs in at just fifty-one kilograms. She is refusing food in protest against an attempt to close down her outspoken magazine: *Adam bol* (*'Be a Person'*) is up in court in February 2015 accused of incendiary reporting that is tantamount to calling for war – not in Kazakhstan, but thousands of kilometres away in Ukraine, where a pro-Russian separatist insurgency is tearing the country apart.

Sitting on a bed set up in her editorial office in Almaty to help her conserve her strength, dressed in jeans, slippers and her trademark tinted oversized glasses, the diminutive Gulzhan Khamitovna (her patronymic) is in characteristic militant mood. She deems the charges that her magazine was trying to stoke war 'absurd' and the case 'a pretext' to close *Adam bol* down 'on orders from on high, very far up on high', as she puts it. 'The point is that our magazine is opposition-minded. We oppose the authorities; we criticise them when they make mistakes,' she explains, with more vigour than might be expected of someone who has been refusing food for seventeen days, as a red sign splashed on the wall behind her indicates. Above her head hang two posters. *'Ashtyk'*, reads one in Kazakh; *'golodovka'*, says another in Russian: 'hunger strike'.

This veteran journalist and political activist is no stranger to attention-grabbing publicity stunts – she once stripped off on video to promote the launch of a news website named *Guljan*, after herself,

under the slogan: 'Better the naked truth than a nicely tarted-up lie.'
Her hunger strike is certainly attracting attention: the court-ordered
closure of *Adam bol* has been roundly condemned by international
organisations ('drastic and disproportionate', says the OSCE) and
free-speech watchdogs (the 'orchestrated throttling' of an independent
voice, protests Reporters Without Borders).[1]

'This is nothing new for me. It's not the first time we've been closed
down,' Gulzhan Khamitovna sniffs, pointing to the string of outlets she
has run over the years which have, after ruffling too many feathers, ended
up shuttered by court order or transferred into hands loyal to the regime.
In 2010, she sold off her most famous publication – an influential, gutsy
and scurrilous tabloid called *Svoboda Slova* (Freedom of Speech) to a
new owner who neutered it by turning it into an anodyne government-
friendly newspaper – though she got a tidy $2.5 million from the sale.[2]

Gulzhan Khamitovna's problems have generally resulted from her
crossing swords with Kazakhstan's ruling classes, but this time geopolitics
are at play too: *Adam bol*'s recent reporting has had in its cross hairs not
only Astana but Moscow as well. 'I've written articles heavily critical of
Russia and of Putin. I'm convinced this doesn't please the Kremlin,' she
says. Speaking in *Adam bol*'s editorial office in a converted blue three-storey
house on a quiet side street in Almaty, 4,000 kilometres from Moscow, the
editor might be over-exaggerating her significance in the Kremlin's eyes,
but she has a point: Moscow is watching its former colonies carefully for
signs of disloyalty after what it sees as 'betrayal' by Ukraine, and critical
coverage of the Kremlin's role in that conflict in the press of countries
'loyal' to Russia, such as Kazakhstan, probably does not escape its beady
eye. It definitely does not escape the Kazakh government's watchful gaze.

The hunger strike is to publicise a last-ditch appeal against the closure
of her magazine, ordered by a court three months earlier. The lawsuit,
lodged by Almaty's city hall, hinged on an interview published in *Adam
bol* with Aydos Sadykov, a rabble-rousing Kazakh political activist living
in Ukraine, who urged citizens of Kazakhstan to go and take up arms
against pro-Russian separatists fighting to wrest territory from Kyiv's
control. The fighting may be geographically distant from Kazakhstan,
but the ramifications are too close for comfort. The sight of Russia –
Kazakhstan's closest ally, as Nazarbayev never tired of saying – annexing
a chunk of a post-Soviet neighbour and facing accusations of stoking

a separatist conflict is not a comfortable one for Kazakhstan's ruling classes. The government is trying to avoid antagonising a bellicose Moscow while steering Kazakhstan through a crisis that has sent shock waves through the post-Soviet region, and the media should toe the line. But Gulzhan Khamitovna is not known for toeing anyone's line: *Adam bol*'s coverage of the Ukraine conflict is markedly anti-Kremlin in tone, and the magazine is publicly raising awkward questions about the implications for Kazakhstan of Russia's aggressive stance.

'Right now our independent line scares both our leadership and Russia,' she suggests. 'The Kremlin's strategy is to create hegemony in Kazakhstan.' That is debatable, but it is beyond doubt that after the debacle of the dissipation of its influence over Ukraine, the Kremlin wishes to shore up its political sway over other post-Soviet states – like Kazakhstan.

Geopolitics aside, there were plenty of people in Kazakhstan who would have liked to silence Gulzhan Khamitovna once and for all. 'I've made a lot of enemies, of course,' she shrugged nonchalantly. 'It's the same people sitting there for twenty-odd years, including our president, and they've always wanted me to go, to disappear.'

Gulzhan Khamitovna came from a distinguished family that was solidly part of Soviet Kazakhstan's establishment – her father, Khamit Yergali, was a famous poet – but in independent Kazakhstan his daughter was a source of vexation to the authorities, not only for her fearless reporting but also for her political activism. A founder member of the DVK reform movement in 2001 and politically active in opposition parties that emerged later, she was a familiar figure at protests on the streets of Almaty, with her pull-no-punches speeches attacking Nazarbayev and his ruling clique ('a mafia that calls itself a ruling power', she railed at one demonstration in 2012, where she was protesting against the results of elections that had shut the opposition out of parliament yet again; she had been disqualified at the last minute from standing, on spurious grounds).

The magazine editor had served short spells in jail for breaching Kazakhstan's strict public assembly laws, and a few days before this interview she had been briefly detained by police to prevent her from holding what she called a public meeting with readers on Republic Square to publicise her appeal against *Adam bol*'s closure. The authorities deemed it an illegal rally, to the consternation of Maina Kiai, the UN rapporteur on freedom of assembly visiting Kazakhstan at the time, who noted in his report how preventive detention to thwart public protest was used as 'a form of intimidation' and was 'a blatant violation of the right of peaceful assembly, as well as the rights to security and liberty'.[3]

Like other journalists critical of the government, Gulzhan Khamitovna had for years been under what she called intense 'financial, physical and moral pressure': websites blocked, print runs seized, access to printing houses denied, costly libel claims lost; personally, she had been subjected to threats, intimidation and physical attack. In 2001 her family was violently assaulted at home by a group of masked men, leaving her husband with head injuries from which he never fully recovered – an attack for which she subsequently blamed Rakhat Aliyev, the president's later disgraced and deceased son-in-law.[4]

After a quarter of a century standing up to pressure and intimidation, Gulzhan Khamitovna had had enough. 'It's clear the authorities want to stop me writing as a journalist; they drop hints that perhaps I should consider my position. I have to think about it, because I'm expending my energy and money. I'm sixty-three. I'm tired, to be honest. If I start another project, they'll only close it down in three months,' she said. 'As long as I'm present, they'll close it down. If I step aside…' She left the sentence trailing.

The next day, Gulzhan Khamitovna halted her hunger strike, and soon afterwards she lost her final appeal against *Adam bol*'s closure: the magazine was shuttered on the grounds that its reporting had contained 'attributes of war propaganda and agitation'.[5]

Adam bol's fate was sealed – but the game of cat and mouse between the powers that be and Kazakhstan's independent-minded journalists would continue.

A month later, in March 2015, *Adam* (Person) hit the news-stands: a new magazine with a markedly similar appearance to *Adam bol*, a name harking back to the old one and Gulzhan Khamitovna's son Ayan Sharipbayev in the role of editor-in-chief. We got the message, he said: 'They wanted Yergaliyeva to leave the project, then your future could be different'. 'They didn't say that directly, we surmised it,' explained Ayan, who had been news editor at the defunct *Adam bol*. 'Now, Gulzhan

Khamitovna isn't involved in the project, but we work as before, by the old rules.' Someone in Nazarbayev's 'close entourage' wanted the veteran journalist off the scene, suggested Ayan, who had an affable, easy-going manner that belied his dogged approach to investigative journalism. There was a lot of 'personal animosity' towards her, and 'if one day someone decides they have to get rid of Yergaliyeva, it will be done', he said, with a wry shrug. So she had handed the mantle over to the next generation.

He was sitting in the editorial office in that little blue house in Almaty in June 2015, and the new magazine had been up and running for three months. Had it felt any pressure yet? 'I don't know if you can call surveillance [by the security services] pressure, for example,' Ayan replied, with a philosophical shrug. 'Our experienced reporters take quite a sanguine view of this. I don't know if you can call delays at the printer's pressure,' he continued. 'I don't know if you can call failure to fulfil contractual obligations pressure.' He meant that the magazine was facing only the usual kind of 'pressure', nothing out of the ordinary, nothing that appeared to threaten its survival – for now.

Adam was now one of a handful of media outlets left trying to play the role of the fourth estate in Kazakhstan after the mass shuttering of *Respublika* and other outspoken outlets in 2012 (in a separate case, Yergaliyeva's news website *Guljan.org* was suspended by court order in 2012, and later folded).[6]

Were there any red lines the magazine would not cross to survive against the odds in this beleaguered media environment? Ayan paused, then sighed, distractedly running a hand over his five o'clock shadow. 'To be honest, for the moment we're a little afraid of criticising Nazarbayev directly – directly, as we used to,' he said slowly, meaning in previous outlets under the 'Gulzhan' brand. 'It's not because we've received some sort of order,' he elaborated, picking his words carefully. 'It's self-censorship. After we've been through all this, lost two [publishing] licences, several lawsuits, huge fines. All the staff have children. Evidently they bashed away at us and bashed away at us and bashed away at us, and got something of what they wanted.' Self-censorship was a tried and trusted survival tactic for Kazakhstan's press – but would it work?

Adam would still uphold the track record of gutsy reporting to hold the authorities to account, Ayan pledged, and it had an important role to play against the backdrop of the conflict in Ukraine: the editor wanted the magazine 'to inform the Russian-language population, because they're receiving some information, but it's distorted and in our view it doesn't reflect the real picture'.

The toppling of a pro-Russian president in Ukraine the previous year had sent the media in Russia into paroxysms of outrage – a mirror image of the Kremlin's indignation. Over a year later, Russian news programmes were still broadcasting a barrage of strident anti-Western onslaughts combined with cacophonous attacks on the 'junta' now in power in Ukraine and the 'fascists' running it: derogatory tags the Kremlin had attached to the new rulers in Kyiv, based on the existence of a few virulently anti-Russian, far-right elements among the protesters who had brought the new pro-Western leadership to power, and also harking back to an old insult which the Soviets used to tar Ukrainian nationalists.

Russian television is beamed into millions of homes around the former Soviet Union every day and is preferred by many viewers for its slicker, more entertaining format compared to the drabber programming on offer on domestic channels – so Ayan was positioning his magazine to push back against the black-and-white narratives being fed to Kazakhstan's Russian speakers and consumed wholesale by many. Tiny *Adam* as the David against the Goliath of Kremlin-backed TV was an uneven match, but he believed his magazine had a role to play, however small, in this battle for hearts and minds.

Adam published its articles in Russian, but had registered as a bilingual magazine because it planned to add Kazakh-language content at some point in the future. The editor wanted to bridge a gap that is the result of a complex linguistic legacy that dies hard in Kazakhstan, and in other post-Soviet countries like Ukraine. The media moulds the mindset, and in Ukraine a gulf in world views that had arisen between Russian speakers and Ukrainian speakers had played a major role in fuelling tensions that had erupted into conflict. In Kazakhstan there were nowhere near as many fault lines between Russian speakers and Kazakh speakers – but still, said Ayan, 'there are ever fewer bridges that could unite the Kazakh and Russian-language populations'. He was seriously concerned that the rift was widening. 'This will all blow up in the end; these two worlds will be living their separate lives. At *Adam*, we're trying to retain this bridge.'

Would *Adam* survive in Kazakhstan's embattled media environment? Ayan sighed again. Alternative voices exist in a 'frail state', he conceded carefully. However, he was cautiously optimistic about the magazine's chances of survival: 'I really want to believe, seriously, because without that belief, you might as well just get up and walk out of the door.'

Six months after hitting the news-stands, in October 2015, *Adam* was closed down by court order. Its crime? Failing to publish in the Kazakh language as well as Russian – an intention it had stated, but had no legal obligation to fulfil.[7]

CHAPTER 9

Bread and Circuses

Almaty, 2005–16

The presidential challenger smiles for the cameras as he drops his voting slip into the ballot box. Mels Yeleusizov is facing off against Nazarbayev for the presidency in April 2011, the incumbent's twentieth year in power as leader of independent Kazakhstan. Who did Yeleusizov vote for, ask the assembled reporters, for form's sake. 'Nazarbayev,' responds the ostensible opposition challenger, with a sanguine smile.

This is a telling snapshot of the type of elections offered to the people of Kazakhstan: monochrome, monotonous, monopolistic and micromanaged to the point of absurdity. Elections are not about giving voters a choice; they are choreographed rituals designed to cement Nazarbayev in office for another few years, and unleash another outpouring of adulation for the *Yelbasy*, the Leader of the Nation. Yeleusizov, a grey-haired environmentalist in his sixties who dabbles in politics only when elections come around, is merely there as a stalking horse to lend a veneer of democracy and a semblance of competition to the stage-managed vote. He cannot be bothered to vote for himself – or even pretend to for the sake of appearances. Casting his ballot for himself is a waste of time, the unrepentant challenger asserts, since Nazarbayev is bound to win.

He is right: Nazarbayev is the sure-fire winner of this election, not least because Yeleusizov and two other apathetic 'rivals' are doing nothing to challenge the incumbent in a yawn-inducing campaign for an election they have no chance or intention of winning. Kazakh elections offer all the traditional political trappings – candidates, manifestos, campaign trails, victory rallies – but lack the most vital democratic element: political choice. In 2011, Nazarbayev is facing off against an ersatz opposition in a pre-scripted election which everyone knows he will win with a crushing landslide. Every election ever staged in independent Kazakhstan has had a foregone conclusion – but they were not always as toothless as this.

'We want something to change as regards domestic freedom – the chance to think and talk freely,' a woman said after casting her vote for the main opposition candidate in the previous presidential election in 2005. She knew her choice, Zharmakhan Tuyakbay, had no chance of beating Nazarbayev, but she relished the fact that she did, at least, have a choice. Another voter walking home through an Almaty park of snow-fringed fir trees on that crisp December day had chosen another challenger, Alikhan Baymenov, wishing to break the old Soviet mould of elections with foregone conclusions. 'My logic was to try not to vote for Nazarbayev,' he explained. 'That's not necessarily because I don't want to, but because it would be good to depart from the kind of tradition where the result is 80–90 per cent.'

In 2005, Kazakhstan was already a political monocracy – but opposition still existed to fight electoral battles, even if it was doomed to defeat. Anti-Nazarbayev forces from across the political spectrum had banded together behind Tuyakbay, a saturnine former senior functionary in Nazarbayev's ruling party in his late fifties who had recently tergiversated to the opposition. Previously speaker of the Mazhilis (parliament's lower house), Tuyakbay had walked out in protest at what he and many other critics said was the rigging of parliamentary elections in 2004 that saw the opposition win just a single seat. Nazarbayev's untrammelled rule was turning 'other branches of power into a fiction', Tuyakbay complained, creating a system that was 'corrupt, irresponsible and leading to totalitarianism and the consolidation of autocracy'.[1] Given his past as a Nazarbayev loyalist and former chief prosecutor of Soviet Kazakhstan, Tuyakbay's miraculous conversion to democracy was not altogether convincing, and he was dogged by rumours that he was a Trojan horse to infiltrate the opposition – but as a big-shot regime defector, he was the man selected by the Za Spravedlivyy Kazakhstan (For a Just Kazakhstan) opposition coalition to challenge Nazarbayev in 2005.

The alliance included Kazakhstan's most prominent opposition leaders: Bolat Abilov, an urbane, well-groomed businessman and former ruling party MP with a nice line in fiery oratory; Oraz Zhandosov, a lanky ex-central bank chairman with a scholarly demeanour; Serikbolsyn Abdildin, leader of the Communist Party; Tolegen Zhukeyev, a former deputy prime minister; Amirzhan Kosanov, a former government spokesman active in opposition politics since the late 1990s; and Vladimir Kozlov of the Alga! party, who was later jailed over the Zhanaozen unrest. Flanking Tuyakbay at the coalition's founding conference were two other opposition leaders, Zamanbek Nurkadilov and Altynbek Sarsenbayev, who would both soon be dead: the former in a suspicious fatality before the election, the latter in a political assassination after it that exposed the pressures on beleaguered government critics.

In 2005, Nazarbayev was facing only his second-ever competitive election in his decade and a half in power. In independent Kazakhstan's first election in 1991 he had run unchallenged, Soviet-style, winning 99 per cent of the vote. He extended his rule by referendum in 1995, and first faced a challenger in 1999, trouncing communist leader Abdildin, a respected elder statesman figure, with 81 per cent. In 2005, Nazarbayev was facing four challengers in Kazakhstan's most competitive presidential election to date – even if they were all trailing far behind in a one-horse race.

Tuyakbay's campaign trail was dogged by dirty tricks.[2] In the city of Ust-Kamenogorsk, he was pelted with bricks and stones; in Shymkent he was attacked in a café by thugs hurling chairs, crockery and bottles, leaving one activist with a fractured rib as Tuyakbay escaped by leaping from a second-floor balcony.[3] His campaign was overshadowed by the disappearance of the teenage daughter of an activist who had recently complained of rebuffing an attempt by the KNB to recruit her as an informer within the opposition headquarters. After the election, Oksana Nikitina was found raped and murdered, and her uncle was later convicted of the crime, although the girl's mother suspected it was somehow connected to her own political activism.[4]

Three weeks before the election, a deadly drama erupted within the opposition camp: Nurkadilov was found dead, sprawled with gunshot wounds on the floor of his billiard room. A bluff former cabinet minister and mayor of Almaty who had worked with Nazarbayev since the mid-1980s, Nurkadilov was a portly, straight-talking 61-year-old with a shock of black hair and a reputation as a maverick, who had defected to the opposition in 2004, accusing the president of monopolising power. He had then positioned himself as an anti-corruption crusader, an image that did not sit altogether comfortably with his lavish lifestyle: he lived in an Almaty mansion which had once been robbed of a million dollars' worth of cash and jewellery (the family fortune, Nurkadilov explained, was earned by his wife Makpal Zhunusova, a blowsy celebrity singer).

Nurkadilov had promised to reveal a 'bombshell' about the Kazakhgate bribery case before the election. Now he was dead, and an orgy of speculation raged over who might have killed him. A relative during a family dispute? Shadowy forces to defuse his 'bombshell'? Powerful players indulging in murderous Machiavellian power games to discredit the president? Or – as Dariga Nazarbayeva, the president's daughter, hinted improbably – even the opposition itself, as a political provocation?[5]

The official verdict came as a shock: suicide. Nurkadilov had shot himself twice in the chest and once in the head after a mercurial family quarrel, investigators declared[6] – to the astonished derision of his widow and the outrage of his opposition allies, who deemed his death a political assassination.

A week later, Nazarbayev romped home in the election with 91 per cent of the vote, the opposition crying foul that it was rigged and international monitors noting an atmosphere of harassment and intimidation in a poll that had fallen far short of democratic standards.[7] Nazarbayev was sanguine, however. Soon afterwards he declared that after 'casting off the totalitarian past', Kazakhstan had 'successfully travelled the difficult route [...] from the dictate of a one-party system to political pluralism'.[8]

The next parliamentary election challenged Nazarbayev's starry-eyed vision of a pluralistic democracy: his party won every single seat up for grabs at the ballot box. Kazakhstan was not a one-party state like the Soviet Union, but it had become a state with a one-party parliament.

All the country's previous parliaments had been multi-party and contained a smattering of opposition – albeit severely curtailed after Nazarbayev dissolved a recalcitrant legislature in 1995 to rule by decree until a more pliant parliament was installed.[9] By 2004, opposition representation had dwindled to one seat, held by Ak Zhol (Bright Path), a centre-right liberal movement that had emerged from the 2001 reform coalition DVK. The party initially boycotted the seat over claims of vote-rigging.

In 2005, Ak Zhol split amid acrimonious disagreements – stirred up, some suspected, by the authorities as a divide-and-rule tactic – between one of its leaders, former government minister Alikhan Baymenov, and all the others. The genial, clean-cut Baymenov led a rump Ak Zhol party and subsequently took up the boycotted parliamentary seat. The others denounced him as a government stooge and formed a splinter movement called Nagyz (Real) Ak Zhol, which later rebranded as Azat (Freedom) under Abilov's leadership.[10] Meanwhile, Tuyakbay, Nazarbayev's former ally, formed the National Social Democratic Party (known by its acronym OSDP), with Kosanov, the veteran opposition leader, as his deputy. Also jostling for space on the crowded opposition scene were Vladimir Kozlov's Alga! party (which could not fight elections since it did not legally exist: the government refused to register it, believing it was backed by Ablyazov), and Abdildin's Communist Party. It was a bewildering array of opposition forces on a political scene dominated by Nazarbayev – lending weight to the criticism levelled at opposition leaders that disunity, infighting and personal ambition were holding back their cause.

The shifting sands and fractured nature of opposition politics contrasted with the well-oiled political machine that was Nazarbayev's Nur Otan party, which loosely translates as 'Ray of the Fatherland' but bears the echo of its leader's first name, Nursultan. By the time of the parliamentary vote in 2007 (a snap election as usual, since the authorities would discard the electoral timetable to suit themselves), Nur Otan's membership had swollen to one million, or 10 per cent of the electorate – including many public-sector workers, whose membership dues were deducted from their pay packets. This was the political behemoth that stormed to victory in the 2007 election, leaving six other parties in the dust. Nur Otan scooped up 88 per cent of the vote, but picked up all elected seats in parliament since it was the only party to clear the electoral threshold of 7 per cent of the national vote.

The election had delivered a one-party parliament that was nothing but a talking shop for Nur Otan, but Nazarbayev was pleased: his party had, he judged, won a 'legitimate and deserved victory' in 'honest, competitive and fair elections'.[11]

When Nazarbayev called a snap presidential election in 2011, the demoralised and fragmented opposition boycotted it in protest against a political playing field in which all the cards were stacked against it. Facing off against three stalking horses including Yeleusizov, who casually admitted to voting against himself, Nazarbayev swept 96 per cent of the vote, triumphantly hailing the election as proof 'that we are building a democratic Kazakhstan'.[12]

Parliamentary election day in January 2012 'was a black day in the calendar of the whole history of Kazakhstan', lamented veteran opposition leader Amirzhan Kosanov. 'On that day democracy was killed, just as in Zhanaozen our peaceful citizens were killed with machine guns!'[13]

Opposition leaders had gathered in a blizzard on Almaty's Republic Square two days after the vote, which took place a month after the shooting of oil workers in Zhanaozen, to protest against an election that had shut them out of parliament yet again. The election had rid Kazakhstan of its one-party legislature – but rather than allow any real opposition in, the decision-makers had reshuffled the political deck to create an astroturf 'opposition' as a token of political diversity. The administration was shrinking the political space and at the same time refining its methods for controlling it.

Rather than go to the trouble of forming a new party, the authorities would just seize an existing one that already had brand recognition among voters. It chose Ak Zhol, the erstwhile opposition party led by Baymenov, which was ready to become 'a worthy sparring partner and a worthy rival to Nur Otan', presidential adviser Yertysbayev opined airily – as if it were quite normal that the government should spearhead the creation of the political opposition.[14] All that remained was to effect a takeover.

On 1 July 2011, Baymenov resigned as Ak Zhol's leader, and a Nur Otan apparatchik named Azat Peruashev resigned his membership of the ruling party and seat on its political council. The next day, Baymenov got a cushy government job and Peruashev was parachuted into the Ak Zhol leadership – a bloodless coup that was acerbically dismissed by pundit Nurlan Yerimbetov as 'political prostitution'.[15]

In the election six months later, Nur Otan scooped 81 per cent of the vote, and two other parties scraped over the 7 per cent threshold to enter the Mazhilis with a handful of seats: Ak Zhol, rebranded as a business-friendly party, and the Communist People's Party of Kazakhstan, a pro-government splinter wing of the Communist Party which political analyst Dosym Satpayev derided as 'Dolly the Sheep' – cloned to create a simulation of political opposition.

The OSDP Azat opposition alliance spearheaded by Tuyakbay, Kosanov and Abilov trailed in with 1.7 per cent of the vote and no parliamentary seats. The day after the results came in, the leaders gathered on Republic Square and set fire to election protocols and Nur Otan flags, the smoke curling up into the air as they voiced their anger at being robbed, in their view, of a fair shot at entering parliament yet again. The election was 'a Rubicon after which all hopes that the current powers that be can reform themselves are lost', remarked Tuyakbay morosely as snowflakes floated down from a heavy grey sky and settled on his flat cap.

Ten days later, around 500 demonstrators turned out near the Soviet-era Hotel Kazakhstan, an Almaty landmark topped with a gold crown, for a rally called by opposition leaders to protest against the election results and the Zhanaozen shootings – a tiny protest by most standards, but large for Kazakhstan. 'Nazarbayev *ket!*' ('Nazarbayev out!') rang out scattered shouts from bolder protesters, a slogan borrowed from revolutions that had toppled presidents in neighbouring Kyrgyzstan in 2005 and 2010. This small, peaceful gathering was no revolutionary uprising, but activists took turns to express their anger at the election and their horror at the Zhanaozen killings: Abilov, Tuyakbay and Kosanov were followed by well-known faces like Ryspek Sarsenbay, brother of the opposition leader Altynbek (murdered six years earlier), and his wife Marzhan Aspandiyarova; Gulzhan Yergaliyeva, a prominent journalist; and Mukhtar Shakhanov, an elderly poet and Kazakh community leader. Conspicuous by his absence was Vladimir Kozlov, the opposition leader whose arrest days earlier, on charges of stoking the Zhanaozen unrest, had ramped up political tensions.

The demonstrators dispersed peacefully – but the police came later for the opposition leaders. They had breached Kazakhstan's draconian public assembly laws requiring protesters to obtain prior permission to gather, and Abilov and Kosanov were jailed for fifteen days on charges of organising an unsanctioned rally. Two weeks after their release, they were back behind bars – this time for organising a demonstration they had not even attended. They were arrested before it began, in a pre-emptive strike, and again jailed for fifteen days in what Kosanov slammed – speaking hurriedly by telephone as he was driven off to jail – as 'political revenge by the regime' on the opposition for proving that not everyone in Kazakhstan agreed with Nazarbayev's rule. The small demonstration of a couple of hundred protesters proceeded without the jailed leaders, and there were scuffles with riot police outside the Hotel Kazakhstan as officers kettled the demonstrators and snatched the most vocal out of the crowd. 'Nazarbayev *ket!*' cried one activist through a megaphone, before black-clad officers scooped him up and carried him aloft to a waiting van to shouts of 'shame, shame!' from protesters.

It was the opposition's last stand in what turned into a bleak year: the protests petered out, and by the end of 2012 Kozlov had been jailed, his Alga! party banned, and almost all the media outlets that had once given a voice to the opposition shut down by court order.

In 2013, the remnants of Kazakhstan's neutered political opposition crashed and burned. The OSDP Azat alliance splintered back into two; Abilov bowed out of politics, leaving Azat a headless chicken; and the OSDP imploded when Tuyakbay ousted Kosanov, leaving one of Kazakhstan's last existing opposition parties moribund.[16] Abdildin's Communist Party limped on ineffectually, but was banned by the courts in 2015 on a technicality involving membership numbers.[17] That left Kazakhstan all but bereft of organised political opposition. A movement called *Forum Jana Qazaqstan* (Forum New Kazakhstan), launched with fanfare in 2018 by former opposition leaders to press for reform, soon fizzled out.[18]

When the parliamentary election came around in 2016, the only opposition party still in existence to stand was Tuyakbay's OSDP. 'There's more lively competition for places in some cemeteries than there is in these parliamentary elections,' remarked the pundit Satpayev wryly.[19] The OSDP put up a lacklustre fight – the leader did not bother running himself – and failed to pick up any seats. The vote delivered an identikit parliament: Nur Otan, flanked by two 'opposition' parties – the tame Communist People's Party of Kazakhstan and the co-opted Ak Zhol, which Satpayev dismissed as 'zombie parties'. 'It reminds me of a Soviet shop,' he quipped (shops in the USSR were notorious for shortages and monotony of choice). 'There would be cans of sprats there, all the same, and you could get food poisoning from any one of them!'

In 2016, Nazarbayev characterised that Potemkin parliament elected in a Potemkin election as 'a great achievement of our democracy in the year of the twenty-fifth anniversary of independence'.[20]

The foregone conclusion of a massive victory did not guarantee a fair fight in Kazakhstan's elections. Although everything tipped the scales heavily in their favour, the authorities never shied away from wielding what is known in the post-Soviet world as the 'administrative resource': abusing the trappings of power to secure a huge landslide and a sky-high turnout to legitimise victory. Appearances matter. The authorities would harness public resources to promote Nazarbayev, and strong-arm millions of people – civil servants, doctors, teachers, students, soldiers – to get out and vote for Nazarbayev or his ruling party to boost the credibility of elections. People were bussed from polling station to polling station to vote multiple times in a system nicknamed the 'electoral merry-go-round'. Students were frogmarched to victory rallies to wave turquoise and yellow pennants (the colours of both Nur Otan and the national flag) and chant victory slogans. When inauguration day came around, Nazarbayev would be sworn into office standing on a piece of white felt – a regal nod to the traditions of the Kazakh khans of old.

Observers from the Organisation for Security and Cooperation in Europe, the main regional election-monitoring body with a credible claim to verifying democratic standards, have never judged a vote in Kazakhstan free and fair in its three decades of independence. They point with monotonous regularity to recurring problems: a lack of genuine choice for voters; severe restrictions on media access, freedom of expression and public assembly that curb the opposition's ability to communicate political messages; pressure on voters to turn out for fear of retribution; and – in case that is not enough to secure a favourable result – vote-rigging and ballot-stuffing on election day.[21] 'My vote's been stolen,' lamented one voter in an Almaty polling station in 2011, perusing a list showing he had already cast his ballot. Electoral officials apologised for the 'technical mistake' committed by a 'short-sighted' polling officer, and offered the man the chance to vote anyway. He declined angrily. This voter had planned to spoil his ballot in protest at the lack of choice – one of the few remaining options for dissenters. A spoiled ballot once doing the rounds on Twitter showed the presidential candidates crossed out and a box ticked beside the scrawled-in name 'Borat', a fictional Kazakh figure of fun made famous by a British spoof film. The authorities can hardly blame voters for not taking elections as a serious exercise in democracy: the party spirit whipped up on election days – with polling stations blaring out cheerful music, cheap cakes on sale outside and voters given gifts ranging from boxes of chocolates to irons – contributes to a lack of gravity. The government rejects criticism out of hand, and touts counter-findings of monitoring missions from organisations not distinguished by their commitments to democratic values, like the Commonwealth of Independent States (a post-Soviet grouping), which sing Kazakhstan's electoral praises. The government woos 'independent' foreign observers who enthuse about Kazakhstan's democratic credentials, like the Western analysts who hailed one election which delivered an opposition-free, rubber-stamp parliament as magically destined 'to carry Kazakhstan forward toward a multi-party political system with strong democratic institutions'.[22]

When taken to task, Nazarbayev was fond of saying – as he remarked during a visit to Astana by British Prime Minister David Cameron in 2013 – that 'full democracy is for us not the start of the road but the end of the road'.[23] Britain had taken centuries to get there; Kazakhstan would get there too, and in less time. Nazarbayev, who did not take kindly to lectures from Westerners about democracy, also retorted that contrary to foreigners' views of Kazakhstan as a 'medieval' country where people ride about on camels, it actually 'assures key human rights' and has free elections, a pluralistic parliament, a functioning opposition and a free media.[24]

'I've been ruling Kazakhstan for quite a few years; I stood at the cradle of independence,' mused Nazarbayev in 2015, playing hard to get about whether he would stand for re-election. 'Perhaps it's time to change the scenery, as they say in the theatre?'[25]

As the septuagenarian leader aged, many were wondering what would follow nearly three decades of this political monocracy. Who would replace the potentate? Would there be a destabilising power struggle, a carve-up of economic assets, political unrest? What would post-Nazarbayev Kazakhstan be like?

The names of possible successors were constantly being floated by the chattering classes – but fixating on names was missing the point, argued pundit Dosym Satpayev: 'It's easy to find a successor. It's far harder to assure the actual succession of power, because power in Kazakhstan has from the outset been created for a particular president: for Nursultan Nazarbayev,' he said in 2015.[26] Nazarbayev had talked of bequeathing a political system that would be 'resilient despite a change of leader'[27] – but would the sclerotic, autarchic system he had fashioned be fit for purpose for his successor?

For years, this concern was brushed under the carpet, but in 2017, months after the death of the long-ruling dictator of neighbouring Uzbekistan, Nazarbayev's contemporary Islam Karimov, the authorities devolved some of the president's all-encompassing powers, a nod to concerns over the system's durability.[28] Yet what resulted from this political calculus was mere constitutional tinkering to hand a few powers over from the presidency to the hand-picked government and the rubber-stamp parliament. Without political pluralism, this reform was meaningless: shuffling powers between a strong presidency and other emasculated institutions would not magically create a robust system of checks and balances to govern Kazakhstan after its founding father was gone.

But in 2015, Nazarbayev was not going anywhere just yet. He stood for re-election in another one-horse race, challenged by two political nobodies. This time the opposition did not boycott the proceedings: it simply no longer existed to field a candidate.

Many people professed delight at the opportunity to keep voting to keep Nazarbayev in power. 'Of course I'm going to vote for Nazarbayev, the *Yelbasy*,' said Salamat Saginbay, a professional boxer jogging in Almaty's Park of the First President near the giant statue of Nazarbayev, the only leader this young man had ever known. 'He's a wise president and we all support him.' Walking out of an Almaty polling station into a heavy April shower, pensioner Valeriy Chernoknizhnyy expressed his confidence in Nazarbayev: 'Let him rule as long as he has his health.' Not everyone agreed, but for dissenters, abstention seemed the only option in the absence of opposition. 'I'm not voting, because I consider myself a democrat, and in a democratic country presidents should only be elected twice,' grumbled one man. 'How long can Nazarbayev rule for? He's been in power since 1989, for twenty-six years.'

In 2015, Nazarbayev boosted his vote share to an eye-popping 97.5 per cent. For that stratospheric result, he offered a pseudo-apology: 'I'm sorry that for super-democratic states such figures would be unacceptable: 95 per cent turnout, 97.5 per cent for me. But I could do nothing. Had I interfered, I would have been undemocratic, wouldn't I?' The triumphant president then headed off to his victory rally in Astana, where hordes of flag-waving students dressed in turquoise and yellow feted the Leader of the Nation with chants of 'Kazakhstan! Nursultan!'

CHAPTER 10

End of an Era

Almaty/Nur-Sultan, 2019–21

A s the president's familiar face popped up on the nation's TV screens one evening four years later, in spring 2019, his compatriots were expecting standard greetings for Nauryz, a public holiday marking the spring equinox and associated with new beginnings. But Nazarbayev had more on his mind than festive salutations: he was about to drop a political bombshell. 'Today I am addressing you, as I have always done at the most important moments in the history of our state that we are building together,' he began, staring solemnly into the camera, flanked by the resplendent turquoise-and-yellow Kazakh flag and the national emblem.[1] 'But today's address is special. I have made a decision that was not easy for me: to relinquish my powers as President of the Republic of Kazakhstan.' It was the end of an era for Kazakhstan, and for Nazarbayev, who had been running the country for some three decades after being 'bestowed by my people with the honour of becoming the first president of independent Kazakhstan'. Now he would hand the reins of power to Qasym-Jomart Toqayev, the Senate speaker, who was constitutionally bound to assume the presidency for the remainder of the term.

Social media exploded in a crescendo of mixed emotions – shock, sadness, elation, confusion – as Kazakhstan processed news of the departure of the leader under whose rule around half the population had been born.[2] There were accolades from admirers; homages from those who respected Nazarbayev's decision to stage a graceful exit; and abundant jokes: 'Nursultan Nazarbayev has left the group,' quipped one Twitter user,[3] while a meme parodying the 'ice-bucket challenge' – depicting Nazarbayev throwing down the gauntlet to other long-ruling post-Soviet presidents, like Vladimir Putin – went viral. There was also a sense of disorientation. 'This world doesn't feel real to me without Nazarbayev. It's like Astana is no longer Astana. It's like snow is no longer snow,' remarked someone – prophetically, it turned out.[4]

Ever the political showman, Nazarbayev donned his glasses, picked up a pen and signed his resignation decree with a flourish, then concluded his valedictory speech by wishing 'every family, every citizen, prosperity, happiness, all the very best, and that you bring up children believing in our wonderful future'. Nazarbayev's oratorical flair had not deserted him at this most portentous of moments in a political career spanning half a century – but this was more 'so long' than 'farewell'. Kazakhstan's Leader of the Nation was endowed with substantial powers – from overseeing policy-making to chairing the Security Council – and would be exercising them as Kazakhstan moved inexorably towards, if not quite into, the post-Nazarbayev future. 'I will', he clarified, 'serve with you to the end of my days'.

The day after Nazarbayev's resignation on 19 March 2019, his name was immortalised to live on beyond the end of his days. Toqayev's first act was to bestow Nazarbayev's name on his pet project. It had long been assumed that Astana (meaning simply 'capital') would one day bear Nazarbayev's name in some form, though most had expected a posthumous rechristening. But parliament unanimously rubber-stamped Toqayev's motion, and out of the blue Astana became Nur-Sultan (the hyphen, not part of Nursultan Nazarbayev's first name, left unexplained). The imperious decision brought protesters onto the streets of 'Nur-Sultan', who became the first of thousands rounded up as the year progressed for daring to peacefully express their opposition to the side-lining of the public at this historic moment. A move cementing the Nazarbayev family's grip on power even as its patriarch relinquished the presidency stoked further ire, as Dariga Nazarbayeva, his daughter, replaced Toqayev as Senate speaker. That positioned her constitutionally second in line to the presidency, leaving many wondering if a dynasty was in the offing for Kazakhstan sooner or later.

Nazarbayev deserved the tribute of the capital bearing his name and more, Toqayev opined, including a statue in Nur-Sultan (he ended up with two, one unveiled for his eightieth birthday in 2020, another for his eighty-first in 2021) and the rechristening of main streets in towns across the land to honour a leader whose 'wisdom and leadership as a great politician, committed to democratic values' had earned him a place in history.[5] Hyperbole and sycophancy perhaps, but Nazarbayev's resignation did mark the end of an era for the country he had steered into independence out of the wreckage of the USSR. He was also making history for the post-Soviet region: the last leader to leave office from the contingent of ex-communist apparatchiks in power since before the USSR collapsed in 1991. In Central Asia, it was generally death or revolution that forced leaders out, but Nazarbayev was embarking on a bold experiment: bowing out of office but not out of power. As founding father, he would steer his country into a new political age while securing his legacy and, hopefully, avoiding a destabilising power struggle that might have erupted had he passed away in office. But the masterplan proved not to the liking of all his countrymen.

'We are the people! What about our opinion?' asked a woman demonstrating in Almaty, when anger spilled out onto the streets after Nazarbayev's resignation. A viral Instagram post captured the sense of dislocation: a young woman called Medina Bazargaliyeva marched around the capital breathlessly chanting words that became a catch-phrase: 'I have a choice! Nur-Sultan is not my town! Toqayev is not my president!'[6]

Although detractors derided his role as puppet to Nazarbayev's puppeteer, most viewed the jowly, silver-haired ex-prime minister and foreign minister, who also had a distinguished international diplomatic career as a former United Nations deputy secretary-general, with either respect or indifference. But while many would accept Kazakhstan's fledgling new mode of governance, others were hell-bent on demanding a say in their political future during this once-in-a-generation opportunity to push for change. Surreal scenes ensued as demonstrators mingled with celebrations of the Nauryz holiday. Masked riot police dodged men strutting around in warrior outfits, women in conical hats walking on stilts and children playing a giant version of a traditional dice game with sheep bones, to rugby-tackle protesters and carry them aloft to police vans. One young man thrust his head out of the window to yell an old slogan assuming a new meaning, reflecting disenchantment with political

arrangements that left Nazarbayev out of office but in control.[7] '*Shal ket*
(old man out!),' he yelled, a blue balloon signalling support for Mukhtar
Ablyazov – Nazarbayev's old nemesis, now stoking dissent from his lair
in France – floating out of his hand into the sky before officers shoved
him inside and drove him off to jail.[8]

Dissenters soon became creative to express their frustration. 'You can't
run away from the truth,' read a banner unfurled as marathon runners
jogged along an Almaty street in April, with hashtags #Ihaveachoice and
#forafairelection, referring to a vote called to legitimise Toqayev's rule.
Those sentiments landed the masterminds of the stunt, Asya Tulesova
and Beybaris Tolymbekov, in prison for fifteen days for breaching public
assembly laws, causing Amnesty International to declare them 'prisoners
of conscience' and creating the first cause célèbre for a new generation
of pro-democracy activists: millennials and Generation Zs born into
Nazarbayev's Kazakhstan who wanted a stake in the post-Nazarbayev
future.[9] Absurdist copycat actions followed. Artist Roman Zakharov
was imprisoned for hanging up a banner quoting Kazakhstan's constitution: 'The people are the sole source of state power.'[10] A young man
held up a blank sheet of paper on a square in the city of Uralsk, to 'put
our authorities' absurdity and insanity under the spotlight' and was
duly detained (but released when the police could not think of a crime
to charge him with).[11]

Young people looked to the past for inspiration and found it in a
rousing century-old poem: 'Wake Up, Kazakh!', penned as a call for
a political awakening by Mirzhakyp Dulatuly in the dying days of the
Russian Empire. Dubbing their movement Oyan, Qazaqstan (Wake Up,
Kazakhstan), the activists earned derision from critics dismissing them
as woke urban hipsters sitting around sipping flat whites while plotting
an Instagram revolution, and their meetings in public places for poetry
readings and guitar strumming provided easy fodder for mockery, even
if their goal of reclaiming the streets for peaceful gatherings was serious.
Tangled up in this protest movement were culture wars and generational
tussles, encapsulated in a sign displayed at a demonstration later that year:
'OK, boomer', the exasperated catchphrase of Western millennials to baby
boomers reinterpreted to signal vexation with Kazakhstan's stuck-in-the-
past Soviet-era dinosaurs who seemed deaf to the younger generation's

voice. Oyan, Qazaqstan had a serious political agenda: a transition to parliamentary democracy as 'the first step to break once and for all with the totalitarian past', said founder member Dimash Alzhanov.[12] With the handover of power a done deal, that seemed a vain hope, but it was not only trendy millennials refusing to accept the new status quo.

'Let's unite! We are the people! I'm not afraid to speak out, I'm afraid to be silent!' cried Zhazira Demeuova, as crowds out celebrating May Day strolled in Almaty's Gorky Park. 'Don't be afraid! Speak out! It's about the future of our children!' Indicating the girl she held by the hand, she warned police standing by: 'I've come with my child, so be careful: pick up the child if you're going to round me up.' A young man chipped in: 'Nur-Sultan is not our capital! Toqayev is not our president! Dariga is not our speaker! We have a choice!'

The instigator of this protest was Ablyazov, the oligarch who had slugged it out through the French courts to have his extradition struck down in 2016. He had since formed the Democratic Choice of Kazakhstan (DVK by its acronym) movement, echoing the name of the pro-reform group that had caused his rift with Nazarbayev nearly twenty years earlier. The courts had banned this latest incarnation of DVK as 'extremist', and convicted Ablyazov *in absentia* on a string of charges that he denied: from corruption to contracting the killing of his ex-business partner who had perished in a mysterious hunting accident fourteen years before investigators spotted anything fishy about the death.[13] The embittered Ablyazov had resumed his baiting of Nazarbayev and Kazakhstan's ruling classes – virtually, from France (where he received political asylum in 2020, a court decrying 'obvious attempts by outside agents to exert influence on the asylum authorities'[14]). He had a small but vociferous fan base inside Kazakhstan who followed his vitupera-tive, rambling social media posts and heeded his occasional calls for street protests, which he made no secret of stoking to push for 'regime change'.[15] Since Nazarbayev's resignation, novice protesters had joined die-hard Ablyazov supporters, and this demo was led by a few mothers with young children in tow. Striking among them was Oksana Shevchuk, a mother of four with flowing waist-length ash blonde hair who had come 'to express my support for mothers and children today', she cried through a karaoke mike – hardly a clarion call for revolution, although that intent would later be ascribed to her in court. In her arms was her seven-month-old daughter, Eva, clad in a pink bonnet – to signal that the protesters had peaceful intentions and important messages for future generations, Shevchuk later said, after she was arrested and brought to trial for supporting a banned organisation.[16]

The protesters began to dance, Demeuova's daughter twirling a ribbon as a smiling woman called out: 'We have a choice, we finally have a choice!' The crowd began marching around the park, big wheel and chairoplanes spinning behind them while giant furry animals who were part of the May Day fun – Mickey Mouse, Deputy Dawg – tried to disrupt the demo. 'Old man out!' 'No to dictatorship!' 'Alga, Kazakhstan!' cried the protesters, taking up a popular patriotic slogan meaning 'Forward, Kazakhstan!' as a blue balloon soared above the marchers' heads. 'We want democracy. We want freedom of speech. We never have democratic elections,' complained Dilyara, a softly spoken teenager attending, with her mother, her first ever protest, wearing a T-shirt scrawled with 'you can't run from the truth'. 'We're here because we want change!'

The presidential election in June would not deliver change, even if it featured, for the first time since 2005, a contender critical of the government: Amirzhan Kosanov, whose involvement in opposition politics dated back two decades. As Kosanov fended off accusations of selling out and legitimising another choreographed electoral spectacle, Toqayev romped home with 71 per cent of the vote – hardly a Nazarbayev-style 98 per cent landslide, but a comfortable margin of victory. This election had 'offered an important moment for potential political reforms, but it was tarnished by clear violations of fundamental freedoms as well as pressure on critical voices', concluded international observers.[17]

'I have a choice!' 'Toqayev is not my president!' 'Boycott! Boycott!' yelled demonstrators swarming onto a hulking Soviet-era statue in an Almaty park on election day, as police dragged them down and hauled them aloft into vans, leaving the park littered with mini Kazakh flags, deflated blue balloons and items of clothing shed in scuffles: a baseball cap here, a loafer there. Police detained 4,000 people over several days of protests; 700 were jailed for short periods.[18] The authorities deemed them dangerous dissenters intent on 'regime change', but many were just thoughtful citizens requesting a political voice. 'I'm against this regime and I'm against those elections [...] because I don't consider them fair elections and true elections,' said a young composer at the protest in Almaty, dismissing the vote as 'theatre' – more bread and circuses. 'I just want to show that I disagree with this regime. I disagree with how our politicians rule our country. I disagree pretty much with everything that's going on right now.' It was an inauspicious start to Toqayev's presidency as Kazakhstan experienced its first power shift as a modern nation state.

'We are the people! We are the power!' chanted a boisterous group outside an Almaty courtroom one November evening, as a police car idled, blue light flashing. Inside, a political trial had just ended with guilty verdicts for three women who had been leading lights in the May Day demo – Demeuova, Shevchuk and Gulzipa Dzhaukerova – and one man, Anuar Ashiraliyev. These ordinary mothers had become unlikely poster girls for the cause of peaceful dissent, their case made more poignant since – deemed dangerous dissenters fomenting rebellion – they were held on remand and separated from their dependent children, including a breastfeeding daughter (Shevchuk's Eva) and a child with special needs (Dzhaukerova's). All had denied being members of Ablyazov's banned DVK, claiming they were being persecuted for voicing their convictions. 'I have the right under the constitution to express my thoughts. I didn't call for any rebellion or anything, I merely spoke about my own social problems, and I was arrested for that,' said Demeuova indignantly in a recess.[19] Shevchuk had gone to the Gorky Park demo 'to express my opinion', she testified. 'I had no political aims.' She wanted 'to talk about my problems, what concerns me' – the socio-economic problems struggling families faced, which had recently become a hot topic.[20]

Not long before, a tragic fire in Astana in which five children had died alone at home while their parents – members of the working poor – toiled on nightshifts had incensed the public, and given impetus to a coalition of mothers demanding greater welfare support for large families (which the government encouraged to boost birth rates in thinly populated Kazakhstan).[21] A mother of four herself, Oksana sympathised with the movement, and that fire 'really shook me up' – it gave her nightmares, she later explained with a shudder, pinpointing the spark for her political awakening that ultimately landed her in the dock. The incident personified a Kazakhstan of haves and have nots: the bereaved parents' ramshackle house and daily struggles contrasting with the fat cats' glitzy homes and cushy lives. Shevchuk's family was certainly not starving, but expected more from oil-rich Kazakhstan – 'I wasn't born in Africa [...] or the North Pole. I was born in a rich country' – as they mulled over problems like corruption eating away at public services while officials on the take got rich quick, or millions splashed on vanity projects while 'there's nothing for my children'. Oksana – a member of the 'Nazarbayev Generation', born in 1989, the year he rose to the helm of Soviet Kazakhstan – had been apolitical, but the revelation that policy at the top affected life at the grass roots struck her. 'It all comes down to politics, whichever way you look at it, because it's all about our lives.'[22]

The defendants said they had been speaking up for the struggling and dispossessed, not acting as Ablyazov's proxies to foment an uprising. 'I'm not a soldier to carry out orders,' scoffed Shevchuk, professing herself no advocate of 'regime change' or 'revolution or bloodshed'. Turning the trial into a soapbox, Ashiraliyev brandished Kazakhstan's constitution and recited, with a scornful laugh: 'Restrictions of the rights and freedoms of citizens for political reasons shall not be allowed in any form.' Unmoved, the judge convicted the four, but spared them prison sentences. They received 'restricted freedom' terms, with bail-like restrictions, and a two-year prohibition on public activism: 'de-activating the activists', said defence lawyer Gulnara Zhuaspayeva exasperatedly. (This counted as leniency: a man named Aset Abishev had previously been jailed for supporting DVK not on the streets but on social media – another piece of human collateral damage in the war between Ablyazov and the state.[23]) After the verdict, supporters streamed out of the courtroom to greet the mothers with a hero's welcome, chants of 'We are the people! We are the power!' echoing down the street before they massed on the steps and burst into a lusty rendition of the national anthem, 'My Kazakhstan'.

These activists may have been 'de-activated', but there were more dissidents out there. On Independence Day in December, protesters rallied again to call for reform. 'Kazakhstan Without the Nazarbayevs!' demanded a silver placard waved by Oyan, Qazaqstan demonstrators, spotlighting how the sway of the ex-president and his family rankled as the year of his resignation drew to a close.

Court proceedings in London in 2020 provided a glimpse into the family's wealth and privilege. The UK had slapped Unexplained Wealth

Orders on three luxury residences owned by Dariga Nazarbayeva and Nurali Aliyev, her eldest son (a businessman), through offshore companies, claiming they were purchased using illicit funds from Nazarbayeva's late disgraced ex-husband Rakhat Aliyev. The pair fended off the allegation, arguing that they had used their own legally acquired wealth to purchase £80 million worth of properties, including a ten-bedroom mansion complete with swimming pool and cinema on a Hampstead street nicknamed Billionaires' Row. Dariga Nazarbayeva declared herself 'vindicated' by the court victory.[24] But the proceedings lifted the veil of secrecy surrounding the assets of the Nazarbayev family, whose global property empire was estimated by journalists to be worth a cool $800 million.[25]

Another family drama making headlines in London took a tragic turn. Dariga Nazarbayeva's youngest son Aisultan had previously revealed his battle against drug addiction, after his devastation at his father's scandalous demise (Aliyev was found hanged in an Austrian cell while awaiting trial on murder charges) had catapulted him into substance abuse, seeking 'solace for the soul from unbearable reality'.[26] Aisultan had been up in the London courts (convicted for biting a police officer) and in and out of rehab in the Priory (luxury haunt of celebrities with a habit) when he took to Facebook in early 2020 to splash a slew of allegations about family corruption and assassination and kidnapping plots against him, topped off with the outlandish-sounding claim – delivered as a curious aside in a stream of posts talking about magic and asking Queen Elizabeth to give Nazarbayev a call – that his real father was supposedly not Aliyev but Nursultan Nazarbayev.[27] The family refrained from comment about this claim of incest, though one minister dismissed these ramblings as the product of a substance-addled mind.[28] The young man's troubled life – perhaps the result of the family traumas of his childhood – ended in tragedy in summer 2020, when he died in London at the age of twenty-nine, leaving his mother 'devastated at the loss of our beloved Aisultan'. A British coroner ruled his death 'the result of natural cause; he died as a result of his addiction to cocaine'.[29]

Tongues wagging about a Nazarbayev dynasty had been stilled with Dariga Nazarbayeva's dismissal from her top job at the Senate in May 2020. The political defenestration of this scion from what had looked like a dynasty-in-the-making perhaps signalled a closing of ranks from rivals wishing to rid Kazakhstan of the Nazarbayev family dynasty option – although, with the post-Nazarbayev future still shrouded in uncertainty, there was no guarantee. In 2021 she returned to parliament as an MP for the ruling Nur Otan party, proving that the family remained a political force to be reckoned with two years after Nazarbayev's resignation. Many were still wondering what would happen when the octogenarian Leader of the Nation passed away. Was Toqayev a stop-gap leader? Would he want to stay in power? Would he be able to, if vested interests lined up against him? Could a member of the Nazarbayev family still have a shot at the presidency? Were other contenders waiting in the wings? How would a future leader cater for political dissent and Kazakh nationalist sentiment? What role would Kazakhstan's powerful security services play as politicians and oligarchs jostled for position – particularly since powers of oversight over key political and security appointments had been handed to the Security Council?[30] Would a power struggle, political score-settling and a redivision of economic spoils – developments Nazarbayev had tried to prevent by stepping down in his lifetime – erupt after his death? Would apocalyptic scenarios play out, or would the reins of power remain in the hands of a Nazarbayev regime stalwart, with the ex-president elevated – even more in death than in life, perhaps – into a cult figure around whom to rally the nation? Ironically, a political transition designed to create certainty and end speculation about the post-Nazarbayev future had done anything but, as uncertainty prevailed over who would lead Kazakhstan and what shape the political scene would take after his death. Rumour-mongers gossiped inexorably about a power struggle between the hawkish Team Nazarbayev (dubbed 'The Library' because it worked out of the Library of the First President and believed to be close to Kazakhstan's security apparatus, spearheaded by intelligence chief Karim Masimov) and the supposedly dovish Team Toqayev ('Akorda', after the presidential palace), which had been cutting its teeth with promises of reform.

In his first state-of-the-nation address in 2019, Toqayev pledged to transform Kazakhstan into a 'Listening State' that would abandon monologue for dialogue and loosen the screws on the political process to establish 'a multi-party system, political competition and pluralism of opinion' – startling talk in a country with no functioning opposition parties, and there was more. Toqayev would guarantee citizens' right to protest, which had become a battleground since Nazarbayev's resignation. But it would be a struggle for Toqayev to reconcile the irreconcilable demands of perpetuating the status quo, as Nazarbayev had appointed him to do, and delivering the change dissenters were demanding. Indeed, the constitution prohibited changes to 'the basic principles' of Kazakhstan's political system, in recognition of Nazarbayev's 'historic mission' as its founding father.[31]

Toqayev's commitment to political plurality failed its first test, when an attempt to form an opposition party descended into farce in February 2020 as activist Zhanbolat Mamay tried to set up the Democratic Party of Kazakhstan. The founding conference floundered as police rounded up would-be delegates, and when Mamay tried to stage a protest rally, he was briefly slung behind bars.[32] The party continued operating without registration, staging street protests that would lead to hours of police kettling but few arrests, leading critics to mutter darkly that it was a faux opposition movement directed by the security services – something Mamay hotly denied.

A few days after that fiasco, a tragic incident cast a spotlight on Kazakhstan's treatment of protesters. On a dark winter's evening, officers came to arrest Dulat Agadil, an activist who was a constant aggravation to local police, in Talapker, a village near Nur-Sultan, for non-compliance with court orders. After an altercation with a protesting, half-dressed Agadil, they cuffed him and marched him into a car. That was the last time his wife and six children saw him alive: hours later Agadil died in a cell, officially of heart failure – but friends and family suspected foul play. This was far from Agadil's first brush with the law: the 43-year-old had spent frequent spells in detention for staging unauthorised protests. A supporter of the recently formed Koshe (Street) Party – banned soon afterwards, deemed another incarnation of Ablyazov's DVK – Agadil had previously embarrassed law-enforcers by escaping through a window while serving his fifth prison sentence within a month.[33] A thousand mourners turned out in a blizzard to bury Agadil in a coffin shrouded in the Kazakh flag, hailing a 'brave son of the Kazakh people' and shouting political slogans as the procession marched to the grave.[34] The burial of an activist who had come to prominence asserting his right to protest did not pass without arrests of mourners, and demonstrations to demand accountability over Agadil's death were also shut down with detentions.[35] 'Dulat is a victim of the system,' read a placard waved as the first anniversary of Nazarbayev's resignation approached.[36]

It had been a bruising first year in office for Toqayev, confronting small but sustained protests demanding political change, and for Kazakhstan, confronting the challenge of moving on from one-man rule while the elder statesman jealously guarded his legacy. Now, along came a cur-veball that would leave Kazakhstan, and the whole world, reeling: the coronavirus pandemic, which would expose both the failings of the system Nazarbayev was bequeathing and the weakness of opposition forces – both nascent and established.

The summer of 2020 saw Kazakhstan engulfed in a devastating wave of infections,[37] leaving the healthcare system creaking as the pandemic 'exposed all the sector's systemic problems', as Toqayev later put it.[38] As hospitals filled up, social media lit up with outrage over what mourn-ing relatives deemed unnecessary deaths resulting from bungling and corruption that had laid the healthcare service to waste over years, and continued thriving during the pandemic, judging by allegations of a conspiracy to skim off $1 million in healthcare funding.[39]

'It's these thieves who steal from the people who are to blame for everything, who steal the whole budget and sit in power,' exclaimed Dauren Mombayev, a lawyer who had just lost his father that July, his voice choking with grief and fury.[40] 'These deaths, this blood, are on them.' He had fought first to get an ambulance, then to find his father a hospital bed. As Dauletbek Mombayev gasped for breath, the registrar had refused admission, citing a lack of medicine, oxygen and beds. 'I was told directly: we have nothing to treat your father with,' explained Dauren, who queued up with other frantic relatives to buy oxygen from workshops that usually supplied carbon dioxide to breweries. He was convinced his father's life could have been saved had corruption not corroded the healthcare system over the years. As people lay dying in overcrowded wards, the government struck a disastrous note on a public holiday honouring Kazakhstan's capital and falling on Nazarbayev's birth-day. On 6 July a lavish fireworks display exploded over Nur-Sultan's glitzy skyline, prompting outbursts at this feast in time of plague: 'dancing on people's bones', remarked one social media user, as Nazarbayev turned eighty with his hands still firmly on the helm of power.[41] Dauletbek Mombayev had officially died of pneumonia, but the family believed his was one of thousands of 'pneumonia' cases that the government later admitted were probably undiagnosed coronavirus infections[42] – one of many statistical obfuscations that left even Toqayev admitting he did not trust the data.[43] Cases numbers and death rates were relatively low, but international studies of excess mortality figures revealed a different picture. One found Kazakhstan to be among the world's leaders for an increase in deaths, 22 per cent up compared to pre-pandemic times.[44] Another suggested the true death count was far higher than 5,620, the government's tally at the time the research was conducted, and actually stood at 81,696. The government rejected the claim.[45]

All countries made blunders fighting the corona-crisis, and Kazakhstan did better than many as it ploughed some of its oil wealth into funding a $14 billion rescue package, covering everything from healthcare spending and danger money for medics to welfare handouts and economic stimulus.[46] But that would not stop the economy from plunging into its first recession for more than two decades in 2020, when the poverty rate was estimated to have more than doubled to 12–14 per cent of the population.[47] That meant about 2.5 million people were living in poverty in a country whose leaders had always boasted of their hydrocarbon riches and consideration for public well-being. No country would emerge unscathed from the economic shockwaves of the pandemic, but Kazakhstan was hard hit by a phenomenon that had struck it before, as another plunge in global oil prices in 2020 again revealed the government's failure to diversify the oil-dependent economy. Prices picked up, but as Kazakhstan's thirtieth anniversary of independence came round in 2021 with its economy still addicted to oil, a yawning rich-poor divide and corruption still running rife, it did not look like the great economic success story that Nazarbayev had hoped to bequeath his people.

As elsewhere in the world, the pandemic magnified problems that already existed but now became glaringly obvious. These included the pitfalls of a sclerotic system that bred loyalty up the chain to the leadership rather than accountability down the chain to the people, and public distrust in unaccountable rulers that made people suspicious of government messaging. Flouting mask-wearing and social-distancing rules, people turned to quack remedies – from the mundane (horserad-ish) to the exotic (dog fat, from Korean medicine). Crackpot conspiracy theories – about helicopters spraying the virus to poison people, or vaccines being part of a global plot to embed chips in humans to monitor them – went viral as the authorities, always so quick to shut down online political dissent with criminal charges, looked on passively.[48]

Kazakhstan was quick off the mark in ordering vaccines (Russian and Chinese), and offered them free to all adults, but anti-vaxxer sentiment and distrust of officialdom led to slow take-up. When the government ordered everyone working with the public – from civil servants to shop assistants and waiting staff – to get jabbed, a trade in forged 'vaccination passports' took off, as people bribed medics to fake the process of jabbing them but pour the valuable substance away, so they could get registered as vaccinated.[49] The perversity of this black market involving people paying not to get a jab that they could have got for free encapsulated two problems that had blighted Kazakhstan for years: the gaping dis-connect between rulers and ruled, and rampant corruption that could quite literally have lethal consequences.

Toqayev's promise of a 'Listening State' notwithstanding, the battle against political dissent continued. As proof of good faith, the govern-ment held up its enactment in 2020 of the reforms Toqayev had prom-ised: the government abolished the requirement to obtain permission for most types of protests, and simplified registration requirements for political parties. This resulted in a sight astonishing for Kazakhstan: pro-democracy protesters gathering in Almaty in October 2020 to shout slogans and wave placards demanding 'yes to reform, no to repression!', unmolested by police. So was the 'pluralism of opinion' that Toqayev had promised finally flourishing? Hardly. The authorities may have reformed the letter of the law, but the spirit of its application remained unchanged. Some demonstrations were allowed to proceed, but the right to protest was granted selectively, sparingly and grudgingly. Harassment of pro-democracy campaigners of all stripes continued, but the toughest meas-ures were reserved for supporters of Ablyazov and his DVK movement. This was a red line for the authorities, because his decades-long personal feud with Nazarbayev was so bitter and because the powers that be were genuinely spooked by his calls for 'regime change'. DVK protests were shut down with arrests (often pre-emptive, so would-be demonstrators could not even approach a planned protest site), and its activists were harassed, prosecuted and imprisoned. By March 2021, two years after Nazarbayev's resignation and eighteen months after Toqayev's promise of a 'Listening State', 270 people were under investigation for what human rights campaigner Bakhytzhan Toregozhina described as 'the public expression of opinions' – clearly opinions the 'Listening State' did not want to hear. Of these, 124 faced charges of involvement with banned Ablyazov-linked political groups labelled 'extremist', which generally led to spells of imprisonment or restricted freedom.[50]

Always hyper-sensitive to manifestations of dissent, Nur-Sultan was taking no chances as it anxiously surveyed the post-Soviet scene in 2020 and 2021: Belarus engulfed in demonstrations against a rigged election; Russians taking to the streets to protest over the arrest of anti-corruption activist Aleksey Navalny; post-election protests in Kyrgyzstan sweeping its president out of office, leaving Toqayev warning against the dangers of 'ochlocracy' – mob rule.[51] In Kazakhstan, though, the civil society that had seemed so buoyant after Nazarbayev's resignation appeared to flag rather than gather momentum. The absence of a credible charismatic leader; disunity between disparate forces; public apathy; crackdowns on dissenters – all were plausible explanations. Whatever the case, protests in 2021, even on Independence Day in December, were mostly able to muster no more than a few dozen people – no wonder the mass demonstrations that erupted in January 2022 blindsided Kazakhstan's complacent leaders.

Toqayev's brave new age of 'political competition' looked hollow when parliamentary elections came round in January 2021. Still no opposition parties had managed to form, and the government had rejected at least eight attempts.[52] Even the last nominally opposition party left standing, the toothless National Social Democratic Party, boycotted the election after Ablyazov endorsed it to sow disarray. It was seventeen years since an opposition party had last won a parliamentary seat, but now Kazakhstan set a dismal new record by staging its first ever parliamentary election in thirty years featuring no opposition parties at all on the ballot. On election day outspoken media suffered cyberattacks, while police detained and kettled demonstrators, holding them in freezing temperatures for hours without access to food, water or toilets. Inside the polling stations draconian new restrictions hampered independent scrutiny of the vote, leading civil society campaigner Maria Lobacheva to dub the election an 'insiders' get-together from which observers and voters are excluded'. The election cemented a parliamentary status quo that had been in place for nearly a decade, delivering the same three pro-government parties into parliament as the two previous elections: Nur Otan flanked by its sidekicks Ak Zhol and the People's Party of Kazakhstan (which had dropped 'Communist' from its name). 'Everything was done to ensure the fairness of the conduct of the elections,' Toqayev opined.[53] 'An election can only be truly democratic when voters have real political options to choose between, and the voice of civil society is heard and appreciated,' reflected international observers.[54] Public distrust in the fairness of elections was sky-high: one poll showed three-quarters believed the results could not be trusted,[55] while 22 per cent only went to the polls to stop someone from stealing their vote and another 11 per cent because they felt coerced.[56] As Kazakhstan celebrated its thirtieth anniversary of independence in 2021, its claim to be a democracy looked like a sham to its own people: only 6 per cent believed their country had become a democracy, while 23 per cent thought the political system had nothing in common with one.[57]

The parliamentary election was a 'symbolic spectacle of democracy', remarked Sofya Omarova, a UK-based Kazakh academic, dubbing Kazakhstan 'a Listening State with a deaf regime'.[58] While the authorities chanted their mantra of stability and continuity, to many this looked more like stagnation. Azamat Junisbai, another academic, cut to the heart of the conundrum of Kazakhstan's political transition, which had raised, then quickly dashed, hopes for change: 'Pursuing major reforms aimed at political liberalisation would be akin to pushing a self-destruct button for the very status quo this transition format was designed to safeguard.'[59]

II

IDENTITY CRISIS

CHAPTER 11

Kingdom of the Kazakhs

Kapshagay, 2015

Blood-curdling war cries wrench the air as a horde of fierce armour-clad warriors bursts out from behind a craggy bluff and, pennants aflutter and swords aloft, gallops furiously into an enemy encampment below. With a thunder of hooves and a clash of swords, a pitched battle breaks out. As the Kazakhs fight it out down on the plain in a life-or-death struggle for their sovereignty, perched on a spur above the tussle a female swashbuckler, attired in an ornate fur headdress and wearing a quiver of arrows on her back, taps furiously away at her smartphone as a shaggy white camel impassively chews the cud.

This is no medieval theatre of war, but the set where a *Game of Thrones*-style historical epic recounting the dramatic tale of the national awakening of the Kazakh nation more than half a millennium ago is being filmed. Shot against the breathtaking mountains and rolling grasslands of south-eastern Kazakhstan, this is *Kazakh Khanate*: a TV mini-series and big-screen film dramatising the tempestuous historical backstory of a kingdom founded in 1465 by two Kazakh rebels that is nowadays considered the precursor to today's nation state – albeit with what pedants sniff at as dubious historical myth-making.

This is the saga of a political and military struggle between warring tribes, complete with valiant heroes, the Kazakhs, and dastardly villains, the Mongols, Uzbeks and other foes with whom they cross swords to win the ultimate prize: a land they can call their own. With its enduring themes of power and glory, war and peace, love and hate, *Kazakh Khanate* has certainly imbibed some creative inspiration from *Game of Thrones*.

Unlike that popular fantasy-based hit series, though, this is based on actual historical figures slugging it out for supremacy and survival. 'We have a real story about seven kingdoms,' enthuses Arman Asenov, the burly, bearded producer, as he steers his jeep over rugged terrain out to the film set not far from Almaty near the Kapshagay reservoir, which flashes by in a glint of sparkling blue on a bright December day in 2015.[1]

The heroes of this tale are Zhanibek and Kerey, two rebels who broke away from territory ruled by nomadic Uzbeks to form their own khanate amid the chaos that reigned on the Eurasian plains following the disintegration of the Golden Horde, the vast Mongol-ruled empire founded by Genghis Khan in the thirteenth century that once governed from the steppes of Asia to the shores of the Danube. 'They decide: we're announcing from this day on "we're the Kazakh Khanate", and they send riders out all over [to spread the news]!' exclaims Arman, with an ebullient flourish as he negotiates a rutted track near the town of Kapshagay, which is jokingly dubbed 'KazVegas' because it is stuffed with casinos.

Why have the film-makers suddenly chosen this ancient topic to entertain the twenty-first-century public? 'The history of my country and the history of my people and how it was born isn't just important but also topical,' Rustem Abdrashev, the thoughtful, baseball-capped director, says later, strolling the ramparts of a fortress on an unusually balmy winter evening while the velvety twilight engulfs a mud-baked medieval village constructed below. On the set, the crew rushes to pack up the gear after a long day's filming, weary extras mounted on sleek horses swearing roundly at recalcitrant camels which refuse to budge.

The director hoped that his on-screen dramatisation of the past would act as an 'awakening' for the younger generation, 'because unfortunately we lived for seventy years with a distorted knowledge of our own history, and now we're trying to inform people about it, correct it, replenish it and recount it'.

The Kazakhs date their history of nationhood back to the foundation of the Kazakh Khanate in 1465, when Kerey and Zhanibek broke away from one of the successor kingdoms to the Golden Horde, the Shaibanid Khanate, which at one point controlled swathes of land stretching across much of what is now Kazakhstan. In the mid-1450s, the Shaibanid Khanate (sometimes called the Uzbek Khanate after Sultan Mohammed Öz Beg, who gave his name to the Uzbeks of modern-day Uzbekistan) was governed by Abulkhair, whose rout in battle by the pugnacious Oirats – the age-old foes of the Kazakhs who lived in what is now western Mongolia – sparked an exodus from the remnants of his kingdom. The revolt was led by Zhanibek and Kerey, descendants of the last khan of the Ak Orda (White Horde), one of the kingdoms that emerged out of the fragmentation of the Golden Horde. The name Nazarbayev chose more than five centuries later for his presidential palace, Akorda, is a nod to that lineage.

The renegades moved into a valley between the Shu and Talas Rivers in a breakaway migration that gave them a new name: these nomadic Turkic tribesmen began calling themselves *kazak*, meaning 'free' or 'wanderer'. That, at least, is the etymology widely accepted in Kazakhstan nowadays; rival theories also exist, for example that '*kazak*' derives from a Turkic word meaning 'to acquire', or from '*kas sak*', meaning 'real Scythian', in reference to the ancient Scythians ('*sak*'), whom the Kazakhs view as distant forefathers. (The 'h' in the English 'Kazakh' came via Russian, which rendered the Kazakh letter 'k' in '*kazak*' differently at the beginning and end of the word. In modern Kazakh the word remains '*kazak*', and the word for the country is '*Kazakstan*', officially rendered in the new Latin alphabet that is being phased in as 'Qazaqstan'.)

The Kazakh Khanate experienced its heyday in the sixteenth century, in the mid-1500s reaching the borders of the fledgling Russian state, which was expanding eastwards as the Golden Horde collapsed, and towards the end of the century conquering the great Central Asian cities of Tashkent and Samarkand. But the khanate's fortunes ebbed and flowed, as did its borders, and by the 1570s it had entered a spiral of decline that continued, with a few comebacks, for three centuries.

In the seventeenth century, the Kazakhs were again losing territory to rivals and struggling to hold off the marauding Oirats, now united into the Dzungar Khanate. In the 1720s, the Dzungars launched crippling raids that led to a disaster remembered as the *aktaban shubyryndy*, loosely translated as the 'barefooted flight': a traumatic exodus of Kazakhs from the lands they roamed as they fled to escape the attacks. These debilitating battles with their centuries-old foes drove the Kazakhs to seek a powerful champion. In the early eighteenth century, they looked north for protection, setting in motion a relationship that would bring their ancestral lands under Russian rule. This, at least, is history as taught under the Soviets and still taught in Kazakh schools today, although some quibble over its accuracy. History is written by the victors, and the idea that the Kazakhs invited the Russians in for protection is one that suited – and still suits – the Kremlin nicely, tying in neatly with a world view still prevalent in Russia of the Russians as benevolent big brother rather than expansionist coloniser.

Kazakh communities were tribal, with different '*ru*' (tribes) grouped into three '*zhuz*' (tribal unions) that were gradually subsumed into the Russian Empire in a protracted process lasting well over a century. Theoretically allied but separately ruled and often acting as rivals, these were: the Uly ('Greater') Zhuz in the south-east; the Orta ('Middle') Zhuz in northern, eastern and central Kazakhstan; and the Kishi ('Lesser') Zhuz in the west. (Although largely formal distinctions nowadays, these tribal affiliations still exist: most Kazakhs know which *ru* and *zhuz* they hail from, and can also list seven generations of their ancestors, as tradition dictates, which serves the practical purpose of preventing intermarriage to keep the bloodline strong.)

First to take an oath of loyalty to Moscow were tribes of the Kishi Zhuz, who became Russian vassals in 1731, and the Orta Zhuz khan swore allegiance to Russia in 1740. In the 1820s, the Russians abolished khan rule over these two tribal unions and assumed direct control. The first tribes of the Uly Zhuz had sworn an oath of loyalty to Russia in 1742 and more followed, until by the 1870s the lands of the Uly Zhuz were also under Kremlin rule. The Kazakhs had been subsumed into the Russian Empire – although, owing to some confusion over Central Asian ethnicities, the Russians called the Kazakhs 'Kirgiz' and the Kyrgyz tribes who lived to their south (in what is today Kyrgyzstan) 'Kara-Kirgiz' ('Black Kirgiz'). These misnomers persisted for several centuries until the Kazakhs were finally given their proper name – and an eponymous Soviet republic – in 1925.

The Kazakh Khanate had a brief resurrection in the 1840s, led by Kenesary Khan, who proclaimed its revival and regained control over swathes of land – but this was short-lived, and the khan's death in battle in 1847 marked its demise.

After the Russian Revolution in 1917, tsarist colonial rule over Kazakhstan segued into Soviet colonial rule. A bid by a group of Kazakh intellectuals to win autonomy through a movement called *Alash Orda*

(*Alash* after a distant Turkic ancestor, *Orda* meaning horde, the name for the ancient nomadic steppe kingdoms) foundered; a separate bid for Central Asian self-determination by the Turkestan (or Kokand) Autonomy under the Kazakh intellectual Mustafa Shokay was crushed. Civil war raged across parts of Kazakhstan until the Reds drove the Whites out in 1920, ushering in seven decades of Soviet rule.

From his vantage point in the Kremlin, Vladimir Putin does not believe that Kazakhstan is over half a millennium old. 'The Kazakhs never had statehood,' Putin declared in 2014, belying the historical narrative of his closest ally about Kazakhstan's long and illustrious history. At face value, Putin was effusively praising Kazakhstan's 'wise leader', who had achieved something 'completely unique': 'he created a state on territory where there had never been a state.'[2] In reality, he was calling into question Kazakhstan's viability as a sovereign state at this very tense time: Russia was on the warpath in Ukraine, and Russian nationalists, fired up by the conflict, had started laying jingoistic claim to chunks of neighbouring states. Parts of northern Kazakhstan in Russia's southern underbelly were a popular target, and remain so – in 2020, a Russian MP falsely claimed that the north had been uninhabited before the Russians arrived, and went on to describe Kazakhstan's territory as 'a great gift from Russia and the Soviet Union'[3] – but the entire region was not immune. Vladimir Zhirinovskiy, Russia's best-known ultra-right firebrand, had proposed subsuming all five Central Asian states into a Moscow-run colony managed from Almaty, which Zhirinovskiy (who was born in the city in Soviet times) insultingly called by its Russian colonial name Vernyy (named after St Vera, but also meaning 'faithful'). Putin's patronising jibe, delivered in a honeyed tone with a snide smile, carried menacing undertones of Kazakhstan as a weak, artificial construct that Russia could gobble up, should it fail to do Moscow's bidding.

Days earlier, Nazarbayev had pledged to pull Kazakhstan out of the Eurasian Economic Union if the new alliance posed any risk to sovereignty. This was intended as reassurance to dissenters at home, but was perceived as a threat abroad. Now, Putin was asked a question that was clearly planted: was a 'Ukraine scenario' – implying revolution, war and a Russian land grab – possible in Kazakhstan in the post-Nazarbayev future? Couching his response in flattering terms, Putin managed to imply that Kazakhstan's sovereignty was so brittle it could snap at the slightest provocation. Nazarbayev, 'a very experienced and wise leader', was well aware of the advantages of being inside the Eurasian Union and smart enough to realise that his countrymen were in favour of remaining part of the 'Greater Russian World' – shorthand for the Kremlin's sphere of influence.

Nazarbayev kept quiet, but an asymmetrical sally followed: an announcement of festivities to celebrate Kazakhstan's long and distinguished history: its 550th anniversary of statehood in 2015. 'Kerey and Zhanibek created the first khanate in 1465, and the statehood of the Kazakhs dates from those times,' Nazarbayev said – perhaps not 'a state in the modern understanding of that term, in the current borders', but 'it was then that the foundation was laid'.[4]

'The leader of a neighbouring country said last year that the Kazakhs in the past did not have a state,' sang Yerkebulan Kaynazarov, melodically strumming his stringed *dombyra*. 'We've answered him, not with words but with deeds, and now we're getting ready to celebrate!' The 3,000-strong crowd gathered in Almaty's main concert hall, the monolithic Soviet-era Palace of the Republic, responded with rapturous applause. This young man was an *akyn* (poet) performing improvised verse to music, and he was singing at an *aytys* competition, a popular form of entertainment where performers compete in pairs to display their musical and verbal virtuosity by trumping each other's witticisms on the hoof – like rap, it requires razor-sharp thinking and ingenious creativity. *Aytys* is always elaborately performed, with the *akyndar* (poets) in traditional attire: for women elegant long dresses and tall conical hats topped with auspicious owl feathers; for men felt waistcoats with Kazakh *oyu-ornek*, ornamental designs based on shapes like the wings of a bird, the hump of a camel or the horns of a ram. At this contest, one *akyn* sported a super-cool modern take on traditional costume: black leather trousers stamped with silver *oyu-ornek*, and biker boots.

In autumn 2015, statehood celebrations were in full swing, and this was the theme on which the *akyndar* (all young – the ancient art of *aytys* is thriving) had to riff to win prizes. It is time, sang *akyn* Maksat Akanov, for patriotic Kazakhs to 'bring your sword and slay those who still call Almaty Vernyy, and destroy Zhirinovskiy as Moscow was destroyed by

Timur!' (the fourteenth-century Turkic warrior known as Tamerlane in the West). The crowd responded with raucous cheers, wolf-whistling and foot-stamping to this riposte to the Russian nationalist's outburst, which had struck a raw nerve. The audience roared with approval when one *akyn* sang a musical plea for Furmanov – an Almaty thoroughfare that still bore the name of a Russian revolutionary – to be renamed after Zhanibek and Kerey. The rumour mill said it was being saved to bear the president's name one day – and in 2017 it was rechristened Nursultan Nazarbayev Avenue, which turned out to be a precursor to the renaming of main streets in cities across the land in honour of the former president after his resignation two years later.

'The 550th anniversary of the Kazakh Khanate shows that the Kazakh nation and the Kazakh state have a long history,' pronounced Nazarbayev, unveiling a statue to Zhanibek and Kerey, grandly seated on thrones befitting the first Kazakh khans, in Taraz in 2015. This pleasant, languid provincial capital, once a pit stop along the Silk Road, is celebrated as the cradle of Kazakh statehood, lying in the valley where the khanate put down its roots in 1465 – over a decade before the Russians shook off their own two-and-a-half-century colonisation by the Golden Horde, which they still bitterly allude to as the 'Mongol-Tatar Yoke' half a millennium later.

With the celebrations of statehood, Nazarbayev was accused of embroidering the facts and indulging in self-serving historical myth-making: the Kazakh Khanate had merely been a loose tribal confeder-ation, hardly a nation state, even if it had lasted in various incarnations for four centuries. Even if Nazarbayev was playing fast and loose with the historical facts, he had astutely harnessed the historical symbolism. Statehood was 'a historic dream for Kazakhstan, an ancient dream that has come true after 550 years', raved Gulnaz Aydynbayeva, a doctor out taking selfies in front of Zhanibek and Kerey. 'We bow before the president,' she continued, genuflecting to make her point as statehood celebrations peaked in Taraz with a bonanza of festivities, while up in Astana one nine-year-old boy celebrated by doing 550 patriotic press-ups. The message had hit home: take pride in Kazakh history, and be grateful to the father of the nation. 'All this came true thanks to our president – this dream of independence,' enthused Nakan Aydynbayeva, the doctor's octogenarian mother, her wrinkled face wreathed in smiles.

'You remember when Putin declared that Kazakhstan was a country that had no history? That probably strongly spurred us on,' acknowledged Arman, the producer of the film about the Kazakh khanate, which was later released as a mini-series called *Kazak Yeli* (Kazakh Nation) and on the silver screen as *Diamond Sword*. 'What we're now filming – it really did start in 1465 […] and then they start saying there was no state!' he guffawed. So was the film a riposte to Putin? 'No way!' he exclaimed, before backtracking. 'I think it was linked, but in what sense? Not in the sense of putting one over on him, but in the sense that Nazarbayev understood that people don't understand that we have such an ancient history and they have to be shown, since an educated person like the [Russian] president doesn't know that.'

'Putin offended us once, saying that Kazakhs have no history and no state,' said Smagul Yelubay, a celebrated Kazakh writer who worked on the screenplay, after the film's release. 'Then our president […] ordered screenwriters to write about the history of the Kazakh Khanate 550 years ago.'5 He jumped at the chance, because 'we'd been waiting for that for a long time, because we love our history', he explained. 'That wasn't allowed before – the Soviet Union didn't need people with their own self-worth. They needed *mankurt*s – people who'd forgotten their language and their history.' In legend, a *mankurt* is someone enslaved by having their head baked in a camel skin under the sun to erase their memory.

This is take two on Kazakh history, then – but is it just another distortion of the historical facts to serve a different master: Nazarbayev, credited as the film's ideological inspiration? Rustem, the director, amiably shrugged off the suggestion with a sanguine smile. He was, he said, combating seventy years of Soviet propaganda to put a new, Kazakh slant on his country's past. 'History is extremely complicated and subjective,' he mused, gazing out over the ramparts of the fortress into the inky darkness that had engulfed the film set below. 'But aside from history, we're making movies, and this should be an artistic production. The priority isn't to distort history, but to tell an interesting story.'

CHAPTER 12

Mother Russia

Ust-Kamenogorsk, 2014

'K azakhstan,' reads the stark message stamped on a green hillside in giant white letters towering over Ust-Kamenogorsk, a gritty industrial north-eastern city just south of the border with Russia. It seems odd for a city to erect a looming reminder to residents of the name of the country they live in – but a glimpse inside a red-brick tsarist-era building down on the main drag offers a clue to the rationale.

Inside a cultural centre on Kazakhstan Street, a new Cold War is raging. Viktor Sharonov, a gruff, burly Slavic community leader, is railing against the West, accusing America and its European lackeys of meddling in Russia's backyard in Ukraine. The other men present – mostly elderly and all leading lights in the city's Slavic communities – agree vociferously. 'The people who have perpetrated an anti-constitutional coup that turfed out a legally elected president are for some reason being feted in the West!' bellows Sharonov, referring to the recent revolution that replaced Ukraine's pro-Russian president with a pro-Western one. 'I personally, and our Cossacks, see this as the desire of Western countries to do the dirty completely on Russia once again!' he growls, while the other Slavic leaders nod vigorous assent.

Sharonov is the *Ataman* (leader) of the Verkhne-Irtyshskaya Russian Cossack Community, which is named after the river that flows through Ust-Kamenogorsk – Irtysh to the Russians, Yertis to the Kazakhs. Sharonov lives up to the image of the Cossacks, a proud and pugnacious people who originated in southern Russia and Ukraine and identify strongly with Slavic traditions. In the Russian Empire, the Kremlin used the Cossacks as an advance guard for imperial expansion and a military force to guard borders and buffer zones – which is why there is a strong Russian presence in northern Kazakhstan today.

The new Ukrainian government is composed of 'fascists', 'ultrana-tionalists' and 'banderovtsy', fulminates Oleg Navozov, another of the Slavic community leaders present, echoing the Kremlin's mantra that the new rulers in Kyiv are products of the far right ('banderovtsy' means supporters of Stepan Bandera, a World War II-era Ukrainian nationalist reviled in Russia for collaborating with Hitler in the hope of winning Ukrainian independence). Wiry, white-haired Navozov is chairman of Lad ('Accord'), a Slavic community group formed in the early 1990s to lobby for cultural and linguistic rights after the USSR's collapse, when Slavs were agonising about how their future would pan out in independent Kazakhstan.

The Cold War ended a quarter of a century ago, but there is more than a touch of its frozen hostilities here, and Sharonov concludes with an apocalyptic prediction: 'If the actions of this Ukrainian junta spill over into bloodshed, that means a fire in the heart of Europe!' As these stalwarts of Ust-Kamenogorsk's Slavic communities vent their anger over the geopolitical stand-off in April 2014, strains of Russian choral music waft in incongruously from a choir practising in another room of the House of Friendship, a community centre used by cultural associations representing Kazakhstan's 125 ethnic groups. 'Friendship of the peoples of Kazakhstan is our country's priceless achievement,' reads a blue banner outside. 'Under one shanyrak,' says another, referring to the crisscrossed wooden top of a Kazakh yurt, a symbol of hearth and home.

Emotions are running high. Despite the geographical distance between Kazakhstan and Ukraine (Kazakhstan is on the south-eastern flank of the former Soviet Union, Ukraine on its western edge), the cause of Ukraine – which has toppled a pro-Russian president, lost a chunk of territory to a Kremlin land grab and become embroiled in separatist strife – is close to the hearts of these men. They grew up in Soviet times, and are – like Putin – nostalgic for the Soviet Union, yearning for its certainties and for the sense of pride that came from living in a country the rest of the world both respected and feared as a great power. These mostly elderly men still look to the 'centre' (as Moscow was known in

Soviet times) and to Russia as a country to admire and to which to aspire. It is, in post-Soviet parlance, their 'historical homeland', the country of their ethnic affiliation, although they ended up outside its borders when the USSR collapsed.

There has been a Russian presence for more than four centuries in the north of what is now Kazakhstan, ever since the Cossacks started pushing south out of Siberia in the late sixteenth century. In 1584 they built a military settlement on the spot that is now the city of Uralsk, tucked into the north-western corner of Kazakhstan just south of the Russian border, and in 1613 Yaitskiy Gorodok ('Yaik Settlement') was founded there, named after the river Kazakhs call the Zhayyk. In 1775 the settlement was renamed Uralsk, after the Ural Mountains, by Russian empress Catherine the Great as punishment for an uprising led out of the town by a Cossack rebel called Yemelyan Pugachev, and the river running through it became the Ural. Kazakhs call the city Oral, but it has not been officially renamed since independence.

Cossacks and Russian traders pushed south to the Caspian Sea and east towards Mongolia and China along the southern fringes of Siberia, reaching what is now Ust-Kamenogorsk, 3,000 kilometres from Uralsk, in the early eighteenth century. In 1720, a military mission dispatched by Peter the Great to prospect for gold set up the fortress and trading post of Ust-Kamennaya, 'Rocky Mouth', which evolved into Ust-Kamenogorsk (Kazakhs call the city by a Kazakhified version of the Russian name, 'Oskemen', although it has never been officially renamed.) Russia was beginning its long push into Central Asia that would see it gradually swallow up the lands ruled by the Kazakh khans, cementing colonial control in its underbelly before thrusting south to conquer the rest of Central Asia more than a century later.

With colonial power came colonial settlers. Imperial Russia encouraged Slavs to move south to secure the territory and work the land, and in the nineteenth century some 400,000 poured into Kazakhstan, including landless peasants freed after the abolition of serfdom in Russia in 1861.[1] The arrival of the railways in 1906 – when the Trans-Aral line opened, linking Central Asia with Siberia across Kazakhstan – sped up the influx, and 2.4 million more settlers arrived from central Russia between 1907 and 1912.[2] With Moscow's backing, the Slavs founded farms on land roamed by Kazakh tribes, dispossessing the nomads and pushing them off the best pastures. This created festering grievances that erupted into violent retribution in 1916, during World War I, when an uprising across Central Asia against the conscription of Muslims for rearguard work (such as digging trenches) saw Kazakhs rampage through villages built by colonial settlers on their roaming grounds in an orgy of death and destruction.

The flood of settlers continued after the Russian Revolution. In the 1930s and 1940s Slavs came to staff new factories and mines in northern and central Kazakhstan that were built to power Stalin's industrial revolution, and non-Slavs arrived in droves when Stalin deported entire peoples – Germans, Chechens, Koreans, Poles, Turks, Tatars and more – from elsewhere in the USSR to Central Asia en masse as collective punishment for perceived disloyalty to the motherland before, during and after the Great Patriotic War (the Soviet name for World War II). Between 1954 and 1962, another 1.7 million settlers were enticed by perks to migrate from European parts of the USSR to plant grain on the plains of northern Kazakhstan under Nikita Khrushchev's Virgin Lands programme.[3]

For Kazakhstan, all this translated into a demographic maelstrom. Between 1897 and 1911, the proportion of Slavs in the population more than doubled, from 13 per cent to 27 per cent, and by 1939 Kazakhs had been pushed into a minority in Kazakhstan, where they remained until well after independence. When the USSR collapsed in 1991, Kazakhstan was the only Soviet republic whose titular group was outnumbered by minorities: Kazakhs made up 40 per cent of the population and Slavs 44 per cent (the latter group composed mostly of Russians, totalling 37 per cent of the population).[4]

Until the USSR disintegrated, it mattered little which of the fifteen Soviet republics people lived in. Whether Russia or Kazakhstan, Ukraine or Belarus, Uzbekistan or Armenia, all were administrative regions of a single country. But its collapse left many anxious for their prospects as minorities in new nation states, and sent some who felt stranded on the 'wrong' side of new borders fleeing to their 'historical homelands' to start new lives. In countries where nationalism reared its head in ugly and sometimes violent forms, they had reason to be fearful, but Kazakhstan was not one of these: Nazarbayev had no wish to antagonise either the Kremlin or the 60 per cent of his people who were non-Kazakhs. Still, there was an exodus as Russians and other minorities, including Germans and Jews, upped sticks and left, spurred by the severe economic crisis and by fears about their futures. In the 1990s, 2.6 million people left Kazakhstan, 1.7 million of them for Russia, and the number of Russians shrank from 6.2 million to 4.5 million (driven by falling birth rates as well as migration).[5] Meanwhile, Kazakhs were arriving from other countries, lured with incentives under the government's *oralman* (returnee) programme to live in their 'historical homeland'. Officially, this was to bring 'home' Kazakhs cast around the world by the winds of history, but it also delivered a stratospheric boost to the Kazakh population. By the end of the 1990s, the ethnic balance had tipped back towards the Kazakhs, who were in a small majority of 53 per cent; by 2021 the figure had reached 70 per cent.[6]

The demographic legacy of four centuries of Slavic settlement is striking along Kazakhstan's 6,846-kilometre frontier with Russia, the world's second longest land border. In 2014, when the conflict erupted in Ukraine, Russians formed 22 per cent of Kazakhstan's population nationwide (by 2021, that figure had fallen under 16 per cent), but in many places in the borderlands they were in large majorities: in Ust-Kamenogorsk, 67 per cent of people were Russians, while in the town of Ridder, further north towards the frontier, the figure was 85 per cent (by 2021, those figures had fallen to 50% and 80% respectively).[7] Nazarbayev had long had his eye on this demographic, which was one of the drivers for moving the capital north from Almaty after independence: officially, Almaty was squeezed for space, plus it lies in an earthquake zone – but the move also shifted Kazakhstan's political centre of gravity into its Slavic-populated northern heartlands, helping cement the president's authority over them. Nazarbayev's decision to move the capital from balmy, buzzy Almaty to frozen, sleepy Akmola (as the city that became Astana and later Nur-Sultan was then called) raised eyebrows at the time and is often depicted in the Western media as the whim of a narcissistic tinpot dictator, but it was dictated by iron logic, even if he soft-pedalled his thinking at the time.

In 2014, with Ukraine plunged into violent turmoil, old anxieties were nagging anew. How far were loyalties divided in Kazakhstan's Russian-majority areas? If push came to shove, where would the fealties of the country's Russians lie?

*

'Down with the separatists of the Ural Cossack Host!' proclaimed placards waved by Kazakh protesters. 'Kazakh land is indivisible!' In September 1991, as the Soviet Union was collapsing, thousands of Kazakhs descended on the backwater of Uralsk in the borderlands between what was about to become independent Kazakhstan and its colonial master Russia, just half an hour's drive away, to prevent what they feared was the imminent threat of the Cossacks declaring a separatist state.

These were turbulent times in the almost defunct USSR, where torrents of pent-up resentments about Soviet rule were being unleashed among its non-Russian inhabitants: officially all the peoples of the USSR were equal, but it was an open secret that the Russians were more equal than others. The USSR did not recognise racial tensions – its mantra was '*druzhba narodov*' ('friendship of the peoples'), and ethnically diverse Kazakhstan was known as the 'laboratory of friendship of the peoples' – but latent frictions came to the fore. In late Soviet times, ethnic clashes erupted in various parts of the USSR, including Central Asia: hundreds died in Kyrgyzstan in Kyrgyz–Uzbek clashes in 1990, and in Kazakhstan five died in the oil town of Zhanaozen when Kazakhs came to blows with minorities from the Caucasus in 1989.[8] Meanwhile, skirmishes erupted with pro-Russian separatists in various Soviet republics, and Georgia, Moldova and Azerbaijan all ended up losing territories which later formed Russian-backed breakaway states.

It was against that backdrop that the Cossacks announced plans to stage a celebration in Uralsk in 1991 marking the 400th anniversary of the Ural Cossack Host's pledge of fealty to the Russian tsar. The declaration rang alarm bells with some Kazakhs, who suspected the festivities were a cover for plans to declare a separatist state in Uralsk, potentially sparking a domino effect across northern Kazakhstan. In September 1991, hundreds of Cossacks flooded into the city from elsewhere in Kazakhstan and from Russia, thronging the streets in their tsarist-era military uniforms topped with trademark shaggy *papakha* hats. They were confronted by thousands of Kazakh protesters who came from all over Kazakhstan, fired up by a nationalist group called Azat (Freedom) to head north under the slogan '*Attanayyk Zhayykka!*', roughly translated as 'saddle up and head for Zhayyk!', '*attanayyk*' being both a traditional battle cry and an evocative reference to the Kazakhs' nomadic horseback heritage. According to Kazakh nationalist lore, it was a Kazakh grandmother who had the presence of mind to stop the brewing violence in its tracks. Carrying her small granddaughter in her arms, Khadisha Karybayeva laid her white headscarf, traditionally worn by married women, on the ground and urged demonstrators marching on the Cossacks' venue to halt. Since cultural taboos forbade Kazakhs from stepping over the scarf, the marchers stopped in their tracks, and the Cossacks hurriedly dispersed.[9]

In Ust-Kamenogorsk, Nazarbayev wrestled with separatist sentiments throughout the 1990s, until in 1999 the authorities made a sensational announcement: they had foiled a plot to seize the local government and subsume the region into Russia. The ringleader was a Russian citizen named Viktor Kazimirchuk, who farcically styled himself 'Pugachev' after the leader of the eighteenth-century Cossack rebellion against Catherine the Great. 'Pugachev' was among thirteen Russian and Kazakh citizens jailed over the conspiracy, but was quietly freed six years into his eighteen-year sentence and returned to Russia.[10]

Sceptics doubted the plot really amounted to much, but it sparked an outpouring of angst in Russia's nationalist press about 'multiple cases of oppression of the Slavic population and discrimination on ethnic grounds' in Kazakhstan, as the far-right Moscow newspaper *Zavtra* thundered in a report grounded more in emotion than fact. Getting a job had become harder for Slavs, *Zavtra* complained, which was true: in the civil service, passing a Kazakh-language test had become a prerequisite for employment, disadvantaging Russian speakers, who had not been required to learn Kazakh in Soviet times and had generally not bothered to do so. *Zavtra* also turned its sights on the *oralman* programme to entice Kazakhs from abroad to live in Kazakhstan. With breathtaking chutzpah, *Zavtra* deemed this a 'creeping occupation' – of Kazakhstan, by Kazakhs. Now that Kazakhs were being given the edge in the new Kazakhstan, *Zavtra* grumbled that this was 'causing particular resentment among the Slavic population because the northern regions of the Republic of Kazakhstan (bordering Russia) have never been territories of traditional habitation for Kazakhs' and 'were until the 1917 revolution part of the lands of the Cossack hosts'.[11]

This echoed an old line trotted out by Russian nationalists, including the writer and Soviet dissident Aleksandr Solzhenitsyn, who in 1990 advocated the creation of a new Slavic state out of the ashes of the Soviet Union, incorporating Ukraine, Belarus and northern Kazakhstan. The late Nobel Prize winner is feted as a hero in the West, but he is reviled by many Kazakhs as a Russian nationalist who refused to respect their post-Soviet sovereignty.

In 2014, with Russian demagogues verbally carving up Kazakhstan as the Kremlin was physically carving up Ukraine, it was no wonder that the government was getting the jitters. 'We are tempted by Russian towns that ended up over the border in Kazakhstan. Starting with Uralsk, a whole uninterrupted chain of Russian towns right up to Ust-Kamenogorsk should become part of Russia,' wrote Eduard Limonov, a far-right rabble-rouser, in an article advocating the dismemberment of Ukraine, not long after Zhirinovskiy had called for Central Asia to be subsumed into a Moscow-run colony.[12] Zhirinovskiy was a clownish figure, but the Kremlin used him to float trial balloons. His idea sounded outlandish, but there were people in the borderlands of Kazakhstan who were keen on the idea of shifting the Russian frontier further south. In 2015, an informal online poll in the Russian-majority town of Ridder found that three quarters of the 500 people who took part were in favour of the region seceding and becoming part of Russia. The Ridder resident who published the poll was jailed for five years on a charge of promoting separatism[13] – a crime suddenly rushed onto the statute book after the separatist insurgency had erupted in Ukraine.

'In Crimea, people were weeping,' said Sharonov, Ust-Kamenogorsk's Cossack *Ataman*. '[Russian] state TV channels showed pictures of people crying when the results of the referendum came out, and saying: Crimea's been returned home! You can't fake that, and you can't explain it any other way. Those were emotions!'

Sharonov was talking about the Crimean referendum a month previously, in March 2014, which voted a resounding 'yes' to Russia's annexation. It was approved by 97 per cent of voters in Crimea, where 68 per cent of the population was ethnic Russian (according to a census held a few months after the referendum in 2014) – not least because Stalin deported the entire population of indigenous Crimean Tatars to Central Asia in 1944; seventy years later, Tatars were still only 13 per cent of the population.[14] Moscow said the annexation was righting a historical wrong: until 1954, Crimea had been part of the Soviet republic of Russia, then Nikita Khrushchev, the USSR's leader, transferred it to Ukraine. Back then it was a fairly meaningless administrative stroke of the pen, but half a century later the ramifications were momentous. When the USSR collapsed, most countries simply accepted the borders in place at the time, for better or worse, and those that did not were plunged into conflict. Russia's argument regarding Crimea called into question post-Soviet border settlements, which Moscow now granted itself the right to revise as it saw fit.

In Ust-Kamenogorsk, just 100 kilometres south of the border with Siberia, there was rock-solid support for the Kremlin's land grab among the Slavic leaders, who interpreted it as Russia re-staking its rightful place in the world following a couple of decades of humiliation by the West. 'People came to understand that it wasn't possible to retreat any further,' opined Sharonov. 'If Russia hadn't taken Crimea, Russia would not only have lost face, Russia would have lost its future!'

On the streets of Kazakhstan, many people expressed delight at the sight of Russia gobbling up a slice of its neighbour – not just Russians, but Kazakhs too. 'Western Ukraine and the *banderovtsy* supported the fascists in their time. You can't call Ukraine a cohesive country,' said Bayan, a fifty-something Kazakh professional woman in the city of Semey, to the north-west of Ust-Kamenogorsk and even closer to the Russian border. Fresh in her mind was a potted history of Crimea repeated almost verbatim from Russian TV. 'Crimea's always been considered Russian,' Bayan explained chattily, erasing in one breath the complex history of a peninsula that had been ruled by a Muslim Tatar khanate for three centuries. 'Khrushchev made a mistake by giving it to Ukraine,' she continued, before leaping back a couple of centuries to the Crimean War. 'Sevastopol and Crimea are real Russian lands,' she went on, becoming quite heated. 'The Russians and the Orthodox defended it from the Turkish yoke, and that's where our Russian soldiers fought.' Although Bayan is a Kazakh, to her, Russian soldiers fighting a nineteenth-century war in far-off Crimea, 5,000 kilometres from her hometown, are 'ours'. What about Russian nationalists' territorial claims on northern Kazakhstan? 'We're not planning to divide anything up!' she blustered. 'Anyway, nothing like that will happen. Russia and Kazakhstan are like brothers.'

Not everyone agreed: 'When Russia needs a war like the one in Ukraine in northern Kazakhstan, it'll make one,' muttered Oralkhan, an Almaty taxi driver, darkly. However, many people deemed preposterous the idea that Moscow would carve up their country. 'I don't think Russia's going to grab a piece of Kazakhstan – what would it want to do that for?' asked Viktor Chernyshev, an engineer in Ust-Kamenogorsk, genuinely puzzled. 'Russia isn't seen as some sort of enemy here,' pointed out Aleksandr Alekseyenko, an amiable academic from an Ust-Kamenogorsk university. 'It's seen as an opportunity.' The vibrant Russian city of Novosibirsk, 700 kilometres to the north, is closer than Astana, a thousand kilometres to the west, and Siberian cities like this are often the first choice for people in Ust-Kamenogorsk seeking opportunities for employment and study. For people in Kazakhstan wanting to live or work in Russia, the Eurasian Economic Union, with its simplified residency requirements, would be a dream come true.

Back in the House of Friendship on Kazakhstan Street, the confab of Slavic community leaders continued. 'There's an illegitimate government in Ukraine,' said Leonid Kartashev, the president of Ust-Kamenogorsk's Russian National Cultural Centre. 'There can be no analogy between Ukraine and Kazakhstan, because in Kazakhstan President Nazarbayev is legitimately elected and in Kazakhstan there's a legitimate government.'

Sitting in the office of the local newspaper he edited, Vadim Obukhov, another Cossack leader, broadly concurred: 'The situation in Kazakhstan is completely different to the situation in Ukraine.' No one was stopping Russians from speaking their language in Kazakhstan, he said, where Russian enjoys a protected legal status under the constitution. That means people have a legally enshrined right to use Russian, not Kazakh, in public life if they wish – in government, parliament and the media, and also to navigate day-to-day officialdom – though some would like to see Russian upgraded to the same status as Kazakh, which the law defines as the 'state language'. Language rights had assumed fresh significance, because Putin had used moves to restrict the use of Russian in Ukraine as another justification for annexing Crimea, granting Moscow a new, self-appointed right to intervene abroad to protect not just Russian citizens but anyone who spoke Russian. In Kazakhstan, that had made Nazarbayev chant his mantra of ethnic harmony ever more insistently.

'It's clearly stated in our constitution: discrimination on any religious, ethnic or linguistic principle is forbidden,' he said after Crimea's annexation: this 'should be written on all walls, here, there and everywhere.'[15]

Putin's self-styled role as protector of Russians worldwide sounded reassuring to some in Kazakhstan who, like all the country's minorities, fretted about the post-Nazarbayev future. Nazarbayev had made ethnic and linguistic inclusiveness a pillar of Kazakhstan's nationhood, but what if a Kazakh nationalist came to power after him? Yevgeniy Cherkashin, a local newspaper tycoon in Ust-Kamenogorsk who was a generation younger than the Slavic leaders in the House of Friendship, was breathing a sigh of relief that for now Nazarbayev was at the helm, with his inclusive attitude towards minorities. 'Nazarbayev pursues a very competent ethnic policy,' he said, but 'certain apprehensions exist, because Nazarbayev hasn't clearly designated his successor'. Choosing his words with the utmost care, he continued: 'Let's put it this way: we're not feeling utter panic, because we don't for the moment see any radicals on the political arena. If this radicalism – and I don't mean the current leadership, because the current leadership in Kazakhstan doesn't want this – but if radicals were to come to power in Kazakhstan, certain hopes exist that someone will step in as our protector – and I don't mean America or the European Union,' he said, with a wry twist of his mouth that was not a smile. For Cherkashin, Russia was 'the guarantor of our security, not against the current leadership but against the possibility of radicals coming to power'.

Kazakhstan was about to join the Eurasian Economic Union, and while opponents panicked that it was a kind of Soviet Union-lite for the twenty-first century, some supporters welcomed it for precisely that reason. 'People hope that we're going to live in one state,' enthused Obukhov. 'Not in Russia, of course,' he added hastily; instead, he explained, he hoped that the fledgling economic alliance would eventually give birth to some sort of federal union state, so that the people of Kazakhstan, Russia and other members of the union would once more be living together under the umbrella of a single country.

In the House of Friendship, the Slavic community leaders were resolute in their backing of the Eurasian Union, and rather disdainful of Kazakhstan's chances of succeeding as a sovereign state without it.

'Of course, with such a small population on such a large territory, Kazakhstan isn't a self-sufficient state, so Kazakhstan's doomed to be in a union with someone,' said Nikolay Plakhotin, a member of the Lad Slavic community group. 'Who's closest? Russia. Who's closest to the Kazakhs in their mentality? Russians.' Navozov, Lad's chairman, had this to add: 'Without this union, Kazakhstan's future is hazy.' And for those fearing that the Eurasian Union heralded a return to the days when Russia was the master and Kazakhstan the slave in the colonial relationship, he also had an answer: the non-Russian republics of the USSR 'had an awful lot of rights – some people forget to talk about that now, but they really had an awful lot of rights at the republican level, and privileges too'. For this old man, the Eurasian Union really was a back-to-the-future moment: 'This is to one degree or another a return – perhaps not entirely, but nevertheless to a large degree – towards what there was in the Soviet Union.'

CHAPTER 13

Death to the Past

Almaty, 2017

When Nurziya Kazhibayeva was six years old, she walked from Kazakhstan to China on a life-or-death march for survival.

'One day back then my mother told me: "We're going to China. You can walk, can't you? You're a good girl. We'll be going there on foot." I asked: "Is it far?"' recalls the old lady of the day eighty-four years previously that she learnt of the mammoth trek ahead.

It certainly was far for a six-year-old child to walk: a fortnight trudging over rugged mountain terrain, moving in silence by night to evade Soviet border patrols that her parents feared would at best capture them and at worst shoot them dead on the spot.

'The day we planned to set off we packed up everything and they said: "Here we are. We'll move today." "Don't speak, don't make a sound," my mother told me. We set off that day. We were about twenty people in total. We left when it got dark, after people had gone to bed. "Move in small groups, because if we're in a big group someone could spot us," they warned. So we set off at night and I was among them. I was the youngest of all – I was six years old. My uncles, my father's younger brothers, led me by the hand. We walked by night and slept by day. [...] It took fifteen days, my mother said.'

It was March 1933 when the family of Nurziya-azhe (*azhe* is a Kazakh term of respect for elderly women, loosely 'granny') embarked on the arduous journey from their ancestral lands in eastern Kazakhstan into north-western China. They were among around a million Kazakhs fleeing for their lives from a man-made catastrophe that was ravaging Kazakhstan in the early 1930s: the *Asharshylyk* (famine).

Her parents had only a hazy idea of what had brought this disaster down on their heads. 'They didn't know how the famine started. Grain was seized, animals were seized, but they didn't know who caused it. People from the government did that – they all had rifles on their shoulders and they were in large groups. There was no one but the Soviet government. If you think about it, there was no one apart from the Soviets.'

This old lady with white hair, bright brown eyes and striking cheekbones is sitting in her daughter's modern, airy, high-rise flat in Almaty dressed in a white headscarf, green woollen waistcoat and Kazakh felt slippers decorated with swirly orange *oyu-ornek* (ornamental designs) on a spring afternoon in March 2017. She is remarkably agile for someone who has just turned ninety-one: she enters the living room shuffling on a walking frame and holds herself erect as she recounts her memories and those passed down by her mother in a sonorous tone, punctuated with deep sighs at the trauma of reliving these eight-decade-old experiences.

Before the famine struck, 'there was a *zharmenke* [country bazaar] around twenty kilometres away, and, and the men used to go there to barter things and to let their hair down,' recounts Nurziya-azhe. But then there was nothing to eat and nothing to barter, and one day her father returned from a fruitless trip to that once thriving market asking: '"Will we survive or not?" Because there were so many dead bodies on the road. [...] They were hungry and they'd stop on the roadside and they'd be wailing and dying there. My father saw many of those. That's what I know about the famine.'

It was that horrific sight that led her father to plan the family's desperate flight for survival. They would not be fleeing completely into the unknown: seventeen years earlier, during the uprising against the Kremlin's forced conscription of Muslims in 1916, he had sought sanctuary in China, returning only after the tsar was overthrown in 1917. Back then, he had been a bachelor dodging the draft from a distant war the Kazakhs saw as nothing to do with them; now it was a matter of his family's survival. Nurziya-azhe recalled the family getting ready for the journey ahead. 'We prepared all winter and made *talkan* [bulgur wheat] out of grain using a hand mill,' she said. 'My mother said we had only salt, water, no other food. She'd mix *talkan* with water to make a sort of semolina to give us, yet it wasn't thick like semolina but far more watery.'

Her parents found a guide who could evade the Soviet border patrols. He would lead them in exchange for food for himself and his ailing son, whom the refugees would carry to China. It was an arduous trek through the Tarbagatay Mountains, whose slopes were coated in ice through which the men hacked footholds, attaching Nurziya-azhe to her uncle's belt to prevent her from tumbling into the abyss.

'We walked for a long time, then we reached the town of Tacheng when our food had finished, my mother said. Our men hid us somewhere [...] and went to the market. We were hungry,' she recalled. 'They exchanged some silver jewellery for food, my mother said. It was nice, white buns.' Her family were among the lucky ones, she believes: they had food to sustain them, possessions to trade and strength to walk. Others – starving, weak and destitute – did not survive the trip.

Relief at escaping the famine was tempered by the realisation that as nomadic herders they were ill-equipped for urban life in China. 'They asked around and realised they couldn't survive in this town because as Kazakhs they couldn't do manual work. Then they learnt that there was an *aul* [village] outside the town, and they should go there. They learnt that this *aul* roamed and bred animals, and my uncle's in-laws were in that village.' There, they bartered their remaining possessions for something far more valuable: cattle. 'We exchanged pieces of gold jewellery – earrings, bracelets – and expensive fur coats for animals and got hold of quite a few. And there we finally escaped the famine.'

'Good that my parents and relatives started thinking and moved early enough, believing we should move otherwise we wouldn't survive,' the old lady adds pensively. 'The Kazakh people were just on the brink of survival – just on the brink.'

'The Kazakh nomads could not imagine an existence without their livestock: they knew of no other kind, and believed that to be left without their animals would mean certain death.' Mukhamet Shayakhmetov was born in 1922 into a family of nomadic herdsmen in eastern Kazakhstan, where until the age of nine he lived the traditional life the Kazakhs had led here for centuries, as he recalled in his memoirs, *The Silent Steppe*.[1]

'The pattern of our year was dictated by the needs of our herds and flocks. In order to provide enough grazing for them, we were always on the move between pastures, following routes established by our forefathers,' he writes of the *kosh*, the seasonal migration.

Each move was like a festival, especially for us children; everyone was happy, and dressed up for the occasion. The caravan was headed by the most respected woman of the aul, who rode on a horse, leading the camels which carried her family's possessions. [...] The other women came next, also leading pack camels, in a long line accompanied by two men who acted as guides. The rest of the men would drive the flocks separately from the caravan, and the young people would play along the way, racing one another on horses, singing songs, and picking flowers and wild berries.[2]

His family followed the centuries-old migration routes of their forefathers, moving four times a year, up to the *kokteu* and *zhaylau* (spring and summer pastures) in warmer weather and down to the lower *kuzdeu* and *kystau* (autumn and winter pastures) in colder seasons. They lived in yurts, circular dwellings similar to a tepee, which Kazakhs call a *kiyiz uy* ('felt home'). Small groups of kinsmen formed one *aul*, and each stuck to its own traditional roaming and grazing lands.

For the Kazakhs, their livestock was their lifeblood. 'For as long as anyone could remember, a stock-breeder's entire life in the steppe had been bound up with his animals,' Shayakhmetov wrote.

Our people always looked after them with great care, because they were our main livelihood, and we knew just about everything there was to know about rearing them. The death of even one of them was always treated very seriously: a kid accidentally strangling itself on its tether would cause great consternation, and the whole family would mourn the loss of a favourite horse or camel, because they were the main means of transport and work force in a nomadic household. Relatives and friends would solemnly express their condolences, just as if a member of the family had died, and help them to cover their loss.[3]

This was how the nomads lived until the calamity of the *Asharshylyk* struck. As Shayakhmetov put it, this 'marked the start of a great catastrophe for the Kazakhs who had no livelihood other than stock-breeding'.[4]

'Come, comrade, and join our collective farm!' exhorted a bright-eyed peasant woman in a red headscarf, standing alongside a burly beaming tractor driver in a cheery 1930s propaganda poster. The reality was less starry-eyed.

In 1927 Stalin declared a grand plan to transform the creaking Soviet economy into a mean modern-age machine: an industrialisation blitz and a root-and-branch overhaul of agriculture. These were the Siamese twins of Stalin's 'revolution from above', which would wreak a social revolution in the USSR. The results were dramatic and traumatic – nowhere more so than in Kazakhstan, where an entire lifestyle was eradicated in the space of a decade in a case of social engineering writ large across the steppe.

The agricultural reform involved driving farmers into state-owned collectives. This collectivisation programme meant that all peasants and livestock breeders had to surrender private property and join a *sovkhoz* (state farm) or *kolkhoz* (collective farm), which would manage all resources – land, grain, machinery, cattle – collectively, for the good of the nation. The nomadic Kazakhs were used to efficient collective management of their resources, but shared them in small groups, the *aul*, formed by ties of kinship. The idea of pooling resources to be run by an amorphous, faceless state was anathema to them – and utterly incomprehensible at that.

Collectivisation tore up the rules of agriculture, but failed to put a functioning system in their place. The terrible price for this blitzkrieg was a devastating famine that swept across swathes of Russia, Ukraine, Belarus and Kazakhstan, killing an estimated six to eight million people.[5]

In Kazakhstan, the famine was presided over by the local Communist Party boss, Filipp Goloshchyokin, whose name is still a dirty word in the country today. A dental technician-turned-diehard revolutionary, Goloshchyokin had distinguished himself as a zealot before arriving in Kazakhstan as its local leader in 1925. As military commissar of the Urals after the revolution, he had been instrumental in orchestrating the bloody execution of the last tsar Nicholas II and his wife, children and servants in a Siberian cellar in 1918 and the disposal of the royal bodies down some nearby mineshafts.

Goloshchyokin (who was later shot in Stalin's purges) arrived in Kazakhstan as a man on a mission: to drag the land populated by the nomadic Kazakhs kicking and screaming into the modern Soviet age. He was also a man with a plan: *Malyy Oktyabr* (Little October). Just as the Bolshevik Revolution had rampaged across Russia and its colonies, sweeping away the past and replacing it with a form of rule unseen before in the world – communism – so Little October would march across Kazakhstan, sweeping away the ancient Kazakh way of life and making good Soviets out of the nomads. The Soviets distrusted a lifestyle that the state could not control: its destruction was not just the price to pay for 'progress', but a prerequisite for it.

For the Soviets, nomadism was synonymous with 'backwardness and savagery, although this was a way of life from down the ages for the Kazakhs', said one Kazakh historian who had been researching the famine since a taboo was lifted after the collapse of the USSR. 'The Kazakhs considered the nomadic life a cultured life, a traditional one, they even took pride in being nomads,' explained Talas Omarbekov, an elderly professor sitting surrounded by books in his office at Almaty's Al-Farabi Kazakh National University on a February afternoon in 2017, the sky leaden with snow outside the window. 'But the attitude of Soviet power was: if you're a nomad, you're the most backward person.'[6]

Goloshchyokin's Little October was the 'prelude to the famine', the historian explained, starting with land and cattle confiscations from the Kazakh *bays*, the richer class, the redivision of land and the 'Sovietisation of the Kazakh *aul*'. But, he added, 'the main reason for the famine wasn't those campaigns. The main reason was the liquidation of the Kazakhs' traditional animal husbandry. At the start of the 1930s, the Kazakhs had almost 40 million head of cattle. Three years later there were 4.5 million left.' In Kazakhstan, this famine is often referred to as the Great *Zhut*, a term implying that it was a natural disaster. A *zhut* (in Kazakh, '*dzhut*' in Russian) is a climatic phenomenon that brings harsh weather conditions that kill livestock en masse. However, Professor Omarbekov argued passionately that this is highly misleading, since the Kazakhs knew how to survive a *zhut* and this famine was strictly man-made: forced requisitioning had decimated Kazakhstan's herds. Requiring meat and grain to feed the USSR's growing urban workforce and to export for hard currency to power the industrial revolution, Stalin ordered mass confiscations that left hitherto self-sufficient local populations desperately short of food. Southern Russia and Ukraine were the breadbasket of the Soviet Union, targeted for massive grain requisitioning, while Kazakhstan was earmarked to become the butcher of the USSR: 'Western Kazakhstan had to supply the North Caucasus with meat; southern Kazakhstan had to supply the cotton-producing centres of Namangan, Samarkand and Tashkent [in Uzbekistan]; and the other northern and central regions sent meat to the centre – to Moscow, to Leningrad, to the shock-work construction centres, to the Red Army.' After those places had been fed, there was very little left over for the Kazakhs to feed themselves. 'Meat requisitioning was particularly alarming and ruinous for the Kazakhs,' because their animals provided everything, from their homes (the practical *kiyiz uy*, made of sheep felt) to their clothing and food. 'The Kazakh, who was a nomad and herder, had always been saved by his cattle, its meat, its milk, its *kymyz* [fermented mare's milk] – so he automatically perished.'

'Their only wealth was their cattle – their only wealth. When their cattle were taken away, they perished.' These were the words of illustrious writer Smagul Yelubay, the first author to chronicle the Kazakh famine in fiction, in his harrowing novel *Lonely Yurt*. Yelubay was speaking in February 2017 inside an Almaty art gallery where a TV crew was rushing around setting up cameras. A friendly character with wispy grey hair, smartly turned out in a suit and open-necked shirt, he was about to give an interview to Kazakh television just ahead of his seventieth birthday. 'My family lived through that famine,' he explained.[7] 'My family, our *aul*, lived in the western part of Kazakhstan, between the Caspian and Aral Seas. They were nomads.' But when the cattle disappeared and with it their sustenance, the proud, self-sufficient nomads turned into destitute migrants. 'When they started to confiscate the cattle, the Kazakhs got alarmed, and they fled with their cattle and their families,' the writer continued, 'some to Iran, some to Afghanistan, others to Uzbekistan. [...] Our *aul* went further, to Karakalpakstan, on the other side of the Aral Sea, the southern side, then onwards into Turkmenistan. We survived the famine in Karakalpakstan [then a Soviet region, nowadays part of Uzbekistan]. I was born there in 1947, and I spent my childhood in Turkmenistan.'

His parents often talked of the famine when he was growing up in Turkmenistan 'in an *aul* on the border with Afghanistan', where they tended cattle on the *kolkhoz*. 'But as schoolchildren we'd open up history books, and there was nothing about that. [...] This didn't exist in history, it was erased.' This gave the budding author creative inspiration – but it was dangerous to fictionalise for posterity the oral history he was hearing. 'Censorship didn't allow anyone to utter the word "famine". That didn't happen, because the famine was a crime committed by the Communist Party.'

Smagul Yelubay wrote *Lonely Yurt* in the early 1980s, but it was not published until 1991. 'I wrote it in secret. I wrote it from the heart,' he explained ardently. 'I followed in the footsteps of the nomads, where our *aul* was from. I talked to people from the older generation, they knew the history, they were alive. Then I went across the Ustyurt Plateau between the Aral and Caspian Seas to Karakalpakstan, and there I found old people from those *aul*s, and I listened to their talk. Now there's almost no one left alive.'

'I took a big risk with this step in my youth,' the author added. 'All the older writers advised me: it's not worth it, it's risky, it's dangerous – but I couldn't not write it. It was burning my soul up too much.'

'*Serp i molot – smert i golod*' ('hammer and sickle – death and hunger') ran a Russian saying coined in the 1930s, a tragic play on words referencing the symbols of the revolution, the tools of worker and peasant.

It has never been established how many people died in Kazakhstan in the *Asharshylyk*, which wrought a demographic disaster on the Kazakhs, not least because Stalin scrapped the results of the 1937 census and had those who ran it shot. Lower estimates put the death toll at one million, but research by the late Kazakh demographer Makash Tatimov suggests that 2.1 million people – more than a third of Kazakhstan's pre-famine population of 6.2 million – died of hunger and disease, and another million fled, of whom maybe 400,000 later returned.[8]

Inside the squat building of the Archive of the President in Almaty, one researcher was spending part of her time looking for a needle in a haystack: sifting manually through hundreds of thousands of dusty documents to extricate the names of individuals killed by the famine. 'It's very difficult,' said Aynash Seysenbayeva, demonstrating on her screen the database collating the information.[9] 'You see a name, but you have to read it and try and work out what that name is [...] and if the person died of hunger or not.' Boris Dzhaparov, the archive's director, offered a poetic allegory for this painstaking task, as he sat in his office in front of a Nazarbayev portrait and a Kazakh flag draped gracefully on a pole: 'It's like gold scattered on the sand. We have to sift through the grains of sand to find those pieces of gold.'[10] This gargantuan endeavour will keep the archivists busy for years: in its first year, the project managed to confirm 415 names out of the couple of million who may have perished.

In Ukraine, the famine – there called the '*Holodomor*' – is officially designated an 'act of genocide' committed by the Soviets, and historian Anne Applebaum argues that it fits the original definition of seeking to destroy the 'essential foundations of the life' of a group, if not the UN definition of 'intent to destroy'.[11] That definition could apply to Kazakhstan, since the Kazakhs' nomadic way of life was obliterated – but the Kremlin-friendly government treats this history gingerly. Here, it is depicted as a common tragedy which should not be 'politicised' because it was the fault of an 'inhumane totalitarian system', in Nazarbayev's words.[12] This conciliatory attitude is much to the chagrin of some who would like to see blame apportioned. 'It was a genocide! The Kremlin thinks it's not their fault – as if we killed ourselves!' complained the writer Yelubay sarcastically. Yet Omarbekov has found no evidence in the archives of Stalin dreaming up a deliberate policy to exterminate the Kazakhs; he described the *Asharshylyk* instead as the tragic result of Soviet 'ineptitude and ignorance of the Kazakh way of life'.

Nurziya-azhe and her family returned to Kazakhstan after six months in China, herding their livestock – a cow and several goats – with them. 'We came to the border post – I remember it – and three or four horsemen came galloping up. They had red armbands on. They were Russians, but one of them was a Tatar who knew Kazakh. He took my father aside and started asking him questions.' When her father explained they were heading home because they had heard the famine had abated, 'these Russians tapped my father on the shoulder and cried: "Well done!

Molodets [good man]!"' and ushered the family across the border into Kazakhstan. 'So we came back to our country safe and sound.'

'The motherland is the motherland', she explained. 'That's why they always returned. They returned with the hope that they'd start living their previous lives.' They would not, of course, as those lives had been eradicated: her parents joined a *kolkhoz*, and later Nurziya-azhe became not a nomadic herder but a bank clerk. She has no time for nostalgia about the vanished past: 'that's the old way of living,' she said, times change and 'that's life'. She married a teacher and is glad her children and grandchildren went to university and can dream of prospects of which her generation, preoccupied by survival, never could.

This dignified old lady, who was at the time one of the last surviving people who could recount first-hand memories of Kazakhstan's terrible famine of nearly a century earlier, would pass away three years later, in 2020, at the age of ninety-four. But now she rose slowly to her feet, then paused before shuffling off on her walking frame to rest, worn out by dredging up these memories of the tragic past. 'I always think that people survived even on the *Titanic*,' mused Nurziya-azhe, who is a fan of the eponymous Hollywood blockbuster. Whenever she saw the old lady in that film recounting how she survived the shipwreck, she would be reminded of something her mother would often say: 'My mother used to wonder: how on earth did we survive? It turns out that if *kuday* [God] wants you to survive, you will survive.'

CHAPTER 14

The Gulag Archipelago

Dolinka, 2013/Malinovka, 2009/Astana, 2017

Stalin's piercing gaze stares down through a watchtower in a sleepy village called Dolinka, testament to a totalitarian past that traumatised and transformed a nation.

His eerie portrait hangs in a grey neoclassical building, topped with a red star, that was once the Karaganda Corrective Labour Camp (Karlag for short), a link in a chain of Soviet concentration camps stretching across Russian Siberia and south into Kazakhstan. Soviet dissident writer Aleksandr Solzhenitsyn, whose experiences as a slave labourer in Karlag formed creative inspiration for his Nobel Prize-winning literature, memorably christened this network *The Gulag Archipelago*.

Nowadays, the former nerve centre of this concentration camp houses a museum which lifts the veil not only on the torments suffered by the prisoners who passed through its gates but also on the tumult of the Stalin era, which left an indelible legacy on Kazakhstan's physical landscape, its demographic make-up and its national psyche.

Past the giant portrait of the *Vozhd* (Leader), Stalin's reverential epithet in his lifetime, the long, echoing halls of the former Karlag headquarters are lined with mug shots of *zeki* staring wild-eyed down from the walls. '*Zek*' is slang for a convict, derived from the Russian *zaklyuchyonnyy*, *z/k* for short in Gulag red tape. During Stalin's rule, from the mid-1920s until the early 1950s, millions of Soviets – 18 million, by some counts[1] – passed through the Gulag, an acronym for the officious-sounding *Glavnoye Upravleniye Ispravitelno-Trudovykh Lagerey* (Main Directorate for Corrective Labour Camps). Between 700,000 and one million prisoners passed through Karlag, and many did not emerge from the camp to tell the tale: shot as traitors, executed for attempting to flee, worked to death as slave labourers, felled by frostbite and disease.

Imperial Russia used Kazakhstan, like Siberia to the north, as a distant dumping ground for undesirables, and Stalin followed suit: Siberia and Kazakhstan became the main hosts of the Gulag, a system designed with the dual purposes of punishing people the regime deemed suspect and fuelling the terror that kept the rest in check. Set up in 1931 in this village 3,000 kilometres south-east of Moscow, Karlag was not a single prison camp but a whole chain of them sprawling over 21,000 square kilometres, a little larger than Slovenia. This was just one of eleven concentration camps in Kazakhstan's slice of the Gulag, which stretched over an area roughly the size of France.[2]

Kazakhstan's camps included one incarcerating women and children accused of no other crime than being the wives, mothers, sisters and daughters of 'enemies of the people': Alzhir, the acronym for the Akmola Camp for the Wives of Traitors to the Motherland. In the village of Malinovka near the capital, there is a haunting museum to these victims of political repression, its entrance poignantly marked by a swooping black and silver statue in the conical shape of a *saukele* (a Kazakh bridal headdress). Inside, a shocking statistic is on display: over its sixteen years of operation, 1,507 children were born in Alzhir to prisoners raped by their guards.

On a summer's afternoon in 2009, two old Russian men were sitting on a bench outside taking the air, boasting chests full of Great Patriotic War medals sparkling in the sunlight. Did the locals feel sorry for the women and children held prisoner here, purely for being related to 'enemies of the people'? 'There was no one around to feel sorry for them,' replied one, taken aback by the question. His own father had been a warder in Karlag; after all, unless a person was a *zek*, 'everyone around here was a prison guard'.

When Svetlana Tynybekova was born in 1939, her grandmother was in the Gulag. 'This is my wonderful grandma,' said the old lady, holding out a photo of a striking young woman with sculpted cheekbones and soulful eyes gazing out from under a fur-brimmed hat. When this picture was taken in the 1920s, Gulyandam Khodzhanova was the wife of a Kazakh intellectual who was high up in the Soviet government ruling Central

Asia after the revolution. Just a few years later Sultanbek Khodzhanov was arrested and shot, and his wife was dispatched to Karlag for the crime of being married to an 'enemy of the people'.

Born into a family of cattle herders in 1894 in a village in southern Kazakhstan, Sultanbek Khodzhanov went to school in the town of Turkestan and to teacher training college in Tashkent in Uzbekistan, from where the Russian Empire ruled its Central Asian colonies. At the time Tashkent was an intellectual hothouse ablaze with political debate, which gathered pace after the Central Asian uprising of 1916 caused a spike in resentments over tsarist rule. There, Khodzhanov mixed with some of the Kazakh intellectuals who later made abortive bids for autonomy after the revolution, imbibing their heady ideas, joining an underground student movement and later editing a radical newspaper.[3] After the revolution Khodzhanov rose up the Soviet ranks to become a *narodnyy komissar* (people's commissar, equivalent of minister) in Soviet-ruled Central Asia, then deputy leader of the regional Communist Party covering the territory that later became Kazakhstan – but in 1925 he clashed with the new Moscow-appointed party boss, Filipp Goloshchyokin. Kazakh intellectuals resisted Goloshchyokin's Little October strategy, seeing it as colonisation by another name. However, soon the critics, who were known as champions of Kazakh language and culture, found themselves accused of nationalism ('national deviationists', in the label of the time) and forced out of Kazakhstan. To correct his views, Khodzhanov was dispatched to Moscow to study Marxism–Leninism, and later returned to Tashkent (the capital of Soviet Uzbekistan), where he worked in various official positions – until Stalin's Terror took his life.

'In summer 1937 the whole family was gathered one morning drinking tea, and suddenly there was a knock at the door,' said his granddaughter, sitting in her flat in Astana eight decades later, in November 2017, a blizzard billowing outside the window. 'Grandma opened the door, and two men came in and said to him: you're under arrest [...] – you're an enemy of the people. He said: the son of a poor man who's spent his whole life serving the revolution and the cause of the party is suddenly an enemy of the people?' Svetlana Borisovna (her patronymic), an elegant 78-year-old with a warm smile, was recounting memories passed down by her mother, Ziba, then seventeen. Ziba recalled being hurriedly dispatched by her mother Gulyandam to ask for help from Akmal Ikramov, the Uzbek party boss (who was later arrested and shot). Ikramov told her 'that it was all a mistake, that everything would be fine' – and her father said the same as officers from the NKVD, the secret police, hauled him off. But in 1938 her grandfather was executed as an 'enemy of the people' for being a member of an 'anti-Soviet, nationalist organisation', she said, showing photographs of him as a dashing young man with a droopy black moustache. After Stalin's death, Khodzhanov was officially rehabilitated, one of many victims of Stalin's Terror deemed not guilty of the crimes that had led to their incarcerations and deaths.

An estimated 100,000 people from Kazakhstan were jailed in the Gulag, and around a quarter were shot.[4] Stalin's Terror wiped out the cream of the intelligentsia across the Soviet Union, and among the Kazakhs who faced the firing squad were famous writers, intellectuals and political leaders, celebrated in Kazakhstan as heroes today – such as Khodzhanov, who, in Nazarbayev's words, 'did a great deal to raise the consciousness of the Kazakh people'.[5]

As relatives of an 'enemy of the people', Khodzhanov's wife and children fell into disgrace. The children were expelled from school, then their mother was arrested and sent to the Gulag. 'They stuffed these wives of government leaders into cattle wagons. They were cold, there was no water, no nothing, everyone weeping,' said Svetlana Borisovna, tears in her eyes as she recounted what she later heard from her grandmother. 'Afterwards I thought: it's unnatural, it's inhumane, that a child should live having never met their grandmother – and never see their grandfather at all,' she said sadly.

Ziba and one brother were taken in by relatives in Kazakhstan, but the youngest brother, nine-year-old Arstan, was sent to a children's home. 'In children's homes for enemies of the people the children were treated really badly. They weren't fed properly, their things were taken away. They were transferred from one children's home to another and their names were changed so they wouldn't be found, and it was drummed into the children that their parents were enemies of the people.' Relatives eventually tracked him down and brought him to live with his siblings in Kazakhstan, but the children struggled to finish their education – Ziba got a place at university but was expelled when they realised who her father was (although later she qualified as a psychiatrist, and Arstan as a mathematician; their brother Nurlan was killed in a bombing during the war). The family suffered 'major trauma', said Svetlana Borisovna, their lives 'broken apart'.

Gulyandam was sent to Karlag, where she lived in a mud hut and slept on a bed of reeds. She spent the next eight years as a slave labourer, first doing agricultural work and later as a seamstress in a workshop, where she once sewed a portrait of Stalin as a birthday present for the Soviet leader who had jailed her and had her husband shot. Upon her release in 1945, she was sent into exile in a village in southern Kazakhstan. 'She survived it,' said Svetlana Borisovna proudly. 'She was a strong-willed woman.'

In 1948 Gulyandam went to live in Alma-Ata, the capital of Soviet Kazakhstan, with Ziba, who had married a Russian artist by this time and had a daughter, Svetlana. When Stalin died five years later, Svetlana Borisovna was astonished by her grandmother's reaction. 'She sat and wept. Stalin was at fault for everything that had happened, and I couldn't understand it at all,' she said. 'She was sitting by the window, weeping and weeping. Perhaps she was weeping at the way her fate had turned out because of Stalin.'

The Gulag was a well-oiled machine designed to serve the Terror – but it also served another purpose. As Solzhenitsyn chronicled in *One Day in the Life of Ivan Denisovich*, the camps provided an endless flow of expendable slave labour to get the wheels of Soviet industry moving. Solzhenitsyn's three years in Karlag – part of his eight-year sentence for disparaging Stalin in a letter written from the front line of the Great Patriotic War – inspired this gruelling novella detailing the back-breaking, mind-numbing daily life of a slave labourer in a camp in the coal basin of Ekibastuz. The Gulag's forced labourers provided manpower for Stalin's helter-skelter industrialisation drive, for under Goloshchyokin's Little October Kazakhstan was becoming a feeder of raw materials for the rest of the USSR. The *zeki* of Karlag toiled in coal and copper mines, laboured in steelworks and electricity plants, slaved in ceramics works and clothing factories, and hacked railway lines and reservoirs out of the steppe. During his incarceration, Solzhenitsyn worked as a miner, foundryman and bricklayer – one small cog turning the wheel of the giant Gulag, where, in his memorable phraseology, 'the law of the taiga' ruled.[6]

Karlag provided more than grist for the mill of industry: it was also a giant *sovkhoz* growing food for the USSR's expanding industrial

workforce and performing agricultural experiments that produced marvels such as a gigantic 200-kilogram ram, an enormous cabbage named
Slava (Glory) and a cow that spurted out phenomenal amounts of milk.
In the surreal Stalinist system, these fruits of slave labour were held up
as sources of pride and emulation.

Like other Gulag camps, Karlag housed a *sharashka*, a research centre
staffed by convicts who had been academics and scientists in their former
lives. These prisoners were still slave labourers, but mental toil in scientific
hothouses was preferable to physical labour in mines and steelworks.
Solzhenitsyn, a mathematician, served part of his sentence in a *sharashka*,
an experience he dramatised in his masterpiece *The First Circle*.

Karlag's twin beyond the barbed wire was Karaganda, a coal miners'
settlement 40 kilometres from the camp headquarters. Designated a town
in 1934, Karaganda mushroomed into an industrial powerhouse and is
still today a city of gritty factories contrasting with grandiose statues and
bold murals lionising the workers who, along with the peasants, were
the backbone of the revolution. Opposite the majestic Miners' Palace
of Culture stands a hulking bronze ode to the working class: Miners'
Glory, two proud pitmen – one Russian, one Kazakh – bearing aloft a
giant slab of coal. It was erected in the 1970s, but epitomises the ideal
which the Soviets posited as a source of aspiration for the Kazakhs: they
were teaching all the peoples of Central Asia 'the ideals of the Leningrad
worker', Bolshevik revolutionary Mikhail Kalinin remarked in 1929,
shortly before the Kazakhs' nomadic way of life was wiped out for good.[7]

The city was built in a place Kazakhs called Karagandy (place of the
caragana bush), which Russians called 'Karaganda'. (They often rendered
the *ty/dy* suffix of Kazakh place names as 'a'. Kazakhstan's Soviet-era capital was 'Alma-Ata', translating loosely – albeit ungrammatically – as 'father
of apples'. This created an enduring misconception that this is the original
meaning, although Kazakhs called the spot Almaty, 'place of apples', the
name it bears today.) Workers' city par excellence, Karaganda was a town
peopled by disparate incomers: Russian and Ukrainian *kulaks*, a 'richer'
class of peasant, exiled by Stalin for supposedly sabotaging collectivisation; Slavic labourers who poured in as manpower for new mines and
factories; prison guards policing Karlag; and former *zeki* who settled
in the city after their release. For when they were finally freed from the
Gulag, the *zeki* were not allowed to return home. After his release from

Karlag following Stalin's death, Solzhenitsyn was exiled to the village of Kok-Terek, following a long Kremlin tradition of using north-eastern Kazakhstan as a place of banishment: a century earlier Russian literary giant and political dissident Fyodor Dostoyevskiy had been banished to the city of Semipalatinsk after his release from a Siberian labour camp. Solzhenitsyn's exile-for-life sentence was later commuted, and he returned to Russia until his forcible exile to the West in 1974 amid a furore over the publication abroad of *The Gulag Archipelago*, his magnum opus interweaving the history of the camps with his personal experiences.

After Stalin's death in 1953, the Gulag was rolled back. Karlag was closed in 1959 after three decades fuelling the terror and feeding the slave labour machine, and the prison headquarters in Dolinka lost its raison d'être. It was used to store agricultural equipment, then in the 1980s reincarnated as 'Brigantina' ('Brigantine'), a jolly nautical name for a former prison far inland. Brigantina was a sanatorium offering rest cures for Soviet workers – an ironic leap from concentration camp to holiday camp.

From the late 1950s to the late 1980s a veil of silence was drawn over the horrors of the Gulag. It was briefly lifted in the early 1960s when Solzhenitsyn's *One Day in the Life of Ivan Denisovich* was published in the USSR, creating an explosive impact, but the author soon fell out of favour. His work became unpublishable again, circulating only in samizdat, until the rise to power of the last Soviet leader unleashed a torrent of debate on hitherto taboo topics – like the atrocities of the Gulag.

'It was like a bomb going off in Karaganda!' exclaimed Yekaterina Kuznetsova, a sprightly 78-year-old, recalling her newspaper's publication of an exposé of the Gulag nearly thirty years earlier. That was in 1988, three years after Mikhail Gorbachev had come to power, ushering in two new policies that would loosen the grip of totalitarian rule and pave the way for its downfall a few years later: perestroika ('restructuring', of the economic and political order) and glasnost ('openness', to discussion and debate). This new spirit of glasnost sparked lively conversations about the Soviet system and its bloody past, which reverberated in Karaganda, the heart of the former Gulag.

At the time, Yekaterina Borisovna (her patronymic) held an influential position at *Industrialnaya Karaganda*, the local newspaper which had started life as the *Bolshevistskaya Kochegarka* ('Bolshevist Boiler Room') in 1931, publishing out of a railway wagon as revolutionary reading fodder for the miners. She was the newspaper's propaganda chief, ensuring it stuck to the Communist Party line – an unlikely job for someone born into a family of former Imperial Russian diplomats who had refused to return home after the Bolshevik Revolution. Born in 1938 in Manchuria, Yekaterina Borisovna had remained there with her family throughout Japanese and Soviet occupation before finally moving in 1954 to the USSR, a country she had never set eyes on, eight years after the Soviets ceded Manchuria to China. After rattling for several thousand kilometres through China and Siberia by train, the family ended up in Kazakhstan, where Soviet apparatchiks dispatched them to work on a collective farm near Karaganda – labour for which her parents, members of the urban intelligentsia, were supremely unsuited. The family later moved into the city, where her parents found jobs at a research institute, and Yekaterina Borisovna became a journalist.

When *Industrialnaya Karaganda* published its first exposé about the Gulag in 1988, 'the newspaper was snapped up at once', Yekaterina Borisovna recalled animatedly, speaking on a dark December evening in 2016 at a thinly attended lecture she was delivering on the camps at an Almaty university. 'The paper was photocopied and sent to towns all over the Soviet Union, and then the letters started coming in: "I served time," "I'm looking for so-and-so," "I want to know where my husband is, where my son is, where my children are." When I started reading them, it was like an abyss opening up before me, only there were no stars above,' she said. 'I understood that we needed to talk about this.'

Glasnost had opened the floodgates, but when Yekaterina Borisovna started seeking out people in Karaganda who had lived through the Gulag, guards and prisoners alike, she met a wall of silence because, she said, of an atmosphere of 'fear' that pervades Karaganda 'to this day'. Nevertheless, she managed to collect some oral testimony and hold something akin to public hearings: in one video clip, a former guard waxes lyrical about the food grown at Karlag, as if it were a utopian model farm rather than a concentration camp. The former guards she spoke to were mostly unrepentant. 'They were enemies,' she was told dismissively by one former boss of the Alzhir camp for wives and children of 'traitors to the motherland'. 'I think they were all afraid,' Yekaterina Borisovna explained. 'They were expecting retribution. They knew that a collective crime had been committed here. But each of them thought they were just following orders: I was ordered, I followed the order.'

At one public gathering, 'I asked them: what's the difference between Soviet camps and fascist concentration camps?' she recalled. 'Everyone jumped up and started shouting "how dare you compare us?". And that was our Karaganda intelligentsia sitting there. Half of them had seen their fathers shot. But they drew no conclusions.' One female guard came up with an answer: the camps of the Gulag were nothing like Nazi camps because 'we didn't have ovens'. 'They didn't take responsibility for themselves, they deflected the blame on those up the chain of command,' Yekaterina Borisovna continued. 'Yet by that principle [...] no one will ever be guilty.'

After independence Kazakhstan paid out small amounts of compensation to former Gulag inmates, and declared an annual day of commemoration for victims of political repression and the famine, marked with solemn words from Nazarbayev about how 'the memory of the tragic pages of our history and of the victims of political repression and famine is, always has been and always will be sacred for our people'.[8]

Yet there has been no debate about individual and collective culpability for the atrocities of the Soviet past in Kazakhstan (or in Russia, where many still revere Stalin as a strongman who made the USSR great); for the Kremlin-allied country, calamities like the famine and the Gulag are collective historical tragedies for which no one is to blame. Some, however, see that as shirking historical responsibility: Yekaterina Borisovna believes Kazakhstan needs a reckoning with the past, with communist-era crimes 'shouted from the rooftops'. For her, historical awareness is key here: 'There's no need to punish anyone, no need to jail anyone, but to create a sense of moral responsibility.' For Kazakhstan, which officially reveres its Soviet-era leader as its founding father, that would be a tough conversation to have.

Instead of truth and reconciliation, Yekaterina Borisovna believes Kazakhstan is engaging in collective amnesia. 'This is the most terrible lesson: that our society is deflected from our past,' she lamented. 'That means oblivion. And that oblivion assures fear. And that fear assures submission, non-resistance to evil, appeasement. We always endorse everything. Then you can do what you want: no one will condemn you.'

CHAPTER 15

Exile of the Innocents

Krasnaya Polyana, 2016/
Tashkent, Uzbekistan, 2014

When Polina Ibrayeva was three months old, Red Army soldiers marched into her mountain village in Chechnya and sent her on a 3,000-kilometre journey across Siberia to the plains of Kazakhstan. This tiny baby was an 'enemy of the people', and her punishment was exile.

'We lived in the foothills of Mount Kazbek. From there we were taken, on 23 February, at night. There was snow and lightning,' says the 72-year-old, sitting in a polka-dot dress and flowery headscarf in her cosy cottage more than seven decades later, in September 2016, her chubby grey tabby purring contentedly beside her. 'We were deported from the Caucasus and thrown off the train. Then, my mother said, from every *aul* carts came, to the station, and we were loaded onto them by the station. [...] A couple of carts came from each *aul*, and we were taken in two carts to a Kazakh *aul*.'

That is why she is now living here in the village of Krasnaya Polyana in northern Kazakhstan, thousands of kilometres from Lyunki, the settlement where she was born in December 1943. It was February 1944 when Soviet troops rounded up the villagers in the Caucasus region of Chechnya, packed them into cattle trucks and deported them to Central Asia, along with half a million others. This was the *Aardakh* (the Exodus), the word the Chechen people use to describe the tragedy that befell them and their neighbours the Ingush.

'They called us enemies of the people,' says the old lady simply. The phrase used to justify sending prisoners to the Gulag was also the justification used for another of Stalin's experiments in social engineering: the deportation of entire peoples from their homelands as collective punishment for alleged treachery to the *rodina*, the motherland. Chechens and Ingush, Germans and Poles, Greeks and Armenians, Kurds and Koreans, Karachays and Kalmyks, Turks and Tatars were just some of the estimated 1.4 million people banished from their homelands before, during and after the Great Patriotic War.[1] Many ended up in Kazakhstan, which became a dumping ground for entire nations against whom the *Vozhd* had a grudge.

'They supposedly deported us to save the Caucasus,' explained Ansar Ibrayev, the genial *akim* (mayor) of Krasnaya Polyana and the son of the old lady deported at the age of three months, sitting attired in a blue velvet Chechen skullcap in his book-lined office in the small town hall.

In 1942, Nazi troops marched on the Caucasus seeking to conquer Soviet oilfields, and Chechnya was a strategic bridgehead. 'The policy was that the Chechens could go over to the side of the Germans in the Caucasus, although the Germans didn't reach Groznyy [the Chechen capital] and they didn't reach the [River] Terek,' explained Ansar Ibragimovich (his patronymic), who qualified as a historian before he became the mayor. Capturing Groznyy and crossing the Terek would have advanced the Nazis towards their prize, but they were forced into retreat and ended up losing the Battle of the Caucasus. 'Nevertheless, Russian policy labelled us traitors and enemies of the people!' he exclaimed, an epithet that still rankles seventy years on. 'There were 50,000 Chechens fighting [for the Soviets] in the Great Patriotic War: that's a historical fact,' said the mayor. 'They were heroes, yet their wives and mothers were deported.'

The Chechens had never been an easy people to colonise and rule, as the Russians knew from centuries of on–off guerrilla warfare since Moscow had started penetrating the Caucasus in the sixteenth century, eventually conquering Chechnya in 1858. During World War II nearly a century later, a Chechen insurgency had been raging, but it started in 1940, when the Soviets were Nazi allies under a pact which lasted until the Germans invaded in 1941. That brought the USSR into the war, after which Hitler gave some backing to the Chechen uprising. However, the tide in the Battle of the Caucasus had long since turned in favour of the Soviets when they labelled the Chechens a fifth column and turfed them out of their homeland. They code-named this blitzkrieg against their own people Operation Lentil (*Chechevitsa* in Russian, which sounds similar to 'Chechen').

'On 23 February 1944 soldiers came into our village under the guise of preparing for forthcoming manoeuvres,' wrote a couple called Sebert and Khalida Abayev, in memoirs exhibited in Krasnaya Polyana's village school. 'The local people, with the hospitality ingrained in them, accepted the soldiers and officers, not suspecting the true aim of their arrival. They surrounded the village and drove all the inhabitants to the railway station, where they were loaded into goods wagons and, without the destination being declared, taken to Central Asia and Kazakhstan.

'On the way people died of hunger and cold. The bodies of the dead were thrown out of the carriages and there was no chance to bury them. Many of our fellow villagers and relatives were left lying in the boundless expanses of Russia and Kazakhstan. When we got to Kazakhstan we were settled around various villages and towns. In the harsh winter conditions and amid the hunger and absence of any sanitary conditions, many people, especially the elderly and children, died. And those that survived, they survived by a miracle.'

There are few people alive with first-hand memories of Stalin's deportations, but in 2014 there was one octogenarian living in Tashkent, the capital of Uzbekistan, another part of Central Asia that the Soviets used as a human scrapheap. He was a Tatar from the Black Sea peninsula of Crimea who was expelled from his homeland in 1944 at the age of fifteen in a tragedy the Crimean Tatars call the *Sürgünlik* (the Exile).

'In the evening some soldiers brought some vehicles – lots of them – to the school,' 85-year-old Rauf Ibragimov (a pseudonym) recalled in a voice trembling with emotion, sitting in his small flat in May 2014, the seventieth anniversary of the *Sürgünlik*. 'We kids were out and about in the evening and we saw the cars. [...] In the morning, really early, two soldiers came: Get ready – you're leaving. Where to? No one knew where. Mum and Dad said there'd been some Germans living not far away from us before, and when the war started the Germans were deported – they're probably going to deport us too.' The villagers were given a quarter of an hour to get ready and ordered to take food for one day, but were told there was 'no need for your things'. One odd memory stuck in his mind: 'My mother ran up to me and said: "You may be taken to dark places." There'd be no light – so she gave me two light bulbs.' He was bundled with his parents and six siblings into a cattle wagon. 'There was manure – it stank.' Many perished from malnutrition and disease on the journey east, or in the harsh and disorientating conditions into which they arrived.

This old man was one of 238,500 people exiled from Crimea in May 1944, including the entire Tatar population and the Greek and Bulgarian minorities, after the Soviets had recaptured the Nazi-occupied peninsula.[2] Even Crimean Tatar soldiers who had been fighting the Germans on the front line were dubbed traitors and packed off into exile in Central Asia as soon as they were demobbed. This demographic gerrymandering had far-reaching consequences: Crimea now has a majority Russian population, which wholeheartedly approved Russia's annexation of the peninsula from Ukraine in 2014.

Most of the Tatars passed through Kazakhstan in cattle trucks and ended up in Uzbekistan, where Rauf Ibragimov's family was sent to live in a mud hut on a *kolkhoz*. 'There were no doors or windows, nothing, just reeds,' the widower recalled. 'We left on 18 May, and on 3 or 4 June we arrived,' he said in a quavering voice, speaking Russian interspersed with snatches of Tatar. 'They took us to a place that's now known as Gulistan [Land of Flowers], but at that time it was known as the "hungry steppe".' The teenager worked as a labourer on collective farms – 'in the cotton fields, digging, whatever' – and 'then they came to recruit us'. Industrialisation was continuing apace, and recruiters fanned out from new factories looking for manpower. Although the expulsions were primarily intended to deracinate groups deemed disloyal and politically suspect, they also served a practical purpose: like the Gulag, they provided influxes of labour for collective farming and industrialisation.

Rauf Ibragimov was sent to work in a textile plant in Tashkent, where he found that the stigma of 'betrayal' stuck: after he lashed out at a female colleague who called him 'a turncoat Crimean Tatar', he ended up in jail for a year. 'At the time we were called turncoats, but now they say we were wrongly deported,' said the old man sadly, sitting in his kitchen in the Tashkent flat where he will live out his days, thousands of kilometres from his birthplace.

Polina-apa (*apa* is a respectful term of address for older women, loosely 'elder sister') has no memories of the *Aardakh*, but the traumatic story was passed down by her mother (her father had disappeared in the Terror, presumed shot). 'Our people went with nothing. My mother told me: we were driven out of the house. She said: I wanted to take a bucket, so we'd be able to gather water and have a drink on the way, but one soldier shoved me out and said: Go!' The villagers of the Chechen village of Lyunki were taken to the nearest town, Itum-Kale, and then on to Groznyy: 'There was a road in the mountains with a chasm underneath, a drop of two or three hundred metres,' said Polina-apa, her sharp brown eyes misting over as she recounted her mother's memories. 'One old man said: I'm not going anywhere, and he jumped from the truck into the chasm. [...] That's how we got to Groznyy.'

Their expulsion was a shock, but with hindsight her mother realised that some Russians billeted with the family – 'medics and a captain, they lived with us, four of them, all Russians' – had been part of an advance guard to prepare the ground for the expulsions. That is how this old lady ended up with a Russian, rather than Chechen, name: her mother named her after a Russian nurse living with the family who helped at Polina's birth.

Three months later, the infant was one of 387,000 Chechens expelled from Chechnya, along with 91,000 Ingush.[3] Most ended up in Kazakhstan, where this family was taken to a village in Kostanay Region in the north, where, according to family lore, the kindness of the Kazakhs kept them alive. 'This babushka came with *kurt* [dried cheese balls, a Kazakh staple] and blankets, and fed us and clothed us. We lived with them for two years, that Kazakh family.' She was so grateful that she brought up her children to be thankful to the Kazakhs. 'They say they survived only because the local Kazakhs helped,' said her son. 'They arrived in March, it was cold, with nothing, without clothes, without food. My mother always tells me: Ansar, you're alive because the Kazakh people didn't let us die.'

The mayor's late father was also a deportee, who ended up in Krasnaya Polyana in 1944. 'He'd always remember how they came here: they arrived in March, him at the age of fourteen. His sister and mother died of starvation, on the same day. He took them to the cemetery, buried them, came home, and his second sister was lying there dead. They're buried here, in our cemetery. All in one day.' The younger siblings 'were left in my father's hands; he worked raising cattle on the *kolkhoz* and helped out in the fields – that's how he fed the family'.

The Chechens were granted permission to return to their homeland thirteen years after their expulsion, in 1957, three years after Stalin's death. (The Crimean Tatars, on the other hand, were not allowed home until 1989.) 'I remember how happy we were!' exclaimed Polina-apa. Aged thirteen, she had been out tending sheep with her cousin, and when they returned to the village, they 'thought the world had been born again – people were weeping and dancing, saying that we were allowed to go home'.

Her family packed up and left for Chechnya. They were unable to return to their home in Lyunki, which had been occupied by newcomers, but settled in a village called Komsomolskoye. There, Polina-apa would have lived out her days but for the intervention of fate, in the form of an arranged marriage. Aged eighteen, she came to Kazakhstan with her family to visit relatives in Krasnaya Polyana, a place distant from where she had grown up in Kazakhstan and where she had never before set foot. 'In 1962, I came here to visit my mother's relatives. My mother and brother went home, but my hand was given in marriage, so I stayed behind,' she said. 'I wasn't thinking of marriage. I wanted to join the party, I was a *komsomolka* [a young communist].'

She bears no grudge against the Soviet system, and still professes admiration for Stalin, the tyrant who branded her a traitor at three months old and banished her from her homeland. 'Stalin was a good man, of course he was! He never offended anyone.' She blames Stalin's henchman Lavrentiy Beria, head of the NKVD, the Soviet secret police which organised the deportations.

Polina-apa and her husband had fourteen children including the mayor, who now has offspring who are the third generation of Chechens to grow up in Kazakhstan. He puts the size of the family down to his father's trauma at burying most of his relatives upon arriving in Kazakhstan. 'Evidently because everyone had died he himself had a big family. We're all still alive. My eldest brother lives in Chechnya, and one sister married over there. The others are all here.'

Krasnaya Polyana is a couple of hours' drive from the nearest town, Atbasar, past undulating golden wheat fields stretching away in a sheet of yellow to the silver-blue horizon. Another legacy of the Soviet past, these fields were planted in the 1950s under the Virgin Lands campaign to sow the steppe with grain. A turn-off onto a muddy track passes through the villages of Poltavka and Spasskoye, where old German ladies in head-scarves tend their hay bales and lean on fences passing the time of day. They are Volga Germans: distant descendants of German settlers invited to Russia by Catherine the Great in the eighteenth century to farm land along the Volga River. Two centuries later, the families of these settlers were deported to Kazakhstan after the outbreak of war with Germany, in case they harboured Nazi sympathies.

Beyond lie the adjoining settlements of Krasnaya Polyana, Arbuzinka and Petrikovka, founded by Russian settlers – many enticed by perks offered by Imperial Russia to farm land on the fringes of the empire – but now almost entirely Chechen. 'Krasnaya Polyana was founded in 1863. After serfdom was abolished in Russia in 1861, the poor people were resettled here, and settlers from central Russia founded this vil-lage,' explained Ansar Ibragimovich. 'Petrikovka was founded in 1915, Arbuzinka in 1925, also by Russian settlers.'

Most Russians left these villages after the fall of the Soviet Union. Most of the Chechens stayed put, partly because they had put down roots and partly because, as the mayor put it, 'the whole of Chechnya was in ruins' after being bombed to smithereens by the Russian military to crush a separatist Chechen state declared after the USSR collapsed.

Nowadays, Krasnaya Polyana is almost entirely Chechen, and the guttural sounds of this Caucasus language – entirely different to Turkic Kazakh or Slavic Russian – echo around the village, which has the only school in Kazakhstan that teaches Chechen as part of the curriculum. In another first, this is Kazakhstan's only dry village: alcohol is not banned, but it is not sold either, not out of religious fervour but out of a desire to protect the village from the rampant alcoholism that blights life in rural Kazakhstan, where villagers have little to do with the long winter nights but drink themselves into oblivion.

The Chechens here have a nickname, the *Beloshapochniki*, the White Hats, because the deportees made sheepskin hats to keep warm in the bitter Kazakh winters, and 'gradually to define us people started calling us the *Beloshapochniki*', explained Ansar Ibragimovich, modelling the shaggy white hat, called a *papakha* in Russian, in his garden. 'According to the sunnah of the Prophet Muhammad, white is purity of the soul – pure intentions,' he added with a smile. In Krasnaya Polyana, new traditions combine with ancient ones that the community keeps alive, most expressively in the *zikr*, the hypnotic Chechen version of a whirling dervish dance, which the villagers perform on special occasions. 'We shouldn't lose our culture,' said the *akim*. 'We don't have the right. That's our rich asset.'

In 2016, all but twenty of the 1,042 villagers in Krasnaya Polyana were Chechens, living alongside fourteen Russians, three Germans and three Kazakhs. The Kazakhs were the deputy mayor, his wife and their 18-month-old son – named Nursultan, after Nazarbayev, a popular namesake in Kazakhstan. At the village nursery, Ansar Ibragimovich lifted Nursultan up for a hug and took credit for suggesting the name to his deputy, in honour of a president to whom the Chechens were grateful for making them still feel welcome a quarter of a century after the Soviet Union collapsed. 'Nazarbayev is my president, and he's a good man,' said Polina-apa. 'I really like him. I always say: let him live as long as we are living here.'

The memoirs of Sebert and Khalida Abayev come to a poignant conclusion: 'Kazakhstan has become our second Motherland, but the yearning for our fathers' distant Motherland is so strong that even those who were born and grew up here dream of it at night.'

Polina-apa and her offspring are happy in Kazakhstan, but did she ever miss her homeland after she was married off here? '*Yeshchyo kak!* [not half!]' she exclaimed. 'I still miss Chechnya. I've been living here for fifty-four years, but I still miss it. It's my place, where my people are.' She used to visit her three siblings there every year, but now she is too frail. 'Sometimes', said the old lady wistfully, stroking her purring cat, 'I sit up at night and weep and I think: why are those three in a different place and I'm here? That's not something you forget. We were cast adrift.'

CHAPTER 16

Sparks of Tension

Yntymak, 2015/Masanchi, 2020

'Kazakhstan is a Land of Unity and Accord,' trumpets the billboard on the main road leading to the villages of Yntymak and Bostandyk in southern Kazakhstan. Harmony between Kazakhstan's myriad ethnic groups is a pillar on which Nazarbayev founded his nation state, but on a wintry February morning in 2015, there is not much sign of it in these two villages near the border with Uzbekistan.

In Yntymak, a Kazakh family grieves for its murdered son. In neighbouring Bostandyk, jittery Tajiks are clearing up after a Kazakh mob rampaged through their village in revenge for the killing of a Kazakh by a Tajik. Houses have been trashed and the potholed lanes are littered with burnt-out vehicles, scars from a night of violence that is an uncomfortable reminder of how quickly intercommunal frictions can tip over into intercommunal violence in multi-ethnic Kazakhstan. 'It's like brother against brother,' sighs an elderly Tajik man attired in a blue velvet *chapon* (robe) and *tuppi* (skullcap), pausing on his way to pray for peace at the local mosque.

It all started with an argument over a greenhouse.

'There were two close friends, a Tajik and a Kazakh,' Umurdin Nazhmiddinov, a Tajik community elder from Bostandyk explained, sitting cross-legged on a *topchan* (a raised seating platform with a low table) over a pot of green tea in a traditional-style teahouse in Yntymak, where he had come to pay his respects to the bereaved Kazakh family.

'They had a fight and the Tajik pulled a knife on the other, and as a result the other died.'

The row began over a debt owed by Navmidin Narmetov, a Tajik from Bostandyk, to Bakhytzhan Artykov, a Kazakh from Yntymak, for the rental of one of the polytunnels that dot the landscape in this fertile region. When the two friends came to blows, Narmetov stabbed Artykov to death. A small group of hotheads from Yntymak blamed not the murderer but the entire local community of Tajiks, a Persian-speaking Central Asian people whose 'historical homeland' is Tajikistan. 'A Tajik kills a Kazakh, and now all the Tajiks are to blame!' lamented one Tajik woman in Bostandyk, standing with her four grandchildren beside her burnt-out car, bought with two years' worth of profits from her vegetable-growing business. 'Why did they attack the whole village? Is the whole village guilty?'

That sentiment was rife among the Tajiks who had suffered as a result of the violence, in which no one was injured but serious damage was wreaked on homes and vehicles. 'Let the guilty man be punished, but it's as if the fault is all of ours: I'm a Tajik so I'm guilty before all Kazakhs,' echoed Sukhrob, another villager whose property was damaged ('they smashed up my car and threw rocks at my house – whatever was in their way'). Sukhrob was a pseudonym, and he was speaking in a cloak-and-dagger interview because he was nervous of publicly discussing ethnic frictions, a taboo topic in Kazakhstan – at least officially. Sukhrob told me to head for a patch of wasteland, where a burnt-out beer delivery lorry stood, and surveyed me from a concealed spot to ensure I was alone before zooming up in a car and ordering me to hop in. As he put it, nervously checking the rear-view mirror, 'we're under the watchful gaze of the *organy*' (*organy* is slang for the KNB, the security service). To meet Sukhrob, I had escaped my own minders – a plain-clothes officer who said he was police but was more likely KNB, and a local official from the nearest town of Saryagash, both extremely amiable, who had attached themselves to me since my arrival. When I refused to let them drive me around, they tailed me in a conspicuous red car 'for your own security', which made the villagers retreat into their homes until I evaded the tail by running down a muddy lane impassable to vehicles.

Following the night of violence, the security forces had the area under lockdown. The authorities insisted the clash was a 'domestic' with no ethnic element – but they had reacted to a few broken windows and burnt-out cars with a massive show of force that belied their soothing utterances. Hundreds of menacing-looking police in full riot gear were patrolling the usually sleepy rural streets, the air crackling with the sound of their two-way radios. Military trucks stood on the main road, controlling access to the villages, and the schoolyard in Bostandyk – where signs greeted children coming to class with 'welcome' in Tajik (*'Kush omaded!'*) as well as Kazakh (*'Kosh keldinizder!'*) – swarmed with police mustering for duty.

To prevent news of the clash spreading and sparking copycat violence, internet and mobile phone communications had been cut off for miles around, even in the city of Shymkent, 120 kilometres away. Predictably, since locals had already uploaded videos online, this led to apocalyptic rumours spreading like wildfire. Nevertheless, the authorities were determined to nip this clash in the bud. The row over the greenhouse was, after all, 'just the spark' that ignited simmering ethnic tensions, said Sukhrob. 'The people are afraid.' Fresh in people's minds were troubling memories of ethnic clashes in neighbouring Kyrgyzstan in 2010, where tensions in the Fergana Valley – another ethnic hotchpotch, like southern Kazakhstan – spilled over into violence between Kyrgyz and Uzbeks, leaving 470 people dead and the whole of Central Asia reeling.[1]

For Nazarbayev, tolerance and harmony between Kazakhstan's ethnic groups (125 or so of them[2]) had always been buzzwords, touted in his speeches at every turn and screaming down from billboards, like the one outside these two villages hailing Kazakhstan as a 'Land of Unity and Accord', or another in Bostandyk trumpeting the slogan 'One People, One Nation, One Fate', with a picture of jolly minorities in national dress holding hands and dancing. 'Ethnic accord is life-giving oxygen. We don't notice it when we breathe, we do it automatically, and we just live. But if the air is poisoned, we'll notice it immediately,' Nazarbayev proclaimed shortly before this unrest. 'We should boost trust between Kazakhstanis and be tolerant towards each other, as we've always been. That's the key to the future of our country.'[3]

For minorities, Nazarbayev was the guarantor of their security and interests, and many Kazakhs also liked living in a country that presented itself as a cosmopolitan utopia. Others were not so sure: some saw this policy as soft-pedalling at the expense of the Kazakh majority. 'People's anger has been building up for years and this murder was just a pretext to warn Tajiks that they have become too audacious,' one Kazakh man told a journalist after the killing in Bostandyk: it was 'a lesson' to other ethnic groups to keep in line.[4] These remarks reflected resentful perceptions among some Kazakhs that too little had been done since independence to redress discrimination Kazakhs suffered in Soviet times, when they were driven into a minority in Kazakhstan and their language and culture were treated with haughty contempt.

It was a delicate balancing act for Nazarbayev: while some Kazakhs griped at his vision of Kazakhstan as a multicultural melting pot in which every citizen is a 'Kazakhstani', minorities chafed at 'Kazakhification', the spread of the Kazakh language and the dominance of ethnic Kazakhs in the civil service, where obligatory knowledge of the Kazakh language gave Kazakhs a leg-up and nepotism did the rest. Nazarbayev was the glue holding the ethnic mix together – but what next? 'Our *Yelbasy* is OK,' said Sukhrob. 'For now the president's got a handle on all this. But what happens after him? Let's hope everything will be fine.'

Kazakhstan's ethnic groups rubbed along together with few discernible frictions. Yet this local conflict in southern Kazakhstan, albeit minor, was a reminder of how quickly ethnic fault lines could fracture into ethnic clashes because of seemingly minor incidents, and how the powers that be preferred to brush frictions under the carpet rather than confront them – since they did not officially exist.

This was not the first time a trifling local conflict had split along ethnic lines: there had been occasional incidents in villages outside Almaty, where the descendants of Stalin-era deportees live in villages strung out along the road to China – like Malovodnoye, where an argument over a game of billiards in 2007 led a Kazakh mob to chase out Chechen families, many of whom had been their neighbours for decades, leaving five Chechens dead.[5]

South Kazakhstan Region (nowadays renamed Turkestan Region), the most populous of the country's provinces, was also a farrago of ethnic groups – Uzbeks, Uighurs and Ukrainians; Tajiks, Tatars and Turks – living crowded together in adjoining villages, competing for scarce jobs and resources like water and agricultural land. Here, Tajiks (who at the time numbered 3 per cent of the local population, and 0.2 per cent of the population nationwide[6]) jostled for space with Kazakhs and other groups due to another piece of Soviet border gerrymandering – an administrative stroke of Nikita Khrushchev's pen six decades earlier, like the one that granted Crimea to Ukraine in 1954.

'The Tajik people have lived here for sixty years. We were resettled here in 1954 from Bostandyk District,' said the old Tajik man on his way to pray for peace. That district nowadays lies over the border in Uzbekistan, because it was moved out of one Soviet Socialist Republic, the Kazakh SSR, into another, the Uzbek SSR, when this octogenarian was twenty-two years old, and some of the Tajiks living in that district were resettled in Kazakhstan. 'Since then we've lived in peace, and we live in peace now – but all of a sudden we're being called outsiders,' he said aggrievedly. This village in Kazakhstan where many of the resettled Tajiks now lived was called Bostandyk (Freedom) after the name of the district they left behind in Uzbekistan. The name of the adjoining village where the murdered Kazakh lived had a hollow ring in the light of the violence: Yntymak means 'accord', a reference to the ethnic harmony chanted as an official mantra in Kazakhstan. Like other minorities, the Tajiks of Bostandyk were fiercely supportive of Nazarbayev, the living embodiment of this policy of inclusion. 'The state is protecting us, as you can see,' said Mels Khizmatov (his was a popular Soviet-era first name, formed from the first letters of Marx, Engels, Lenin, Stalin). This middle-aged Tajik, a child psychologist, was standing outside his house as dusk fell in Bostandyk, not far from the home of the murderer whose crime had put the state on alert. 'We're Kazakhstani Tajiks. Thank God the state protects us,' he said, gesturing at a group of tooled-up riot police beginning a night patrol to ensure the security of this man and his neighbours against the angry Kazakhs in the next village. 'Thank you to the police, who are staying up at night to make sure we're safe, thank you to the state, and a big thank you to Nazarbayev.'

Five years later, violence that pitted Kazakhs against another minority community elsewhere in southern Kazakhstan ended with tragic consequences.

As the sun set on the village near the border with Kyrgyzstan one evening in February 2020, a family was deep in mourning. 'I have lost my son,' lamented a middle-aged man, his face contorting with grief and disbelief as well-wishers passed sombrely through his courtyard to pay their respects, heads bowed, hands on hearts. 'I have only one son.' As he choked on his words, his eighteen-month-old grandson toddled out into the courtyard chuckling merrily, unaware that his father had been killed in a night of deadly violence that had engulfed Masanchi, a village inhabited by Dungans: Mandarin-speaking Muslims of Chinese ancestry (called 'Hui' in China) who fled to Imperial Russia-controlled Central Asia in the nineteenth century during the Dungan Revolt.

The spark for the violence was prosaic, as in past incidents when local disputes had split along ethnic lines. This time it was a bout of road rage, as an argument between Kazakhs and Dungans over right of way erupted first into an argument, then into fisticuffs, then into an orgy of shooting, beating and burning that left eleven people dead. Masanchi was a scene of devastation, with charred hulks of homes and shops lining the main street as locals stood around murmuring about the horrors of the attack in the sing-song tones of the Dungan language (this chafes with some of their neighbours, who would prefer them to speak Kazakh). 'Today some of the dead were buried and some people are missing. People are looking for them,' said one young man. Another man out searching for two elderly relatives who had disappeared from their burnt-out house said he had been praying at the mosque on the Friday evening when he heard a commotion. He came out to see a mob attacking the village. 'They immediately set fire to five or six homes. Our guys came out to try and restrain them. Then they started shooting [...] We were all in shock.' Around 20,000 Dungans fled over the border into Kyrgyzstan, ten minutes' drive away. Others stayed behind and battled the attackers – among them the young man who was one of ten Dungans to lose his life. 'I was beside him. I told him, you go home and I'll stay. He said: dad, you go and I'll stay. I said: you go, you have children,' said his father (who requested anonymity, for fear of reprisals). The young man refused, and soon afterwards he was shot dead. 'He died from a gunshot wound to the back,' explained the bereaved man, as the attack turned into 'a bloodbath'.[7]

What had led to this outburst of deadly violence? The mutual recriminations went far beyond the road rage incident that had sparked the turmoil, in which an elderly Kazakh man had been hospitalised with a broken rib in an assault for which two Dungans were later jailed.[8] Some Dungans complained of being made to feel like guests in Kazakhstan despite their community – just 76,000-strong nationwide, most living in four villages in this area – having founded the first Dungan settlement in Central Asia in 1878 (it went through several names before being christened Masanchi after a Dungan Soviet revolutionary). 'They always say: this is our Kazakhstan. This belongs to us, so what we say you do. It's always been like that,' said one young Dungan, voicing a common complaint from minorities about an unwritten law that Kazakhs are first among equals in Kazakhstan. A Kazakh man in the village of Karakemer, a ten-minute walk from Masanchi past bucolic scenes of sheep grazing on rolling green pastureland in front of a snowy alpine panorama, certainly believed minorities should know their place. 'Kazakhstan is a multi-ethnic country. We are all Kazakhstanis, like Americans are all American. I don't distinguish by ethnicity,' he began. But there was a catch. 'These people, the Dungans, had started to get cocky. This didn't happen in one day – it has built up over years and years. Patience snapped. They got rich, and when people get rich, they start looking down on other people. They started saying to us: "Though the land is yours, the power is ours."' Both villages looked pretty prosperous by the standards of rural Kazakhstan: this man, an engineer, had just parked his expensive jeep in the driveway of his well-appointed house. But here, as around Yntymak, families were large, settlements were crowded and competition over resources was fierce – especially land, which typically Dungans used for agribusiness and Kazakhs for livestock breeding. Toqayev had his own explanation for the violence: a tussle over smuggling in these borderlands, though he did not elaborate on how that translated into mobs of Kazakhs attacking Dungan villages.[9] And it was only the four Dungan-inhabited villages that were attacked, and all but one of the fatalities were Dungans. Wild conspiracy theories circulated – the attacks had been prepared, outsiders had come from far and wide to join in – but nothing was proven, although all sides agreed that WhatsApp messages inciting violence had gone viral on the night of the attacks. Most of those who called for bloodshed, many from far afield, got off scot-free. 'It's those who fell for those provocations who are on trial – cannon fodder,' Khusey Daurov, a community leader who suffered a broken arm during the unrest, said later.[10]

The judicial proceedings over the violence left a bitter taste for the Dungans, who argued that they had been acting in self-defence after mobs attacked their villages while police, who said they were over-powered until reinforcements arrived, stood by. 'It was not they who attacked those villages, burned down houses and killed people. On the contrary, they were saving people and protecting themselves,' Bolatbek Omarov, a defence lawyer at a mass trial of fifty-one defendants, said. 'They were doing the work of the police.'[11] Dungans accounted for thirteen of the fifty-seven people convicted on charges ranging from murder and participating in mass unrest to looting in two trials, some of whose defendants alleged they had been tortured after arrest.[12] Five of the twenty-six people who received jail terms of between five and twenty years were Dungans (one defendant was acquitted; the others got non-custodial sentences). 'This is not justice. This is a circus,' said a shell-shocked Mukharme Daurov (no relation to Khusey), after his son Ersa was imprisoned for sixteen years on charges that he denied of attempting to kill police officers.[13] 'He went out to protect his home and his family, and he has been convicted.' The term was reduced to ten years on appeal, but a sentence of sixteen and a half years handed to Dungan defendant Shchimar Sanguy on a murder charge was upheld despite his lawyer producing evidence in court that he had not been present at the scene of the killing of the one Kazakh man who died in the unrest. Eight of the twenty-one Kazakhs jailed had their sentences commuted to non-custodial terms on appeal, though others would remain behind bars for many years.[14]

The authorities refused to characterise the worst ethnic violence Kazakhstan had witnessed in its three decades of independence as an intercommunal clash and did not respond to concerns raised by the United Nations Committee on the Elimination of Racial Discrimination,[15] although much was said about promoting ethnic harmony and healing wounds. But for the bereaved family, where a young wife had been widowed and two small children left fatherless, the wounds would never heal. And the most crucial question, which Omarov eloquently put to the court, was left unanswered: 'Why in the twenty-first century, in civilised Kazakhstan, did bestial instincts awake in some citizens and why, in defiance of the law, did they vent their rage on peaceful people guilty of nothing?'[16]

CHAPTER 17

December of Discontent

Almaty, 2011/2016

Talgat Ryskulbekov vividly remembers the day his brother was sentenced to death. It was 16 June 1987 when a judge ordered 21-year-old Kayrat Ryskulbekov executed by firing squad, and what sticks in his younger brother's mind is the sight of his mother trying to stop her condemned son being removed from the court. 'After they'd passed the death sentence on him […] my mother fell on her knees in front of the van, so they wouldn't take him away,' the tough-looking amateur boxer says quietly, frowning at the painful memory. 'They wanted to frighten the people,' he adds more defiantly, sitting in Almaty in December 2011 recalling events of a quarter of a century ago. 'But you can't break the spirit of the Kazakh people.'

Kayrat had been sentenced to death for his role in fomenting an anti-Soviet uprising in Kazakhstan in the deep dark days of winter 1986 which came to be known as '*Zheltoksan*', Kazakh for December (the word means '90 winds', evoking the gales that buffet the land during that ferocious season). The rebellion was brutally suppressed, killing scores of people and bringing ruthless reprisals against the mainly Kazakh protesters, who were vilified across the USSR for what the Kremlin deemed a violent outburst of anti-Russian nationalism.

Kayrat spent nearly a year on death row, but won a reprieve when his sentence was commuted to a long jail term. Yet the young man did not live to see his twenty-third birthday: he was found hanged in a prison cell in what the authorities classified as suicide, but his family have always suspected was foul play.

Six months before his sentence of execution was passed, Kayrat was a carefree young man, happy to have finished his national service in the Soviet army, part of which he had spent on the toughest of front lines: fighting in the doomed war in Afghanistan. With that behind him, he was enjoying student life in Alma-Ata, the capital of Soviet Kazakhstan (he and his brother had moved there to study from a village in south-eastern Kazakhstan). But on 16 December 1986 momentous events erupted that would soon end Kayrat's short life, rattle the foundations of the Soviet state and leave a traumatic scar on Kazakhstan's national psyche. Kayrat died because of a chain of circumstances set in motion by *Zheltoksan*, which with hindsight is viewed in Kazakhstan as a harbinger of the collapse of the Soviet Union five years later. Towards the end of the 1980s, there was rioting and rebellion against Soviet rule elsewhere in the USSR – Georgia, Azerbaijan, the Baltic States – but many Kazakhs take pride in the little-known fact that it was they who first rattled the Soviet cage. '*Zheltoksan* was the first democratic movement in the whole of the Soviet Union,' muses Mukhtar Shakhanov, an elderly poet who is revered by many Kazakhs for his role in lifting the veil of secrecy on a Soviet cover-up of *Zheltoksan*. Sitting in 2016 in his office near Almaty's central mosque, the call to prayer that was banned in Soviet times drifting melodiously through the window, the imposing septuagenarian adds: 'It was an uprising that sowed the seeds of the destruction of the Soviet Union.'[1]

It all started with what seemed like a piece of inconsequential news.

Kayrat heard on the radio the tidings that would lead to his untimely demise: Soviet Kazakhstan was getting a new leader. In the Kremlin, 4,000 kilometres away, machinations were afoot that would bring political change to Kazakhstan, overseen by Mikhail Gorbachev, the USSR's new reformist leader. The Politburo had decreed that Dinmukhamed Kunayev, the long-serving first secretary of the Communist Party of the Kazakh SSR, would be replaced by Gennadiy Kolbin, a Soviet official and regional party boss in Russia. This reshuffle came as an unwelcome shock in Kazakhstan, and it brought thousands of people flocking out to Alma-Ata's main square to stage a spontaneous protest of a type highly unusual in the USSR.

The demonstrators saw two things wrong with Kolbin: one, he was an outsider with no links to Kazakhstan; two, he was a Russian – or rather, he was not a Kazakh. By appointing Kolbin, the Kremlin had broken the unspoken rule that a Kazakh would lead Kazakhstan, like Kunayev: he was born and bred in Alma-Ata (born, rather, into tsarist Russia in 1912 in the city then called Vernyy). Seen as the grandfather of Kazakh politics, Kunayev had been Kazakhstan's leader for well over two decades, and although most leaders prior to him had been non-Kazakhs, his long tenure had fostered the expectation that Kazakhstan would have a Kazakh leader – like Nazarbayev, perhaps, who was Kunayev's political protégé.

But Kunayev fell victim to a new broom sweeping through the Soviet Union, brandished by a new leader trying to brush away the cronyism and corruption that had embodied the '*Epokha Zastoya*', the 'Era of Stagnation' that had preceded Gorbachev's rise to power, when the USSR had turned into a sluggish gerontocracy under Leonid Brezhnev's long rule. It was crucial for Gorbachev to eject entrenched leaders of Soviet republics who seemed to embody the ills of the age – but he had not reckoned on grass-roots opposition from the Kazakhs to the imposition of a Russian outsider as ruler of Kazakhstan.

As news spread around Alma-Ata, young people began streaming into the central square, nowadays called Republic Square but at that time named after Brezhnev, who in the 1950s had been Kazakhstan's first secretary before later becoming Soviet leader. Many were students, but they were joined by a disparate bunch of demonstrators from all walks of life: blue-collar workers downed tools in factories, white-collar workers walked out of offices, and even actors walked off film sets.

Gulbakhram Zhunis was a young performer filming on the set of *Pesnya o Turksibe* (*Song about the Turksib*), a socialist realist silver-screen ode to the Turkestan–Siberia railway linking Central Asia with Russia. 'I was filming at the Kazakhfilm studio,' she recalled thirty years later, standing on the square where the rebellion unfolded, 'and we were told on the radio that Kunayev had been ousted. We were shocked: What?! The filming was cancelled right away, and I started saying: Send everyone to the square!' Hearing that 'young people had already started gathering there', she took a bus from the studio and sneaked through a police cordon. 'I reached the square through those fir trees,' she said, pointing towards the snow-dusted branches near Almaty's city hall, which was then the headquarters of the Central Committee of Soviet Kazakhstan's Communist Party. 'We stood here, and more and more young people gathered,' she remembered, gesturing around the square where she had come to lay flowers on a dazzling sunny morning on 16 December 2016, the thirtieth anniversary of the protests and the day Kazakhstan was celebrating its quarter of a century of independence. 'We hadn't come here to smash anything up or break anything apart or beat anyone up or kill anyone.' The protesters were angry 'because Kunayev was being removed and some Kolbin appointed, who not only didn't know the city of Almaty or Kazakhstan – he didn't even know what kind of nation this was, our traditions and culture'.

'When Kolbin was put in, the whole Kazakh people rose up,' explained Talgat Ryskulbekov, sitting in an Almaty café and looking back on the painful events that led to his brother's premature death in the dying days of the USSR. 'We weren't rising up because Kolbin had been put in, but because it wasn't a Kazakh who'd been put in.'

In theory, that should not have mattered, but Kolbin's appointment appeared to confirm something many Kazakhs had long believed: that their Russian rulers looked down on them as second-class citizens. 'This was the last straw, you see,' recalled Dos Kushim, who was then a young lecturer and became a prominent Kazakh community leader after independence. 'For years this discontent had been accumulating inside us, that we'd become second-rate. The affront had been building up in our souls.'

The USSR was, theoretically, a union of equal states whose citizens all enjoyed equal rights. It was, however, an open secret that Russians were first among equals, the 'elder brother' in the family, and to some Kazakhs the relationship felt more like master and slave. 'We were colonies of Russia; you can't escape this,' said Kushim in 2011, speaking on the twenty-fifth anniversary of *Zheltoksan*. 'Although the Soviet Union was called that, it was a Russian state, and the Soviet Union continued the Russian imperial course, only in a more sophisticated and cunning way.' The poet Mukhtar Shakhanov offered a starker view: 'Kazakhstan has been under Russian influence for about 300 years. Over this time, the issues of the destruction of the language and of the nation have always been on the agenda.'

Nowhere had seventy years of Soviet colonisation wrought such demographic and linguistic upheavals as in Kazakhstan, where the Soviets had wiped out the traditional nomadic way of life, driven Kazakhs into a minority in their eponymous republic and, doomsayers believed, left their language teetering on the verge of extinction. Russian was the USSR's lingua franca, and took especially deep root in Kazakhstan, with its ethnic medley, even supplanting Kazakh as the native tongue for many Kazakhs. This has left an enduring legacy in Kazakhstan, where around a third of people still could not speak Kazakh nearly two decades after independence, while knowledge of Russian was near universal.[2]

'They wanted to make us all Russian speakers,' said Talgat, who grew up in a Kazakh-speaking village before moving as a student to Alma-Ata, a Russian-speaking city where – partly due to discriminatory housing and employment policies – Kazakhs numbered only 22 per cent of the population.[3] Shakhanov also recalled the disdain in which some of the townspeople held his native tongue: 'Once I was on the tram and a friend came up and he talked to me in Kazakh. This burly Russian guy came up to us and said: What are you going on about? Why don't you talk in a comprehensible language? A comprehensible language meant Russian. He actually said those words. The friend was a sportsman, and he said: Mukhtar, let me break his nose. I barely managed to stop him.' Gulbakhram, born almost sixty years before in a village then called Karl Marx in south-western Kazakhstan, also had tales to tell of linguistic discrimination in those days: 'We were absolutely strictly forbidden from talking in Kazakh, in our own language, on buses or in public places, although we were from villages and our Russian was ropey. They'd laugh at us, they'd reproach us, they'd even insult us: What are you chuntering on about in your monkey language? Speak in a normal language!' With her halo of smartly styled blonde hair and brown fur coat, it is hard to imagine this formidable-looking woman being intimidated, but 'that's the way it was'.

The protest on Brezhnev Square quickly swelled to several thousand people, waving hastily fashioned placards with slogans like: 'To each people its own leader!' and – alarmingly for the apparatchiks in the Kremlin – 'We demand self-determination!' 'Perestroika is under way, where is democracy?' wondered a third. Perestroika was one of Gorbachev's buzzwords; the other was glasnost, which encouraged people to air their problems openly. Optimistic that the winds of change were blowing through the USSR, the young Kazakhs saw this as their chance to make their voices heard and register their dissatisfaction with Moscow's diktat. 'We were simply, I think, showing our attitude to society, to the Soviet Union, to the totalitarian regime,' explained Kushim. But the regime reacted with a massive onslaught of violence: Brezhnev's old Era of Stagnation was about to collide head-on with Gorbachev's new age of glasnost.

Operation *Metel* (Snowstorm) was about to begin.

At first, the demonstration was light-hearted. The high-spirited pro-testers linked arms and sang the song that became the anthem of their protest: 'Menin Kazakstanym' ('My Kazakhstan'), an uplifting ballad written in 1956 about the Virgin Lands campaign, which later became independent Kazakhstan's national anthem. As word spread, demonstrations erupted in other towns: Talgar and Taldykorgan near Alma-Ata; Tselinograd ('Virgin Lands Town', as the city that later became Kazakhstan's capital was then called), Pavlodar and Kokchetav (nowadays Kokshetau) up north; Chimkent and Dzhambul (now Shymkent and Taraz) down south; and Dzhezkazgan (now Zhezkazgan) and Karaganda (Karagandy in Kazakh, but never officially renamed) in the central industrial heartlands.

On Brezhnev Square, police struggled to contain the rising tide of protest, and factory workers (mainly Slavs) armed with shovels, hammers and picks were bussed in to help face down the protesters (mainly Kazakhs). 'There were a lot of workers from the factories there,' who came 'prepared with steel rods', recalled Gulbakhram. As police moved in to break up the demo, she was arrested and hauled off to the police station – but she had a lucky break. She was spotted by a policeman who was her brother's friend, who 'let me out of the back door, put me in a taxi and told the driver to take me right to the door [of her home] – he gave the address and paid the money'. But after the taxi had left the police station, she jumped out, 'covered in blood, with all my clothes ripped', and made her way back to the square, where she ended up arrested again – and this time she would not escape from the police's clutches so easily.

As the protest entered its second day, thousands of extra police and paramilitary forces (7,618, according to one count[4]) flooded in from all over the Soviet Union – Siberia, the Urals, the Caucasus, other parts of Central Asia – and riot police, special forces and troops from the Ministry of Internal Affairs equipped with anything from truncheons to sappers' shovels began clashing with demonstrators armed with stones, branches and Molotov cocktails. Helped by 10,000 'volunteers' ushered (or ordered) into civilian militias and using guard dogs rounded up from all over Alma-Ata, they chased down the rioters and dispersed them using water cannons. Some of the drenched protesters were driven out of town and dumped out on the freezing steppe in bitter temperatures; others suffered savage beatings as they were hauled off into custody. 'A lot of people think those are wrinkles,' Gulbakhram joked, pointing to a scar running under her eye, 'but those aren't wrinkles.' The scar is from a smashed cheekbone, one of four broken bones she sustained during beatings on the square and in police cells.

Nowadays, *Zheltoksan* is mythologised in Kazakhstan as an outpouring of resentment against colonial dictatorship that set the country on the path to independence: a 'resolute protest at the abuse and hypocritical policy of the totalitarian system', as Nazarbayev once said, glossing smoothly over his own part in that system as Soviet Kazakhstan's political number two at the time.[5] Yet many *Zheltoksanshylar*, as the protesters are known, did not hold anything against him. Talgat remembered Nazarbayev as the only leader who got up close to the protesters to appeal to them directly. After the apparatchiks emerged from the government building in Brezhnev Square to address the demonstrators from the top of a podium usually used during parades, Nazarbayev chose to mingle with the crowd. 'Nazarbayev was the only person – you have to give him his due – who stepped down and calmed us down,' Talgat recalled, pushing the salt and pepper pots around the sugar bowl on the table in the café to demonstrate how Nazarbayev walked around urging the demonstrators to disperse, telling them: 'I fear they may use force against you.' Gulbakhram bore no malice towards Nazarbayev either, believing that 'it was Moscow that dictated to us' so those in positions of power in Kazakhstan 'couldn't defend us'. Arrested for a second time as the protests turned nasty, she was fingered as a ringleader, a crime that carried a long jail term.

Meanwhile, in the world outside the jails holding thousands of protesters, rumours were circulating that hundreds of people had died in the violent clashes. But no one knew precisely how many.

'Yesterday evening and today a group of young students, incited by nationalist elements, took to the streets expressing disapproval of the decisions of the plenary session of the Central Committee of the Communist Party of Kazakhstan which occurred several days ago. Hooligans, parasites and other antisocial persons took advantage of this situation, committing unlawful actions and behaviour against law enforcement officers, and also perpetrating arson against a food shop and private cars, and committing insulting actions against the towns-people.' This was how the first official report, by Soviet news agency TASS, described the protest on 18 December 1986. It made no mention of casualties, but two months later Nazarbayev (at that time chairman of Kazakhstan's Council of Ministers) told Western journalists, granted permission to visit Alma-Ata from Moscow, that the official death toll was two and 200 people had been injured.[6] But in Kazakhstan, rumours abounded of secret graves out on the steppe.

Gorbachev's glasnost notwithstanding, it was clear from the tone of that first report that the response would be in the old Soviet style: a cover-up, with blame attached to rogue members of society. In Soviet-speak, this meant 'hooligans', 'parasites', 'anti-social elements', '*alkashy*' (alcoholics) and '*narkomany*' (druggies), with a dash of censure for 'nationalist elements' thrown in. Kazakhs were vilified to the rest of the USSR as nationalists who had breached the 'friendship of the peoples'. Talgat refuted this indignantly, however: 'We weren't rising up against the Russian people, but against the regime.'

After Operation Snowstorm came the reprisals. Around 8,500 people were hauled into interrogation centres.[7] Some failed to emerge alive: sixteen-year-old Lyazzat Asanova died after supposedly throwing herself off the roof of a KGB interrogation centre in Alma-Ata, and another young woman, Sabira Mukhamedzhanova, lost her life after allegedly hurling herself out of a detention centre window in Ust-Kamenogorsk. The vast majority of those detained – 92 per cent by one official count – were Kazakhs.[8]

Among those arrested was Kayrat Ryskulbekov, who had been caught on camera taking part in the disturbances. He was charged with the murder of Sergey Savitskiy, a Russian engineer killed while serving as a volunteer in the civilian militias formed to battle the protesters. Kayrat confessed but later recanted, claiming his confession was extracted under torture from KGB interrogators. He acknowledged being present, drawn by curiosity and rumours the security forces were beating up Kazakh girls, and admitted to striking a policeman 'because he was brutally dragging some girl by her hair'. But, he stated, 'as God is my witness, I didn't kill anyone'.[9]

On 16 June 1987, Kayrat was convicted of murder and condemned to death. His brother felt that he had been made a scapegoat, because the authorities 'wanted to frighten the Kazakh people, so the people wouldn't rise up again'. An old black-and-white photograph shows Kayrat standing in the dock looking defiant, a proud tilt to his head as his death sentence was read out. The photograph caused such a stir when it was published in Soviet Kazakhstan's press that the photographer and several others involved lost their jobs, because the authorities were enraged at its potential to make martyrs out of the 'hooligans'.[10]

The grapevine was also abuzz with talk of a missing piece of TV footage that the KGB spent years trying to ferret out. A Kazakh official had colluded with journalists to conceal it from Moscow, to protect the protesters caught on camera and for fear of the explosive consequences if it was seen, since it contradicted the official version of events. It showed not drunken, drugged-up hooligans attacking the security forces but young people being manhandled by police. The footage spent five years buried in a garden until it was dug up in 1991.[11]

Protesting his innocence from death row, Kayrat appealed for clemency, and won a reprieve: his sentence was commuted to twenty years in jail. Still, the thought of spending two decades behind bars drove him to despair: 'This twist of fate might, perhaps, have brought cheer or comfort to someone,' he wrote in his last letter to his mother. 'But to me personally this announcement brought no joy. Dear Mama, you cannot fail to understand me! The thought that I must sit it out, innocent, in this dungeon is unbearably hard for me.' He was 'drained to the limit' by eleven months on death row. 'I have no strength left. And I don't want to put up with twenty years of torment for anything.'[12] Kayrat also wrote poetry, and the last poem he penned before his death rails against the fate that has 'stolen [his] youth', offering instead 'putrefaction and decay', before presenting a lyrical reflection on the need to stay strong to clear his name. It could be read either way: a mutinous message that he will fight on, or a suicide note hoping truth will win out after his death.

Had he survived, Kayrat would have been released after the USSR collapsed and Nazarbayev 'rehabilitated' the *Zheltoksanshylar* by wiping clean their criminal records. However, less than a month after his sentence was commuted, he was found hanged from a vest in his cell in Semipalatinsk in north-eastern Kazakhstan, where he was being held en route to a prison camp in Russia. His body was swiftly buried and his death classed as suicide – but his brother has always suspected he was murdered on orders from on high. 'They killed him in prison to break the spirit of the Kazakh people,' said Talgat. Although he believes the murder was probably committed by the '*zek*' (prisoner) who was his cellmate, 'it was the system that killed him'.

'You can accuse 5,000 people, 10,000 people, 100,000 people – but you cannot accuse the entire Kazakh nation of nationalism! The words "Kazakh nationalism" are an accusation against the entire Kazakh nation! We therefore request that justice be done, that these harsh and undeserved accusations against the nation be lifted! The Kazakh nation has shown more than once in its history and through its blood its devotion to "friendship of the peoples"!'[13]

This was the poet Mukhtar Shakhanov, speaking in 1989 at the Congress of People's Deputies, the USSR's new parliament which had been created under Gorbachev's reforms and was holding its first session in Moscow. Shakhanov had tricked Gorbachev into giving him the floor, and he was now taking a risky step that could have landed him in jail, in order to blow the *Zheltoksan* cover-up wide open.

As a parliamentary deputy from Kazakhstan, he begged the Soviet leader to find him five minutes in a busy agenda to speak about a Central Asian environmental disaster, the shrinking Aral Sea – but given the floor, he used the slot to call for a probe into *Zheltoksan*. 'It was like a bomb going off,' he recalled proudly. 'At the time Gorbachev was boasting: I'm creating a democratic union, the Soviet Union's going to work democratically.' The poet, who in 2016 still cut an impressive figure at the age of seventy-three, with his mop of jet-black hair and sharp suit, decided to hold the Soviet leader to his word. Smashing the conspiracy of silence surrounding *Zheltoksan* was a hazardous undertaking, even though Shakhanov – who started writing as a tractor driver on a collective farm before finding fame as a poet – was an illustrious member of the Soviet Union's literary establishment with impeccable socialist credentials.

Since *Zheltoksan*, the mood in the Soviet Union had changed. As Gorbachev wanted, glasnost had unleashed debate, and in 1989 a controversy was raging over the violent quelling of pro-independence demonstrations in Georgia. This was glasnost at its boldest, playing out on the stage of the USSR's new parliament, whose stormy debates stand in stark contrast to the docile yes-man show that is Kazakhstan's parliament today.

When Shakhanov threw down his gauntlet to the Kremlin, with a national audience watching on live television, he did not mince his words. Roundly rejecting the accusation of Kazakh 'nationalism', he led a countercharge. 'At the first challenge against it, the Era of Stagnation bared its evil teeth,' the poet (attired in a snazzy purple tie and blue jacket) railed, effectively accusing Gorbachev of retreating into the repressions of the past. Hundreds of young people – killed, imprisoned, expelled from their universities, dismissed from their jobs – had had their lives 'ruined forever', he said. According to later findings, 900 people were convicted of crimes ranging from murder and assault to hooliganism (82 of the 900 were jailed), and 1,400 people received reprimands that blighted their records as good Soviet citizens.[14]

Among those who suffered reprisals was Gulbakhram: badly injured during her arrest, the performer spent eight months languishing in jail while the authorities tried to pin on her the charge of being a ringleader – but eventually she got off with a fine. That was a stroke of luck, but she had been fired from her prestigious job at Kazakhstan's main concert hall, and as a convicted *Zheltoksanshy* had no chance of finding work in the arts or anywhere else: she was even cut out of scenes in the film she had been shooting when the protests began. 'It was upsetting, really upsetting – when we'd believed in our "older brother" [Russia] and looked to Moscow, and then they trampled upon our honour and our national dignity,' she said. 'It's really upsetting when your brother offends you, whom you'd considered close and trusted – that affront is really, really painful. It is, you know, an incurable pain.'

Shakhanov's attempt to smash through the wall of silence surrounding *Zheltoksan* caused a ripple of shock around the Soviet parliament, but, as video from the session shows, one person sat poker-faced: Nazarbayev.[15] *Zheltoksan* had done nothing to harm his career prospects: he was about to take over the top job in Kazakhstan. Two weeks after Shakhanov's speech, Gorbachev appointed Nazarbayev to replace Kolbin, still in the job three years after the *Zheltoksan* protests against his appointment, as first secretary of Kazakhstan's Communist Party, a position which would subsequently pivot the rising star into the presidency of independent Kazakhstan.

Nazarbayev was later quick to harness the *Zheltoksan* uprising as a founding myth of independence, but at the time he was more ambivalent. In 1990, he was calling the demonstration 'hooliganism' and claiming protesters had attacked police.[16] However, he made a remarkable U-turn in memoirs published the following year:

> In every person's life there are moments when they are suddenly faced with the problem of a serious choice, making them break with something habitual and comfortable, boding unpredictable difficulties or trials [...] When the people gathered on the square made a rush for the city, I understood I was facing such a choice: either I had to resolve to take action, or calmly return to the Central Committee building. The latter seemed to me an unpardonable betrayal of the people – they were right! I marched with them, at the head of the column.[17]

Thirty years later, Shakhanov, who has a long track record of opposition to Nazarbayev, refused to be drawn on the president's role in *Zheltoksan*, beyond a scornful sound bite: 'He's a two-faced person.'

Shakhanov's bold sally paid off: finally, three years after *Zheltoksan*, Gorbachev agreed to form a commission to investigate. According to testimony provided by one KGB officer, the death toll was not two, as Nazarbayev had stated in 1987, but 168 (155 civilians and 13 members of the security forces).[18] The final injury toll was 1,700.[19]

But there was constant pushback against the commission's work from the powers that be, and that death toll was never officially confirmed. Many *Zheltoksanshylar* did not believe the truth had been established, or that it ever would be. Much that might shed light still remains locked in archives in Moscow, leaving some muttering darkly that it remains a mystery who gave the orders to quell the rebellion so viciously. This is rather convenient for politicians like Nazarbayev, who were top dogs in Kazakhstan's communist leadership at the time.

Kazakhstan was the last Soviet republic to declare its independence in 1991. This was not, as frequently claimed, because Nazarbayev was clinging on to the sinking ship of the USSR, but because he chose with typical political savvy to wait for a portentous date: he declared independence on 16 December 1991, five years to the day after the *Zheltoksan* protests erupted.

The ousted Kunayev, who died in 1993, now has a place in the pantheon of Kazakhstan's founding fathers, and a museum honouring him in his old flat on a leafy Almaty boulevard, where exhibits include a giant vase featuring his portrait and a carpet with his jowly face woven in.

Nowadays, a statue to Kayrat Ryskulbekov stands in Semipalatinsk, where he died on his way to a Russian prison camp. Granted a posthumous medal as a Hero of Kazakhstan, he is no longer a 'hooligan' and 'parasite' but, according to the inscription, a 'fighter for the freedom and independence of Kazakhstan'.

CHAPTER 18

Lure of the Land

Almaty, 2016

Awoman in a bright pink T-shirt is singing snatches of Kazakhstan's rousing national anthem as she is frogmarched away by police in Almaty, her arms twisted painfully behind her back. 'Let go of my arms!' she shouts at the officers, before bursting defiantly into song: 'My country, my land!' she sings spiritedly as they drag her off.[1]

This woman's crime is that she has taken to the streets of her country to mount a defence of its land, which she and hundreds of other demonstrators around Kazakhstan believe is about to be stolen from beneath their feet. This ordinary woman in her thirties is among over a thousand people whose patriotic sentiments will land them behind bars for daring to express their views peacefully on this sunny Saturday morning in May 2016. '*Ni hao!*' chant some of the protesters to the tooled-up security forces arresting them – 'hello' in Mandarin, the language spoken by the people the demonstrators believe are about to grab their land.

'The fate of the land is the fate of the nation!' 'Selling land is selling the motherland!' scream placards waved at rallies around the country, as people from all walks of life march through towns and cities in a show of defiance unseen since the *Zheltoksan* demonstrations three decades earlier. The patriotic spirit has been roused: these national-anthem-singing, *ni-hao*-chanting demonstrators are part of a grass-roots protest movement that has taken the complacent government in Astana by total surprise.

The point at issue seems obscure: the government plans to introduce auctions to expand the sale of farmland to private investors and extend the length of land leases. Some opponents are against land sales per se, believing land is a national asset that should be publicly owned. Others fear the reforms will provide foreigners, hitherto banned from owning land, with a back-door route to buying it up. First in the queue to snap up slices of Kazakhstan, so the logic goes, will be its huge neighbour China, which is buying and leasing farmland around the world to feed its expanding population. The two countries enjoy a cosy partnership, but China is viewed with suspicion by many ordinary people in Kazakhstan, where Beijing's economic footprint has been firmly planted for years. China already controls over a quarter of Kazakhstan's oil.[2] Now anxious Kazakhs fear that acquisitive Chinese are going to grab another of their national assets – their land.

'Sky of golden sun, steppe of golden grain,' sang a thousand-strong crowd gathered on the main square in Atyrau, an oil city in western Kazakhstan, in April 2016.[3] 'My country, my country,' begins the chorus of the national anthem – but, like the woman in the pink T-shirt in Almaty, these protesters sang their own version: *'menin yelim, menin zherim'* ('my country, my land'), before finishing up with the resounding last line: 'My native land – my Kazakhstan!' This was the protest song chanted by the *Zheltoksanshylar* three decades earlier, 'Menin Kazakstanym' ('My Kazakhstan'). For the last ten years, it had been the national anthem, the original amended to include lyrical contributions from Nazarbayev himself.

It was no coincidence that the protesters had chosen this ballad as their protest anthem: it is a rousing ode to the open sky and the bountiful steppe that describes the powerful attachment of Kazakhs to their land. 'Menin Kazakstanym', written in 1956, is widely held to be a sonnet praising the Virgin Lands campaign to make Kazakhstan a breadbasket of the USSR. However, the son of composer Shamshi Kaldayakov disagrees that this was the motive behind the song: he says it was actually a passionate plea against grain being planted on swathes of virgin Kazakh land.[4]

Whatever the original motivation, the song was symbolic, and so was the spot where the Atyrau protesters massed to make their stand: in the shadow of a statue of Makhambet Utemisuly and Isatay Taymanuly, who in the mid-1830s led an uprising against a khan who imposed restrictions on nomads' grazing rights. Nearly two centuries later, the question of sovereignty over the soil had riled Kazakhs again, and protests, often involving just a handful of people or a single person, were breaking out all over Kazakhstan as news spread that land was about to go under the hammer.

For Kazakhs, land had always been an emotive issue. For their nomadic ancestors, the encroachment of foreigners (first Russian colonial settlers, later the Soviets) on their ancestral roaming grounds had ended in the death and displacement of millions of people and the destruction of their traditional way of life. Protests over land rights were certainly nothing new: a century before the Atyrau protests, when Muslims across Central Asia had rebelled against an Imperial Russian conscription order, the uprising had unleashed festering resentments that sent Kazakhs rampaging through villages built by colonial settlers on their roaming grounds. If officials had forgotten that distant grievance, they might have paused to remember a more recent protest, in 2010, when demonstrators in Almaty had used eye-catching stunts to communicate their displeasure at plans to lease land to China: a performance artist ripped the head off a toy panda, and attendees were served up the national dish of *beshbarmak* ('five fingers', hunks of meat on a bed of pasta slabs) made with Peking duck instead of the customary horsemeat or lamb, eaten with chopsticks instead of the hands.[5] Yet still in 2016 the government was caught unawares by the groundswell of public opposition.

Wrong-footed bureaucrats belatedly started explaining that auctioning off land would magic up the cash to kick-start an agricultural revolution, essential to wean Kazakhstan off its addiction to oil. Furthermore, foreigners would merely have limited ownership rights as minority partners, and there were absolutely no plans to sell land to them outright. But the government struggled to bridge its disconnect with the people: they did not believe a word their leaders were saying.

The demos not only refused to die but began spawning new tentacles, and – with the economy in a nosedive because of low oil prices and recession in Russia – what had begun as a small protest movement over a misunderstood agricultural reform was fast becoming a platform to air all manner of grievances: poverty, joblessness, corruption, low wages, soaring debts. Social media were ablaze with outrage, and firebrands began circulating a slogan guaranteed to rattle the government: '*shal ket!*' ('old man out!').

A nationwide day of protest was announced for 21 May, and it threatened to unleash a torrent of discontent.

First, Nazarbayev tried the carrot: he ordered a U-turn, of sorts. Firing two ministers and berating his minions for failing to communicate properly with the recalcitrant public, he slapped a moratorium on the reforms and announced a public debate on what shape they should take. But for those convinced that Kazakhstan was about to sell off its national heritage for a song to a horde of hungry Chinese, it was too little, too late.

It was time for the stick. 'Kazakhstanis don't want Ukrainian events in Kazakhstan, I know that,' Nazarbayev intoned – in his view, where there are demonstrations, revolution is not far behind. He warned people not to 'undermine peace and stability in our common home', threatening the 'toughest measures, so that people know and don't say I didn't warn them'.[6]

Two days before the nationwide demonstrations, police arrested around forty of the most vocal would-be land protesters all over Kazakhstan and slung them in jail for up to fifteen days. They were being punished for a thought crime, guilty not of breaking Kazakhstan's stringent public assembly laws, but merely of thinking of doing so. 'Even the thought of doing something is a criminally punishable offence,' objected Zhanargul Bokayeva, the sister of Maks Bokayev, an activist detained in Atyrau. 'My family and I don't understand how you can punish a person who roots for the fate and future of his country.'[7]

The authorities hoped to decapitate the protest movement, which had sprung from the grass roots since there was no political opposition left in existence to organise it – but it gathered steam: opponents wanted the abolition of the reforms, not a suspension. On 21 May, demonstrators took to the streets of towns and cities across the country, singing the national anthem. They were greeted by tooled-up riot police, who swooped in to make blanket arrests, with squads of masked, balaclava-clad officers – dubbed 'ninjas' by the demonstrators – snatching protesters off the streets, twisting their arms behind their backs and frogmarching them off to throw them into police buses. It was 'the overall atmosphere of a police state', bewailed lawyer Yevgeniy Zhovtis, Kazakhstan's most prominent human rights campaigner, now out of jail after serving his sentence over the fatal traffic accident.[8] The demonstrations were small: here a few dozen people, there a few hundred. The show of force was immense.

Well over a thousand people around Kazakhstan were rounded up, according to tallies compiled by human rights campaigners (no official figures were ever released).[9] 'This is a legal travesty,' complained Marzhan Aspandiyarova, a political activist who – as the sister-in-law of opposition leader Altynbek Sarsenbayev, murdered a decade earlier – had known some dark times. 'I've been an opponent of the current regime for many years and much has happened over these years, and every time you think it can't get worse. But every time it turns out worse. It's very sad. It's very dangerous for the future of the country.'[10] For the third time in a month, she and her husband Ryspek Sarsenbay had been arrested in Almaty, accused of demonstrating against the land reforms, this time on the day of the nationwide protest. Both were found guilty of breaching public assembly laws and given fines. By the government's logic, the protesters were committing a crime simply by being there: rallies required official permission, and no one had permission since the authorities had refused it in all towns where activists had applied – so everyone was breaking the law. Yet all citizens enjoy the right to free and peaceful assembly under Kazakhstan's constitution; arresting them for exercising it was legal nonsense, countered Zhovtis.

Most of the detainees were eventually released without charge, often after spending hours in detention without access to food, water, toilet facilities and lawyers. Fifty-one were tried, of whom four were jailed for short periods, twelve were fined and the others were cautioned.[11] To the government, the detention of more than a thousand peaceful demonstrators was a model policing operation: a crime-prevention exercise, in fact. 'There were no unsanctioned rallies, there were no conflicts with the police, there were no violations of public order,' claimed Igor Lepyokha, a top official in charge of policing (with Orwellian logic, since detaining people had prevented them from committing the crime of staging an 'unsanctioned rally').[12] 'If Mr Lepyokha says there were no unsanctioned rallies, can we ask who those people they arrested are?!' countered an exasperated Zhovtis.[13]

They were quislings with ill designs on the motherland, responded Kazakhstan's TV channels, as a barrage of hysterical innuendo-filled coverage drowned the airwaves. The demonstrators were 'traitors' whose aim was 'to sacrifice our independence', thundered KTK TV, to a drumbeat of ominous music and a backdrop of heart-stopping footage of death and destruction from Middle East war zones.[14] Switching channels, there was swivel-eyed newsreader Aymira Shaukentayeva denouncing the demonstrators as paid stooges acting in foreign interests.[15] The shadowy conspiracy theories seemed to have official backing: Shaukentayeva was the newsreader on First Channel Eurasia, a TV station jointly owned by the Kazakh and Russian governments in which the president's daughter Dariga Nazarbayeva was rumoured to have interests.[16] Called upon to prove these egregious allegations, the channel broadcast hazy footage of dollar bills changing hands that proved nothing at all.

Fake news was in full swing, and the media mud-slingers were using techniques straight out of the Kremlin's playbook, honed on Russian TV in the propaganda war over Ukraine. Although some in Kazakhstan pooh-poohed this binge of poisonous sensationalism, others – reared on a diet of Russian propaganda about the evil conspiracies of the wicked West – swallowed it hook, line and sinker.

In Nazarbayev's Kazakhstan, there was no such thing as public disaffection, so it was a short step from grass-roots protests to heinous conspiracy.

Next came the official explanation: this was not an outpouring of public discontent over land reforms but a plot to topple Nazarbayev, just as the unrest in Zhanaozen had been five years earlier. 'Their ultimate goal was not to hold peaceful meetings and seek changes to the land code, but to destabilise the sociopolitical situation, incite ethnic strife and seize power,' stated the prosecutor's office. 'They knew full well that mass unrest could lead to pogroms, violence, marauding and human casualties. Libya, Syria, Egypt and a number of post-Soviet countries offer graphic examples of the consequences of such events.'[17]

Every plot needs an evil mastermind. Who was behind this one?

To widespread amazement, the ringleader was named as brewery owner Tokhtar Tuleshov, a businessman from Shymkent in southern Kazakhstan who had been little known until his arrest a few months earlier on charges of weapons and drugs possession. This relative unknown had been plotting an audacious coup d'état from behind bars, prosecutors claimed. The 'beer king' had been arrested three months before the protests had begun, but, undeterred, had continued to foment his conspiracy from his cell. Perusing the techniques of revolutions that had toppled presidents in Kyrgyzstan in 2005 and 2010, Tuleshov had latched on to discontent over the land reforms to stir up unrest with the aim of provoking sufficient chaos to get himself installed as vice-president of Kazakhstan as a springboard into power – no matter that this position had been abolished twenty years previously. Sympathetic military officers stationed in southern Kazakhstan had acted as the muscle behind this plot, helping him form a private militia using the armed forces – all apparently unbeknown to the Defence Ministry.

The theory sounded 'fanciful', as political pundit Tolganay Umbetaliyeva remarked.[18] However, investigators were adamant this was Tuleshov's plan. To prove his lust for power, the KNB produced a trump card: a photo of Tuleshov sitting in a chair gazing at Akorda, Nazarbayev's presidential palace. This was touted as iron proof of the ambitions of a man they depicted as a criminal kingpin with links to the Russian mafia.[19] His mishmash of motives for seeking to overthrow the state included a striving for power and a need for cash to pay off millions of dollars in debts run up through his 'bohemian lifestyle'.[20] In Soviet-speak, 'bohemian' was a derogatory term for nonconformists that was often associated with dissidents; here it was psychobabble to blacken the defendant's character. Tuleshov was yet another 'bohemian' with his sights on Nazarbayev's throne: opposition leader Vladimir Kozlov had been described as a 'bohemian personality' when he was jailed over the 2011 Zhanaozen unrest-cum-coup conspiracy. Tuleshov admitted everything, although his explanation of his desire to raise his own pro-file by overthrowing Nazarbayev (to 'boost my image', as he put it) was rather hazy.[21] Many were baffled at this theory, as it appeared so riddled with holes. Perhaps it was a sign of political clan warfare, with Tuleshov a 'pawn' in a power game, puzzled pundit Dosym Satpayev.[22]

Tuleshov's trial in a closed military court left no one any the wiser. The litany of crimes of which he was convicted – coup plotting, murder, kidnapping, running a crime ring and possession of weapons and drugs – landed him a 21-year jail sentence.

Next up in the dock were Maks Bokayev and Talgat Ayan, the alleged foot soldiers of Tuleshov's revolution. Both men were civil society campaigners from Atyrau, known for their activism in causes both high-flown (political freedoms) and practical (oil workers' rights, the price of electricity). Now they were charged with three serious crimes, all carrying long jail terms: disseminating false information, breaching public assembly laws and incitement.

The incitement charge falls under a broad crime outlined in Article 174 of the Criminal Code: 'incitement to social, ethnic, tribal, racial, class or religious strife', which human rights campaigners had previously called on the government to abolish because, as Zhovtis had put it, the charge can, 'given the desire, be used against inconvenient dissidents and political opponents'.[23] Indeed, it had been; this was one charge under which Kozlov had been jailed for allegedly fomenting fatal unrest in Zhanaozen five years earlier. It had also been wielded against social media users for writing posts officials deemed suspect: from two opposition activists briefly jailed in 2016 for discussing on Facebook snatches of an unpublished book written two decades previously, to the man incarcerated in 2016 for three years for calling Putin a 'fascist' and accusing him of stoking separatism in Ukraine.[24] In Zhovtis's words, this abuse of Article 174 'for the persecution of dissidents' risked turning Kazakhstan 'into a police state moving closer to totalitarianism'.[25]

Bokayev and Ayan had been vocal at the Atyrau demonstration against the land reforms in April, and now investigators claimed the two had taken $100,000 from the power-mad businessman-cum-crime boss Tuleshov to do his bidding. They protested that they had never met the entrepreneur, but Tuleshov testified that he had talent-spotted them as rabble-rousers from media reports and headhunted them into his revolutionary plot. 'I'm a teacher, and not even my schoolchildren believe the fairy tale that Tuleshov from Shymkent gave my son $100,000 after once seeing him on television during his one-man picket against utility tariff rises!' Ayan's shocked mother exclaimed.[26]

In the eyes of the authorities, the two activists were dangerous demagogues whose grass-roots activism had nearly toppled the foundations of the state. In the eyes of their supporters, they were scapegoats who were now facing a kangaroo court because the protests had embarrassed the powers that be. In the eyes of Amnesty International, they were 'prisoners of conscience detained solely for peacefully exercising their rights to freedom of expression and peaceful assembly'.[27]

'I am a Kazakh who has died a thousand times and been resurrected a thousand times,' proclaimed Talgat Ayan in a lofty last statement to the court, referencing the famous Soviet-era poem 'Men Kazakpyn' ('I Am a Kazakh'). 'Our ancestors didn't spare their lives for the sake of defending the land and the motherland. Kazakhs are a resolute, bold, courageous and heroic people. Our history, our boundless expanses and our land are confirmation of this. Defending it is not a crime. So my conscience is clear: I am not guilty.'[28]

This lyrical defence did not wash with the judge, who proclaimed Ayan and Bokayev guilty and sentenced them to five years in jail. They greeted the verdict with defiantly raised fists.

'How can the right to assemble, the right to freedom of speech and the right to take part in government – these are three fundamental rights, aren't they, which are enshrined both in the constitution and in international agreements, the International Covenant on Civil and Political Rights – be shifted onto the level of criminally punishable deeds?' asked Zhanargul Bokayeva, sister of Maks Bokayev, sipping a cappuccino in Starbucks in a flashy Almaty mall shortly after her brother was incarcerated. 'These are basic rights which should be treated very carefully, because the line is very fragile. But here the constitution and constitutional rights were treated lightly.' (Eighteen months later, in April 2018, Ayan's sentence was commuted after he had served a third of the term, and he was released from prison to serve the rest of the sentence with restrictions on his freedom of movement, but Bokayev remained behind bars).[29]

A smartly turned-out paralegal with a gentle manner, who eschewed emotion in favour of precise references to the letter of the law, Zhanargul was on her lunch break: she was back in her day job after a gruelling six weeks fighting on her brother's defence team at the trial in Atyrau, which had ended with a lengthy sentence despite what she believed should have been an unimpeachable defence: 'They were simply exercising their rights according to the constitution, that's it.' In Kazakhstan, 'expressing a negative opinion about government policy is not a crime', as Human Rights Watch had pointed out before the trial.[30] The watchdog slammed the verdict as a 'miscarriage of justice', while the EU deemed it the 'criminalisation of dissenting opinions'.[31]

'You know, everyone harbours hope,' said Zhanargul, brushing aside a strand of her stylish, short, wispy hair with manicured scarlet nails. She had harboured two types of hope: 'when you believe as a relative' in a fair outcome, and 'when you believe absolutely in the abstract' in the justice system delivering justice. 'But when the verdict was delivered on 28 November, these two pillars collapsed, to be honest.'

Her 43-year-old brother would serve his sentence in a penal colony in the city of Petropavlovsk in northern Kazakhstan some 1,500 kilometres from home, so family visits would be difficult. To make matters worse, he was in ill health, suffering from hepatitis C. Yet she was looking on the bright side; 'otherwise, how can you go on living?' she asked rhetorically. 'There are a lot of negative aspects,' she conceded, but 'our late father always taught us to seek positive aspects in negative things and negative aspects in positive things – to maintain that balance. And our mother is the ripe old age of seventy-five, so we need to support our mother. If we just give up and weep, what kind of example will we be showing? So we stay quite positive and believe.'

That seemed hard, with her brother serving a long jail term for a peaceful demonstration over land reforms that had by now been kicked into the long grass (Nazarbayev had shelved them until 2021), but Zhanargul could make the leap: 'What I've found to be positive for myself about this is that my brother is not broken. He's not broken, and we are not broken. And the worst thing, I think, is to crush a person morally, to kill off the human being in him. We have remained human beings.'

When Bokayev finally walked out of prison on a freezing, foggy day in February 2021, he headed straight back to that symbolic spot where it had all begun: the square in Atyrau, named after two local heroes who had led a nomads' rebellion against an imperious khan over land rights two centuries previously and where Bokayev had staged a peaceful demonstration against land reforms five years earlier that had set him on a collision course with the government and landed him in jail. Fist raised in a symbol of defiance, the veteran activist pledged not to abandon his fight for democratic freedoms – despite draconian restrictions slapped on him now he was free. His three-year ban on engaging in public activity after his release, part of his original sentence, prohibited him from joining movements, including political parties; participating in community events, including peaceful protests; working with civil society groups and doing voluntary work; and giving media interviews. The courts had also placed a host of limitations on his private life, such as a night-time curfew and a ban on going to restaurants.

True to form, Bokayev was defiant: he considered himself 'illegally convicted and innocent' and would not bow to such 'ridiculous restrictions'. 'I did not serve four and a half years in prison to come out and keep quiet,' Bokayev said with a chuckle after his release. 'When I deem it necessary, I am going to express my opinion. When I deem it necessary, I am going to go out to peaceful demonstrations. I reserve the right to act within the constitution of Kazakhstan and the International Covenant on Civil and Political Rights.' After all, 'if I had preferred to keep quiet, I might not have served time at all'.[32]

That sensitive topic of land was back on the agenda, as the moratorium on reforms imposed to stem the protests in 2016 was expiring. 'I'm not against market relations,' Bokayev clarified, but 'I am convinced, and I was convinced then, that it was very dangerous to entrust the sale of land [...] to our bureaucrats.' Of course, 'no one can put land in their pocket and take it away', but rampant corruption among officials who would be responsible for land distribution and shoddy oversight made sales and leases to foreigners risky. Acutely sensitive to these concerns that had sparked mass protests five years earlier, shortly afterwards Toqayev approved a law banning sales and leases of land to foreigners altogether.[33] So the 2016 protests achieved their aim in 2021, though Bokayev had paid the price with his stint in jail.

While he had been inside, Kazakhstan had changed presidents, but Bokayev was unimpressed with the new political arrangements. Nazarbayev pulling the strings as *Yelbasy* – 'something like a king' – was an 'archaism', he said, shrugging off reforms enacted by Toqayev to create his 'Listening State' as 'cosmetic'. Bokayev listed a litany of reforms he believed essential for his country: 'We need supremacy of the law; we need democratic institutions; we need a modern electoral system in which the most varied parties can participate; we need to change party legislation; we need decentralisation.' He had had ample time in prison to hone not only his political philosophy but also his skill at communicating it in layman's terms. In jail, where many prisoners practised boxing, he would reach for a sporting analogy to explain the value of democracy. Just as a boxer cannot land a strong blow without getting his stance correct, 'if we want our country to develop, our petrodollars not to disappear in vain, the homes our builders construct not to fall down in a year, our roads not to be washed away at the first snow, we need democratic institutions, we need a free press, we need freedom of assembly'.

Standing up for his convictions trumped any concerns he harboured about facing another spell in jail for breaching those draconian restrictions. 'I don't want to go prison, of course,' concluded Bokayev. But 'what remains to be done, if our country is such that a person can go to prison for his convictions?'.

CHAPTER 19

Homeward Bound

Almaty, 2016/2014/
Olgiy, Mongolia, 2009/
Lake Kanas, China, 2007

For Amangul Akilbek, Kazakhstan is the land of promise. She was born in a far-flung village in China, but moving to Kazakhstan has turned her life around. 'It's actually called Kumak, but I call it End of the Road,' she jokes, speaking of her birthplace in Xinjiang on China's north-western fringe.

Amangul, slight, bright-eyed and looking younger than her thirty-two years, arrived in Kazakhstan in 2004 at the age of nineteen, driven by a determination to escape a life of drudgery in a village where she saw no prospects. 'There's nothing, there's no work, there's no opportunity to work,' she says. 'People just survive day by day. They only live off the land. [...] Because that's the only income.'

There are around 1.5 million Kazakhs living in China.[1] For much of the twentieth century they were cut off from their brethren in Kazakhstan by the Sino-Soviet border – but nowadays the government is luring them to come and live in the motherland. Amangul is one of over a million Kazakhs who have resettled here from foreign lands in the three decades since independence, uprooting from countries near and far to throw in their lot with the new Kazakhstan. She is a '*kandas*', which means 'blood relation' and is the official status given to foreign-born Kazakhs who have, with the government's encouragement, chosen to make Kazakhstan their home. Informally, they are often called '*oralman*', which means 'returnee', implying a 'return' to their 'historical homeland', although many of them have never set foot in Kazakhstan before.

Amangul's first glimpse of the country came after she gave up her old life in China and uprooted 1,500 kilometres west to make a new one in Kazakhstan. Chafing at the limitations of village life in Xinjiang, she could have opted to join China's rural-to-urban exodus and moved to the bustling provincial capital, Urumqi, or further afield to the industrial powerhouses on China's eastern seaboard. Instead she looked west, to her 'historical homeland', enticed by the prospect of new opportunities in a country that welcomes Kazakhs from around the world with open arms.

Like many *oralmandar*, Amangul found settling into a strange country a struggle: she faced not only a massive culture shock, but also a totally unexpected language barrier in Kazakhstan, where the lingua franca is not Kazakh but Russian, of which she spoke not a word. Yet despite a few hiccups acclimatising, Amangul has never really looked back. 'I feel here is home,' she says contentedly, looking out of the window of her flat in Almaty at the snow-dusted trees on a February evening in 2016.

When the Soviet Union collapsed in 1991 there were around 5 million Kazakhs living outside the borders of newly independent Kazakhstan, across Europe and Asia, from the shores of the Caspian to the coast of the Black Sea. Some were living on ancestral lands their forefathers had roamed for centuries, in countries bordering Kazakhstan like Russia, Uzbekistan, Turkmenistan, Mongolia and China. Others were descendants of Kazakh families sent scattering around the world by war, revolution, famine and repression, who ended up in countries as distant and disparate as Afghanistan, Turkey, Iran and China.

Amangul's grandfather Dinmukhamed Dospayuly was born into the famine in the early 1930s in a village in eastern Kazakhstan near the town of Ayagoz, 275 kilometres from the Sino-Soviet border. 'He was the first child,' Amangul said, recounting the tale passed down by her grandmother, Aysha Mukhametkyzy. 'When he was only one and a half years old, his mother carried him across the mountains. She walked for many, many days.' Fleeing the *Asharshylyk*, Amangul's great-grandmother stole across the Chinese border with her baby in her arms, travelling with her mother-in-law (her husband had disappeared, presumed dead). After walking for days, fearing attack by starving wolves, they came across some nomadic Kazakhs, who took them into their *aul* and saved them from starvation.

Her great-grandmother later remarried and settled in a village called Zhylan Til ('Snake's Tongue'), where her grandfather got an education and became a teacher. He married Amangul's grandmother, who had had a sad life: Aysha Mukhametkyzy had been thrown out of her home by her mother-in-law because her husband had run off to Kazakhstan in the 1950s, and her husband's family had kept her two sons. 'They blamed her for her husband leaving. They thought my grandma was bad luck for this home,' Amangul explained, showing photos on her mobile phone of a striking old lady with an aquiline nose. 'She was a lost soul.' After her grandfather died, Amangul suggested searching for the two sons her grandmother had been forced to abandon all those years ago, but the old lady refused, and in 2016 she passed away. 'She never saw her [first] two children again.'

Aysha Mukhametkyzy started a new family with Dinmukhamed Dospayuly and gave birth to Amangul's father, but in 1962 a political upheaval occurred that landed her husband in jail. Mao Zedong's China and Nikita Khrushchev's USSR fell out amid geopolitical rivalry and disagreements over communist doctrine in what became the Sino-Soviet split. Moscow threw open the border, to encourage the Turkic peoples of Xinjiang to immigrate into the Soviet Union, intending to undermine China and foment nationalism on its borders. Uighurs (the region's most numerous people) and Kazakhs crossed into Soviet Kazakhstan in droves. Amangul's grandfather and the other men in the village 'took all the horses to the border and left', planning to send for their families later – but for reasons family lore has not recorded, he soon returned. He was arrested by the Chinese authorities, deemed a ringleader of the flight of able-bodied men from Zhylan Til and thrown into jail, where he spent the next seventeen years. After his release, the family moved to Kumak, where Amangul was born.

'I don't think there was a normal life for me in China,' mused Amangul. 'I wanted to somehow get connected to Kazakhstan.'

Ironically, it was to escape the expectations of her traditional Kazakh family – an early marriage, children and a lifetime of filial and parental duty – that Amangul moved to Kazakhstan in 2004, eyeing her independence and the opportunities created by the oil boom in her new homeland. She was bright and ambitious, but her chances of getting a decent education and forging a career at home were slim. Brought up in a family of four children (her parents exempt, as members of an ethnic minority, from Beijing's one-child policy), Amangul did not go to school until she was nine. 'Nobody thought I should go to school. I was taking care of my brother, because in my village a boy is the biggest treasure in life. I became responsible for my brother's life. [...] I took care of him, so I had no time to go to school.' She almost started school when she was eight, but her grandfather, who by then was the village mullah, ordered her instead to spend her days helping out in the home of her pregnant aunt. 'I said: no, I'm going to school! But my grandpa ordered: you, child, go to take care of your aunt, because she's more important. Children's studies – they can study any time; and girls – you don't need to study.'

Amangul eventually went to school and managed to complete her secondary education, but there was no money for her to go to university. There was not much cash in the family, not least because her father gambled it away at cards, and any spare would go on tuition fees for her brother, who went to university and went on to join the police force in Urumqi. Deprived of opportunities at home, Amangul dreamed of Kazakhstan as the land where she could stand on her own two feet.

News of the *oralman* programme reached villages in outlying areas of China both from Kazakh diplomats, who toured Kazakh-inhabited regions publicising the perks the government was offering, and also by word of mouth, from tales brought back by those who had made the move to Kazakhstan returning to visit relatives – which is how Amangul heard of it. In the teeth of opposition from her parents, she badgered an *oralman* uncle who was a cross-border trader between Xinjiang and Kazakhstan to take her to live with his family in a village in south-eastern Kazakhstan. It was a scary move, but also an exciting one. 'I didn't know my destiny,' she says. But through sheer grit and determination to make a better life, she arrived in Kazakhstan as an *oralman* at the age of nineteen.

Amangul is one of over a million[2] Kazakhs who have answered the clarion call the new country put out after independence to its brethren around the world: come 'home' to Kazakhstan, your 'historic homeland'. 'The doors of Kazakhstan are always wide open for every Kazakh who loves their motherland,' as Nazarbayev put it in 2017.[3] The emotional tug on their heartstrings was backed by hard-nosed financial perks, which have varied over the years but have included relocation payments, travel subsidies, housing, fast-tracked citizenship, support in finding jobs and credit to start businesses.

Astana presented its *oralman* programme as a way for Kazakhstan to do its historical duty by the Kazakhs blown abroad by the winds of history – but it was also a response to the demographic conundrum the country confronted when it was parachuted into independence.

Kazakhstan's demographic potpourri was a national security concern, albeit one the government avoided voicing for fear of affronting the Kremlin and its own minorities. But with Kazakhs in a minority and separatist sentiments erupting along the Russian border, there was a nagging worry that the ethnic mix could prove combustible. Luring some of the Kazakhs living abroad at the fall of the Soviet Union (around 5 million, compared to 6.5 million in Kazakhstan at the time) to their 'historical homeland' could ease the demographic legacy. Officially, it was an economic imperative to boost the tiny population of this massive country, where at independence 16.5 million people were living in a state the size of western Europe – but as Nazarbayev cast around for a way to redress a demographic balance knocked out of kilter by the tumult of the Stalin era, the *oralmandar* were the answer.

Amangul arrived full of high hopes for a new life in Kazakhstan, but culture shock soon set in. For many *oralmandar* accustomed to village life in rural China or Mongolia, modern lifestyles in Soviet-influenced Kazakhstan, particularly its Russified urban areas, came as a surprise. 'For me everything was shocking,' laughed Amangul – but nothing more so than the unexpected language barrier that arose to cut her off from her new countrymen. 'I thought for me it wouldn't be difficult, I speak Kazakh,' said Amangul, her eyes widening in amazement at the memory over a decade later. 'But in Almaty everybody spoke Russian! It really struck me. When I first came here I only survived by speaking Kazakh.' At independence, many Kazakhs who grew up speaking Russian at school and at home were unable to speak Kazakh at all. (There is even a derogatory term for such people: *shala kazak*, a 'halfway' Kazakh who has lost the language and culture.)

Many *oralmandar* speak Russian because they grew up in other former Soviet states such as Russia, Turkmenistan and Uzbekistan – but for Kazakhs from countries like China, Mongolia and Iran, the language barrier is immense. 'Russian is not my language!' exclaimed Bekzat Dalilbek, another young *oralman* from Xinjiang. 'Why should I speak Russian in my own homeland?!'

Ironically, Bekzat's family relocated to Kazakhstan from their village in Xinjiang when she was eighteen partly because her parents feared the children were losing their native tongue. 'We were learning Chinese at school and at home we were speaking Chinese,' she said, describing an assimilation process identical to that undergone by Kazakhs in Soviet Kazakhstan. 'My parents didn't like it. They told us: at home you should speak Kazakh,' explained the young professional, sitting one evening in summer 2014 in a trendy café in Almaty, where she worked as a translator for a Chinese oil company. Yet moving to Kazakhstan to safeguard their language, the family wound up in a country where many people speak no Kazakh, and her parents still had to communicate with Russian speakers using sign language. Both Bekzat and Amangul ended up paying for private language lessons to navigate life in Kazakhstan, and are now fluent in Russian as well as Kazakh, Mandarin and English. Without Russian, says Bekzat, *oralmandar* are squeezed out of the job market, and 'they also feel like visitors, not like people who are living here – they're not accepted'. (To address this problem of acceptance, Toqayev decreed not long after he became president that the term *oralman*, with its connotations of coming from outside, should be officially replaced with the term *kandas*, with its connotations of kinship.[4])

Worse still, some of the new arrivals cannot even read their own language: in Kazakhstan, Kazakh is written in Cyrillic, like Russian, while in China the Arabic script is used (as it was in Kazakhstan until 1929, when the Soviets ordered it replaced first by Latin then, in 1940, by Cyrillic). That is changing again – after Nazarbayev in 2017 decreed a switch to Latin for Kazakh by 2025, later postponed to 2031, the gradual introduction of a modified Latin alphabet has begun – but for now it is another barrier. 'I couldn't read anything, I couldn't even write. I just thought I must be very dumb – I just can't do it!' recollected Amangul.

There were times when the language and culture shock became too much for her. 'I couldn't speak properly, it's from so much struggling in my life, changing my country, totally different people, my voice could get blocked,' she said quietly. 'I stopped speaking, I couldn't even cry.' Compounding the language barrier were cultural differences between the life she was used to and life in Kazakhstan. 'I even have a barrier of understanding with the local Kazakhs. I feel I'm smaller than them. Kazakhstan Kazakhs – they're very proud, they're all European even though they're Asian!' she joked.

Nazarbayev hoped his countrymen would welcome the *oralmandar* with open arms, but some have been less than enthusiastic. Some migrants have settled in easily – particularly those from former Soviet states, who make up well over half of the total. Of the 1.08 million *oralmandar* who arrived in Kazakhstan over the first thirty years of independence (to make up nearly 6 per cent of the national population by 2021), half (49.9 per cent) came from one Central Asian neighbour, Uzbekistan (most from Karakalpakstan, a region of Uzbekistan abutting western Kazakhstan); 6.8 per cent came from Turkmenistan; 1.5 per cent from Russia; and 0.7 per cent from Kyrgyzstan.[5] They have found it fairly easy to integrate linguistically and culturally into a similar post-Soviet society, but others from countries like China (32.8 per cent); Mongolia (5.1 per cent); Afghanistan (1.2 per cent); and Iran (0.8 per cent) have often faced serious problems fitting in with what is, to many, a very different way of life. This has fuelled a widespread perception that the 'returnees' are uneducated freeloaders cashing in on the government's generous incentives to lure them to the motherland. In fact, of those who arrived in the programme's first twenty-five years, 80 per cent had completed their secondary education and 10 per cent had a higher education; only 10 per cent had no education at all.[6]

The perks have varied over the years, but these are vastly inflated in the popular imagination: fear of migrants is not limited to Western countries. *Oralmandar* are criticised by some Russians and other minorities who resent the influx of Kazakhs that is altering the country's ethnic and linguistic mix, but also by some Kazakhstan-born Kazakhs who begrudge the provision of financial incentives to incomers. This is not helped by stories – many apocryphal, some true – of *oralmandar* moving to Kazakhstan to pick up the cash then immediately heading back home. Yet many *kandastar* are the opposite of the stereotype, like Amangul and Bekzat: bright, ambitious, determined and go-getting – qualities any country would dream of harnessing for its workforce. Bekzat, who has a degree in Mandarin and English from a Kazakh university, is used to taxi drivers complaining to her: 'Why does the government give people from China and Mongolia so much money? Why don't they give it to people from Kazakhstan to make their lives better?'

Kazakhstan should, she says, 'celebrate as a country' the arrival of the *kandastar*; after all, the reunification of Kazakhs scattered far and wide was made possible by the fall of the Soviet Union. Her family is a case in point: her father had been separated from his sister for three decades by geopolitics until the USSR collapsed, making contact possible again. In 1965, her aunt left China for Soviet Kazakhstan during the Sino-Soviet split, and her father did not see his sister again until he visited her in Kazakhstan in 1993.

Eleven years after his emotional reunion with his sister, Bekzat's father moved the family from their village in Xinjiang to his sister's adopted village in eastern Kazakhstan. 'If we'd stayed in China, we also could have got a good job and had a good life,' Bekzat said, but the family embraced the *oralman* life out of a sense of 'patriotism'.

The *oralman* programme has combined with an exodus of Russians and other groups in the post-independence years to cause a tectonic shift in Kazakhstan's demographics. By 2021, the share of Kazakhs in the population had risen from 40 per cent to 70 per cent and the share of the other largest ethnic group, Russians, had fallen from 37 per cent to just under 16 per cent.[7] Kazakhstan's two main cities used to be predominantly Russian; now Kazakhs dominate. Nur-Sultan's Kazakh population hit 80 per cent in 2021, up from 17 per cent at independence (when it was a still a backwater called Akmola and not yet Kazakhstan's capital); Almaty's Kazakh population had risen from 22 per cent to 62 per cent.[8] In the north along the border with Russia, the number of pockets where Kazakhs remain in the minority is shrinking, leaving only two provinces in which Kazakhs were outnumbered by other groups in 2021 (North Kazakhstan and Kostanay). Since 2014 the government has (with limited success) targeted incentives to shift the flow of *oralmandar* northwards, officially to combat a looming labour shortage in regions depopulated by emigration – but this would also 'Kazakhify' towns along the

Russian border, boosting the Kazakh population and making these areas linguistically and culturally more Kazakh.

This made some Russians nervous, but for Kazakhs frustrated at slow progress in reversing centuries of Russification in Kazakhstan, the inflow of *kandastar* has been welcome. Some view Kazakhs from non-Soviet countries like China and Mongolia as the guardians of Kazakh language and culture that were eroded in Kazakhstan during colonial times. *Oralmandar* have not only swelled the ranks of Kazakh speakers in Kazakhstan, but they have also 'brought with them the culture that we forgot when Russification occurred', as Kazakh community leader Dos Kushim once put it. 'They've brought with them the culture of our ancestors, the culture of our grandparents.'[9]

At a family party in western Mongolia in August 2009, the guest of honour toddled along, her legs tied together with sheep innards. Kazakhs celebrate milestones in a child's early life with a series of festivities, from the *besik toy* (cradle party) after the birth to the *tusaukeser* ('cut the shackle') ceremony when the child starts walking. At this festivity, a symbolic string is tied around the child's ankles and snipped by a respected person whose laudable qualities the parents hope will rub off on their offspring. At this party in the Altay Mountains of western Mongolia, sheep innards were being used as string to make it extra special: this was a *besik toy* and a *tusaukeser* rolled into one, since many relatives were seeing the child for the first time. She was born a Kazakh citizen to *oralman* parents from western Mongolia who had settled over the border in eastern Kazakhstan.

Sparsely populated Mongolia lost nearly half of its population of ethnic Kazakhs to Kazakhstan in the first couple of decades of the *oralman* programme, lured by the magnet of a country in the midst of an oil boom.[10] 'There are more prospects there,' said Adilbek, a young driver from the town of Olgiy, who was mulling making the move himself. This is the provincial capital of the province of Bayan-Olgiy, a sleepy place where yurts jostle for space with houses and paved roads peter out into muddy tracks. This is where most of Mongolia's Kazakhs live, 1,600 kilometres west of the capital Ulaanbaatar. The closest city is Ust-Kamenogorsk in eastern Kazakhstan (500 kilometres as the crow flies across the Altay Mountains, or 850 kilometres by road through Russia), whose hustle and bustle contrasts with Olgiy's laid-back rural vibe.

Here, the nomadic way of life that was wiped out in the 1930s in Kazakhstan lives on. In August, the Kazakhs were still up in the *zhaylau* (summer pastures), and the rolling green lowlands were strewn with belongings they had left behind to return to when the time came for the autumn *kosh* (migration). In one meadow, a wooden *shanyrak* – the crisscrossed wooden top of a yurt – stood propped against a cattle stockade alongside a sheepskin and a lone cowboy boot.

In Bayan-Olgiy ('Rich Cradle' in Mongolian), 90 per cent of the population was Kazakh, and the exodus of *oralmandar* to Kazakhstan had had a tangible, albeit hard to quantify, knock-on effect on their country of origin. Popular prejudices in Kazakhstan notwithstanding, far from all *oralmandar* are uneducated shepherds, and emigration had left a 'negative impact' on the local community, said a journalist at the broadcasting centre in Olgiy. 'We've already experienced an outflow of members of the intelligentsia, and our political and intellectual potential has decreased,' explained Ospan Nabi, taking a breather to chat between radio shows. Seriktes Shadet, the province's deputy governor, estimated that 87,000 Kazakhs had left Mongolia between 1991 and 2009, leaving around 100,000 still there. (By 2020, the Kazakh population of Mongolia numbered 120,000.)

The Kazakhs and Mongols rub along with few frictions, despite speaking different languages and practising different religions – the Mongols are Buddhists, the Kazakhs Muslims, as the minaret of Olgiy's mosque nestling against the dramatic alpine backdrop suggests – but the economic pull of oil-rich Kazakhstan was making many turn their faces west. 'We don't have discrimination,' said Adilbek. 'The problem is we have limited jobs, and lots of students and young people are joining the workforce every year.'

In China, it is a different story.

'We were born here, this is our homeland – but now we have to buy it,' grumbled an elderly Kazakh man in August 2007, sitting by the shore of the crescent-shaped glacial Lake Kanas glittering turquoise in the Altay Mountains in the north-western tip of China, not far from where Amangul was born. Surrounded by dense taiga giving way to sweeping meadows, this is a prime area for livestock breeding, which is the mainstay of the Kazakh nomadic lifestyle – but this way of life was under threat in this far-flung corner of the world. 'Pressure's increasing with every year,' complained Kayrat, a twenty-something Kazakh speaking under a pseudonym for fear of reprisals from the Chinese government. 'We have to move out of here.'

Kayrat's ancestral roaming grounds fell inside a national park created to promote tourism and protect the delicate ecosystem, but now the Kazakhs were being displaced by development. It was late summer and the family had moved to the *kuzdeu* (autumn pastures), where four generations of his family were living in their small wooden house, but he believed it would not be long before they were pushed out of the park and off their ancestral lands altogether. Others told similar tales: they had been 'requested' to relocate their homes, or banned from pitching their yurts in parts of the park. There were yurts in the main tourist village in the middle of the park, but they were kitschy souvenir shops rather than family dwellings.

The Kazakhs complained that they were the last to cash in on the tourist boom that was driving them off their land: most of the tourist-trade workers hailed from elsewhere in China, and the cash was swelling the coffers of Han Chinese businessmen from outside who owned the luxury hotels and fancy restaurants that had mushroomed around the lake, their orange and yellow facades garish against the green taiga.

To make a few yuan from the passing trade, Kazakhs like Kayrat's family had resorted to sending their children out with the family goats to offer photo opportunities for visitors, who were mostly from the swelling middle classes driving China's domestic tourism boom. Tourist buses noisily plied a new road through the park to the once tranquil lake, and the air rang with the shouts of rafters clad in fluorescent life-jackets, zooming down the pristine waters of the Kanas River.

Lake Kanas is part of the Ili Kazakh Autonomous Prefecture, where Beijing would a decade later open a sprawling network of concentration camps as part of an iron-fisted crackdown on minorities in a region where the government had for years struggled to quell a separatist insurgency waged by Uighurs fighting for their own homeland on the borders of post-Soviet Central Asia. The Kazakhs of Xinjiang would be among an estimated one million people caught up in a dragnet of detentions and dispatched to undergo political indoctrination in what the world dubbed 're-education camps' while the Chinese government tried to pass them off as 'vocational training centres'. The pressure on their lifestyles that the Kazakhs living around Lake Kanas in 2007 so vividly described was a harbinger of this policy of mass incarceration of ethnic minorities in Xinjiang which later shocked the world. Beijing had long since been encouraging migration into the region from other parts of China, which had brought Han Chinese flocking there. This signature policy, officially part of a strategy to encourage economic development but also a tacit plan to coax recalcitrant minorities to integrate their lifestyles with the Chinese mainstream, was nicknamed Go West. But the Kazakhs of Xinjiang could already Go West – to Kazakhstan.

The *kandas* programme has had its hiccups, but it has certainly been a game changer for Kazakhstan's demographics.

It has also changed individual lives. Amangul achieved her dream of obtaining a higher education. She passed the Kazakh school-leaving exam, helped by teachers who coached her free of charge, then won a government grant to do a teaching degree in English and Mandarin at an Almaty college. She went on to work in a company in the oil sector which needed her language skills, and she also privately tutored students in Mandarin. 'I'm glad I'm through this difficult stage and I've come out a better person,' she said, of her years adapting to life in Kazakhstan. 'All my life I learnt to be a survivor,' she added with a smile. 'At least I can change my own life!'

Bekzat, the oil company translator, was also positive about her move to her 'historical homeland': 'It's a great step my parents took for me in my life, bringing me here.' And it is good for Kazakhstan too. 'People from other countries love Kazakhstan more than the locals, I think. The people who come here – we will love our country. My children will love this land also. They'll be ready to give their blood for this motherland.'

CHAPTER 20

Behind the Red Wall

Almaty, 2017–21

'Don't torture Kazakhs!' 'Freedom!' The chants shatter the calm of a residential street in Almaty that is shimmering in the heat one morning in May 2021. Police link arms to create a human shield to prevent a small group of protesters from advancing towards their target: the consulate of the People's Republic of China, whose red flag flutters proudly against the bright blue sky. The half dozen people picketing the consulate are demanding answers from Chinese diplomats about the fates of their relatives, who are among a million or more members of ethnic minorities sucked into the vortex of a sprawling network of 're-education camps' in China's Xinjiang province, which borders Kazakhstan. To these Kazakhs who were born in China and now live in Kazakhstan, that red flag flying above the consulate is less symbol of pride in their country of birth and more red rag: the icon of a state that has incarcerated their relatives. Today marks the 100th straight day that members of Almaty's community of Chinese-born Kazakhs who have answered the government's call to move to Kazakhstan have been picketing this diplomatic mission demanding freedom for their relatives.

A little old lady with a big voice pushes at the police line and harangues the officers, her head, swathed in a white headscarf, not reaching their chests. Three of this widow's four sons are locked up in Xinjiang: one in prison, two in one of the detention facilities that the world has taken to calling 're-education camps', since they are political indoctrination centres designed to re-programme detainees' brains to think in a manner the

Chinese leadership deems acceptable for its citizens. Beijing, eventually forced to admit to the existence of these facilities, has a different name for the barbed-wire-encircled sites: 'vocational training centres' that are benevolently teaching the minorities of Xinjiang – mainly Turkic-speaking Muslim peoples, like the Kazakhs – skills to better themselves in life. These people picketing the consulate use a less euphemistic name: 'concentration camps'. 'China, release my children! Shut down your camps!' cries Khalida Akytkhan, the old lady, in her sonorous voice. 'Stop imprisoning Kazakhs!'

Gulzira Auelkhan knows what it is like to undergo 're-education' in one of these camps. In July 2017 she decided to pop over the border from Kazakhstan into Xinjiang to deal with some paperwork, because officials kept ringing her relatives demanding she come in person. Little did she know that her week-long visit would turn into an eighteen-month nightmare, as she was caught up in the dragnet of detentions sweeping Xinjiang. 'I decided to go there for a week. My daughter, aged three, was left behind,' she said, pointing at a little girl called Bayan running around in a pink onesie, who once featured in a heartrending video posted online pleading with the Chinese authorities to release her mother. 'Then they detained me at Korgas.' Korgas in Kazakh and Khorgos in Russian, this is the main border crossing between Kazakhstan and China, and the site of a free trade zone held up as a symbol of the Sino-Kazakh alliance. For China, this cog in its flagship Belt and Road global infrastructure project is a gateway to the west for its consumer goods. For Kazakhstan, it is a tangible symbol of the role it desires to play as the 'buckle' in the Belt and Road, a crossroads on the east-west transit route that officials dream of turning into a new Silk Road. As Gulzira crossed into China, she was immediately detained, one of many Kazakhs lured back under false pretences to deal with paperwork only to be thrown behind bars. 'I was taken alone in a car with the siren on to the village where I had registration. They took fingerprints and blood samples from my fingers, and they took pictures of me from different angles,' she said of her surprise detention at a time when the existence of the nascent camp system was not common knowledge. The data harvested from her would be part of a Xinjiang-wide programme to collect biometrics for a Big Brother-style mass surveillance campaign that would flag up behaviour deviating from the government-approved norm to allow the authorities to pick out 'untrustworthy' citizens.[1]

Speaking in Almaty in January 2020 in an interview in the office of Atajurt Eriktileri (Volunteers of the Fatherland), an organisation collecting testimony and publicising the plight of the detainees, Gulzira remembered her relief when she was allowed to go and spend the night with her brother-in-law. But when she went to the police station to ask for her ID to travel to a nearby village, she heard some shocking news. 'I went to the police to tell them I wanted to go to see my father, but they told me that I would go to learn to write in Chinese for fifteen days. I told them that I wanted to see my father and spend a night there, but they didn't let me,' recalled Gulzira, dressed in a black woolly dress against the winter chill and a loosely tied green and purple patterned headscarf. She was driven to a camp housing around 800 women. 'They put camp clothing on me. When I got there they interrogated me, asking why I had gone to Kazakhstan. They asked if I had relatives in prison or in the courts or in the police, how many children I had.' She had no idea why she had been detained, but the interrogation contained a clue that she would not have picked up on. Contacts with people abroad were now considered suspect, and Kazakhstan – although a loyal Chinese ally – was one of twenty-six states included on a list of 'sensitive countries' drawn up by the Chinese government. 'People who have been to these countries, have families, or otherwise communicate with people there' would be 'interrogated, detained, and even tried and imprisoned', Human Rights Watch later reported.[2] This automatically made every single Chinese-born Kazakh living in Kazakhstan and their relatives in China objects of suspicion in the eyes of a paranoid, all-controlling state. 'I have not heard their voices since 2017,' said Khalida Akytkhan, the widow protesting at the Chinese consulate in Almaty in 2021, of her fourteen grandchildren left behind in China, some of whom had ended up in a children's home while their parents were in the camps. She dreamt of seeing her sons and grandchildren again. 'If all three sons come [to Kazakhstan], my heart will probably burst with joy,' she said. 'They have not managed to scatter so much as a fistful of earth on the grave of their father. I do not know if they will even manage to bury me. If I manage to bid farewell to my children and grandchildren before death, surely I cannot dream of more?'[3]

Bemusing as her incarceration was, Gulzira could at least count the days until her release. Yet when the time was up, there was more bad news: she would be 'volunteering' for more time behind bars. 'After fifteen days I wasn't released,' she said. 'They told me I would be sent to do some studies for a year, and that I was signing up for it voluntarily. I asked why. They said: you've been abroad. In Xinjiang there are restrictions on visiting twenty-six countries. Kazakhstan is a country posing a security threat.' This was news to Gulzira, and no doubt to the Kazakh government, which had never given China cause to doubt its loyalty – and was not about to jeopardise that strategic relationship over abuses perpetrated against Kazakhs in Xinjiang. It would find itself in an increasingly awkward position as news of China's system of concentration camps exploded in the international media, and the Atajurt organisation became a focal point for publicity as one of the few places where foreign journalists (barred from Xinjiang) could meet ex-detainees and prisoners' relatives and hear about their experiences.

In the camp, the rules were strict, and enforcement was harsh. 'We were fifty women in a class and there were five teachers and two guards, so seven people in charge,' Gulzira explained. 'We had to raise our hands to get permission to scratch our bodies. We had to raise our hands to ask permission to reach out for something. Otherwise the guards would punish us. We had to ask permission to use the toilet. Fifty women were given two minutes each within half an hour [...] If we used it for three or four minutes, they would taser us.' They lived on potatoes, dumplings and rice, and were made to eat pork, a forbidden food for Muslims. 'They warned us against not eating it, they threatened us.'

In the classroom, lessons alternated between Mandarin language and political indoctrination to inculcate a love for China and for Xi Jinping, the president whose rule has been characterised by an uncompromising stance on bringing those seen as wayward into line across that vast country: from Xinjiang in the north-west to Hong Kong in the southeast, non-conformism is not tolerated, be that the distinctive lifestyles of minorities or the aspirations of pro-democracy campaigners. 'We praised Xi Jinping and the party. We thanked the government. They told us to write *mea culpas* for going to Kazakhstan,' Gulzira recalled. 'In the mornings we sang red songs' – odes to communism and the party. The inmates were told that to become model citizens – and get released – they must learn to speak Mandarin fluently, and abandon their faith. 'They told us not to have religion: don't consider yourself Muslim.' They were lectured about integrating with the Han Chinese in Xinjiang, where the different communities had tended to live separate lives: they should 'eat together, sleep together and visit each other'. The authorities would take that principle to extremes by billeting Han Chinese 'guests' in the homes of minorities in Xinjiang – Uighurs, Kazakhs, Kyrgyz and Hui, Mandarin-speaking Muslims of Chinese ancestry who also have their own distinctive lifestyle and culture – in a dystopian campaign with the cheery-sounding name 'Becoming Family'.[4]

Whenever Gulzira asked the guards about her release date, 'they told me that they were suspicious of my ideology, that I hadn't changed my ideology'. What did they want from her? 'They wanted us not to think about anything, to think that I'm not Kazakh, that I don't have any religion, that I belong to the Chinese, that I am living thanks to the party and to Xi Jinping. But I thought I was Kazakh, and maybe Allah would protect me.' Then an astonishing thing happened: 'They just all of a sudden released me – I don't know why.' She suspected that her husband raising a hue and cry in Kazakhstan, with Atajurt's assistance, had helped.

Still her ordeal was not over. 'I spent five days at my father's house. Then they told me that I wouldn't go back to Kazakhstan yet, but would work for three months. So they took me to a slave factory.' Gulzira became one of many ex-detainees despatched, along with other Xinjiang residents, as forced labourers to factories and cotton fields in the region and beyond.[5] She was promised a monthly wage of 600 yuan to sew gloves destined for Western markets, but was paid around a third of that – '0.1 yuan for one pair of gloves' – and forced to sign a pledge to work in the factory for a year. But in January 2019, she was allowed to return home to Kazakhstan without explanation, and in 2021 she left with her family to seek asylum in the United States.[6]

So had those months of indoctrination worked – what did Gulzira feel for the Communist Party and Xi now? 'Hatred,' she responded, without missing a beat. Life in Xinjiang was freer before Xi launched this blitzkrieg to change mentalities and lifestyles, she believed. 'We had our own customs and traditions.' That will not be the case for the minorities of Xinjiang for much longer, if China's programme of social engineering succeeds.

Singing, dancing, painting, rug-weaving and flower-arranging: Gulzira did not mention these activities featuring on her daily agenda during her months in a camp. But once Beijing was forced to abandon denial in favour of damage control, it claimed this was the type of activity on offer in 'education and training centres' teaching minorities vocational skills such as hairdressing, garment-making and car maintenance as part of an anti-extremism programme in Xinjiang.[7] 'Many trainees have said that they were previously affected by extremist thought and had never participated in such kinds of art and sports activities, and now they have realised that life can be so colourful,' gushed Shohrat Zakir, the head of Xinjiang's government (an Uighur himself), in 2018.[8] The world's media was now full of harrowing stories about the detention without charge of at least a million innocent people in up to 1,400 internment camps across Xinjiang, where torture and sexual abuse were reported to be rife.[9]

In Chinese doublespeak, these places were a benign tool in a campaign to win hearts and minds in a restive region plagued by violence, rather than a brutal instrument designed to eradicate the culture and identity of minorities in order to fashion model Chinese citizens out of them in a process akin to a Cultural Revolution for the twenty-first century. 'Xinjiang officials claim the root of these problems is the "problematic ideas" of Turkic Muslims,' Human Rights Watch reported in 2018. 'These ideas include what authorities describe as extreme religious dogmas, but also any non-Han Chinese sense of identity, be it Islamic, Turkic, Uighur, or Kazakh. Authorities insist that such beliefs and affinities must be "corrected" or "eradicated."'[10] For the Kazakhs as a people, this was the second time in nearly a century that they had faced an integration drive specifically designed to uproot their way of life. There are disturbing echoes here of the eradication of the nomadic lifestyle in Kazakhstan in the 1930s by a government determined to corral a wayward minority into conformity with the Soviet mainstream.

Long-standing tensions between Xinjiang's Han community and minorities – particularly the Uighurs, the most numerous – have given rise to a Uighur separatist movement and sparked bouts of violence over the years. The tensions are rooted in resentments that the officially encouraged influx of Han settlers, combined with government policies to suppress the speaking of indigenous languages and stringent controls on religion, jeopardises minorities' traditional cultures and lifestyles.[11]

The share of Hans in Xinjiang's population rose from 7 per cent in 1949, when the People's Republic of China was born, to 42 per cent in 2020, while the Uighur community shrank from 75 per cent to 45 per cent.[12] Intercommunal tensions have spiralled into ethnic violence, most devastatingly in 2009, when 200 people died in clashes between Uighurs and Hans.[13] Couching its policies in the language of fighting the 'three evils' of 'terrorism, separatism and extremism', Beijing points to violence associated with a separatist movement demanding independence for a region that secessionists call 'East Turkestan' or 'Uighurstan' as justification for its actions.[14] (At one anti-China protest in Almaty in 2019, demonstrators displayed a map showing a dismembered China without 'Uighurstan', Tibet and some northern territories.) There have been fatal attacks with proven or suspected links to Uighurs using explosives and knives in the region itself and in other parts of China, and Uighur militants have joined up with global jihadi groups fighting in the Middle East and Afghanistan.[15] But iron-fisted clampdowns, known as 'Strike Hard' campaigns, have failed to break the cycle of violence and fuelled further resentments as ever more innocent people have been caught up in the repressions, which have expanded beyond the embattled Uighur community to the region's other minorities, including the Kazakhs, since Chen Quanguo – notorious for suppressing the restive region of Tibet – became Xinjiang's Communist Party secretary in 2016. The 're-education camps' opened soon afterwards. By 2019 the government, now in damage-control mode, was claiming the 'vocational training centres' had virtually emptied out as most inmates had 'graduated'[16] – although many had 'graduated' to become slave labourers, like Gulzira, or been sent to mainstream prisons to serve lengthy terms on spurious charges.

Tactics to force the people of Xinjiang to fit the official mould have not been limited to incarcerating them in institutions. Out on the streets, old-fashioned police-state methods of coercion and control have been combined with modern hi-tech surveillance technology to create an Orwellian living environment, so 'the treatment of all Turkic Muslims in Xinjiang – those held inside detention facilities and those ostensibly free – bears disturbing similarities', according to Human Rights Watch.[17] This includes political indoctrination sessions both inside and outside the camps; restrictions on freedom of movement 'ranging from house arrest, to being barred from leaving their locales, to being prevented from leaving the country'; sanctions for worshipping that have 'effec-tively outlawed Islam'; and snooping by 'neighbours, officials, and tech-enabled mass surveillance systems'. There have also been reports of forced sterilisation and abortion campaigns in Xinjiang, to suppress birth rates among minorities.[18] China resolutely denies all such abuses.

As claims of these atrocities trickled out to the outside world, an interna-tional furore erupted – albeit one divided along the lines of realpolitik. China's foes lined up to vilify it, while allies and client states – including many of the world's most powerful Muslim-majority nations – rushed to defend the camps as part of 'counter-terrorism and deradicalisation measures in Xinjiang' and 'commend China's remarkable achievements in the field of human rights'.[19] The US administration has accused China, a chief rival and geopolitical foe, of perpetrating 'genocide' – a claim Beijing dismissed as 'outrageous lies'.[20] Other Western governments have joined the United States in imposing sanctions on Chinese officials,[21] but shied away from the 'genocide' label amid hot debates about whether this onslaught against minority lifestyles fits the definition. China's critics have argued that it fits not only the original definition of trying to 'destroy the essential foundations of the life' of a people, but also the UN's definition of 'intent to destroy, in whole or in part, a national, ethnical, racial or religious group'.[22] Some have argued that what the powers that be are perpetrating against minorities in Xinjiang is at the very least a cultural genocide, since it appears designed to eradicate minority life-styles and cultures. China has hit back in the combative 'wolf warrior' style of diplomacy which Beijing has adopted under Xi. The 'basic facts show that there has never been so-called genocide, forced labour or religious oppression in Xinjiang', Wang Yi, the foreign minister, told the UN Human Rights Council in 2021. 'Such inflammatory accusations are fabricated out of ignorance and prejudice, they are simply malicious and politically driven hype and couldn't be further from the truth.' Xinjiang was now a haven of 'social stability and sound development' after four years without any 'terrorist case'.[23]

The international furore left Kazakhstan tiptoeing along a diplomatic tightrope as it tried to pacify calls to protect ethnic Kazakhs abroad while avoiding antagonising its mighty neighbour and ally. It quietly declined to put its name to letters fawning over Beijing, but refrained from publicly

criticising China in favour of behind-the-scenes diplomacy, while pointing out that it had limited room for manoeuvre to help Kazakhs who
were Chinese citizens. The government, which had for decades been
encouraging Kazakhs abroad to move to Kazakhstan, was not always
generous to Kazakhs fleeing from Xinjiang to seek sanctuary. Several
were tried and convicted for illegally crossing the border – like Sayragul
Sauytbay, a whistle-blower whose public testimony during her trial in
Kazakhstan about goings-on in the camps in China, where she had
worked as an instructor, caused a sensation in 2017. Sweden granted her
asylum when Kazakhstan failed to step up – a sop to China, supporters
assumed – and, conveniently for the government, she moved there – to
a place of safety, albeit one with a language and lifestyle alien to her.[24]

The government's hands may have been tied by the niceties of diplomacy, but it has not welcomed more forthright efforts to publicise the
plight of Kazakhs in Xinjiang, namely from Atajurt. As the international
furore mounted, the government's solution would not be to press China
to stop the repression but to pressure Atajurt to shut up.

'There are two dangers – first the Chinese side kidnap me or kill me, second
the Kazakhs arrest me,' said Serikzhan Bilash airily as he strode around the
Atajurt office in front of a wall plastered with photographs of detainees on
a snowy afternoon in January 2020. The flamboyant founder of Atajurt,
a Chinese-born Kazakh who had moved to Kazakhstan as an *oralman*
two decades earlier and was a naturalised citizen, was making dangerous
enemies on two fronts from his high-profile activism over the Xinjiang
camps. He had recently been released from a six-month spell of house arrest
with a conviction on incitement charges – and was not supposed to be
fronting Atajurt at all anymore. One of the conditions for his release under
a plea bargain that saw him escape a prison term on charges of stirring up
racial hatred was that he would halt the activism that was a thorn in the
side of both the Kazakh and Chinese governments. 'It was that or seven
years in jail,' Serikzhan said after his release in August 2019.[25] 'I had no
choice.' But here he was months later, back at Atajurt, greeting a stream of
visitors arriving to give testimony about detained relatives. After breaking
off to shake hands with the son of an imam incarcerated in Xinjiang, he
recalled how one day in 2018 Atajurt had stayed open until the early hours
recording testimonies from 147 relatives of detainees. Reporters from the

world's top media outlets had tramped through Atajurt's premises, and the distressing tales they heard there formed the basis of stories about the 're-education camps' that were beamed around the world at a time when reporting from inside Xinjiang was impossible.

The resulting international outcry had not been to the liking of China, which had accused Serikzhan of harbouring 'ulterior motives to make things up'.[26] Nor was the Kazakh government a fan of his firebrand style of activism, which became grounds – or pretext – for his arrest in March 2019. Security officers detained him in a dramatic swoop on a hotel in Almaty, and spirited him a thousand kilometres north to the capital to face charges of incitement that he denied, related to a fiery speech in which he had called for 'jihad' against China. This rabblerousing side of Serikzhan, which went down a storm with listeners when he got onto an oratory roll in his native Kazakh, was a far cry from the clean-shaven, besuited man with the jokey persona who would meet and greet foreign journalists in his fluent but idiosyncratic English at Atajurt. In fact, there had been some judicious editing of the video of his speech to justify his arrest – 'trickery', in his words. Yes, he had called for a 'jihad' against 'infidels', 'communists' and 'godless people' – but he had specified a non-violent one. 'Today's jihad is an information and ideological jihad,' he had cried. 'Are we ready for this jihad?!'[27]

Serikzhan's arrest made headlines around the world and was later criticised by the United Nations Working Group on Arbitrary Detention, which found that he had been detained in violation of international law for 'the exercise of his freedom of expression and freedom of association'.[28] With characteristic bombast, Serikzhan said he had been jailed for his power to influence public opinion through his brilliant oratorical skills: 'I could let [Kazakhs] believe in their power as a nation', in the 'fight for a just cause'. No wonder his critics – and there were plenty of them – accused him of demagoguery and hubris as he appeared to revel in the role of martyr to the cause, using his final court appearance to accuse China of committing 'genocide' in Xinjiang – a word he had been warned by Kazakh officials to stop using, he said – while supporters gathered outside chanting for his freedom. Those sticking up for him were almost all Xinjiang-born Kazakhs, for whom this man with a larger-than-life personality was an idol, while the rampant abuses against their brethren in China had not gained much traction among wider society in Kazakhstan, which seemed to see it as something of a niche concern. But such was Serikzhan's international clout that he was released with a plea bargain, an unusual act of clemency in a criminal justice system that usually treats dissidents harshly.

Atajurt was down but not out: a government-backed splinter group had been granted registration, in a typical divide-and-rule tactic that the authorities had previously used to split political opposition, while the Serikzhan-loyal wing, Nagyz Atajurt Eriktileri (Real Volunteers of the Fatherland), continued operating without registration, which had been refused every time they had applied. But what was Serikzhan doing there at all, since his sentencing conditions included a pledge not to head a public organisation for seven years – which was supposed to end his activism once and for all? 'I'm a cleaner and a driver and a translator, not the leader,' he shot back, with an irrepressible grin.

Just as Serikzhan would not let up on his advocacy, the pressure would not let up on him. In August 2020 he was fined for involvement with an unregistered organisation, and – facing possible further criminal charges, as well as surveillance and harassment – he left Kazakhstan for Turkey, then moved on to the United States.[29] He carried on publicising the cause via social media while his organisation kept up its work in Kazakhstan, though international interest had waned as the world, by now in the grip of the pandemic, moved on.

But Atajurt had been instrumental in getting the word out to the world about China's internment camps. Someone had to speak out, said Serikzhan, reaching for a sound-bite and reprising the famous Nazi-era quote about shrugging off responsibility for atrocities. 'Before they were arresting Kazakhs, they arrested Uighurs. Before they arrested Uighurs, they arrested the Tibetans. Before they arrested the Tibetans, they arrested the Falun Gong,' he declaimed. 'While Falun Gong was arrested by the Chinese Communist Party, we kept silent because we are not Falun Gong. While they began to kill millions of Tibetans, we kept silent because we are not Tibetans. [...] While they began to arrest and kill millions of Uighurs, we kept silent because we are not Uighurs, even though we are [of the] same origin, Turkic people.' And when they arrested the Kazakhs, he concluded with a flourish, there was nobody left to 'listen to our cry'.

His words were brimming with characteristic hyperbole, but that last part was not true. Serikzhan and Atajurt had provided a glimpse beyond the veil of secrecy into the horrors unfolding in Xinjiang – so someone did hear the cry of the detainees.

The first day of July 2021 was a special day for China: the centenary of the Chinese Communist Party, which the country was celebrating with pomp and ceremony – and Kazakhstan was determined to ensure nobody would spoil the party mood.

When Baibolat Kunbolat, a well-known face among relatives of detainees who had been picketing the Chinese consulate in Almaty for months, left home that morning, he was plunged into a terrifying situation. 'I left home and went towards my car, and I immediately noticed two people walking beside me, without police uniforms. I immediately thought: maybe they're Chinese secret service,' he explained a week later, sitting in the sunshine on the terrace of an Almaty café on a summer's morning. 'I had the feeling that maybe someone would grab me and take me somewhere, and I didn't know what would happen next. I was very afraid.'

This affable, mild-mannered man had started protesting at Chinese diplomatic missions in 2020, after learning of the incarceration of his younger brother in China, initially turning up for pickets dressed in a black jumpsuit with his hands in symbolic shackles. Police had already arrested him five times, and twice he had been jailed for short periods over what were deemed illegal public assemblies. He had walked free from his latest prison term two days earlier, and had intended to go and film a picket at the consulate on the day of the centenary (he was no longer participating in case of arrest, but simply videoing the action). But when he heard that the would-be participants had all been rounded up when leaving their homes to thwart the protest, he set off to visit his mother instead.

Accustomed as Baibolat was to run-ins with the police, he felt there was something very wrong when the two men in plainclothes snatched his mobile phone, grabbed his arms and pushed him towards an unmarked car. A man in police uniform appeared and joined the fray, but refused to show ID because it was 'left behind in the police station', which made Baibolat 'even more frightened'. The trio bundled him into the unmarked car and handcuffed him, he recalled, demonstrating the scars on his wrists from where the cuffs had cut into them, still visible a week later. Baibolat had moved to Kazakhstan as an *oralman* two decades earlier and was a naturalised citizen, but one thing that flashed through his mind was recent attacks on two Chinese-born Kazakhs who had fled repression in Xinjiang and been violently assaulted on exactly the same day in Kazakhstan but a thousand kilometres apart.[30] Against this backdrop of violence, Baibolat feared the worst. 'I asked them: why are you arresting me? They didn't say. I asked: where's the warrant? They didn't show anything. So I harboured very big suspicions. They could be people working for China who wanted to do something to me. They could kill me, they could beat me up, they could put me in a box and send me to China – anything could happen.'

Fortunately, none of that did happen. The men drove Baibolat to a police station, where a Kafkaesque interrogation lasted throughout the day and into the evening, with his mother and wife also hauled in for questioning. The interrogator would ask him why he had disobeyed police orders; he would reply that he had no way of knowing these people were police, then ask why he had been detained; the interrogator would respond that he would be told in due course. This circular line of questioning continued – with a break for lunch, brought from the police canteen – until evening, when an officer drove them home after their twelve-hour ordeal, 'and that was it'. 'I asked: why did you arrest us? Tell us the reason.' said Baibolat. 'They said: no reason, we just wanted to treat you to lunch.' As Baibolat said: 'It was the 100th anniversary of the Chinese Communist Party. They just didn't want us to go to the consulate.'

Baibolat, now aged thirty-nine, had dreamt of moving to his 'historical homeland' since he was a child. 'When I was little I thought all Kazakhs lived where we were living', in a village in Xinjiang where there were only two Han Chinese, he laughed. 'When I heard there was a place called Kazakhstan in the world [...], a homeland for us Kazakhs, Kazakhstan, I immediately wanted to come to Kazakhstan,' he remembered with a smile. 'All my relatives were against it. They said: why go to Kazakhstan? You don't have any relatives there, you don't know anyone, and we've heard that everyone speaks Russian!' But he was obstinate: 'I'm still going to Kazakhstan.' It took him three years to jump through the bureaucratic hoops to get a passport in China, but in 2002, aged nineteen, he crossed the border. 'When I saw the flag of Kazakhstan fluttering at the Korgas border crossing, I was really happy. I came to

Almaty on that same day, and I've been living in Almaty since.' His parents moved over a few years later, followed by his younger brother, Baimurat Nauryzbek, who started studying at university but returned to China to look after his ailing aunt and uncle (who had brought him up, so he used their surname). By a strange twist of fate, he ended up recruited by the police as an assistant, at a time when they had urgent need of good Mandarin speakers as the crackdown on minorities began in Xinjiang. 'He worked there, then in March 2018 he was taken to a concentration camp,' said Baibolat flatly. 'They were arresting people every day – some days fifteen, some days twenty, by order.' The family was shocked but kept quiet, hoping Baimurat would do his stint in the camp and then be freed. But after eighteen months they heard some terrible news: the young man had not been released from the camp but sent to serve a long sentence in prison. 'When I heard that he had been sentenced to ten years, it was awful for me and my parents,' said Baibolat. The family could not obtain information from relatives in China, because it was too dangerous for them to talk to people in Kazakhstan and they would hang up the phone. That was when Baibolat started picketing Chinese diplomatic missions in Kazakhstan, and that was how he learnt what had happened to his brother. Chinese diplomats promised to look into the case, then sent him a message explaining his brother had been sentenced to ten years over an article inciting racial hatred that he had allegedly posted online in 2012. 'I don't think he did, because in 2012 he was at university in Kazakhstan. How could he write it?' And even if he had, why did it take so long to arrest him, wondered Baibolat, pointing out that China's security services are assiduous in tracking down online dissent, so 'why six years later, when this Chinese genocide was starting?'. His brother would have automatically fallen under suspicion for having been in Kazakhstan, and perhaps for the 'crime' of having WhatsApp on his phone: it is deemed suspect because residents are expected to communicate via China's homegrown WeChat, which conveniently doubles up as a surveillance tool.[31]

Baimurat is one of many detainees who have been released from re-education camps only to be swallowed up in the prison system to serve long sentences on spurious charges, a development that Gene Bunin, the creator of the Xinjiang Victims Database,[32] has described as 'Xinjiang's next great human rights catastrophe'. Noting efforts 'to whitewash the camps – through media propaganda, Potemkin tours, and solicited diplomatic approval', he wrote in 2019 that official statistics and relatives' testimony suggested that 'an incredible number of those detained in 2017 and 2018 are now being given lengthy sentences and transferred to major prisons'.[33]

By summer 2021 Baibolat was hearing unofficially that the Kazakh authorities were tiring of his outspoken advocacy and were thinking of bringing criminal charges against him that could see him put behind bars for several years. 'My mother would suffer most: one son locked up in prison in China and if another gets locked up in Kazakhstan, this would be a great misfortune for my family,' he acknowledged sadly. But he would not stop, he said, quoting a Kazakh proverb: 'The fatherland starts with the family.' 'If I can't defend my family today, how will I defend my homeland tomorrow?' asked this man who had spent his childhood in China dreaming of living in Kazakhstan. 'I have set myself the goal of defending my brother, because he is innocent. I am not going to stop until he comes to Kazakhstan.'

III

STORIES FROM
THE STEPPE

CHAPTER 21

Keeping the Faith

Korobikha, 2010

Valentina Murzintseva is a strong believer in the power of faith. 'True faith existed in the past,' she says, gesturing dramatically around the glinting icon-stuffed church she has built with her own hands in the shadow of the brooding Altay Mountains. 'And it still does!'

Valentina Mikhaylovna (her patronymic) should know: she erected this little church twenty years ago in the hamlet of Korobikha, near where the borders of Kazakhstan, Russia and China collide, to give thanks to God for healing her from a life-threatening illness. As this devout 75-year-old remembers it, God obliged by sending a star to raise her from her sickbed.

'I was very ill for three months and I was lying in bed, and then a star lifted me up,' she explains chattily, a reverent look passing over her wrinkled face as she relives the memory on a summer's day in 2010. 'I was lifted up by that star – I didn't need hospitals or anything like that. I got better, and now it's been twenty years, no hospitals.' She cannot recall the exact diagnosis, but 'it just passed on its own and I got better – God forgave me and extended my life'. To thank the Almighty for his divine intervention, she decided she was destined to build a church. 'Maybe it's not much of a church,' she adds modestly, 'but it's still a church. The cross was raised over it!' Atop the wooden roof, the cross glints against the forested slopes rising behind the Peter and Paul Church, a neat white building with door and window frames gaily painted blue and green. 'I painted it and whitewashed it. I did everything,' she says. 'I bought everything with my own money.'

Valentina Mikhaylovna is an Old Believer, and her presence here in the deepest recesses of the Altay Mountains can be traced back to a dispute within the Russian Orthodox Church nearly half a millennium ago, though she speaks of it as if it were yesterday. 'We're Old Believers,' she says proudly, perched on a bench beside a green plastic bowl she uses to baptise babies, gilded icons and crosses glinting in shafts of August sunlight pouring through the windows after a rain shower. 'When Patriarch Nikon was there, he started to involve everyone in his innovations, and then this happened and everyone started to flee in different directions.'

The 'innovations' are over 450 years old, liturgical reforms introduced in 1653 by the head of the Russian Orthodox Church, Patriarch Nikon, whose name is still a dirty word for Old Believers today. The changes caused uproar among traditionalists who rejected the newfangled ways, and they became known as *Starovery* (Old Believers) or *Staroobryadtsy* (Old Ritualists). The reforms ended up sparking the *raskol* – the schism – in 1666 that sent dissenters scattering to the fringes of the Russian Empire to escape reprisals for sticking to the old ways. 'They're *Nikonovtsy* and we're *Starovery*, and that's that,' sniffs Valentina Mikhaylovna of the millions of Russian Orthodox mainstream faithful, using a dismissive term that loosely translates as 'Nikonov acolytes' to reinforce that the old grudges still die hard. 'We can't pray together!'

'This happened in the times of Patriarch Nikon, when the Old Believers were persecuted,' explained eighteen-year-old Viveya Kazachenko, a devoted member of the faith who is living proof that it is not only the older generation that harbours this centuries-old grievance. 'They had to run away from the long arm of the tsar, they had to run to different corners of the world.' Viveya is the daughter of an Old Believer priest in Ust-Kamenogorsk, Korobikha's nearest city, and she knows all about the seventeenth-century ecclesiastical drama because the memories were passed down from generation to generation as the persecution of Old Believers served only to harden their faith.

The detested Patriarch Nikon may have ended up causing the *raskol*, but his intention was actually to boost Orthodox unity through his reforms, by driving the practices of the Russian church into line with those of the Orthodox Greeks. The changes covered liturgical fine points like how many fingers should be used to make the sign of the cross, whether processions should circle the church clockwise or anticlockwise and how many letters the name Jesus should contain – details which may appear abstruse to outsiders, but still matter a lot to Old Believers in the present day.

'The Russian Orthodox Church does it like this,' explained Viveya, standing in her father's church and demonstrating the curved two-fingered cross of mainstream Orthodoxy. 'And our cross is like this,' she continued, showing the straighter-fingered sign of the Old Believers. 'This finger represents God the father' – she showed her index finger – 'and this' – the middle finger – 'is the human being, the son he sent to us in human form, and this finger is bent, because the human being bows to the divinity. And these three fingers' – the thumb and last two fingers of her hand – 'represent the holy trinity: the father, son and holy spirit. And so,' concluded Viveya with a flourish, 'we cross ourselves: first on the forehead, then on the stomach, then on the right shoulder and then on the left!'

Viveya was standing, fresh-faced and with a mane of chestnut hair in a ponytail, in front of a panel of elegant icons and a gold incense holder in the Church of Protection of the Holy Mother of God, built in a quiet residential neighbourhood in gritty Ust-Kamenogorsk by Father Gleb, the priest who is her father. Sent to northern Kazakhstan by his church from his native Belarus two decades previously, Father Gleb was in charge of the diocese of Kazakhstan's Old Believer community, based in the north-eastern part of the country where the dissenters settled in far-flung spots offering natural refuges from persecution. After nearly half a millennium of ecclesiastical acrimony, he was not hopeful about the chances of a reconciliation between the mainstream Orthodox Church and the *Starovery*. 'What kind of relations can there be?' asked the priest. 'Simply none, you might say. Because this difference of opinion has long since taken shape, this attitude to these totally unnecessary reforms of the seventeenth century, and this hasn't changed. I see no sign of rap-prochement. And it's not even necessary for the moment.'

Valentina Mikhaylovna's family had lived around here for generations: she was the descendent of Don Cossacks who fled the persecution of Old Believers in Russia and ended up in Kazakhstan, 4,000 kilometres from the Kremlin and the headquarters of the Russian Orthodox Church in Moscow. The hamlet of Korobikha was founded in 1792 by an Old Believer named Korobitsyn, as the dissenters pushed into ever more remote areas to escape the scrutiny of the state. That was over a century after the schism, which scattered the *Starovery* much further around the world than this: there are communities as far afield as the United States, Canada, Australia and South America.

Even nowadays, Korobikha is a challenge to reach. It lies in Kazakhstan's easternmost corner 1,400 kilometres from the capital, eight hours' drive from the nearest city, Ust-Kamenogorsk, and a couple of hours from the nearest town, Katonkaragay, at the end of a rutted track lined with birches, poplars and sunflowers that swayed brightly in the summer breeze as the Bastyrma River churned alongside.

This bucolic setting with its spectacular alpine backdrop looked idyllic, but life was hard in this isolated community. Korobikha had no running water, and the villagers survived by growing their own food and harvesting Altay honey, famed for its quality, which they sold for cash or bartered in Katonkaragay for clothes and household goods. These days, many villagers (who are almost all Russians) were escaping the harsh rural life to move to towns in Kazakhstan or over the border in Russia, but some still preferred a traditional life, living off the land. 'I get insomnia in the city,' said Yevgeniya Kashkarova, Valentina Mikhaylovna's 49-year-old daughter, who preferred to be called by her diminutive name Zhenya. 'I've been there and I couldn't sleep – what a racket! So many people!' said this softly spoken, delicate-featured woman, with her hair tucked into a silvery-green headscarf. 'Here we work for ourselves and live for ourselves. There you have to work from morning until night, indoors all the time, not in the outdoors, in nature. I don't like that.' Here, the only sounds were the thwack of her burly teenage sons chopping wood and the gentle lowing of the family's cows.

After milking her cows in the morning, Zhenya headed up to her beehives, an hour's march up the mountainside along a track squelchy with mud after the summer shower. At the top stood a clutch of hives that her parents inherited from the *kolkhoz* where they used to work when it went bankrupt after the USSR collapsed – history going full circle, since these hives must have been seized from Old Believers during collectivisation. 'Beekeeping's interesting work,' said Zhenya enthusiastically, donning her meshed mask and thick gloves. 'It's labour-intensive, but it's interesting.' As the bees swarmed out to greet her in a buzzy, fuzzy mass, she elaborated on their missions in the hive: 'Each bee has a job to do: some bring up the children, some bring water to the hive, some bring nectar.' Casually gesturing up the slopes as her vicious-looking dog began barking menacingly, Zhenya added: 'There's a bear around somewhere. The dog barks and the bear senses there's something fierce in the beehive, and it won't go there.'

In a good year, her bees made fifty kilograms of honey, and the family also sold the pollen, little brown grains that taste like flowers, and propolis, a resin which humans rate as a health balm. 'They feed themselves and they feed us!' said Zhenya admiringly, looking fondly at the furry creatures buzzing around.

In Korobikha not everyone was an Old Believer, and not all the Old Believers were practising, but the faith was strong in the family of Valentina Mikhaylovna, a widow with five children, ten grandchildren and five great-grandchildren. Her daughter Zhenya was brought up in a strong religious tradition, and she was raising her own three offspring in the same spirit. 'Of course I am, so the children know where they've come from, what their faith was, what to adhere to, what holidays to observe,' she said in her kitchen back in Korobikha, over a glass of mead produced by her bees, while the Soyuz TV channel run by the mainstream Russian Orthodox Church kept up a steady stream of chanting in the background. 'I tell mine, but I don't know how it'll work out in future.'

The Old Believers' staunch faith has seen them through centuries of persecution under the Russian Empire that continued into Soviet times, when this oppression was directed at religion in general ('the opium of the people', in Karl Marx's dismissive definition) rather than their faith specifically. 'When Soviet power came, they hid everything,' said Raisa Sagdiyeva, a 72-year-old relative who had dropped round for tea, swaddled in two headscarves and a padded purple jacket: it was chilly up in the mountains, even in August. 'My grandfather was in Katonkaragay. They gathered all the icons and they told him: take them away. He went round the houses and distributed them all around, my grandfather did, my mother's father.' The icons were buried to save them from destruction by the militant atheists of the Soviet state, she explained in a tremulous voice, and the older generation passed down their traditions to keep the faith alive. 'Each house had its grandmother, and they continued to pray,' concurred Zhenya. 'Those who continued and believed, they'd gather in someone's house and pray. They still stuck to their faith.' The old lady, who was born in these parts in 1938, recounted family lore to back this up: 'I don't remember the 1940s, but I heard from my grandfather that they stuck to their faith, they hid from the authorities.' There were no churches around here when she was young: the Old Believer church in Katonkaragay was smashed up by the Soviets, and she still remembered tales of how people who stole items from the debris would run into bad luck: breaking their arms or legs, suffering the death of a loved one. Undeterred by the Soviets' distaste for religion, this old lady had her son secretly baptised as an Old Believer in 1957, four years after Stalin's death. By then, she said nonchalantly, 'it was calm – there was no strong persecution.'

These days, Old Believers face no persecution in Kazakhstan – but they face a different challenge. 'The size of the congregation's fallen sharply, because many leave for Russia,' explained Father Gleb, referring to his church in Ust-Kamenogorsk. 'There is, of course, one main reason: the future for the younger generation.' Drawn by better economic prospects over the border in Siberia or by the emotional pull of living in their 'historical homeland', Russia, many Old Believer families had left villages they had inhabited for generations, and the exodus had led to dwindling congregations of *Starovery*: since he had become priest two decades previously, Father Gleb's flock in Ust-Kamenogorsk had shrunk by more than half, from about 150 to 70. No one knew how many Old Believers were left in Kazakhstan, he said: a rough guess would be 1,500, most in the villages they founded in the Altay Mountains hundreds of years ago.

Ironically, freedom to practise their faith for the first time in centuries had made many Old Believers attach less importance to it, the priest believed. 'At the time when the faithful were persecuted, people aspired more to spirituality, young people and everyone. Now, when you have the possibility to manifest your spirituality, people are turning away, and different values have emerged among young people: material values, values of the flesh, non-spiritual values.'

Father Gleb was optimistic, however, that 'the congregation will remain one way or another' in Kazakhstan, and his daughter Viveya was one of the young people the dwindling community hoped would keep the faith alive. 'Most likely I'll marry someone who's also a believer,' she said with a shy laugh, 'and of course I'll raise my children as they should be.'

In the Peter and Paul Church in Korobikha, Valentina Mikhaylovna also bemoaned the changing times. 'The older folk who pray aren't left any more, and everyone's leaving for the towns,' complained the old lady, who held the ecclesiastical title of *matushka* ('little mother'), which permits women to perform some liturgical rites. 'No one understands religion now. They drink, they have fun, they do anything they want on Sundays. They go to a funeral and they don't want to pray, they just want a good lunch!'

'People should believe in God,' she said sternly, but few in the village – where she was viewed as something of an eccentric – actually came to her church to pray. 'I've built it, and if they're not prepared to come to it, the sin will be on them, not on me,' she sniffed. 'It's said that if people die without repenting, it would have been better if they hadn't been born at all.'

With a sigh, Valentina Mikhaylovna rose and padded to the door of her little church, which she padlocked before shuffling into her cottage a few steps away. Inside the gloomy interior cluttered with icons, bibles and ecclesiastical calendars, she picked up a prayer book and started reciting in the solemn tones of Old Church Slavonic, the language used by the mainstream Russian Orthodox Church and the Old Believers.

Valentina Mikhaylovna was trying her best to keep the faith alive in this outlying corner of Kazakhstan, but there were constant reminders that times were changing. A few years previously the last old lady bearing the name of Korobitsyn, the religious dissenter who founded this village on the edge of the Russian Empire over two centuries ago, had passed away, taking another piece of Kazakhstan's Old Believer history to the grave with her.

CHAPTER 22

Opium of the People

Ridder, 2014

Aleksandr Kharlamov arrives tailed by intelligence agents. The bespectacled 63-year-old, dapperly turned out in a brown suit with a gold tiepin, does not look like a man who merits a security detail, but the authorities in his home town of Ridder, nestling in the foothills of the Altay Mountains just south of the border with Russia, are taking no chances. They have tried many tactics to shut him up – from throwing him behind bars to locking him up on a psychiatric ward – but nothing has cowed him. 'Everything's been tried to neutralise me,' he says, chuckling gleefully, 'yet here I am, safe and sound!'

Aleksandr Melentyevich (his patronymic) has clashed with the state over a principle: a militant atheist who believes all religion is 'idiocy', he defends his right to keep saying so whenever and wherever he wishes. But the state thinks otherwise. Prosecutors have accused him of fomenting religious strife with his diatribes against religion and the 'fools' who believe in it, and he is facing criminal charges of incitement. The amiable oddball says Kazakhstan, a secular state with a majority Muslim population that touts itself as a bastion of religious freedom for all, is riding roughshod over his rights to freedom of conscience and freedom of speech. 'I'm an atheist – there's no crime in that!' he cries in a ringing tone designed to be overheard by the two men in black leather jackets ostentatiously taking notes at the next table in the large and otherwise completely empty restaurant to which he has invited me for lunch on a breezy spring day in April 2014. 'They're *KNBshniki*,' he says nonchalantly, with an airy wave of his hand – slang for agents of the KNB, the security service. 'Let them listen, let them write. I've nothing to hide.'

A year earlier, Aleksandr Melentyevich had been arrested and jailed on charges of stoking religious strife on his blog by claiming that all religions are 'obscurantist and primitive'. 'My criticism of religion was interpreted as incitement of religious enmity and strife. There's no crime. There's no incitement of religious enmity. I criticised all religions – I didn't choose just one,' he complains bullishly. 'Karl Marx was right: religion is the opium of the people!'

For a man facing the prospect of seven years in jail under the notorious Article 174, the incitement charge that has been wielded to muzzle anyone from dissidents to land protesters, Aleksandr Melentyevich was remarkably cheerful. Over lunch he embarked on a meandering lecture taking in world religions, philosophies and political systems. He ripped scathingly into Islam and Orthodox Christianity – Kazakhstan's two main religions – and other mainstream faiths, then expounded on the moral teachings of Jesus Christ and the egalitarian principles of communism: of these, he wholeheartedly approved. 'To this day I serve the ideals of communism and socialism!' he declared, with emphatic finger-wagging. Under the case against him, Aleksandr Melentyevich had recently spent six months in detention, mostly in prison but also a month on a psychiatric ward. This had spiced up the controversy over his case, amid headline-grabbing claims that Kazakhstan was practising Soviet-style abuse of psychiatry against dissidents. The atheist had turned into an unlikely poster boy for the cause of religious freedom, his case a startling litmus test of Kazakhstan's professed commitment to freedom of belief. He was clearly revelling in the limelight as the United Nations Human Rights Council, the European Parliament and a US government commission lined up with human rights campaigners to express concern.[1]

So what was it about the obscure case of a maverick atheist from a sleepy out-of-the-way town in the north-eastern corner of Kazakhstan that had catapulted him into the international spotlight, making waves far beyond the Altay Mountains?

Nazarbayev always painted a rosy picture of Kazakhstan as a cosmopolitan, tolerant country that prided itself on its ethnic and religious diversity. 'The lofty values professed by every religion – Islam,

Orthodoxy, Catholicism, Protestant faiths, Judaism, Buddhism and others – have always been supported by the state of Kazakhstan,' he told the Congress of the Leaders of World and Traditional Religions in Astana, a forum to promote interfaith dialogue and showcase Kazakhstan as a model of religious tolerance, in 2012.[2]

Yet at the same time the government was engaged in a clampdown on minority faiths that would see around a thousand congregations forced out of existence.

In a small plain evangelical church in a quiet Almaty suburb, Pastor Vasiliy Shegay closed his eyes in a state of rapture and raised his arms to the heavens. A flow of rhythmic sounds poured from his mouth, as his flock responded with cries of 'Hallelujah!' and 'Amen!' The air rang with the sound of the grey-haired pastor speaking in tongues from his wooden pulpit as the lively Sunday morning service reached a crescendo, the congregation enraptured by the passionate oration. This service at the Sun Bok Ym Pentecostal Church looked like a vibrant display of that religious diversity which Nazarbayev loved to tout – yet among the flock were nervous worshippers who feared their right to believe was under threat. 'Formally, under the law, there is freedom [of conscience], but in effect it's hard to exercise it in our realities,' sighed one young man after the service. A 'purge' of religious groups was under way, intended 'to abolish faiths that are inconvenient to the state', he complained, speaking anonymously for fear of bringing the congregation under scrutiny. After a lengthy battle, in autumn 2012 his church had just managed to obtain official permission to worship, but a sister church had been refused and faced closure. This was one of hundreds of small congregations spanning the religious spectrum – from evangelical Christians to Muslims worshipping outside state-approved mosques – whose existence was threatened by a draconian new law governing religious affairs.

Around 70 per cent of people in Kazakhstan identified as Muslim and 25 per cent as Russian Orthodox at the time.[3] After seven decades of aggressive state-sponsored atheism under the Soviet Union, though, religious identification for many is more of a cultural marker than a strict doctrine. The number of people piously practising their faiths has grown since independence, however, and as Islam has experienced a revival,

Kazakhstan has not been immune to the penetration of extremist ide-
ologies that have gained ground elsewhere in the world. In May 2011,
Kazakhstan witnessed its first ever suicide bombing, an attack on the
KNB headquarters in the western city of Aktobe (which killed only
the bomber).[4] That was followed by a spate of armed attacks targeting the
security forces, and in November the same year a gunman ran amok in
the southern city of Taraz, killing two civilians and four members of the
security forces before blowing himself up.[5] In 2016, Kazakhstan suffered
its deadliest attack to date: a shooting spree on a National Guard base
in Aktobe that left four civilians and three soldiers dead, plus eighteen
suspects killed in the manhunt.[6] The trial of the survivors found that
they were inspired by Islamic radicalism, although their methods were
chaotic and their motives hazy.[7]

As in many countries, there is much debate in Kazakhstan about the
scale of the dangers Islamic extremism poses and how to respond, but
one of the government's default reactions has been to keep tightening up
the law governing all matters religious. In 2011, as the government kept
chanting its mantra of religious tolerance, a new law was passed stipulating
stringent requirements for all religious communities and introducing a
wafer-thin definition of what is permitted to constitute a congregation.
The law also banned prayer in public buildings – from government
offices, schools and universities to military barracks – and established
vetting over religious literature and missionary activity that critics said
amounted to a state veto over what religions may and may not preach.
Nazarbayev used to be fond of boasting that Kazakhstan welcomed over
40 faiths and 4,500 religious groups, but nowadays it recognises only 18
faiths, and over a thousand congregations were forced out of existence
because they could not meet the draconian new requirements.[8]

The religion law was ostensibly a tool to combat a rising tide of
Islamic radicalism, and some extremists have probably been caught
in its net – yet it has been wielded with alacrity against communities
that appear to present no conceivable extremist threat but simply fail
to conform to the state's rigid ideas of what religion should be. Police
regularly raid places of worship and private homes where believers are
praying, and worshippers often end up in court, where they are usually
fined but sometimes jailed. The security services expend considerable
manpower and resources for often dubious results – such as a sting on

a 61-year-old Jehovah's Witness who was jailed for five years in 2017 for proselytising to seven undercover KNB informers posing as students.[9]

By 2013, when Aleksandr Melentyevich was arrested under an investigation opened against him in 2012, the country's reputation as a haven of religious tolerance had eroded so far as to prompt Robert George, the chairman of the US government's Commission on International Religious Freedom, to offer a damning conclusion: 'Kazakhstan, once a leader in Central Asia on freedom of religion or belief, is a leader no more.'[10]

Putting the atheist behind bars seemed a disproportionate response to his diatribes against religion, and the controversy was fuelled by claims that he had been subjected to forced psychiatric treatment. This prompted comparisons with the abuse of psychiatry practised in the USSR against Soviet dissidents such as the famous physicist Andrey Sakharov by a state that thought dissenters must be mad to disagree with it. The idea of 21st-century Kazakhstan resorting to such mind games was extraordinary, and Aleksandr Melentyevich was not the only one: Bakhytzhan Kashkumbayev, a 67-year-old Presbyterian pastor from a church in Astana who was arrested in 2013 on suspicion of driving one of his parishioners insane through his preaching had also been forced to undergo psychiatric tests. Nazarbayev 'promotes his country's record of religious tolerance', remarked George, the head of the US government commission, but the cases of the atheist and the pastor 'reveal a different truth'. In fact, he concluded: 'The use of forcible psychiatric exams is reminiscent of the worst methods that the Soviets used against dissidents.'[11] The practice was still ongoing in 2018, when Ardak Ashim, an outspoken blogger who (like Kharlamov) was being investigated for incitement under Article 174, was forcibly confined in a psychiatric clinic in the southern city of Shymkent.[12]

In fact, Aleksandr Melentyevich demurred at the suggestion that he was forced to undergo psychiatric treatment. 'No!' he exclaimed emphatically: he agreed to tests to determine his sanity because 'it was interesting to me', as he put it. 'They wanted to declare me a fool. It didn't work out. Why not? Because I'm no fool!' he chortled. He was tested twice, with psychiatrists in Ust-Kamenogorsk, Ridder's nearest city, diagnosing him with a 'delusional disorder' but doctors in Almaty declaring him sane. The latter test was deemed conclusive, otherwise he might have been committed to a psychiatric institution for twenty years. Pastor Kashkumbayev was also declared sane, and was sent for trial. (He was no stranger to run-ins with the law: the police had once raided his church and accused him of feeding parishioners a red hallucinogenic liquid that turned out to be herbal tea.[13]) In 2014, he was convicted of inflicting harm on the health of a member of his congregation, although the parishioner he had allegedly driven insane – who was also subjected to forced psychiatric testing – denied this. After nine months in prison, the pastor was released with a suspended sentence and a hefty fine of $10,800, bringing to an end what his lawyer described as 'one of the strangest cases I have seen in terms of legality'.[14]

Aleksandr Melentyevich had spent six months behind bars, and since his release on bail he had been campaigning to have the case against him dropped. He had never incited religious strife, he claimed, brandishing a letter he had recently sent to the local police. 'On the contrary, I Urge People to Tolerance – Love Thy Enemy, including religious people, which means do not commit any crimes against them!!!' it read, with emphatic and erratic capitalisation and punctuation. 'Love your enemies, I say!' he cried gleefully. 'And I do love them, even though I criticise them!'

The atheist had certainly made plenty of enemies in Ridder, a quiet town of 55,000 people named after a Russian officer who discovered the gold and silver deposit around which it grew in the eighteenth century. Most of the townspeople (85 per cent in 2014, down to 80% in 2021[15]) were ethnic Russians, including Aleksandr Melentyevich: he was a descendent of Old Believers, although this was another faith that aroused his antagonism.

This man was on a self-proclaimed mission to expose wrongdoing in Ridder and bring justice to the downtrodden – and he believed it was this that had riled the local political authorities and security forces. They could not really care less about his religious beliefs or non-beliefs, his theory went: they had opened the criminal case with the aim of jailing him to muzzle a gadfly who kept making waves. 'They had to latch on to something, because I'm inconvenient,' he said breezily. 'Who would like me? Imagine you've done something, committed some crime, and I've written about you in the newspaper. Would you like that? No, you wouldn't!' Inside Aleksandr Melentyevich's office, where a bicycle jostled for space with a pair of red dumbbells, he displayed a pile of cuttings from a scurrilous local news-sheet of his corruption exposés. 'On one hand we say: let's fight corruption; on the other we say: who's this fighting corruption?' he tutted, with mock shock at the hostile reception his antics had received in Ridder. The atheist was also writing a whimsical treatise about science and philosophy called *The Most Ingenious Book*, which he intended to self-publish. (The book's self-publication later sparked fresh charges of inciting religious strife, although these were eventually dropped.[16])

As well as an outspoken atheist, he was also an anti-corruption crusader with a taste for vigilantism that had landed him in jail even before his troubles over his anti-religion crusade began: in the 1990s he served a two-year sentence on hooliganism charges over a citizen's arrest he made when running vigilante patrols to stamp out anti-social behaviour among his fellow townspeople – another bugbear of his. The vigilantism had stopped, no doubt to the relief of the people of Ridder, but he demonstrated the jacket he and his volunteers used to wear (camouflage, with labels reading 'Secret Service Agency' and 'Civil Militia') and the weapons they wielded, which lay on the windowsill: pepper spray, an airgun and a long knife in a sheath.

Aleksandr Melentyevich had another string to his bow – he was running an organisation dedicated to righting legal wrongs for members of the public, for a fee. Outside the flat he used as an office hung printed signs advertising the services of the quirkily named Sekret Servis (a cannibalised version of 'secret service') that provided assistance in 'independent investigations' and 'representation in court and with law-enforcement bodies to defend citizens' rights'. With a chuckle, he revealed that he used to be a police officer himself, in Soviet times, but was fired for disobeying orders. He was still a frequent visitor to the police station, albeit now on the wrong side of the law. 'Just visiting today?' quipped the policeman on the front desk jovially, when the atheist took me to meet his investigating officer. The officer was out, and later he refused in a resigned tone to discuss the case by telephone.

For the oddball atheist, an important principle was at stake, and he certainly did not intend to back down. 'The principle of freedom of conscience has been violated. I have the right to believe, and I have the right not to believe,' he said, before scurrying off to court to act as a public defender for a Sekret Servis client. 'They're making me believe, show respect towards religion, respect God. What is this, a theocratic state? No! So they're infringing my rights!'

Aleksandr Melentyevich's doggedness paid off in the end: in 2018, after an ultimately pointless six-year legal tussle between the state and the atheist, the investigation launched back in 2012 was suddenly dropped and the case was closed.[17]

CHAPTER 23

Culture Wars

Almaty, 2014

Dariya Khamitzhanova is up in court, accused of offending the nation's collective moral values. Her crime? Overseeing the creation of an advert depicting a gay kiss between two nineteenth-century cultural icons. When her agency dreamt up the poster depicting Russian poet Pushkin and Kazakh composer Kurmangazy in a clinch, Dariya did not expect to find herself on the front line of a culture war – but here she is, at the epicentre of a moral panic in Kazakhstan.

The ad designed in August 2014 by creatives at Almaty's Havas Worldwide advertising agency was far from graphic. It showed the familiar faces of Kurmangazy Sagyrbayuly (a cultural hero in Kazakhstan, more usually depicted playing his stringed *dombyra* in statues across the land) and Aleksandr Pushkin (a literary giant revered as one of Russia's greatest writers) exchanging a passionate kiss, the Kazakh composer's flowing beard pushed aside so he could lock lips with the curly-haired Russian poet. The ad purported to be promoting a gay nightclub in Almaty called Studio 69, but it had not been designed for public consumption: it had been entered in an advertising competition in Kyrgyzstan, where it won an award before the furore broke out.

The image was an in-joke: Studio 69, a nightspot with a flamboyantly camp floor show that was popular with Almaty's small gay community, was located at the crossroads of Kurmangazy and Pushkin Streets. It was also an artsy allusion to a real-life embrace that took place at the height of the Cold War: a lip-smacking bear hug between Soviet leader Leonid

Brezhnev and East German president Erich Honecker, caught on camera in 1979. Creative types love to riff on this snapshot, from the graffiti artist who daubed it on the Berlin Wall in 1990 to the street artist in Lithuania who painted a mural of Vladimir Putin smooching with Donald Trump in 2016. So the Kurmangazy–Pushkin poster was simply a jokey take on an iconic image in a display of cultural creativity intended for a private audience – but when it started circulating on Facebook, the flippant piece of PR shocked some people's sensibilities in Kazakhstan.

'Close the club, fine the owners, and throw the advertisers behind bars for this type of propaganda!' 'It's perverts who've dreamt up this poster. [...] How disgusting!' 'Beyond the pale, vulgarity and cynicism. [...] No shame!'[1] These were some of the more polite comments aired in the social media storm that blew up. The government joined the tide of public outrage: 'unsavoury', 'inhuman', 'impermissible' and 'to some degree a crime', railed Arystanbek Mukhamediyuly, the culture minister.[2] Politicians in Russia weighed in, with the nationalist Rodina (Motherland) party condemning 'aggressive LGBT propaganda', which aimed 'to discriminate against people with a traditional sexual orientation and besmirch the historical legacy' of both Russians and the 'fraternal' people of Kazakhstan.[3]

A spirited defence of the poster based on its artistic merits and the right to exercise freedom of speech, followed shortly after by a grovelling apology, failed to win a reprieve for Dariya and her agency: soon they were up in court, facing two lawsuits. Almaty's city hall sued them for breaching advertising law, arguing that the picture 'offends the image of these great artists and violates widespread moral standards and behaviours' by showing 'non-traditional sexual relations which are unacceptable to society'.[4] Separately, thirty-four staff, students and musicians from Almaty's Kurmangazy Conservatory launched a class action for moral damages because they felt insulted as members of an august institution named after the great musician. Strangely, their lawsuit precisely echoed the Russian nationalist party's complaint that the poster had 'besmirched the historical legacy' of the Kazakhs and the 'fraternal' Russians.

A trial putting gay rights in the legal spotlight was a fresh departure for Kazakhstan, but homophobic outbursts were nothing new. People with a 'non-traditional sexual orientation' should be banned from working in schools and the civil service and from serving in the military, suggested youth activist Dauren Babamuratov as the controversy raged. They could be spotted because they wander around in 'colourful trousers', and should be DNA-tested for 'degeneracy', he told a meeting in Almaty organised to urge the government to legislate against homosexuality. There was no subtlety in the message being shouted out: behind him on the wall was a poster of two stick men having sex with a red line scored through it, accompanied by the slogan 'homosexuality is a threat to the nation'.[5]

The push for anti-gay legislation was no coincidence: in 2013, Russia had adopted a controversial law banning the 'propaganda of homosexuality' to children, which critics decried as an assault on gay rights that created a climate of hostility for the LGBT community – and where Moscow treads, other authoritarian ex-Soviet states often follow. Frosty political relations between Russia and the West had helped spawn a backlash against 'Western' values that had found fertile ground in many ex-Soviet countries, placing gay rights on the front line of a new culture war. In Kazakhstan, the self-styled guardians of the nation's moral values had already started to huff and puff before the 'gay kiss' row erupted.

Homosexuality was 'amorality of the highest degree', MP Aldan Smayyl blustered in parliament in 2013, and Kazakhstan should pass a law that would designate homosexuals 'criminals against humanity'.[6] Meanwhile, MP Kairbek Suleymenov called for measures to counteract gay marriage, describing it as 'alien' to Kazakhstan's psychology, ideology and traditions, although there was no legal mechanism for gay marriage, nor any planned.[7] (He had been fired up by a symbolic 'gay marriage' staged by two flamboyant lesbians in the city of Karaganda to celebrate their relationship, which came to a tragic end when one later murdered the other in a jealous rage.) Legislation was needed to 'root out homosexual relations', railed parliamentarian Bakhytbek Smagul, offering the most confused smorgasbord of arguments yet: he rambled from 'national mentality' and family values to demographics and Kazakhstan's location in Central Asia 'where ancient cultures intersect', before citing the inability of gay men to guard borders.[8] He need not have worried on that count: the defence minister had already clarified that gay men cannot serve in Kazakhstan's military, since homosexuality is classified as a 'disorder of sexual desire'.[9]

The government kept quiet, but these MPs were from Nazarbayev's party, Nur Otan, and their homophobic outbursts were spooking Kazakhstan's low-profile gay community.

'I consider this unacceptable. It's like fascism. If we start persecuting one group, then it'll be another – Jews, then Uighurs,' asserted Roman, a 28-year-old designer based in Almaty, Central Asia's most gay-friendly city. 'I think the state should treat all citizens equally and doesn't have the right to discriminate against people according to their affiliation.' The gay-bashing made him think of Borat, the star of the satirical 2006 film featuring a fictional Kazakh journalist famous for making shocking non-PC comments. 'Everyone laughs at Borat and the damage this did to Kazakhstan, but this is another Borat moment,' complained Roman. He had a point: not long before an American gay rights activist called Will Kohler had published an article whose headline screamed: 'CALL BORAT! – Kazakhstan considering copying Russia's anti-gay laws.' In it, Kohler had commented acidly: 'Perhaps Borat was a documentary and not a comedy.'[10] 'I think Kazakhstan should be aspiring to a civilised model, if we want to be a developed, modern state,' sighed Roman. 'I really love my country, I'm a patriot, but if they adopt such laws I might start thinking that this isn't a country I want to live in.'

Yuliya, a young Almaty professional in a long-term lesbian relationship, joked that it was 'a great advert – that's propaganda in itself' for MPs to be gay-bashing as they pushed for a ban on propaganda of homosexuality. But seriously, she said over breakfast in a trendy café, the community felt 'a sense of insecurity' that was not so prevalent before, when it flew more under the radar – even if the environment had never exactly been gay-friendly. 'It's convenient to have an enemy,' said Yuliya, with a philosophical sigh. 'We always fear what we don't understand.'

In 2015, the Kazakh parliament passed a law banning 'propaganda of homosexuality', designed, homophobic MP Aldan Smayyl said, 'to protect children from information that kills off the sentiment of warmth and humanity, damages the psyche and health [...] and lays spiritual waste to the growing generation.'[11]

The gay community was fearful – but salvation came from an unlikely quarter. Kazakhstan was bidding to host the 2022 Winter Olympics, the type of prestigious world event Nazarbayev loved to stage to put the country on the map, and when international sports celebrities lined up against its bid, citing the anti-gay bill, suddenly the law was history.[12] The Constitutional Council struck it down, on a technicality over wording rather than human rights concerns[13] – but the gay community breathed a sigh of relief, especially when it stayed off the agenda even after Kazakhstan lost its Olympic bid.

But the gay-rights row had already turned Dariya Khamitzhanova's life upside down. She and her agency were convicted of breaching advertising law and fined $1,700, then the agency was found guilty of insulting the musicians from the Kurmangazy Conservatory by design-ing a poster showing their namesake in a gay clinch. For that, it was slapped with damages of 34 million tenge, or $190,000 – calculated at a million tenge for each of the thirty-four individuals behind the class action, none of whom had shown their faces in court. 'I'm simply in shock!' exclaimed Dariya. The ruling was 'unjust', the damages 'cosmic' and 'disproportionate'.

The advertising agency closed down, and its director, complaining that there was no space for creative freedom in Kazakhstan, announced that she was emigrating to Ukraine. The authorities had sent a clear message, she said: 'Think a hundred times before you express yourself.'[14]

CHAPTER 24

The Curse of Corruption

Shymkent, 2012

Seven-year-old Azamat is enjoying a rambunctious game of rough and tumble with his twin sister, the children shrieking and giggling as they chase each other around the family home in Tassay, a village near the southern city of Shymkent. But soon the game will have to stop: Azamat has to take his medicine. The little boy is HIV-positive, and he must take antiretroviral drugs several times a day to keep the infection at bay.

Azamat is one of at least 150 children who were infected with HIV in hospitals in Shymkent in a corruption scandal that engulfed the health service and outraged the nation in 2006. Doctors and nurses had been selling blood for personal profit, and reusing disposable syringes and catheters to cream off cash allocated to buy medical equipment. As a result, the HIV virus made its way into hospitals and was pumped via contaminated syringes and drips into the veins of sick children, who must now live with the consequences of this corruption-driven malpractice for the rest of their lives.

Azamat (a pseudonym – the family's names have been changed to protect their privacy) was just eight months old when he was diagnosed with HIV. The first hint of trouble came in a TV news report, which said that cases were being detected among children in Shymkent. Aynur and Marat, the twins' parents, thought little of it until medics came knocking at their door demanding blood samples, claiming they needed to run tests because the twins had frequently been ill (which was not true). The parents refused, but, after a sleepless night, they drove to Shymkent the next day and had blood samples taken from the eight-month-old twins. That is how they learnt that Azamat was HIV-positive.

'We were in utter hysterics,' recalls his mother Aynur in October 2012 as she watches the twins play with their two younger siblings in the living room of their small house in Tassay. Panic broke out as the scandal erupted, and no coherent information was forthcoming. They could not understand how Azamat had been infected with a virus known in the public mind as predominantly affecting drug users and sex workers, or why his twin sister had been given a clean bill of health. The only advice doctors offered initially was 'eat apples', recalls Aynur, wide-eyed at the memory six years on. As the frantic parents sought answers, the doctors kept saying 'wait, wait', says Marat. 'To be honest, we were plunged into a total depression.' To make matters worse, the families were at the centre of a media storm, with journalists publishing the names of infected infants as speculation raged that the virus had been transmitted through their mothers.

Azamat, it turned out, had been infected with HIV at a Shymkent hospital when the twins caught pneumonia and were hospitalised for treatment in 2006. Only Azamat had received a blood transfusion, and he contracted the virus from a contaminated drip. Now, his parents' anguish was compounded by doubts that there were ever valid medical grounds for the procedure: transfusions were prescribed willy-nilly, partly because of corruption – medics charged parents $20 for the blood and pocketed half – and partly because of a medical practice considered outdated in the West, based on the belief that transfusions flush out the organism. Contaminated catheters were inserted into the arms of children who had no need for transfusions: one infant was pumped with twenty-five transfusions of no medical value, according to documents later filed in court.[1]

A total of twenty-one people ended up in the dock, accused of malpractice and negligence: sixteen medics and five local health officials. No national officials took the legal rap, although health minister Yerbolat Dosayev was fired (he later made a comeback as economy minister, then chairman of the central bank). When the verdicts were delivered in 2007, hysterical scenes broke out in court when all but one of the doctors and nurses were jailed (the longest term was eight years) while all five officials walked free with suspended sentences.[2]

Some saw the jailed medics as scapegoats for systemic corruption and negligence in an underfunded health service whose doctors and nurses scraped by on a pittance – and some suspected it was a case of political patronage delivering selective justice. Among those who received non-custodial sentences were Nursulu Tasmagambetova, the local healthcare chief, and her husband Ryskulbek Baykharashev, formerly responsible for overseeing the quality of healthcare services. Tasmagambetova was the sister of one of Kazakhstan's most powerful politicians, Imangali Tasmagambetov, who was mayor of Almaty at the time and was tipped as a possible successor to Nazarbayev. Tasmagambetova and her husband denied any responsibility for the infection of 150 infants with HIV in hospitals under their watch, ten of whom were already dead.

The child HIV scandal lifted the veil on the open secret of corruption in public services, where cash-strapped medics routinely demand kick-backs to top up meagre salaries, teachers and university lecturers often require sweeteners to award decent grades, and bent cops let criminals off in exchange for bungs. 'A lot of people extort money,' agreed Isidora Yerasilova, a healthcare professional specialising in HIV/AIDS, at the time of the Shymkent trial. 'Of course it's a crime, but the one thing [low salaries] generates the other [bribery].'[3]

'I'm warning my relatives, children and friends that there will be no untouchables here,' said Nazarbayev in 2015, claiming that Kazakhstan was 'mercilessly' waging a battle against corruption.[4]

Many people are blasé about graft, seeing it as a necessary evil to keep the wheels of state moving, and believing the example is set from the top: by the government's own admission, bribery runs riot in the highest echelons of the state. The anti-corruption agency estimated in 2017 that graft could be costing Kazakhstan $3.8 billion every year, which dwarfed the $10 doctors were making from selling blood in Shymkent.[5] In the first half of 2017 alone, 900 civil servants were arrested for taking bribes – 150 a month – and that was just those who were caught.[6] Crooked bureaucrats see the public purse as a trough to dip into for personal gain, and the 'everybody's at it' ethos percolates down from the highest government officials to the lowliest teachers and doctors. It is an open secret that some jobs are 'sold' since they can make venal officials a fortune in kickbacks: in 2002, the going rate for a post in the customs service reportedly ranged from $2,000 for a lowly officer to a whopping $500,000 for a cushier post.[7]

Corruption turns the criminal justice system into something more akin to a state-run racket, with police, prosecutors and judges up for sale if the price is right. How much does it cost to swing investigations, convictions and sentences? Anything from a few hundred dollars to several thousand: $9,000 was the going rate to reduce a prison sentence on appeal in one routine provincial trial in 2017,[8] while (as discussed earlier) $20,000 changed hands to cover up the murder of Ablyazov's business partner in 2004. This rampant and avaricious consumption of kickbacks not only makes a mockery of the idea of rule of law and prevents the delivery of justice, but also creates incentives to manufacture situations where suspects are coerced to pay backhanders to achieve rulings that they should have received by law – and even the innocent sometimes have to bribe themselves out of jail. Small wonder that vested interests within a system grotesquely distorted by corruption resist attempts to root out the graft that fills their pockets.

The culture of corruption is fuelled by a perception that when the sword of justice comes crashing down on those who take bribes, it is frequently selective: that people end up in the dock not because of their venality but because they fall victim to political intrigue, economic asset-grabbing and the power games of rivals. The state has fought multi-million-dollar banking fraud cases around the globe in its pursuit of Nazarbayev's foe Ablyazov – but ignored claims in 2017 that deposits in the ailing Kazkommertsbank (an institution close to the government which had recently received a $7.5 billion state bailout) had been illegally raided to fund the business projects of an offshore company.[9] 'As long as the country continues to be ruled by personal decree, then the fate of this or that businessman, public figure or high-ranking government official depends entirely on the decisions of somebody up above,' human rights campaigner Yevgeniy Zhovtis remarked in 2016, referring to contention surrounding the jailing of prominent journalists Seytkazy and Aset Matayev on corruption charges.[10]

The Kazakhgate scandal, with tentacles reaching to Nazarbayev personally, set the tone for independent Kazakhstan, when it was established that millions of dollars had been taken from US energy companies in kickbacks in exchange for oil contracts in the 1990s and secreted in Swiss bank accounts, with a US indictment fingering Nazarbayev as an unindicted co-conspirator.[11] In 2007, officials reached an agreement with the US and Swiss governments to give the $84 million in bribery proceeds to charity.[12] The sum rose to $115 million, with interest accrued.[13] That should have made investors leery of greasing palms in Kazakhstan; however, since then France has spent years probing claims of a $12-million bung shelled out by Eurocopter Group (later renamed Airbus Helicopters) to secure a contract in an investigation that was still ongoing in mid-2021, and Rolls Royce has admitted to paying bribes to win lucrative deals in Kazakhstan.[14]

Top officials are regularly jailed for taking multi-million-dollar bungs, like former prime minister Serik Akhmetov, handed a ten-year prison sentence in 2015 for accepting sweeteners worth $2.4 million and embezzling millions more. His sentence was later cut to eight years, after $15 million was repaid, and he walked free after just two years.[15] That was a drop in the ocean compared to the $32 million siphoned off from funds to build exhibition facilities in Astana, for which an official was jailed for fourteen years in 2016.[16] Those whose job it is to fight corruption sometimes have their fingers deep in the pot: take Amirkhan Amanbayev, former director of Almaty's financial police, jailed in 2014 for his involvement in an organised crime ring that turned over $240 million in illicit proceeds in two years.[17] Sometimes, corruption has implications for national security, as well as human life: in 2013, Major General Almaz Asenov received eleven years in jail for his part in awarding contracts worth $35 million to Ukraine's state-owned arms exporter to maintain military aircraft in exchange for bribes worth $1.5 million, of which Asenov personally was to receive over $1 million.[18] (These sums are in line with a figure often cited anecdotally as the percentage of a contract's value that must be paid in kickbacks to secure a deal, which is 3–5 per cent.) This case came to light after a military plane crash in which equipment failure was a factor killed Border Service director Turganbek Stambekov and twenty-five others in 2012. Asenov walked free after just three years.[19]

Kazakhstan pursues fugitive corruption suspects around the world – but selectively, making it easier for them to avoid extradition by citing political motivations (it was on these grounds that France struck down Ablyazov's extradition, for example). Viktor Khrapunov, a former Almaty mayor and cabinet minister, became the target of an Interpol warrant on embezzlement charges in 2012, four years after he had emigrated from Kazakhstan to Switzerland, where he lived in style (off the fortune, he said, of his wife Leyla, a one-time Kazakh media magnate and entrepreneur). Kazakhstan filed the warrant after Khrapunov, who was related by marriage to Ablyazov, had – extremely belatedly – gone public with a stream of corruption allegations against Nazarbayev. In 2014, a decade after Khrapunov left his mayoral post, Almaty's city hall sued him in the US, alleging that he had looted millions of dollars from the coffers and laundered it around the world, including through the purchase of residences in Trump SoHo, a Manhattan property linked to Donald Trump before he became US president.[20] The Trump name was later removed from the project,[21] and the Trump Organization said it was 'not responsible for the sale of units at Trump SoHo.'[22] Khrapunov's alleged looting of Almaty city funds had gone unnoticed for years, although sleaze allegations had long swirled around him.[23] In 2018 a Kazakh court convicted him and his wife *in absentia* on charges of involvement in organised crime and corruption which they denied,[24] but the Swiss authorities later cleared them of money-laundering charges and granted them asylum.[25] The family was heavy embroiled in cases related to Ablyazov: in 2018 the High Court in London ordered Ilyas Khrapunov (Viktor Khrapunov's son and Ablyazov's son-in-law) to pay BTA Bank $500 million in damages after finding that he had helped Ablyazov dodge an asset-freezing order.[26] Khrapunov, his wife and son have always denied any wrongdoing, claiming all cases against them are politically motivated.

It is an open secret that billions of dollars from Kazakhstan – some of it clean, some dirty – is stashed away in offshore accounts and luxury overseas property. Nazarbayev has repeatedly urged the wealthy to repatriate it. 'If you earn money, invest it in Kazakhstan,' he said in 2013. 'Don't be afraid. Live here, build a future for your children here, and have a care for the future and well-being of your own country.'[27] In 2016, it emerged that his grandson Nurali Aliyev (a businessman and banker who is the son of Dariga Nazarbayeva and the disgraced late Rakhat Aliyev) was tied to millions of dollars of assets registered in the British Virgin Islands, and in 2018 there were revelations that the president's daughter Dariga had also held financial interests offshore.[28] There was no suggestion of anything illegal, and in 2020 the pair won a case in the London courts which had alleged that £80-million-worth of luxury UK properties that they owned had been purchased with dirty money,[29] but so much for 'no untouchables'. Nazarbayev was surrounded by loaded relatives: Dinara and Timur Kulibayev, his middle daughter and her husband, are worth a combined $6 billion, according to the 2021 *Forbes* rich list; Dariga Nazarbayeva, his eldest daughter, was once listed by *Forbes Kazakhstan* as worth $600 million;

and his brother Bolat is a tycoon who sued his ex-wife in Manhattan for conning him out of his $20-million condominium (she was released from house arrest in Kazakhstan, where she had been held on charges of fraud, extortion and kidnapping, under an out-of-court settlement which saw her hand back the property).[30]

Recurrent cases of graft involving stratospheric sums notwithstanding, were lessons about the dangers of corruption learnt in the health service, particularly the part of it dedicated to fighting HIV/AIDS? In 2015, Bill Gates's Global Fund to Fight AIDS, Tuberculosis and Malaria announced that $5.4 million had been creamed off funds allocated to Kazakhstan through a murky scheme involving four unidentified individuals 'who submitted fake bids from smokescreen companies and colluded with each other to create the impression of fair competition'.[31] The money was quietly repaid.[32] No one was prosecuted. Corruption continued to cripple the health service during the coronavirus pandemic, amid claims of embezzlement of healthcare funds[33] and the emergence of a thriving black market in fake coronavirus tests and vaccination passports.[34]

Small wonder, perhaps, that doctors demand small sweeteners to do their jobs. Yet the Shymkent HIV scandal proved that the backhanders dismissed by many as an irritating but inconsequential part of life contribute to a toxic corruption problem that is eating away at the fabric of the state – with devastating consequences for some.

Eighteen-year-old Kanat learnt that he was HIV-positive at the age of twelve, soon after the outbreak in Shymkent was discovered in 2006. Like Azamat, he was infected through a catheter during hospital treatment. 'I quickly got used to the idea of my HIV status,' said Kanat, a softly spoken, smartly dressed young man who was studying electronics and harboured ambitions of working in the telecoms sector. Still, he dreamt that one day 'there'll be a medicine that will cure it'.

He was sitting around a table where a self-help group was discussing how best to break the news to infected children. Kanat had recently told a twelve-year-old boy that the child was HIV-positive, under a system whereby older sufferers would break the news and talk the children through the implications. 'He reacted fine,' the boy's mother Dinara (a pseudonym) said. 'He probably suspected. We told him not to be afraid, but to keep it secret, because society's mentality isn't ready.'

Stigma was a huge problem for these families – in many cases the fathers of infected children had abandoned the family, and their communities had ostracised them. 'At the beginning they didn't even let us in the shop,' said Dina (a pseudonym), the mother of a seven-year-old HIV-positive boy, explaining the hostile reception a group of families got when officials moved them to a village to help them by providing them with housing. The name of the village is Dostyk, which means 'friendship', but their reception was anything but friendly. 'The neighbours yelled at us, and they didn't accept even my older ones at the school – the healthy children,' she said, with a sad shrug. Yet she bore no malice towards them. 'They didn't understand at first. We didn't understand ourselves what this is. But gradually people have got used to it.'

The state provided the children with free antiretroviral drugs that prolong life expectancy, and funded medical treatment at a state-of-the-art paediatric hospital in Shymkent refitted in response to the 2006 outbreak (no bribes were demanded here) as well as psychological counselling. Families received one-off compensation of up to $10,000 (some got much less), and each child was entitled to benefits until the age of eighteen. 'The state has to be thanked for taking radical measures,' said Zhanneta Zhazykbayeva, director of the Protection of Children from AIDS Foundation. But the compensation payments were long since spent, and the parents fretted about what their offspring would do when they reached adulthood, if stigma prevented them from finding work.

Even after six years, it was a constant battle to keep the issue on the state's agenda – and anxiety about the children's futures tormented their parents. Since the initial outcry, said Marat, 'society's become indifferent [...] we've been basically left in isolation'. As the years went by, the parents felt their children slipping down the list of priorities. They worried about whether the free antiretroviral therapy their children relied on would continue, and what kind of healthcare would be available in the future. 'The situation's very difficult,' sighed Marat ruefully, watching a giggling Azamat continue his boisterous game with his siblings. 'What will happen tomorrow, what will happen in ten years? We don't see any future.'

As for Dinara, she preferred not to dwell on the future at all. 'We try not to talk about HIV,' she said, her mask of good cheer slipping for a second. 'We don't want to be reminded of it. When you remember, it's sad. And when you forget, it's possible to live somehow.'

CHAPTER 25

The Shrinking Sea

Aral Sea, 2009

'APOCALIPSES', reads the piece of graffiti scrawled on the rusting hulk of the *Lev Berg*, formerly one of the prides of the Soviet Union's fleet of research vessels and now a wreck beached in a once bustling harbour. The misspelt scrawl neatly sums up the apocalyptic scene viewed through the gaping portholes of this rotting vessel: an expanse of litter-strewn, salt-encrusted sand stretching for miles across a lunar landscape. This was once the bed of the Aral Sea – but now there is not a drop of water in sight.

Here in the deserts of Kazakhstan, stretching over into Uzbekistan, lies the scene of one of the world's worst man-made environmental disasters, caused by imperious Soviet central planners who gerrymandered the mighty rivers of Central Asia to suit their grandiose agricultural designs. Lev Berg, the namesake of the ship listing forlornly on the sand, would be turning in his grave if he could see the state of his beloved sea today: Berg was a celebrated Russian geographer with a passion for Central Asia's waterways who conducted a study of the Aral at the turn of the nineteenth and twentieth centuries. Now, there is no sign of the sea anywhere near the harbour in the town that is named after it, Aral in Kazakh and Aralsk in Russian, which is deserted but for the ghostly shells of the trawlers which were once part of a formidable fishing fleet. In the mid-1970s, the waters disappeared from Aralsk, leaving the fishing port stranded high and dry without its raison d'être.

'Even if the water is gone from the bottom of the Aral, its song has not gone from the hearts of its people,' reads a mournful sign standing in

March 2009 on the desiccated harbour bed. The sentiment is true: local people hark wistfully back to a time when the sea lapped the shores of their town. 'It was like a fairy tale,' sighs a middle-aged man called Arman. 'Everything was different. The air was different. The climate was different. There were more people here. Now what's changed? Everyone's left, gone to live elsewhere. The weather's changed. Dust and wind, and that's it.'

Starved of water, the sea has retreated miles away into the desert. Camels roam the seabed where its waters used to flow, and outside town a dromedary skeleton lies incongruously on parched sand that was once the ocean floor.

It was in the 1960s, under Soviet leader Nikita Khrushchev, that central planners in Moscow started a gargantuan push to divert Central Asia's rivers to water the thirsty cotton crop, which would cause the Aral Sea to begin its disappearing act after surviving for 5.5 million years. A century earlier, tsarist Russia had turned its newly conquered province of Turkestan in Central Asia into the heartland of the Russian Empire's cotton industry, after the American Civil War had strangled the US supplies on which the textile mills of St Petersburg relied. Cotton was planted mostly in Uzbekistan, whose climate – warm, arid and sunny – was perfect for the crop. Uzbekistan had a long history of cotton pro-duction dating back to ancient times, but that was on a small sustainable scale. Soviet mass production was in a different league. It was in 1918, after the Bolshevik Revolution, that the Soviets first started changing the courses of Central Asia's rivers to irrigate land under cotton cultivation; Stalin later drove cotton output up to make the USSR self-sufficient in the crop, a target which was reached in the 1930s. But three decades later, in the 1960s, the death warrant was signed for the Aral Sea, with a push to ramp up cotton output to meet domestic needs and to generate foreign currency from exporting a crop so lucrative it was dubbed 'white gold'. That was under Khrushchev – a man with a passion for grand agri-cultural designs, like his Virgin Lands campaign to transform northern Kazakhstan into wheat fields.

The arid deserts of Central Asia lay along the waterways which were the lifeblood of the Aral Sea. In 1963, before the Soviets embarked on the most zealous phase of this agricultural engineering experiment, the Aral Sea was the world's fourth largest lake, stretching over 66,000 square kilometres, around the size of Ireland. By the early 2000s, its level had plunged by twenty-three metres, its surface area had contracted by half, and what was left of it was no longer a single body of water: in the late 1980s – by which time more than half of its water had disappeared – the shrinking sea had split into two parts, separated by a swathe of toxic, pesticide-strewn, salt-encrusted desert that was growing all the time.[1]

At first people saw no cause for concern as the waters retreated, recalled Temirbolat, a middle-aged man who grew up in Aralsk by the sea that then disappeared and now made his living driving reporters around the dry seabed. (They were not guaranteed a friendly reception: people were understandably tired of featuring in Western media sob stories, and irritated fishermen sometimes demanded wads of cash to be photographed in their boats.) People lived in a communist state that provided for everyone and Moscow would take care of the problem, so the thinking went – until one day they woke up and 'there was no sea, there were no fish, and life was hard'.

Fishing had been the lifeblood of the town since the industry was established by Russian merchants when Aralsk was founded in the early twentieth century, at the site of a Kazakh *aul* called Altykudyk (Six Wells). Initially the townspeople were not too worried by the slow retreat of the waters: as the sea shrank a little further from the harbour every year they shrugged philosophically and carried on with their lives. The fishermen dug channels through the sand to get their boats out to sea, mooring a little further from the harbour each time as the waters inched away. But in 1975, with the sea far distant and hardly any fish left to catch, the port closed down and Aralsk's cannery began processing fish from the Baltics and Russian Far East, working at a loss to provide jobs for the townspeople.

'My father was a fisherman and he used to take me fishing. I was a fisherman at the age of fourteen,' reminisced Zholdas Ayapbergenov, nostalgically casting his mind back four decades to the days when the sea, bountiful with fish, was a source of prosperity for his family. He grew up expecting to follow in his father's footsteps, but the life he imagined was not to be: by the 1970s, what was left of the sea had turned into a toxic brew that was killing off the fish, poisoned by pesticides washed into its waters and rising salinity as the freshwater flow dried up. Once the sea had swarmed with fish, but all the native species gradually died off, poisoned by the grand designs of Soviet planners. They had known all along that the economic benefits would come at the cost of a devastating ecological impact, but believed the environmental price worth paying for the agricultural rewards – so the Aral Sea was replaced by the Aralkum: the Aral Desert.

The catch of the Aral fishing fleet had once provided one sixth of fish supplies for the entire Soviet Union, hauled in on famous vessels like the *Kirov* and the *Kommuna* (*Commune*), which were famous for firing the shots that had turned the tide of a Civil War battle in 1919 by preventing a train carrying drinking water to the Whites from reaching the thirsty troops. But in the 1980s these once illustrious vessels had no more waters to sail on, and the prides of the Aral fleet were scrapped.

'We had top-quality fish like nowhere else,' Zholdas said in an elegiac tone, gesturing at some sepia photos of fishermen hauling in their catches which harked back to the glory days of the maritime past. They were displayed on the walls of the Tastak fish farm out in the desert, once a major breeding centre for Aral Sea fish but now just spawning from catches netted in the Syrdarya River. Zholdas had worked here for the last forty years, since the life he had expected to lead as a fisherman had evaporated along with the sea.

The Aral fishermen enjoyed mythological status in the Soviet Union, feted nationally for more than once coming to the rescue of their starving countrymen with their bountiful catches. In 1921, Lenin, leader of the revolutionary state that was embroiled in a fight for its survival with the White Russians in the Civil War that followed the 1917 revolution, sent a heartfelt begging letter to the Aral Sea fishermen, appealing to them to feed people starving to death in famine-wracked parts of Russia and Ukraine: 'Millions of people, labouring peasants and workers, and millions of cattle are preparing to die and are dying already. Russians and Muslims, settled people and nomads, the same cruel death awaits everyone if their comrades – workers, labouring peasants, shepherds and fishermen from better-off places – do not come to their aid.' The starving were placing their hopes 'in great proletarian solidarity' and 'in those who, like they themselves, are working people with calloused hands, earning their subsistence with their own bent back, not sucking anyone's blood'. By sparing some of their catch for 'those bloated with hunger', Lenin wrote, 'you will show the whole world, and above all our labourers, that the power of the toiling Soviet state […] is indestructible.' 'This,' he concluded, 'is the only way we will preserve Soviet power and protect that freedom won against all the nefarious assaults of the capitalists of the entire world.'[2]

According to Soviet legend – embellished, perhaps, for propaganda purposes – the Aral fishermen rose to the challenge and sent fourteen railway carriages of fish to the Volga in a *podvig* (heroic feat) celebrated around the USSR. It is remembered today in a bold mural at Aralsk railway station showing burly fishermen hauling in their catch from the deep blue sea and handing it into the arms of upright Red Army soldiers waiting onshore.

Twenty years later, the Aral village of Bogen became a national symbol of proletarian solidarity and sacrifice in the Great Patriotic War, celebrated for supplying fish to nourish soldiers battling it out with the Nazis on the front line.

In 2009, Bogen lay fifty kilometres inland from the sea, and on a wind-blown March afternoon it was engulfed by one of the dust storms that have become more frequent and severe since the sea began to shrink, bringing climate change in its wake. 'This is how we live here. You see how it all goes up here when the wind blows,' said an elderly man who worked in the cannery until it closed down, gesturing at the clouds of dust, salt and toxic residues billowing around.

The environmental disaster has wrought a terrible toll on the health of the millions of people living around the sea in Kazakhstan and Karakalpakstan, the region on the Uzbek side of the Aral. Studies have detected higher rates of respiratory, thyroid and kidney diseases as well as tuberculosis, typhoid and anaemia. There has been a spike in some types of cancer: according to research conducted in Karakalpakstan, between 1981 and 1987 liver cancer shot up by 200 per cent, throat cancer by 25 per cent and infant mortality by 20 per cent.[3] Scientists struggle to quantify the precise influence of the environmental disaster on human health – but there is no doubt that local people have suffered serious ill-effects as a result of breathing the toxic pesticides and fertilisers that were once sprayed with abandon onto the cotton fields and are now tossed through the air during the dust storms.

There were few residents out and about on the streets of Bogen as the dust storm surged through: a few elderly people hunched over walking sticks, heads bent against the driving wind; two boys driving a donkey cart loaded up with canisters filled from the village standpipe (there was no running water here). Life was more comfortable in some villages around the Aral; Tastubek, for example, was full of wealthy camel breeders, their stockades full of tethered beasts snorting and stomping, but breeding the ships of the desert (prized for their wool, milk and meat) took expertise and capital that villagers in places like Bogen did not have. Here, young people upped sticks as soon as they could – for Kyzylorda, the nearest city 500 kilometres away, where there were jobs in the oil business and a comfortable life with running water, paved roads, shopping centres, bars and restaurants; onwards to Astana or Almaty if they could. 'What can they do here? There's no work,' said the widow of a fisherman whose photograph hung, draped with silver and purple tinsel, on the wall in her spick and span home, where she lived alone because her children had joined the exodus. 'It was good when the sea was here,' she sighed mournfully.

The sea was miles away, and yet, amid the desolation, there was a whiff of hope in the salty air. It seemed impossible to believe, but at the spot where the Aral split into two in the 1980s, the sea was surging back.

The dust storm that had hit Bogen passed as suddenly as it blew in, and over in the haze where the blue horizon met the golden sand rose a new construction hailed as the saviour of the sea: the Kokaral Dam, looming up in the Berg Straits – named after that Russian geographer whose namesake ship stood rotting in Aralsk – which once linked the northern and southern basins. The sluice gates were slammed shut, and a deep blue body of water was collecting in the reservoir.

The idea of damming the straits to save the northern part of the Aral was mooted in the 1980s, after the waters dried up and left the sea bisected, its northern section in Kazakhstan and its larger southern part in Uzbekistan. In 1992, by which time the USSR had collapsed and there were two independent countries surrounding the two separate seas, a dyke was built on the Kazakh side in the first attempt to arrest the departure of the waters. A flimsy structure fashioned out of sand

and reeds, the makeshift dam collapsed several times and was rebuilt over the next decade until disaster struck: in 2002 a massive storm hit, with high winds whipping up huge waves that washed away the dyke, drowning two workers and leaving others stranded on top of trucks and cranes until they were rescued by boat and helicopter. It was time for a more serious approach to saving the sea – time for the Kokaral Dam.

The dam is named after a former island which became an isthmus when the sea split into two: Kokaral means 'green island', a nod to the once verdant wetlands around these parts. Aral means 'island', and the sea is full of them: the number has changed along with the size of the sea, but there were once around 1,100 here, including the notorious Ostrov Vozrozhdeniya (Resurrection Island), where the Soviets sited a now defunct germ warfare facility, now part of the mainland because the sea around has dried up. According to one theory, the name 'Aral' refers not to this scattering of islands but to the wetlands of the Amudarya delta, christened by nomads who viewed their watery habitat as an island among the surrounding rivers, lakes and marshes. This is the ravaged ecosystem that the Kokaral Dam is now trying to rescue, along with the sea.

'We're saving the lake system,' said Sergey Krasilnikov, a bluff official from the Russian company operating the dam, sitting in his office out in the desert surrounded by charts and maps. 'When we close the sluice gates, the lake system fills up,' he explained, jumping up from his desk to demonstrate on a wallchart. 'This is so local people can fish, but the main thing is that reeds can grow.' The rejuvenation of the wetlands should again bring climate change to the Aral region – this time for the better: more rains, fewer dust storms and better water, air and soil to grow crops and raise cattle.

Opened in 2005, the 13-kilometre, $86-million dam had already exceeded some of the wildest hopes invested in it. The water level in the northern, Kazakh part of the sea had shot up by 12 metres, reaching 42 metres from its low of 30 metres in 2003; the water surface had increased by half, to 3,300 square kilometres; and salinity levels had been slashed by half as fresh water flowed in from the Syrdarya.[4] Huge amounts of water were still being diverted upstream to irrigate the cotton fields, but new hydro-facilities lined the riverbanks to get the water flowing back into the delta and to turn the tide back towards Aralsk. When the

Kokaral Dam was built, the seawater had retreated 94 kilometres from the harbour, but it soon started inching back. In 2009, the sea was 40 kilometres away, and coming closer every year. By 2015, after the dam was extended, the sea was just 17 kilometres away,[5] and a scientific expedition in 2019 concluded that the restoration of the sea was well under way and the 'Northern Aral is alive.'[6]

To the astonishment of local people, the fish were also swimming back. 'Now we're fishing again in winter and summer!' said Tolyk, a former fisherman from Bogen. Although the giant Aral fleet trawlers rotting in Aralsk harbour would not be taking to the waters any time soon, there was fresh bounty in the sea for small fishing boats. 'There used to be lots of fish, now there are fewer,' the fisherman acknowledged, 'but still, last year we caught a lot.'

The catch from the northern, Kazakh part of the Aral had increased in the five years since the dam opened, from 52 tonnes in 2004 to nearly 3,000 tonnes in 2009, and four new canneries had opened in Aralsk to cope with the surge in demand.[7] This was a tiny fraction of the Aral Sea's record 34,000-tonne catch of 1961, but offered a glimmer of hope that the once moribund fishing industry could bounce back.[8] 'The fishermen brought a lot of fish last year,' said Sagyda, a cheerful market trader in Aralsk who was enjoying the novelty of selling Aral Sea fish alongside her usual fare of river fish from the Syrdarya and imported sea fish. 'I hope they'll bring more this year.' Her optimism was not misplaced: by 2015, the catch had increased by around twenty times compared to the days before the dam – and some Aral Sea fish were even being exported.[9]

Amid all the excitement about the fledgling resurgence of the sea, it was easy to forget that the resurrection of the northern part of the Aral in Kazakhstan did nothing to help the southern side in Uzbekistan, now dammed off from its sister sea and almost certainly doomed to die a slow death. The picture in Karakalpakstan was even more forlorn than on the Kazakh side, and the dam brought no fresh hopes of revival for the depressed town of Moynaq, which like Aralsk was once a thriving fishing port but was now stranded miles inland. Critics argued passionately that damming the Kazakh section had signed a death warrant for the Uzbek side of the sea, whose water volume had by 2011 shrunk by

80 per cent compared to the late 1980s.[10] The Uzbek side had itself split into two parts, an eastern and western section. That meant that there were three divided bodies of water where once there had been the Aral Sea, and since 2014 the eastern section of the Uzbek side had also been drying up in years when the water flow was weak.

Supporters of the dam countered that it was 'practically impossible' to save the shrinking Uzbek section of the sea, as Nikolay Aladin of the Russian Academy of Sciences – who had been studying the Aral for three decades – said regretfully over the telephone from Moscow in 2009. 'It has a different fate,' he added. The water blocked off by the Kokaral Dam was not in any case flowing over to the Uzbek side: the two sides of the sea had long since split, and the waters flowing from the Kazakh side into the Berg Straits were seeping uselessly away into the desert. 'This is called a medical compromise,' said the pragmatic professor: better to amputate the hand that has gangrene than let the poison spread and kill the whole body.

It was still a long ride out to the sea from Aralsk's derelict port: a couple of hours' drive bumping in a jeep across the scrubby seabed, where camels roamed routes the Aral Sea fleet once sailed; through villages that used to lie on the seashore but were now stranded miles inland; past a 'graveyard' of rusting hulks being slowly picked apart by scrap metal foragers – all melancholy reminders of the disappeared maritime past.

But finally, in a glint of silvery blue, there it was, the elusive water, rising out of the reedy wetlands: first, brackish puddles popping up among scrubby sand dunes, then little ponds gleaming among waving fronds, and finally a whole expanse of shimmering water stretching away into what was left of the sea that nearly shrank into oblivion.

Back in Aralsk, a billboard beside the railway tracks captured the new mood of cautious optimism. '*Suyinshi*' ('Good news'), it read, against a backdrop of a fishing trawler riding the ocean waves as seagulls circled overhead. 'The mother sea is coming!'

CHAPTER 26

The Wasteland

Semipalatinsk, 2016/2009

In the village of Znamenka, a huddle of houses engulfed in the eerie snowy landscape of north-eastern Kazakhstan, many people have tales to tell of the days when mushroom clouds used to explode on the horizon during their childhood. It often happened on a Saturday morning, when they would be rushed out of school to cower in the open air before an earth-shattering blast ripped through the atmosphere.

'We'd be sent outside, and we'd crouch in ditches. We saw mushroom clouds: big and terrifying ones,' recalls pensioner Galina Tornoshenko, shaking her head at the traumatic memory and gesturing upward at the sky, clear blue against the snow swallowing the village streets on a March day in 2016. 'I was small at the time, but I remember it well, oh my goodness me.'

This old lady was born around here in 1949, the year Stalin's Soviet Union detonated its first atomic explosion. That milestone was celebrated by a jubilant Kremlin as a turning point in the burgeoning arms race: Washington had ended World War II four years earlier by dropping atomic bombs on Nagasaki and Hiroshima, and Moscow was determined to acquire nukes to catch up with its arch-rival – fast.

Code-named Operation *Pervaya Molniya* (First Lightning) by the Soviets and Joe-1 by the Americans (after their nickname for Iosif Stalin, 'Uncle Joe', because his forename was commonly Westernised as 'Joseph'), that first explosion was detonated at a new top-secret nuclear *polygon* (testing ground) opened in 1947 which would become the key for Moscow to unlock its atomic ambitions. It was located at a site selected by Stalin's chief of secret police Lavrentiy Beria, on the grounds that it was 'uninhabited'.

At least that was the official line. But the spot chosen for the *polygon*, at 18,500 square kilometres slightly bigger than Kuwait, lay on the doorstep of Kazakhstan's industrial heartland: the city of Semipalatinsk was 120 kilometres away, and a little further afield lay the urban centres of Karaganda, Ust-Kamenogorsk and Pavlodar. For hundreds of kilometres around, there were also agricultural and herding communities living off the land.

The *polygon* went on to detonate 456 atomic explosions over the next 40 years, releasing energy 2,500 times that of the bomb dropped on Hiroshima. 'The drama of the test site is also the drama of the Kazakh land,' as Nazarbayev once put it.[1] This drama is still being played out for the people living on that land, which was not 'uninhabited'. The blasts scattered radioactive fallout over swathes of northern, eastern and central Kazakhstan as well as southern Russia. They exposed hundreds of thousands of people to dangerous levels of radiation, damaging the health of people who had not even been born when the testing ended.

Soviet rulers always put the motherland ahead of the people, the collective ahead of the individual, and the atomic weapons programme was no different. Little may have been known about the effects of radiation sickness in the early days, but the devastation wrought in Nagasaki and Hiroshima had offered a glaring clue about the destructive impact of nuclear explosions on human health and the environment. Nevertheless, scant thought was given to the effect of radiation raining down on the people living around Semipalatinsk-21, the name for the top-secret research centre built on the edge of the *polygon* 60 kilometres from ground zero. Around the research centre grew a new 'closed' town, also called Semipalatinsk-21, existing only to service the research facility and shown on maps simply as '*Konechnaya*' ('Last Stop'). For the Soviet rulers pursuing an atomic bomb at all costs, the people living around were at best inconveniences whose presence would not stand in the way of national nuclear glory, at worst hapless guinea pigs in a giant scientific experiment to win the nuclear arms race.

Znamenka lies in one of the areas worst affected by the nuclear fallout, a couple of hours' drive from the city of Semey (formerly called

Semipalatinsk) down a lonely road from which a turn-off led onto a bumpy byway that melted away as a howling wind blew snowdrifts across it. On the wide horizon, under a blue sky streaked with dramatic cloud, stood the silvery snow-flecked humps of the Degelen Mountains, where underground nuclear tests were once performed in 181 tunnels drilled into the rock, some still containing high-grade plutonium sealed inside.

'Welcome to Znamenka!' said the sign at the entrance to the village of squat houses dotted along potholed, ice-encrusted tracks. Outside one home, three weather-beaten men in their mid-fifties – collective farm workers in Soviet times, now unemployed – sat on a bench passing the time of day, huddled in woolly hats and thick jackets against the biting wind howling through the streets. When they attended the village school in the late 1960s and 1970s, nuclear explosions were a fact of life, even if they did not know what they were. 'On the radio they'd say: go out into the streets, there's going to be an earthquake,' recalled Serikkazy Baribayev. 'How would we know what an earthquake was?' shrugged Zhomart Mukhamedzhanov. 'How would we know what they were blowing up?' Mendibay Umirkhanov, born in a village called Sarapan in 1961, offered a bizarre example of the hopelessly inadequate measures bureaucrats sometimes dreamt up to protect the villagers against the hazardous explosions: they would gather children in groups and cover them with felt, a textile made of sheep's wool that was to hand in any village.

The villagers would be herded out of their homes by soldiers, who would sometimes circle overhead in helicopters, ordering residents out through loudspeakers. Seysenbey Zhantemirov, a local man who was at the time a lorry driver for the Semipalatinsk waterworks, remembered being sent to Sarapan to deliver spare parts in 1975, by which time the explosions had moved underground following an international ban on atmospheric testing in 1963. 'It got late, so I stayed the night,' recalled Seysenbey. 'In the morning, a helicopter came and there were soldiers with loudspeakers on it shouting: go outside, go outside. It happened on a Saturday at around nine in the morning. We went outside, then there was a huge explosion – dudoo! I flew into the air! There was no mushroom cloud like they show on TV. By then these were underground explosions. After that blast, everyone just went home. They said it happened every Saturday around nine in the morning.' The villagers were sent outside 'so the houses didn't fall on them – people could have died', he added, with a sardonic smirk at the irony of apparatchiks fretting about rubble injuring people they were zapping with massive doses of radiation. Many people had no idea what was going on at the *polygon*, and if they did suspect something was amiss, fear of retribution kept them quiet. 'Whether you're afraid or not, you have no choice – if you speak out, they'll soon shut your mouth!' said Seysenbey, with a matter-of-fact shrug.

The *polygon's* existence was classified, but by the late 1980s it was an open secret to those living around it. Times were changing: Gorbachev's glasnost encouraging debate on hitherto taboo topics was in full swing, and public opposition to the nuclear explosions emerged from the shadows. In February 1989, following a leak of radioactive gases from the *polygon*, a grass-roots anti-nuclear movement sprang up, its popularity fuelled by memories of the calamitous explosion of a nuclear reactor at Chernobyl in Ukraine three years earlier. Called Nevada-Semipalatinsk after the American and Soviet nuclear testing grounds and led by Kazakh poet Olzhas Suleymenov, the movement held rallies in Alma-Ata and Semipalatinsk which galvanised public opinion against atomic testing. Nazarbayev, who became Kazakhstan's communist boss in June 1989, was won over by the public mood, or perhaps the prevailing wind. He threw his support behind the anti-nuclear movement, and a moratorium was slapped on nuclear testing at Semipalatinsk. On 19 October 1989, forty years after Operation First Lightning, Semipalatinsk detonated its last atomic explosion, and in 1991 Nazarbayev signed the *polygon* out of existence. The USSR was collapsing, and Moscow washed its hands of this testing ground that had staged two thirds of the blasts in the Soviet atomic bomb programme and nearly a quarter of tests worldwide.[2]

In 2016, Kazakhstan was marking a quarter of a century since the site was mothballed, but the people around were still living with the nuclear fallout.

Semipalatinsk may be a byword for a nuclear wasteland, but the city that gave its name to the *polygon* is a pleasant, laid-back place that wears its heritage proudly. Founded in 1718 when the Russians built a fort by the Yertis River, Semipalatinsk has a famous literary tradition: nineteenth-century Kazakh poet Abay Kunanbayuly lived here, twentieth-century Kazakh novelist Mukhtar Auezov was born here, and Russian literary giant and political dissident Fyodor Dostoyevskiy was exiled here by tsarist Russia. In Semey (as it is now officially called, by its Kazakh name), tsarist-era municipal buildings and one-storey gingerbread cottages straight out of a Russian fairy tale jostle for space with Soviet-era tower blocks and glossy modern business centres. Lined up on one square stands a quirky collection of statues from the pantheon of communist heroes: multiple Lenins, minute to massive, alongside other revolutionary leaders and a bushy-bearded Marx. The city's newest and most poignant monument lies in the middle of the broad Yertis River, where ice fishermen huddled over holes teasing out winter's last catch. On a small island stands a towering statue called Stronger Than Death, depicting an exploding mushroom cloud containing a silver atom under which a mother kneels tending a baby in her lap.

In a small apartment in a drab suburb not far away, Mayra Zhumageldina was tending her disabled daughter, massaging her twisted limbs. 'If you don't do massage, they freeze up,' Mayra said brightly, smiling down fondly at her daughter as she manipulated her tiny deformed hands, the fingernails painted a cheerful red. Zhannur Zhumageldina was born in the village of Olzhabay, a couple of hundred kilometres from the *polygon*, in 1992 and was now twenty-four. The test ground was history before she came into the world – but the tests conducted there had left her unable to walk or talk, or to feed or dress herself. Zhannur was a second-generation victim of nuclear testing, diagnosed at the age of fifteen months with microcephaly, a neurological condition in which an abnormally small head impedes brain development, and later with kyphoscoliosis, severe spinal curvature that had left her paralysed.

Kazakhstan was 'a victim for [the sake of] the Soviet Union's wider security', Erlan Idrissov, the foreign minister, said in 2016, the twenty-fifth anniversary of the *polygon*'s closure. 'They used the local population as guinea pigs.'[3] One such guinea pig was Eliugazy Nurgaliyev, who was among forty-three young men kept under medical observation for years after being ordered to remain behind when their village was evacuated ahead of an explosion in the early 1950s. 'The military people took us to the middle of the steppe, gave us a tent, food and music and told us to enjoy the picnic,' the octogenarian told a journalist decades later. 'Suddenly the sky turned red and a big red storm gathered above our village. We lost our minds.'[4] Yet owing to secrecy surrounding the nuclear programme, researchers say it is hard to quantify how widespread the deliberate use of local people as research subjects was. 'I would not be able to say that it was deliberate, that they really had this menacing plan to use the local population as guinea pigs,' said Dr Togzhan Kassenova, originally from Kazakhstan and a fellow at the Nuclear Policy Programme at the Carnegie Endowment for International Peace in Washington.[5] 'But I do think they had little to no knowledge at that point on how radiation impacted humans. That's why, for example, they were using all these animals on the testing site – to see what the impact on humans would be.'

The deleterious effects of nuclear explosions on living creatures are displayed in a chamber of nuclear horrors in the town once called Semipalatinsk-21, now renamed Kurchatov after the Soviet physicist in charge of the nuclear bomb programme. 'I am happy that I was born in Russia and have dedicated my life to the nuclear science of the great Country of the Soviets,' reads an inscription on Igor Kurchatov's bust outside the National Nuclear Centre, nowadays the powerhouse of Kazakhstan's thriving civilian nuclear industry. A museum inside displays horrifying exhibits: damaged vocal chords and cerebral cortices of various animals; haemorrhaged hearts, bladders and lungs of dogs; disfigured pig and sheep heads. 'The risks everybody was taking for the sake of equalising with the United States – I don't think the health of the local population was high on their priority list,' said Dr Kassenova. But there is no doubt that a medical institution opened in Semipalatinsk in 1957 was there not to provide treatment but to conduct top-secret research into the effect of radiation on human health. Anti-Brucellosis Dispensary Number 4 was ostensibly monitoring brucellosis, an infectious disease found in animals that can spread to humans, but, in Dr Kassenova's words, 'they were not there to treat people – they were there to observe people'.

The litany of health problems associated with radiation exposure detected by studies conducted around Semipalatinsk ranges from heart and thyroid disease to chromosomal aberrations and congenital deformities, and from neurological disorders to leukaemia and cancer of the breast, colon, oesophagus, liver, lung and thyroid. One study, conducted by Kazakh and Japanese researchers in 2008, concluded that levels of cancer were 25–30 per cent higher among those exposed to nuclear testing around Semipalatinsk than elsewhere in Kazakhstan.[6] Then there is the psychological trauma: researchers have, says Dr Kassenova, detected symptoms similar to those of the survivors of the Hiroshima and Nagasaki bombs.

Still, scientists cannot draw firm conclusions as they lack clear data: 'for years, what happened at the Semipalatinsk test site and its effects on human health and the environment were treated as classified information,' explained Dr Zhaxybay Zhumadilov, a professor from Nazarbayev University in the capital who alongside scientists from Hiroshima University has researched the impact of the Semipalatinsk tests.[7] In Soviet times, the national authorities in Moscow kept swathes of information about the nuclear programme secret from the local authorities in Kazakhstan, and the veil of secrecy remained drawn after the USSR's collapse. It has never even been precisely established how many people the tests affected. The Kazakh-Japanese study calculated that at least a quarter of a million people in Kazakhstan were exposed to dangerous levels of radiation, but Nazarbayev has estimated that at least half a million of the 1.5 million people living in areas of Kazakhstan affected by the nuclear explosions 'that caused colossal damage to our land and the health of the nation' suffered radiation exposure in some form.[8]

Many people in Semipalatinsk only learned of the *polygon*'s existence shortly before it was shut for good. 'We never knew it was [nuclear] tests taking place. They normally took place on Saturdays and Sundays. We'd wake up and the light fittings would be trembling. We never supposed that there was a *polygon* right beside us,' said Zhanna Zhibrayeva, a Semey-based civil society campaigner who had worked extensively with victims of nuclear testing. 'We were quite calm about it at first: OK, a *polygon*. We knew about Nagasaki and Hiroshima, but we were never told about the terrible consequences. [...] When we started to receive information, when we started to understand, then we got frightened. We started encountering people who were sick and dying early, children were born deformed – then we started to understand.' Her husband died aged fifty-two of brain cancer caused by radiation exposure.

The ecological impact of the atomic testing is also hard to determine precisely. Nazarbayev has said that a ninth of Kazakhstan's territory, equivalent to the size of Germany, 'was turned into a toxic wasteland, crippled by hundreds of nuclear explosions', causing environmental damage that will last for centuries.[9] Kazakh nuclear scientists are more optimistic: they said in 2021 that much of the *polygon's* land was already salvageable, though they were still finding "dangerous concentrations" of radioactive isotopes in some areas thirty years after the testing ground closed down.[10] Three missions dispatched to Semipalatinsk by the International Atomic Energy Agency in the 1990s found that 'most of the area has little or no residual radioactivity directly attributed to nuclear tests'.[11] But suspicions persist that people still live on radiation-contaminated land: from a helicopter flying journalists and diplomats to Kurchatov in 2009, herders could be seen grazing their flocks on the scrubby steppe and watering them in the Shagan River south-east of the *polygon* in areas identified by the National Nuclear Centre as badly affected by radiation.

Kazakhstan has 'the absolute historic and moral right to act as one of the leaders of the world anti-nuclear movement', Nazarbayev said in 2009, addressing a crowd in front of the mushroom-cloud monument in Semey at a ceremony marking the sixtieth anniversary of the first explosion and the twentieth anniversary of its last test, two years before it was shut for good.[12] Around 25,000 city residents – schoolchildren in spotless uniforms, spruced-up students, besuited office workers and war veterans sporting medals – had been bussed out for a rally in the middle of the working day, waving Kazakh flags and anti-nuclear placards: 'No to nuclear testing!' 'We are for world peace!' As Nazarbayev appeared, waving magnanimously, an organiser implored the crowd: 'Chant the slogans!' It responded with obedient rallying cries of: 'Kazakhstan! Nursultan! Semey! Otan! [Fatherland!]' After delivering his address, Nazarbayev listened to eulogies from speakers lauding his anti-nuclear stance – for this anniversary was not only a solemn tribute to the victims but also another occasion to hijack the limelight for some positive PR.

At independence, Nazarbayev not only closed down the *polygon*; he also relinquished the world's fourth largest arsenal of nuclear weapons. Kazakhstan enjoys a well-deserved global reputation as a responsible nuclear player, and lobbies tirelessly for nuclear disarmament under its ATOM ('Abolish Testing – Our Mission') project, whose ambassador is Karipbek Kuyukov, a Kazakh artist who was born without arms as a result of radiation exposure and paints with his feet and mouth. 'Based on its experience, Kazakhstan has legitimacy in this area,' said Dr Kassenova. 'In terms of what it means for the common good and for the international system as a whole, it's actually very beneficial that Kazakhstan wants to be so active in these issues.'

But the government also milks Kazakhstan's reputation as a cheer-leader for non-proliferation to burnish Nazarbayev's image as a promoter of world peace – and as he basked in the glory, the victims of nuclear testing seemed to take a back seat.

In 2016, in a cramped musty flat in a grey Semey suburb where the roads between shoddy apartment blocks were covered in thick sludge as the snows melted, 37-year-old Berik Syzdykov whiled away his days listening to music videos and strumming on his traditional stringed *dombyra*. He was born blind and with severe facial deformities in Znamenka in 1979. 'Once there was a big explosion,' his 73-year-old mother Zina Syzdykova remembered, leaning back on a scruffy couch in their rented flat and closing her eyes. 'It was the winter of 1979, and I was pregnant. Two months later, Berik was born like this.' She could not recall her son's diagnosis. '*Polygon*,' she shrugged. 'We didn't know anything about it. How would we know? When Berik was born I cried and cried, but how would I know what was wrong with him? They tried to treat him, but...' She tailed off and looked away.

Like other victims of nuclear testing here, Berik and his mother eked out a living on benefits: the compensation the Kazakh government paid out to victims in lump sums in the 1990s, mostly worth a few hundred dollars, had long since been spent. Berik rarely went outside the dingy flat, other than for medical check-ups. He started undergoing operations at the age of seven and had been through surgery in Europe (funded by foreign charities) as well as Kazakhstan (funded by the government), but still he dreamt of seeing what the world looks like. 'If I could see, it would be good,' he said longingly. 'If not, there's no need for any more surgery. I hate the anaesthetic. It plays on your nerves.'

In her flat across town, Mayra, a smiley, homely-looking woman in her forties, kept massaging her disabled daughter's limbs to stop them from atrophying. When doctors told her in 1993 that Zhannur was a victim of nuclear testing, it came as a bolt from the blue to Mayra, pregnant at the time with her second child (a son, born healthy). 'I didn't even know the *polygon* existed until Zhannurka was fifteen months old,' she said, affectionately using her daughter's diminutive name. 'They said: you know there's the *polygon* nearby? I was in shock,' remembered Mayra, massaging her daughter's legs, which were encased in red leggings and woolly socks. 'Everyone said I should abandon her – the doctors, my husband, my mother-in-law. I said: no, I'm going to look after her.'

Mayra's husband later disappeared, and the family survived on Zhannur's disability benefits. Mayra thanked her lucky stars that she had state-subsidised housing, for which she paid just $8 a month, a tenth of the market rate, for a flat consisting of one living room-cum-bedroom plus kitchen and bathroom. Airy and spotlessly clean but sparsely furnished, Mayra and Zhannur's flat was in a smart-looking block on a new social housing estate in the suburbs, but it had no hot running water. Mayra would have liked a kettle, but money was tight, so she boiled water in a pan on the stove. 'The main thing is that we've been given this flat,' she kept repeating – but she spent nineteen years begging the local authorities to get it.

The victims of nuclear testing are entitled to free healthcare, and Zhannur was sometimes sent to Astana for treatment in Kazakhstan's best hospitals. 'Zhannur's not going to walk and that's it. I just want some treatment,' said Mayra, who dreamt of sending her daughter to China, where she believed treatments were available that could alleviate (although not cure) her condition. 'Sometimes I cry,' she said wistfully, before adding stoically: 'I'm used to it. The main thing for me is Zhannur. She'll soon be twenty-five.' She flicked through a photo album showing pictures of her daughter growing up, laughing at a shot of a furry orange fox hugging Zhannur at a New Year party. 'Zhannurka means everything to me,' whispered Mayra softly. 'She's my precious one.'

In summer 2020, when Kazakhstan was in the grip of the coronavirus pandemic and the healthcare service was creaking under a devastating wave of infections, Zhannur fell ill. She had a sore throat and a hacking cough, then she began struggling for breath. As her daughter ailed, Mayra began to panic, and in the early hours she called an ambulance – but she was told there were none available to respond to her call. The next morning she rushed Zhannur to hospital – but there were no beds to take her. Mayra tried to call out a duty doctor – but a home visit was not possible. The doctor gave a consultation over WhatsApp, advising some medication to alleviate Zhannur's symptoms and promising to send a medic round to check on her – but no one came. That night, as Zhannur's condition deteriorated and she gasped for breath, Mayra again called for an ambulance. This time one arrived – but it was too late for her daughter. 'They came after Zhannur had already died in my arms,' said her mother, sobbing as she explained how her beloved daughter had passed away at the age of twenty-eight.

Medics identified the cause of death as heart failure, although the symptoms she displayed at a time when coronavirus infections were raging led to lingering doubts. Mayra fretted that her daughter might have survived, had medical assistance been forthcoming: 'Maybe if doctors had done something to her heart, Zhannur wouldn't have died.' Zhannur's death would not feature in the official coronavirus fatality statistics, but she was certainly a victim of the pandemic.[13] The struggling healthcare service had failed this vulnerable young woman and her mother, who had devoted nearly three decades of her life to bringing up a victim of Soviet nuclear testing with minimal support from the state. Mayra was left bereft. 'I don't need anyone but Zhannur. What should I do? My head is spinning,' she grieved. 'I miss Zhannur so much.'[14]

CHAPTER 27

The Ranch

Yesik, 2012

Former nuclear physicist Yevgeniy Chaykovskiy is lovingly tending his brood of ostriches as they strut about on his farm, casting long gangly shadows that dance around the yard in the dazzling midday sun on a May afternoon in 2012. As the sprightly septuagenarian approaches, the birds crowd inquisitively towards him with an ungainly ruffle of their feathery torsos, crested heads craning, beady eyes flashing. 'The African ostrich is quietly colonising the Central Asian steppe!' jokes the farmer, with a wondering shake of his shock of white hair.

He has owned this farm, a couple of hours' drive from Almaty towards China through bucolic countryside, for over a decade – but still he marvels daily at the sight of his beloved birds galumphing across his land. 'We've proven that the African ostrich can survive and thrive in the climatic and biological conditions of Kazakhstan,' he says, with a broad grin. This is a dream come true for the nuclear physicist-turned-ostrich farmer, an aspiration he could never have imagined would become reality when he first fell in love with the gawky bipeds four decades ago.

It was nuclear weapons, not ostriches, that brought Yevgeniy Vladimirovich (his patronymic) to Kazakhstan nearly half a century ago. He was dispatched from Moscow to the *polygon* at Semipalatinsk in 1970, during the Cold War, when talented young scientists were ordered to the secret site to try and power the USSR to victory in the nuclear arms race. Put to work testing rocket engines for nukes, Yevgeniy Vladimirovich became an acclaimed scientist involved in the pursuit of atomic glory for the

Soviet Union, and at one point was the mayor of Semipalatinsk-21, the closed town housing the top-secret nerve centre of the nuclear operation.

His job included travelling abroad with scientific delegations, and it was on one such trip that the young scientist lost his heart to his first ostrich. Visiting Belgium in the 1970s, he toured a farm breeding *struthio camelus* ('winged camels', the scientific name evoking their arid habitats) as part of a cultural programme for the Soviet scientists, and his enduring fascination with the flightless birds was born.

When the *polygon* closed in 1991, Yevgeniy Vladimirovich had the fleeting thought that losing his day job could free him up to see if his avian dream could take flight. However, although he had done his scientific duty to his motherland (the USSR) to the last, his contribution to his adopted homeland (newly independent Kazakhstan) was yet to come. He was among a group of nuclear physicists who lobbied Nazarbayev – at that time basking in global acclaim after giving up the country's arsenal of nuclear weapons – not to abandon Semipalatinsk-21 but to transform it into a scientific endeavour more suited to the post-arms-race age. Nazarbayev was won over by their plan to turn the former nuclear weapons research and testing site into a centre of excellence for Kazakhstan's civilian nuclear industry, and Yevgeniy Vladimirovich's career in the field was not finished after all: he spent the next decade labouring with other scientists to transform the secret research facility into Kazakhstan's National Nuclear Centre.

By 2001, Kurchatov was home to a flourishing atomic industry developing peaceful technologies that was putting Kazakhstan on the map as a responsible nuclear player – and the time had finally come for Yevgeniy Vladimirovich, then pushing sixty, to follow his dream. 'It was time to bid farewell to nuclear affairs, and I returned to the idea of creating a new type of agricultural business in Kazakhstan: ostrich farming.'

Yevgeniy Vladimirovich sank his savings into leasing farmland on the lush plains near the small town of Yesik, then flew off to Holland in search of ostriches. First, he needed to learn more about the 'winged camels', so – like a true scientist – he adopted a technique of total immersion. 'I lived in the building where the ostriches lived,' he said of his sharp learning curve on a Dutch ostrich farm. 'I asked them to put a bed in there with the ostriches and I watched everything they did and wrote it down. I learnt everything about them.' It sounds like quite a career change, but to the former nuclear physicist's scientific mind, the leap from testing rocket engines to raising ostrich chicks was not such a huge one. 'The methodology was one and the same,' he insisted: empirical evidence, look and learn, trial and error.

These hardy birds, which evolved on the dry plains of Africa, adapted quite easily to life in Kazakhstan, even to the cold winters: their downy bodies, developed to survive chilly nights in the desert, work like an eiderdown against the cold, and their thick eyelashes, evolved as protection against sandstorms, help them blink away the snow. They certainly seemed to be thriving, crowding eagerly up to the mesh enclosing their pen as a farmhand approached rattling a pail of feed, and pecking away greedily at the troughs as the farmer looked on indulgently.

Each of his seventy bipeds had its own personality, he said, and he could read their changing moods: some were bashful and retiring, some flirtatious and gregarious, some serene and sedate, some raucous and rambunctious – but the main thing to remember was that if you treated them right, they would return the favour. 'There are birds that are calm and greet visitors with pleasure, and there are aggressive birds. But the Almighty probably made everything that lives on earth – no matter if it's domestic or wild – capable of telling good from evil,' he declared with conviction. 'So if you treat a bird well, it will return that good to you.'

Ostrich breeding was his core business, one that the Soviet agricultural planners who once controlled every detail of what could be farmed on the land mass of the USSR could never have countenanced. The chicks were mainly sold to other aspiring breeders: a handful of ostrich farms had popped up elsewhere in Kazakhstan, and a dealer from Kyrgyzstan had recently bought some chicks to set up a breeding centre there. The farm also ran a tidy sideline in selling ostrich meat, whose health benefits the farmer extolled: high in protein and iron, lower in cholesterol and fat than other meats of which Kazakhs are fond, which include horse and camel as well as beef and lamb. Kazakhs are avid carnivores: an old joke goes that they are the second biggest meat eaters in the world, after wolves. They would benefit from heaping the less fatty ostrich flesh on *beshbarmak*, the national dish of pasta piled with hunks of meat, jested Yevgeniy Vladimirovich. He also sold ostrich eggs, which make a gigantic omelette that can feed thirteen people – best enjoyed, he grinned, 'with a shot of vodka and warm company'.

Business was booming, and to accommodate rising demand the farm needed a cash injection. Yevgeniy Vladimirovich had just turned seventy, and it was time to pass on the baton. He was selling up to an Almaty construction magnate who had pledged to keep the ostrich farm in business, under the tutelage of its founder for the first few years. 'I'm so sorry to say goodbye to it that I'm moved to tears,' said the old man in a choked voice. 'Intellectually and emotionally – all my input is here.'

As he glanced devotedly at his lanky brood in the pen, two ostriches suddenly began mating in a furious flutter of feathers. 'Look at his rubbery neck, his rubbery wings!' he blurted out with undisguised delight. 'It's love: he's making baby ostriches!'

CHAPTER 28

The Slumbering Steppe

Kalachi, 2015

Viktor Kazachenko was zooming across the steppe on his motor-bike one fine summer's day when his world suddenly went black. The next thing he knew, it was five days later. 'My brain switched off,' he says simply, of the moment the 'sleeping sickness' struck. Viktor had just become the latest victim of a mystery ailment plaguing Kalachi, a speck on a vast flat landscape in the far north of Kazakhstan.[1]

The villagers of Kalachi, which consists of a few rows of tidy Siberian-style cottages, keep dropping off for days on end, and no one can fathom why. 'We're all in fear of falling asleep,' sighs Tatyana Pavlenko, another resident. 'Children, old people, adults – they've all been falling asleep.' Since the perplexing affliction first struck two years ago, scores of people have plunged into comas lasting for days. 'It's not clear what's making people fall asleep, but fall asleep they do!' says Viktor, a bluff, camouflage-clad man in his late forties, standing alongside his sturdy, weather-beaten wife in front of their snow-shrouded cottage.

On this freezing day in February 2015, Raisa Kazachenko, a straight-talking woman swathed in a black fur coat and woolly hat who used to be a milkmaid on the *kolkhoz* in Soviet times, has a better recollection of the moment her husband was struck down. It was dramatic for her too: she was riding pillion on his motorbike when he fell into his coma. 'We were planning to go to town together. I locked the door. He was smoking, and he was shaking on his legs. His cigarette fell from his hand,' she recalls, revelling in the drama of the retelling. 'I said: Vitka, what's wrong? He said: my head's spinning. But we set off anyway, and we were driving across the steppe and then he just flopped over and we both went flying!' she concludes, with a flourish of her furry arm. 'It's good it wasn't that foreign car,' quips her husband with a chuckle, pointing to his small Opel parked in the garden. 'That's fast – a motorbike isn't so fast!'

Viktor is joking about his disorientating experience, but it is no laughing matter. The sleeping sickness leaves victims suffering debilitating after-effects, from blinding headaches, nausea and exhaustion to dizziness, hallucinations and amnesia. 'After this slumber, my blood pressure started going up for no reason,' says Viktor, still feeling under the weather six months later. 'Headaches – that's not the word. For six weeks, I didn't know where to put myself. It strongly affects your mentality. I'm very on edge.'

The boffins were baffled. Scientists were parading through Kalachi running tests on everything from the air, soil and water to the construction materials and animal feed. Yet neither scientists nor doctors had managed to answer the question preying on everyone's mind: what was causing the sleeping sickness, which had felled 120 villagers in the two years since it had first struck, around a quarter of Kalachi's population – some of them, including Viktor, more than once? A few months prior to passing out on his motorbike and losing the next five days of his life, he had dropped into a coma at home which lasted three days. All kinds of theories had been floated: from radiation sickness and carbon monoxide poisoning to contamination by radon, a radioactive gas, or a toxic concentration of heavy metal salts. All seemed possible in a country blighted by environmental devastation caused by reckless Soviet industrial and agricultural policies. Victims of the sleeping sickness had been dispatched to Kazakhstan's top medical centres in Astana and to the National Nuclear Centre in Kurchatov for tests, but the cause of the ailment remained a mystery. 'We're in shock. We're all afraid of it,' said an anxious-looking Tatyana Shumilina, a housewife in her fifties. 'How should a person be treated if they don't even know what it is?' In the absence of hard scientific fact, rumour and conspiracy theory abounded. 'They know what it is but they're not saying,' muttered Viktor darkly – a common sentiment in the village, where an ingrained distrust of officialdom was making the problem harder to tackle.

Many believed that the solution to the puzzle lay right on their doorstep, in the ghost town next door to their village: Krasnogorskiy, a dystopian townscape of spectral ruins casting spooky chiaroscuros on the wintry landscape.

This is the site of an abandoned Soviet-era uranium mine from which local people believed toxic emissions could be seeping. 'We've been thinking it was radiation,' said Tatyana. 'We have a uranium mine here, although it's been a ruin for years.' But if it was the abandoned mine, why had her parents and other miners working it in Soviet times never fallen asleep for days on end? This urban wreck was once a humming town inhabited by miners brought from all over the Soviet Union to extract the uranium that powered the USSR's atomic weapons programme and nuclear power stations – yet none of their descendants in Kalachi recalled any miners ever being struck down by the sleeping sickness.

When the mine closed in the dying days of the Soviet Union, the miners lost their jobs and Krasnogorskiy lost its raison d'être. Now it looked abandoned, but there were still several dozen families scratching out a living amongst the ruins. An old woman carrying a shopping bag scurried alongside the shell of an abandoned building looming eerily out of the snow, as the windows of desolate blocks of flats nearby gaped emptily against the bright blue sky.

If the authorities had their way, soon Kalachi would also be a ghost town. With lots of questions and no answers to the medical conundrum, the local government, backed by the central government in the capital, had come up with a radical solution: evacuation of the villagers to move them out of harm's way. But far from welcoming this concern for their welfare, many residents were up in arms. Even some who had suffered the sleeping sickness were adamant that they would not leave their homes.

'I'm not going anywhere,' said Viktor, who was brought to Kalachi as a child by his Russian miner parents, folding his arms stubbornly at the prospect. 'Why should I go? I've been here for forty years. I'm going to die here.' His wife, whose parents moved here from Russia to extract uranium in the 1950s, was equally defiant. 'I've lived in this house for twenty years. I've lived on this street for sixty years,' she exclaimed indignantly. 'Now where will they send me? What's awaiting me there?'

Life in Kalachi looked hard to an outsider. Temperatures plunged to minus 40 in winter, there was no running water indoors in most houses – Raisa had just returned with a sledge after hauling water home from a standpipe in the village – and there was little work. Since the uranium mine and the collective farm closed with the collapse of the Soviet Union, the villagers had scratched a living from their land and livestock. Yet Kalachi was home, and the evacuation was ripping the community apart as some families upped sticks and others dug in their heels.

The Kazachenkos had just been listing the litany of ill-effects Viktor still feels from his comas, yet they were blasé about the health hazards of staying put. 'It was nothing. We woke him up,' said Raisa, with an airy wave of her gloved hand. 'I've lived here all my life and I'm fine. I'm not sleeping yet!'

This oblivion to the health hazards and dogged resistance to the evacuation plans was making Kalachi's young, no-nonsense female *akim* (mayor) sigh with frustration. Asel Sadvokasova, a smartly dressed woman in her thirties with a cascade of dark hair and a brusquely efficient manner, was adamant that if the health threat could not be identified and eliminated, the people had to go.

'We can't sit with our arms folded watching people fall asleep here,' she said exasperatedly. She knew first hand what she was talking about: the mayor had herself succumbed to a bout of sleeping sickness that had knocked her out for several days. No one was being forced to move out, she said: resettlement was 'all on a voluntary basis'. Her focus was on encouraging the recalcitrant residents to see the relocation not as a threat, but as an opportunity to start new lives in more prosperous places. Everything was being done to meet the villagers' needs in their new locations, she promised: new houses, new jobs and places in Russian-language schools for their children (the villagers were mostly Slavs, while the mayor was Kazakh). Not everyone was buying into her sales pitch, however. 'What sort of voluntary resettlement is it if it's forced?' grumbled Victor truculently.

The government has a policy of encouraging rural people to resettle from dying villages, to save resources on providing public services for dwindling populations – and the local rumour mill had it that the authorities were deliberately concealing the cause of the sleeping sickness to drive the residents out, using the affliction as a pretext to wipe another village off Kazakhstan's map.

'There's no mystery, no secret,' rebutted the harassed mayor wearily, frustrated by the conspiracy theories: as soon as scientists found out the cause, the villagers would be the first to know. As for talk of a government plot to close the village, it was baseless, she insisted: 'All social facilities – the hospital, the school, the mayor's office – will work as long as the last resident is here.'

The local government was bending over backwards to help the inhabitants find somewhere else to live: it had conducted a door-to-door survey of every family asking them where they would like to go and what sort of work they could do. Villagers were being awarded relocation costs and helped to find homes and employment elsewhere in Akmola Region, the massive province (about half the size of Poland) surrounding Kalachi. A hundred or so people had snatched the chance to move out, many to the nearest town of Yesil, a bone-juddering hour's drive through an empty silvery landscape along a road that evaporated under snowdrifts in the middle of winter.

There were still 180 families – 425 people in total – living in Kalachi (and in 2020, there were still 124 families left residing in this village, which nevertheless looked as if it would eventually disappear from the map – even if no cases of the 'sleeping sickness' had been reported for quite some time[2]). Some were getting ready to leave, others were stubbornly resisting abandoning their homes for a step into the unknown. 'Where will we go? We're old!' exclaimed pensioner Vera Matselko, who was reluctant to start a new life at the age of sixty. 'They say "we're giving you a home", but what are they giving me? It's not mine!' she sniffed. 'Then you have to do everything from scratch – paint the house, get the household up and running.' Like others, she feared officials were making big promises because they were under pressure to find a solution, but would fail to deliver – even though the government was behind the plans and said the enigmatic problem was on Nazarbayev's radar. Still, this woman was apprehensive about uprooting from her home in the village where she had lived her whole life, where all her friends were, for an unknown future in a town, without land to grow the food upon which she relied to supplement her pension.

'It's hard for us. We're used to having our own home with its little vegetable plot,' said Tatyana, who was nervously eyeing the prospect of being uprooted for the second time in her life due to forces beyond her control. Nine years previously, her family had been resettled from Krasnogorskiy, where she had lived for forty years ever since her parents had moved there as miners with the five-year-old Tatyana in tow. That time the authorities had shifted residents out of the dying town to Kalachi to save resources, and now she felt strong-armed into contemplating another move against her will. 'We lost our home then,' she said dejectedly. 'And now we're being resettled again.'

The mood in the village veered between angry and sad, but the mayor was determined to put an optimistic spin on events. 'Things are generally positive in terms of the resettlement,' she insisted, with a toss of her long hair and a show of cheery optimism that flew in the face of the evidence. 'There are families who are not agreeing to move,' she conceded, with impressive understatement, when pressed. 'While the matter isn't resolved yet, for now we're working with the families that do want to resettle.'

A few months later, in July 2015, scientists finally established the cause of the sleeping sickness: it was indeed the abandoned uranium mine at Krasnogorskiy. Concentrations of carbon monoxide, carbon dioxide and hydrocarbons were building up periodically, creating a toxic formula that caused people to drop into comas – a phenomenon exacerbated by Kalachi's geographical location and climatic peculiarities.[3] But identifying the problem was a far cry from solving it; beyond relocation, officials had no solution to offer the residents. The sleeping sickness came in waves when carbon monoxide built up in the derelict mine – so although this wave had ebbed, experts believed it would strike again.

'It's like living on a volcano!' groused Raisa, afraid that the life she had lived for sixty years could be turned upside down at any moment. 'They say it affects the brain. They say it gives people headaches,' she barked. 'But our headache now is where we're being resettled!'

CHAPTER 29

The Collective Farm

Karakemer, 2014

When Zeynulla Kakimzhanov took over a wilting vineyard in Kazakhstan's Assa Valley in 2006, the surroundings looked pretty bleak. Abandoned vines straggled over the soil in unkempt bunches, and the winery was crumbling into a state of disrepair. Eight years on, the sight is very different: what was once a Soviet collective farm that churned out plonk for the masses now looks like an age-old vineyard basking in a sun-drenched corner of Tuscany.

Zeynulla, an ebullient government minister-turned-viticulturalist, is a man on a mission: to bottle fine wines to tickle the taste buds of the most discerning wine snobs. The idea of putting Kazakhstan on the oenophile's map may raise eyebrows, but Zeynulla is convinced he can shatter stereotypes about a country better known for its gushing oil than its flow of vintage wines. 'Here, taste this,' he says, proffering a glass of Merlot fresh from the barrel. 'Smooth, easy drinking – it's a divine wine!'

The conditions in the Assa Valley – 'high altitude, good sun, fresh air, good water, superb soil' – are perfect for viticulture, says the suntanned 55-year-old with an air of infectious confidence as he strolls energetically around his vineyard one afternoon in June 2014 after cycling there from Almaty, an 80-kilometre journey under the burning sun. 'We're at a similar latitude to the Rhone Valley, but we're higher – it means it's more sun-intensive,' he elaborates. Even Kazakhstan's bitter winters are a godsend, he says: the diseases and parasites that ravage vines in Europe are no match for the freezing temperatures here. The frosts protect the plants from disease, and to protect the plants from the frosts, Zeynulla has come up with an ingenious solution: 'We bury them.' When the mercury starts plunging, he and his staff embark on the painstaking process of gently folding thousands of vines and covering them with a protective coating of soil, upon which layers of snow fall throughout the winter. When the snow melts in spring, the vines emerge intact, ready to sprout new grapes.

When Zeynulla took over the Kirov Collective Farm in the village of Karakemer in 2006, it had suffered from two decades of wanton destruction and neglect. Opened in the 1950s by Soviet central planners who spotted southern Kazakhstan's potential as a viticultural hotspot, for three decades the *kolkhoz*, named after a Bolshevik revolutionary, produced rivers of plonk until it fell victim to an anti-alcohol crusade which saw vines ripped out of the soil across the USSR.

'*Sukhoy zakon*' (dry law) was intended to wean the hard-drinking Soviet public off the bottle. This was partly for health reasons, but mainly because of lost productivity caused by absenteeism and employees working in a haze of alcohol-fuelled oblivion. Introduced in 1985 by Gorbachev, dry law involved ratcheting up booze prices, restricting sales and slashing production. Vodka was the tipple of choice for most hard drinkers, and Gorbachev set the target of halving production with a view to halving consumption – but wine also joined the list of alcoholic beverages upon which the state frowned. The new spirit of abstinence was summed up in a propaganda poster of the time: a clean-cut young man firmly declining a tempting shot of vodka with an outstretched hand, accompanied by the slogan 'NET!' ('NO!').

Dry law was a flop: desperate drinkers turned to anything from moonshine and glue to boot polish and perfume to get their fix, the state lost millions in alcohol taxes, and Gorbachev certainly won no popularity points with the long-suffering Soviet public. But by the time the anti-alcohol campaign was quietly abandoned in the late 1980s, the damage had been done. Zealous apparatchiks targeted Kazakhstan along with better-known Soviet wine-growing regions such as Georgia, Armenia and Moldova, and by the end of '*sukhoy zakon*' over two-thirds of Kazakhstan's vineyards had been destroyed. Even four decades on, Kazakhstan still had less than half as much land planted with vines as it did before the prohibitionists marched in and ripped them up in a spirit of temperance.[1]

The Kirov Collective Farm survived the onslaught of dry law and limped on into independence, but suffered years of neglect as state funding dried up and Soviet-era managers struggled to adapt to the new economic realities of the free market.

Enter Zeynulla, who had been a Soviet central planner before the USSR collapsed. Born in the small town of Charsk near Semipalatinsk, where he once worked as a carpenter on the railways, he went from humble beginnings to graduate in economics from the prestigious Moscow State University, before returning to Kazakhstan to work at a research institute attached to Gosplan, the Soviet central planning agency. When the USSR collapsed, he embraced capitalism with a vengeance and made a mint in Kazakhstan's fledgling financial sector. In the late 1990s, Nazarbayev invited the successful financier to join his administration, first as an adviser, then finance minister, then director of an investment fund – and unlike some of the 'Young Turks' who were his contemporaries he managed to survive the experience without falling foul of the president. A flamboyant character on Kazakhstan's political scene, Zeynulla made plenty of headlines, especially when in 2001 he pledged to take advantage of a nationwide amnesty on undeclared earnings announced by the government in which he was serving as minister of revenues to bring his own revenue out of the shadows (he brushed aside allegations of wrongdoing, and said he had merely used legal mechanisms to minimise tax liability).[2] Fifteen years later he was back in the news when his family became embroiled in an ugly business dispute, and went on to win a libel suit in 2017 against *Forbes Kazakhstan* over allegations that family-linked companies were mired in sleaze. When some commentators allegedly refused to cease and desist, he launched a criminal case in 2018 threatening journalists with jail terms for the 'dissemination of knowingly false information' – a step roundly condemned by the OSCE's media freedom representative as an 'act of intimidation'.[3] He won the case and was awarded damages.[4]

Zeynulla had survived the cut-throat world of business and walked the tightrope of politics in Kazakhstan, but making wine was the hardest thing he had ever done. 'A thousand different factors influence the quality of the wine,' he explained. 'If you make one mistake, you'll kill the wine.' The financial sector looked 'very simple, even primitive', by comparison, he joked – 'just sums, loss or profit'.

After Zeynulla took over the old *kolkhoz* in 2006, he was astonished, while tramping across the forlorn terrain with Mario Fregoni, an Italian winemaker he had hired as a consultant, to stumble upon some long-abandoned vines that had survived two decades of destruction and neglect. A closer inspection revealed that there were quite a few rows of these hardy plants that had lain dormant for years, clinging tenaciously to life by roots clawing deep into the soil – and they were ripe for revival. 'Your future is in these old vines planted in Soviet times!' Zeynulla recalled Fregoni exclaiming excitedly. The plants had been brought to Kazakhstan from the USSR's premier wine-growing region in Georgia to kick-start the winemaking industry sixty years earlier – now they would get a new lease of life.

Painstakingly replanted, the old vines were now thriving, growing grapes like Saperavi, which produces a rich red, and Rkatsiteli, which yields a crisp white. Nowadays, the vineyard grew these Georgian varieties that are much loved in the former Soviet Union alongside grapes more familiar in the West, imported from Europe: Cabernet Franc, Shiraz, Pinot Noir, Merlot, Malbec, Gewürztraminer. 'This one will be ready in five years, but better in seven,' said the vineyard owner, lovingly stroking an oak barrel of Merlot Reserve maturing in the fermentation room in the old collective farm that he had transformed into a state-of-the-art winery. 'It's not a potato,' he joked with a grin. 'You can't just dig it up and eat it!' It took seven years for his company, Arba Wine, to produce its first bottling for commercial sale, and it would be many more yet – maybe another decade – before the vineyard broke even, let alone made a profit. 'I always dreamt of having this in Kazakhstan,' mused Zeynulla, serious all of a sudden. 'We believe in what we're doing, and we believe it'll work out really well for us.'

Kazakhstan is no big wine-quaffing nation – most drinkers prefer beer or vodka. 'The culture of wine is undeveloped in Kazakhstan,' noted Zeynulla ruefully. 'This has been one of the challenges: to promote not only our wine, but the culture of wine itself.'

But times are changing: Arba Wine's classy shop-cum-wine bar in Almaty does a steady if not roaring trade, and wine bars have started popping up as a taste develops among Kazakhstan's new oenophiles. One warm evening later that summer, Timur Tulebayev, a connoisseur, was leading a wine-tasting evening on the terrace of a trendy Almaty restaurant. 'Wine's considered a luxury,' he said, as several dozen young professionals chatted while sampling the varieties on offer. 'People consider that if you drink wine you must have lots of money or something, but slowly this habit is changing. You can see more middle-class people starting to explore.'

Zeynulla started the vineyard as a hobby, but now he was aiming for the sky: after conquering the Kazakh market he wanted to 'target world-class wines' and win over the palates of foreign bon viveurs. Timur agreed it was possible: 'There is potential to produce good wine' in Kazakhstan. When he travelled abroad, people had either never heard of his country at all or proffered associations that made him roll his eyes ('Borat, corruption, oil!'), but he knew Kazakhstan had so much more to offer than that. 'If I go to some country maybe in ten years and somebody says "I tried that wine from Kazakhstan and it was good", I'll be proud.'

Viniculture is not an art that sits well with nomadic culture: to tend vines and cultivate wine from them requires a settled lifestyle, and in times gone by the Kazakhs favoured other beverages more practical for supping on the hoof, like *kymyz* (fermented mare's milk) and *shubat* (camel milk) – drinks still beloved in Kazakhstan today, now available pre-bottled in supermarkets. But wine has a long tradition in this part of the world: grapes and vinicultural expertise passed through Kazakhstan as goods and know-how migrated eastwards from Europe towards China along the Silk Road (it was two-way traffic that plied that ancient trading route) and winemaking also spread north from other areas of Central Asia inhabited by settled peoples.

In fact, evidence of wine consumption dating back thousands of years has been uncovered right here on the land where this vineyard now stands: in 1959, Soviet archaeologists unearthed an amphora containing wine traces from an Iron Age Scythian kurgan, a burial mound in which the ancient nomads interred illustrious warriors alongside their treasures. A couple of millennia ago, nomadic tribes used this awe-inspiring landscape as a necropolis for their great and good: there are many more kurgans dotted around these parts, and it is not far from here that the Golden Man was found: a Scythian prince interred draped in 4,000 gold ornaments, who has been adopted by Kazakhstan as a glittering national symbol.

Here on this vineyard in the Assa Valley in south-eastern Kazakhstan, the Scythian kurgan loomed up among glistening emerald vines that rippled away to a kaleidoscopic horizon, melting into the purple haze of the snow-crested Tian Shan Mountains against a cloud-streaked sapphire sky. An ancient burial ground that became a Soviet collective farm has been reborn as a boutique Kazakh winery. How times have changed in Kazakhstan.

The Endgame

Almaty, 2022

As Kazakhstan celebrated New Year in January 2022, a blaze of violence convulsed the country, its epicentre in Almaty. City hall was stormed and set alight; the airport seized; TV studios occupied; police stations attacked. Security forces opened fire; gunfights erupted on the streets; Toqayev called in Russian troops. Days of turmoil left 227 people dead nationwide, according to an early death toll, which many believed an undercount. How had the festive season in easy-going Almaty – where at this time of year the snowy streets are usually packed not with gunmen and looters but families strolling and hedonistic revellers heading to hipster bars – degenerated into these apocalyptic scenes?

The roots of the turmoil lay in Zhanaozen, where a decade earlier security forces' shooting of striking oil workers had exposed fault lines that now ruptured with even more deadly consequences. Rocketing fuel prices brought demonstrators onto the streets. When rallies spread to other cities, the government caved in to demands and re-introduced subsidies to lower the cost of fuel. But the protests were already snowballing around Kazakhstan, and the demonstrators' complaints were snowballing too. All those socioeconomic grievances that citizens had been complaining about for years poured out: low salaries; high prices; joblessness; corrupt officials robbing the country blind while the rich got richer and the poor poorer. Next came political demands, protesters taking up an old slogan: '*shal ket!*' – 'old man out!'. Now 81, Nazarbayev was approaching the third anniversary of his resignation with Kazakhstan still under his thumb, even if his hand was increasingly doddery. But the slogan had imbued a broader meaning: people wished to rid themselves of the unaccountable, self-serving political establishment that had ruled them for thirty years – Toqayev and his hollow 'Listening State' included. The state had turned a deaf ear to public grievances over and over again. Now, they would explode into catastrophe for Kazakhstan.

In Almaty, people from all walks of life joined political activists on the streets and eventually converged on Republic Square, where tear gas and stun grenades failed to disperse them. What this mass peaceful movement might have turned into will never be known, because mobs hellbent on violence with links to mafia groups arrived on the scene, seemingly directed by malevolent forces. Marauders attacked police and civilians; stormed and set alight to city hall and the presidential residence; seized the airport and broadcasting facilities; attacked police stations; set cars and buildings ablaze; looted shops and businesses. Security forces opened fire, even before Toqayev made public – amidst a communications blackout – that he had issued a shoot-to-kill order. Seeking military or political support or both, he summoned a contingent of Russian-led forces. Just how did these peaceful protests demanding political freedoms and social justice spiral into this deadly violence?

Toqayev's explanation was perplexing: 20,000 'terrorists' and 'bandits', including foreigners, had emerged from sleeper cells to join a pre-planned operation to topple him. While the orchestrated occupation of strategic facilities lent weight to the suggestion of a coordinated attack, the theory sounded far-fetched, and no evidence was forthcoming. The names of over 200 dead civilians (19 fatalities were law-enforcement officers) remained under wraps, but peaceful protesters and passers-by, including children, were certainly among them. Toqayev angrily denied the shooting of non-violent demonstrators – but eyewitnesses said the army had opened fire on people holding up a banner reading: 'We are ordinary people – we are not terrorists!' Some of the 12,000 people arrested emerged from detention displaying horrific injuries sustained under torture. Others faced serious charges of terrorism and fomenting unrest. Some were probably guilty; others perhaps not. The 'guilty until proven innocent' culture of Kazakhstan's justice system and the torture of detainees cast doubt on Toqayev's pledge that the truth would be laid bare and justice served.

The gaping hole in Toqayev's attempted coup theory was his refusal to name names: who had fomented a plot to topple him? But actions speak louder than words. He ousted Nazarbayev as Security Council chairman; fired the defence minister; and had security chief Karim Masimov arrested on treason charges, saying the KNB security service had gone rogue. But one senior KNB figure got off lightly, with a dismissal: Masimov's deputy Samat Abish, who was Nazarbayev's nephew. The rumour mill was in overdrive with chatter that Nazarbayev family members had been plotting against Toqayev. Revanchist forces close to the ex-president had, so the theory went, been anxiously eyeing the end of the Nazarbayev era, when he would no longer be around to protect their security and assets, so they hijacked peaceful protests and summoned mafia-linked mobs from their powerbase around Almaty to stoke chaos. Their endgame was to oust Toqayev and install their own president. There was no evidence, but if it were true, Toqayev had reason to keep quiet. How could he reveal that cronies of the father of the nation were responsible for this deadly violence? Nazarbayev washed his hands of the whole affair, the Leader of the Nation emerging after a protracted silence to announce that he was nothing but a 'pensioner' and power was in Toqayev's hands.

Toqayev may have cut a deal to protect shadowy figures, but he also embarked on 'de-Nazarbayevification', ousting Nazarbayev's relatives from businesses and official positions and promising 'de-oligopolisation' of the economy, and political reforms down the line. But would Toqayev be up to the job? Would he again tinker with the system, or embark on the root-and-branch reform that Kazakhstan so desperately required and for which its people were clamouring? Nazarbayev's legacy was in tatters, as calls resounded to strip the capital of his name so Nur-Sultan would revert to Astana. The system Nazarbayev had fashioned to serve himself and his cronies had not only failed his people miserably, but failed him as well. He had bred a monster, and bequeathed it to Toqayev to tame. Kazakhstan was at a watershed as it finally started moving into the post-Nazarbayev era. What that would be like was anyone's guess.

Notes

All references to websites were correct at the time of writing, unless otherwise indicated.

Introduction

1 Craig Murray, *Murder in Samarkand* (Edinburgh, 2006), p. 341.

1. Arise, Kazakhstan

1 Nursultan Nazarbayev, *Без Правых и Левых* [Without right and left], (Moscow, 1991). Also available online at the official site of the President of the Republic of Kazakhstan, p. 9, http://personal.akorda.kz/images/file/f1a45bf03d51ef225240 cc06bdf1b3b1.pdf.

2 'Биография и Семья' [Biography and family], official site of the President of the Republic of Kazakhstan, http://personal.akorda.kz/ru/category/detstvo.

3 Jonathan Aitken, *Nazarbayev and the Making of Kazakhstan: From Communism to Capitalism* (London/New York, 2009), p. 27.

4 Nariman Gizitdinov and Torrey Clark, 'Nazarbayev weighs new run to extend longest ex-Soviet tenure', Bloomberg, 12 February 2014, http://www.bloomberg.com/news/articles/2014-02-11/nazarbayev-considers-fifth-term-to-extend-longest-ex-soviet-rule.

5 World Bank data, https://data.worldbank.org/country/kazakhstan.

6 Gizitdinov and Clark, 'Nazarbayev weighs new run'.

7 Michael Parks, 'Kazakhstan and its leader gain in stature', *Los Angeles Times*, 15 September 1991, http://articles.latimes.com/1991-09-15/news/mn-3686_1_soviet-union.

8 World Bank data, https://data.worldbank.org/country/kazakhstan.

9 Ron Stodghill, 'Oil, cash and corruption', *New York Times*, 5 November 2006, www.nytimes.com/2006/11/05/business/yourmoney/05giffen.html.

10 Colby Pacheco and Swathi Balasubramanian, 'Achieving development impact with an inclusive asset-return model', IREX, 2015, https://www.irex.org/sites/default/files/node/resource/bota-case-study-executive-summary.pdf.

11 Aygerim Abilmazhitova, 'Сколько детей родилось в независимом Казахстане' [How many children have been born in independent Kazakhstan], *Tengri News*,

1 June 2016, https://tengrinews.kz/strange_news/skolko-detey-rodilos-v-nezavisimom-kazahstane-295520/.

12 'Названа численность казахстанцев после переписи населения' [Number of Kazakhstanis announced after population census], *Tengri News*, 8 December 2021, https://tengrinews.kz/kazakhstan_news/nazvana-chislennost-kazahstantsev-posle-perepisi-naseleniya-456004/.

13 'Мемлекет басшысы Нұрсұлтан Назарбаев Тұңғыш Президент, Ұлт көшбасшысы туралы заңнамаға өзгерістер мен толықтырулар енгізу жөніндегі заңдарға қол қойған жоқ және осыған байланысты Қазақстан азаматтарына, ел Парламентіне, "Нұр Отан" Халықтық-демократиялық партиясының Саяси бюросына үндеу жолдады' [Head of state Nursultan Nazarbayev has not signed laws on amendments and addenda to legislation on First President and Leader of Nation and in this regard has made an address to citizens of Kazakhstan, country's Parliament and Political Bureau of Nur Otan People's Democratic Party], official site of the President of the Republic of Kazakhstan, 3 May 2010, http://www.akorda.kz/kz/events/memleket-basshysy-nursultan-nazarbaev-tungysh-prezident-ult-koshbasshysy-turaly-zannamaga-ozgerister-men-tolyktyrular-engizu-zhonindegi-zand.

14 'Президент предложил пересмотреть возраст выхода госслужащих на пенсию' [President proposes reviewing civil servants' retirement age], *Tengri News*, 18 November 2015, https://tengrinews.kz/kazakhstan_news/prezident-predlojil-peresmotret-vozrast-vyihoda-284289/.

15 Nikolay Ivashenko, 'Казахи никогда не жили так, как сейчас – Назарбаев' [Kazakhs have never lived as they do now – Nazarbayev], *365info.kz*, 26 May 2016, http://365info.kz/2016/05/kazahi-nikogda-ne-zhili-tak-kak-sejchas-nazarbaev/.

16 'Правительству Казахстана поручено сократить разрыв между богатыми и бедными' [Government of Kazakhstan ordered to narrow gap between rich and poor], *Tengri News*, 10 April 2013, https://tengrinews.kz/kazakhstan_news/pravitelstvu-kazahstana-porucheno-sokratit-razryiv-bogatyimi-231889/.

17 'Average wages in Kazakhstan rise by 7.6 per cent in 2013', Interfax-Kazakhstan, 15 January 2014. Available at http://ilo.ch/moscow/news/WCMS_247345/lang--en/index.htm.

18 'Средняя зарплата выросла в Казахстане' [Average wage grows in Kazakhstan], *Zakon.kz*, 30 July 2021, https://www.zakon.kz/5077563-srednyaya-nominalnaya-zarplata-vyrosla.html.

2. A Family Affair

1 Joanna Lillis, 'Death in Kazakhstan', openDemocracy, 22 February 2006, https://www.opendemocracy.net/democracy-protest/kazakhstan_3293.jsp.

2 'Akezhan Kazhegeldin announces candidacy for the presidency of Kazakhstan', PR Newswire, 10 October 1998, http://www.prnewswire.co.uk/news-releases/akezhan-kazhegeldin-announces-candidacy-for-the-presidency-of-kazakhstan-156073115.html.

3 'Но пораженья от победы ты сам не должен отличать' [But you yourself must not distinguish your victory from your defeat], *Vremya*, 23 October 2003.

4 Rafael Balgin, 'Вторая неделя процесса' [Second week of trial], *Delovaya Nedelya*, 23 June 2006, http://www.dn.kz/main/economo1.htm. The original link is no longer working, but the article can be found at http://www.qwas.ru/kazakhstan/akzhol-party/id_26946/.

5 See quote from Associated Press, 'The victim was believed to be behind allegations five years ago that Aliyev was plotting to depose Nazarbayev', http://www.foxnews. com/printer_friendly_wires/2006Jun24/0,4675,KazakhstanPresidentapossDa ughter,00.html. This allegation was also discussed in 'Петр Своик. Фрагменты истории власти и оппозиции в Казахстане, нанизанные на собственную жизнь. Часть 16' [Petr Svoik. Fragments of the history of the authorities and the opposition in Kazakhstan, threaded into my own life. Part 16], *Zona.kz*, 25 April 2018, https://zonakz.net/2018/04/25/petr-svoik-fragmenty-istorii-vlasti-i-oppozicii-v-kazaxstane-nanizannye-na-sobstvennuyu-zhizn-chast-16/.

6 Quoted in Joanna Lillis, 'Murders and maneuvers', *TOL*, 12 May 2006. Available to subscribers at http://www.tol.org/client/article/17122-murders-and-maneuvers.html.

7 Balgin, 'Вторая неделя процесса'.

8 Statement broadcast on Khabar TV, 21 February 2006, quoted in Joanna Lillis, 'Death in Kazakhstan'.

9 Quoted ibid.

10 'Статья, за которую, якобы, Ержан Утембаев "на протяжении длительного времени вынашивал мысли отомстить" Алтынбеку Сарсенбаеву' [The article for which Yerzhan Utembayev allegedly 'for a long time harboured thoughts of revenge' against Altynbek Sarsenbayev], *Zona.kz*, 28 February 2006, https://zonakz. net/2006/02/28/статья-за-которую-якобы-ержан-утембае/.

11 Lillis, 'Murders and maneuvers'.

12 Dariga Nazarbayeva, 'Дежа Вю' [Déjà vu], *Karavan*, 10 March 2006.

13 Balgin, 'Вторая неделя процесса'.

14 'Письмо Ержана Утембаева Президенту РК' [Letter from Yerzhan Utembayev to president of RK], *Ratel.kz*, 27 January 2014, http://www.ratel.kz/raw/pismo_ erjana_utembaeva_prezidentu_rk. Link no longer working.

15 Ibid.

16 Statement at public hearings in Almaty, 29 August 2006.

17 Joanna Lillis, 'Kazakhstan: Political reshuffle involves president's son-in-law', *Eurasianet*, 8 February 2007, https://eurasianet.org/s/kazakhstan-political-reshuffle-involves-presidents-son-in-law.

18 Idem, 'Kazakhstan: Officials keep looking for a way to prosecute Rakhat Aliyev', *Eurasianet*, 13 August 2007, https://eurasianet.org/s/kazakhstan-officials-keep-looking-for-a-way-to-prosecute-rakhat-aliyev.

19 Quoted ibid.

20 Idem, 'Kazakhstan: Government keeps legal heat on disgraced former presidential son-in-law, *Eurasianet*, 3 February 2008, https://eurasianet.org/s/kazakhstan-government-keeps-legal-heat-on-disgraced-former-presidential-son-in-law.

21 Idem, 'Kazakhstan: Coup trial may have dented government's image', *Eurasianet*, 30 March 2008, https://eurasianet.org/s/kazakhstan-coup-trial-may-have-dented-governments-image.

22 Bruce Pannier, 'Kazakhstan: Coup plots alleged as former presidential son-in-law battles authorities', Radio Free Europe/Radio Liberty, 20 April 2008, https://www. rferl.org/a/1109603.html.

23 Sultan-Khan Akkuly, 'Гульжан Ергалиева: "Эскадроны смерти" давно стали реальностью Казахстана' [Gulzhan Yergaliyeva: 'Death squads' have long since become a reality of Kazakhstan], Radio Azattyq, 6 December 2008, http://rus. azattyq.org/a/Gulzhan_Ergalieva/1356642.html.

24 'Absurd accusations': Lillis, 'Kazakhstan: coup trial may have dented government's image'; 'puppet justice system' and 'rubber-stamps decisions': Idem, 'Kazakhstan: Government keeps legal heat on disgraced former presidential son-in-law'.

25 Idem, 'Kazakhstan: Rakhatgate plot thickens as police identify body of missing television host', *Eurasianet*, 8 August 2007, https://www.eurasianet. org/kazakhstan-rakhatgate-plot-thickens-as-police-identify-body-of-missing-television-host.

26 Guy Norton, 'Kazakhstan: Nurbank looks to leave school for scandal', *Euromoney*, 3 November 2010, https://www.euromoney.com/article/b12khw7k4z0j7r/ kazakhstan-nurbank-looks-to-leave-school-for-scandal.

27 '50 богатейших людей Казахстана – 2012' [50 richest people in Kazakhstan – 2012], *Forbes Kazakhstan*, May 2012, https://forbes.kz/ranking/50_bogateyshih_lyudey_ kazakhstana_-_2012.

28 Nariman Gizitdinov and Torrey Clark, 'Kazakh president Nazarbayev says power won't be family business', Bloomberg, 23 November 2016, https://www.bloomberg. com/news/articles/2016-11-23/kazakh-president-nazarbayev-says-power-won-t-be-family-business.

29 Aleksey Ryblov, 'Киллер Рустам Ибрагимов рассказал, кто заказал убийство политика Алтынбека Сарсенбаева' [Killer Rustam Ibragimov recounts who ordered politician Altynbek Sarsenbayev's murder], KTK, 27 January 2014, https:// www.ktk.kz/ru/news/video/2014/01/27/26382.

30 'Remarks of Ambassador Ordway, chargé d'affaires a.i. at the press conference with the Deputy Procurator General of the Republic of Kazakhstan on December 20, 2013', United States Diplomatic Mission to Kazakhstan, 20 December 2013, http:// archive.is/I5OPn.

31 Joanna Lillis, 'Kazakhstan: Retrial fails to put political killing to rest', *Eurasianet*, 11 February 2014, https://eurasianet.org/s/kazakhstan-retrial-fails-to-put-political-killing-to-rest.

32 Ibid.

33 Manas Kayyrtayuly, '15 лет без Алтынбека. Нераскрытое политическое убийство' [15 years without Altynbek. Unsolved political murder], Radio Azattyq, 11 February 2021, https://rus.azattyq.org/a/kazakhstan-altynbek-sarsenbaiuly-15-years-after-the-political-assassination/31097066.html.

34 Johannes Dell, 'Epic murder trial tests Austrian justice', BBC News, 10 July 2015, http://www.bbc.com/news/world-asia-32922277.

3. Don't Mess With the Boss

1 Interview with author, 15 October 2009.

2 Skype interview with author, 16 May 2018.

3 Dashuta Drachinskaya, 'Тайна аблязовских миллионов' [Mystery of Ablyazov millions], *Доживем До Понедельника*, 6 December 2002, http://www.nomad. su/?a=13-200212060017.

4 Vadim Boreyko, 'Новейшая история: восстание элиты против Рахата Алиева' [Modern history: uprising of elite against Rakhat Aliyev], *Ratel.kz*, 20 September 2016, www.ratel.kz/outlook/novejshaja_istorija_vosstanie_elity_protiv_rahata_ alieva?page=3. Link no longer working.

5   Vladimir Ardayev, 'В Казахстане обострилась борьба за власть' [Struggle for power intensifies in Kazakhstan], BBC Russian Service, 21 November 2001, http://news.bbc.co.uk/hi/russian/news/newsid_1669000/1669376.stm.

6   'Аблязов о причинах его ареста в 2002 г' [Ablyazov on reasons for his arrest in 2002] [video], 16 12. Available on YouTube (recorded 2003, uploaded 18 September 2013), https://www.youtube.com/watch?v=nftAY1aI2oQ.

7   'Kazakhstan: country reports on human rights practices', US Department of State, 31 March 2003, https://www.state.gov/j/drl/rls/hrrpt/2002/18373.htm.

8   Farida Akhmetova, 'Ф.Ахметова: Мистер Лицемер. Заслуженный конец карьеры экс-банкира Мухтара Аблязова' [F. Akhmetova: Mr Hypocrite. Deserved end of career of ex-banker Mukhtar Ablyazov], *Kazakhstanskaya Pravda*, 25 February 2012, http://www.centrasia.ru/newsA.php?st=1330246200.

9   Skype interview with author, 16 May 2018.

10   'Экс-лидер ДВК Аблязов не намерен возвращаться в политику' [Ex-leader of DVK Ablyazov does not intend to return to politics], *Karavan*, 14 May 2003, https://www.caravan.kz/news/ehkslider-dvk-ablyazov-ne-nameren-vozvrashhatsya-v-politiku-184778/.

11   'Аблязов плюнул в лицо своим друзьям, считает президент Назарбаев' [Ablyazov has spat in faces of his friends, President Nazarbayev believes], *KazTAG*, 26 February 2012, http://online.zakon.kz/Document/?doc_id=30579897#pos=0;0.

12   Joanna Lillis, 'Kazakhstan: Ex-nuclear boss sentenced amid claims of political reprisals', *Eurasianet*, 16 March 2010, https://eurasianet.org/s/kazakhstan-ex-nuclear-boss-sentenced-amid-claims-of-political-reprisals.

13   'Kazakhstan: Death of prominent banker sparks rumors', WikiLeaks, 4 January 2005, https://wikileaks.org/plusd/cables/05ALMATY24_a.html.

14   'Муратхан Токмади назвал заказчика убийства банкира Ержана Татишева' [Muratkhan Tokmadi named murderer of banker Yerzhan Tatishev], *Tengri News*, 25 October 2017, https://tengrinews.kz/crime/murathan-tokmadi-nazval-zakazchika-ubiystva-bankira-erjana-329408/.

15   Skype interview with author, 16 May 2018.

16   Almaz Kumenov, 'Kazakhstan: Government's exiled bête noire sentenced to life in jail', *Eurasianet*, 28 November 2018, https://eurasianet.org/kazakhstan-governments-exiled-bete-noire-sentenced-to-life-in-jail.

17   'Семья Татишевых сделала заявление' [Tatishev family makes a statement], *Forbes Kazakhstan*, 5 April 2018, https://forbes.kz/process/spravedlivost_kotoraya_pobedila_vremya/.

18   Veronika Dorman, 'Abliazov: "Le plus avantageux pour le Kazakhstan aurait été que je sois liquidé en Russie"' [Ablyazov: 'The most advantageous thing for Kazakhstan would have been if I had been liquidated in Russia'], *Libération*, 13 December 2016, http://www.liberation.fr/planete/2016/12/13/abliazov-le-plus-avantageux-pour-le-kazakhstan-aurait-ete-que-je-sois-liquide-en-russie_1535095.

19   Skype interview with author, 16 May 2018.

20   Kirsten Ridley, 'Kazakh oligarch Ablyazov to be jailed in UK', Reuters, 16 February 2012, https://www.reuters.com/article/us-ablyazov-jail/kazakh-oligarch-ablyazov-to-be-jailed-in-uk-idUSTRE81F1L220120216.

21   '£1.5 million a month': Skype interview with author, 16 May 2018; information about the High Court judgement: Katy Dowell, 'Teare J refuses to recuse himself

from Ablyazov case', *The Lawyer*, 1 November 2012. Available to subscribers at www. thelawyer.com/issues/online-november-2012/teare-j-refuses-to-recuse-himself-from-ablyazov-case/.

22   Jonathan Russell, 'Banker Mukhtar Ablyazov "fled to France on coach"', *Telegraph*, 24 February 2012, www.telegraph.co.uk/finance/financial-crime/9104787/Banker-Mukhtar-Ablyazov-fled-to-France-on-coach.html.

23   Charles Forelle, 'Billions vanish in Kazakh banking scandal', *Wall Street Journal*, 1 January 2014. Available to subscribers at www.wsj.com/articles/billions-vanish-in-kazakh-banking-scandal-1388632446.

24   Skype interview with author, 16 May 2018.

25   'Kazakh dissident Ablyazov's family allowed back in Italy', BBC News, 28 December 2013, https://www.bbc.com/news/world-europe-25528466.

26   Katy Dowell, 'Addleshaws client Ablyazov debarred from defending $6bn claim', *The Lawyer*, 6 November 2012. Available to subscribers at www.thelawyer.com/issues/online-november-2012/addleshaws-client-ablyazov-debarred-from-defending-6bn-claim/.

27   Skype interview with author, 16 May 2018.

28   Nigel Morris, 'Kazakh dissident loses UK refugee status after David Cameron's trade mission – sparking claims the government is attempting to curry favour with the oil-rich country', *Independent*, 17 April 2014, http://www.independent.co.uk/news/uk/politics/kazakh-dissident-loses-uk-refugee-status-after-david-cameron-s-trade-mission-sparking-claims-the-9268490.html.

29   Joanna Lillis, 'Kazakhstan: Nazarbayev-linked billionaire sucked into UK court battle', *Eurasianet*, 2 December 2020, https://eurasianet.org/kazakhstan-nazarbayev-linked-billionaire-sucked-into-uk-court-battle.

30   Nariman Gizitdinov and Jason Corcoran, 'The $5bn heist', *Bloomberg Markets*, September 2012.

31   Kirstin Ridley, 'English judge says fugitive oligarch defrauded Kazakh bank BTA', Reuters, 19 March 2013, http://uk.reuters.com/article/uk-ablyazov-ruling-idUKBRE92I11J20130319.

32   Charles Forelle, 'Billions vanish in Kazakh banking scandal', *Wall Street Journal*, 1 January 2014. Available to subscribers at https://www.wsj.com/articles/SB10001424052702304367204579270600129884802.

33   Simon Tomlinson, 'Pictured: The glamorous Ukrainian blonde who led to fugitive oligarch's capture after detectives tailed her from London's High Court to his luxurious French hideout', *Daily Mail*, 2 August 2013, http://www.dailymail.co.uk/news/article-2383713/Pictured-The-glamorous-Ukrainian-blonde-led-fugitive-oligarch-s-capture-detectives-tailed-London-s-High-Court-luxurious-French-hideout.html.

34   Nikolay Svetlov, 'Болтливую партнершу Мухтара Аблязова сдал брошенный муж' [Garrulous partner of Mukhtar Ablyazov ratted on by ditched husband], *Moscow Post*, 2 September 2013, http://www.moscow-post.com/redactor/boltlivuju_partnershu_muxtara_abljazova_sdal_broshennyj_muzh12398/.

35   'Feu vert de la France à l'extradition du Kazakh Abliazov' [France's green light for Kazakh Ablyazov's extradition], *Europe 1*, 12 October 2015, http://www.europe1.fr/societe/feu-vert-de-la-france-a-lextradition-du-kazakh-abliazov-2528299.

36   'CE, 9 décembre 2016, M. O...', Conseil d'État, 9 December 2016, http://www.conseil-etat.fr/Decisions-Avis-Publications/Decisions/Selection-des-decisions-faisant-l-objet-d-une-communication-particuliere/CE-9-decembre-2016-M.-O.

37 Skype interview with author, 16 May 2018.

38 'Kazakhstan: Police crack down on anti-government rallies', *Eurasianet*, 10 May 2018, https://eurasianet.org/s/kazakhstan-police-crack-down-on-anti-government-rallies.

39 Dorman, 'Abliazov: "Le plus avantageux".'

4. *Fault Lines in the Feel-Good Factor*

1 'Сегодня в день 20-летия Независимости Республики Казахстан Глава государства Нурсултан Назарбаев принял участие в торжественной церемонии открытия Триумфальной арки "Мәңгілік Ел" в г.Астана' [Today, on the day of the 20th anniversary of independence of the Republic of Kazakhstan, head of state Nursultan Nazarbayev took part in the formal opening ceremony of the 'Mangilik Yel' triumphal arch in Astana], official site of the President of the Republic of Kazakhstan, 16 December 2011, http://www.akorda.kz/ru/events/segodnya-v-den-20-letiya-nezavisimosti-respubliki-kazahstan-glava-gosudarstva-nursultan-nazarbaev-prinyal-uchastie-v-torzhestvennoi-ceremoni.

2 Joanna Lillis, 'Kazakhstan: Labor dispute dragging energy production down,' *Eurasianet*, 13 October 2011, https://eurasianet.org/s/kazakhstan-labor-dispute-dragging-energy-production-down.

3 'Striking oil, striking workers', Human Rights Watch, September 2012, www.hrw.org/sites/default/files/reports/kazakhstan0912ForUpload.pdf.

4 'Kazakhstan: Lawyer freed, but rights restricted', Human Rights Watch, 14 March 2012, https://www.hrw.org/news/2012/03/14/kazakhstan-lawyer-freed-rights-restricted.

5 Joanna Lillis, 'Kazakhstan: Violence in Zhanaozen threatens Nazarbayev legacy', *Eurasianet*, 21 December 2011, https://eurasianet.org/s/kazakhstan-violence-in-zhanaozen-threatens-nazarbayev-legacy.

6 Idem, 'Kazakhstan: Police claim exonerating video from Zhanaozen – so where is it?', *Eurasianet*, 26 December 2011, https://eurasianet.org/s/kazakhstan-police-claim-exonerating-video-from-zhanaozen-so-where-is-it.

7 [video], YouTube (uploaded 20 December 2011), https://www.youtube.com/watch?v=yo9RnHo-lBo&feature=plcp. Link no longer working.

8 'Заявление Генерального Прокурора Республики Казахстан по событиям, имевшим место в г. Жанаозен 16.12.2011 года' [Statement by General Prosecutor of Republic of Kazakhstan on events that took place in town of Zhanaozen on 16.12.2011'], General Prosecutor's Office, 25 January 2012, http://prokuror.kz/rus/novosti/press-releasy/zayavlenie-generalnogo-prokurora-respubliki-kazahstan-po-sobytiyam-imevshim.

9 'Nazarbayev. Live.' [video], KTK. Available on YouTube (recorded 4 July 2013, uploaded 5 July 2013), https://www.youtube.com/watch?v=2U2pz2iklFg.

10 'Назарбаев: Участники беспорядков в Жанаозене получили по 20 тысяч тенге' [Nazarbayev: Participants in unrest in Zhanaozen received 20,000 tenge each], *Tengri News*, 23 December 2011, https://tengrinews.kz/kazakhstan_news/nazarbaev-uchastniki-besporyadkov-janaozene-poluchili-20-204486/.

11 Lillis, 'Kazakhstan: Violence in Zhanaozen threatens Nazarbayev legacy'.

12 Skype interview with author, 16 May 2018.

13 Sean Michaels, 'Sting cancels Kazakhstan concert over "repression" of striking workers', *Guardian*, 5 July 2011, https://www.theguardian.com/music/2011/jul/05/sting-cancels-kazakhstan-concert.

14 Igor Vinyazvskiy, 'Пока горит свеча!' [While the candle is burning!], *Vzglyad*, 18 January 2012.

15 Joanna Lillis, 'Kazakhstan: Authorities free newspaper editor under amnesty', *Eurasianet*, 15 March 2012, https://eurasianet.org/s/kazakhstan-authorities-free-newspaper-editor-under-amnesty.

16 Atabayev and Mamay's release: 'Release of activists in Kazakhstan underscores need for due process', Freedom House, 13 July 2012, https://freedomhouse.org/article/release-activists-kazakhstan-underscores-need-due-process; Mamay's 2017 conviction and ban: 'Kazakh editor convicted of money laundering, banned from journalism', Committee to Protect Journalists, 7 September 2017, https://cpj.org/2017/09/kazakh-editor-convicted-of-money-laundering-banned.php.

17 Joanna Lillis, 'Kazakhstan: Rights activists urge halt to Zhanaozen trial amid torture claims', *Eurasianet*, 23 April 2012, https://eurasianet.org/s/kazakhstan-rights-activists-urge-halt-to-zhanaozen-trial-amid-torture-claims.

18 'Суды в Актау и свидетельства подсудимых о пытках во время проведения следствия' [Trials in Aktau and defendants' testimony of torture during investigation], Open Dialog Foundation, 21 June 2012. Available at https://bureau.kz/monitoring_2/mejdunarodnye_otchety_2/article_4598/.

19 Lillis, 'Kazakhstan: Rights activists urge halt to Zhanaozen trial'.

20 Joanna Lillis, 'Kazakhstan: Zhanaozen police trials spark scapegoat accusations', *Eurasianet*, 18 May 2012, https://eurasianet.org/s/kazakhstan-zhanaozen-police-trials-spark-scapegoat-accusations.

21 Idem, 'Kazakhstan: Five police sentenced for Zhanaozen shootings', *Eurasianet*, 28 May 2012, https://eurasianet.org/s/kazakhstan-five-police-sentenced-for-zhanaozen-shootings.

22 Idem, 'Kazakhstan: New Zhanaozen verdicts cause shoes to fly', *Eurasianet*, 4 June 2012, https://eurasianet.org/s/kazakhstan-new-zhanaozen-verdicts-cause-shoes-to-fly.

23 Erlan Idrissov, 'A perspective from Kazakhstan', *The National Interest*, 6 April 2012, http://nationalinterest.org/commentary/perspective-kazakhstan-6742.

24 Joanna Lillis, 'Kazakhstan: UN Rights Commissioner urges Zhanaozen probe', *Eurasianet*, 12 July 2012, https://eurasianet.org/s/kazakhstan-un-rights-commissioner-urges-zhanaozen-probe.

25 Robert Mendick, 'Tony Blair gives Kazakhstan's autocratic president tips on how to defend a massacre', *Telegraph*, 24 August 2014, www.telegraph.co.uk/news/politics/tony-blair/11052965/Tony-Blair-gives-Kazakhstans-autocratic-president-tips-on-how-to-defend-a-massacre.html.

26 Anar Bazmukhametova, 'Актау: Эксперт рассказал о психологических портретах Козлова, Сапаргали и Аминова' [Aktau: Expert gives psychological portraits of Kozlov, Sapargali and Aminov], *BNews.kz*, 28 August 2012, https://bnews.kz/ru/news/obshchestvo/aktau_ekspert_rasskazal_o_psihologicheskih_portretah_kozlova_sapargali_i_aminova.

27 'Kazakhstan: opposition leader jailed', Human Rights Watch, 9 October 2012, www.hrw.org/news/2012/10/09/kazakhstan-opposition-leader-jailed.

28 Robin Paxton, 'U.S. says Kazakh verdict silences opposition', Reuters, 9 October 2012, http://af.reuters.com/article/worldNews/idAFBRE89809I20121009.

29 Shuttering of trade unions: 'Kazakhstan: trade union shut down', Human Rights Watch, 10 January 2017, https://www.hrw.org/news/2017/01/10/kazakhstantrade-union-

shut-down, and 'Kazakhstan must stop attacks on unions', IndustriALL, 4 February 2021, http://www.industriall-union.org/kazakhstan-must-stop-attacks-on-unions; jailing of union leaders: Mihra Rittmann, 'Trade union leaders freed in Kazakhstan', Human Rights Watch, 6 June 2018, https://www.hrw.org/news/2018/06/06/trade-union-leaders-freed-kazakhstan; expressions of concern from the International Labour Organisation: International Labour Conference Committee on the Application of Standards, 15th sitting, 12 June 2017, http://www.ilo.org/wcmsp5/groups/public/--ed_norm/---relconf/documents/meetingdocument/wcms_557884.pdf.

5. Publish and Be Damned

1   'Ермухамет Ертысбаев: 3 апреля станет великим днем' [Yermukhamet Yertysbayev: April 3 will be a great day], *Ekspress K*, 4 March 2011, http://old.express-k.kz/show_article.php?art_id=49943.

2   'Court convicts suspects in firebombing of opposition weekly', Committee to Protect Journalists, 28 March 2003, https://cpj.org/2003/03/court-convicts-suspects-in-firebombing-of-oppositi.php.

3   'Что случилось с Лейлой Байсеитовой?' [What happened to Leyla Bayseitova?], *Internews Kazakhstan*, 1 August 2002, http://old.internews.kz/rus/bulletin/143/page01.htm.

4   'Opposition journalist accused of rape is jailed for three and a half years', Reporters Without Borders, 28 January 2003, https://rsf.org/en/news/opposition-journalist-accused-rape-jailed-three-and-half-years.

5   'Exiled editor of Kazakh opposition weekly detained for two days', Committee to Protect Journalists, 25 April 2005, https://cpj.org/2005/04/exiled-editor-of-kazakh-opposition-weekly-detained.php.

6   'Прокуратура Алматы просит суд закрыть ряд оппозиционных СМИ' [Almaty prosecutor's office asks court to close several opposition media outlets], *Tengri News*, 21 November 2012, https://tengrinews.kz/kazakhstan_news/prokuratura-almatyi-prosit-sud-zakryit-ryad-oppozitsionnyih-223826/.

7   'Глава МИД: Казахстан имеет право на защиту от информационных атак Аблязова' [Foreign Minister: Kazakhstan has right to defence against Ablyazov's information attacks], *Tengri News*, 1 February 2013, https://tengrinews.kz/kazakhstan_news/glava-mid-kazahstan-imeet-pravo-zaschitu-informatsionnyih-227713/.

8   'Заявление о недопустимости уничтожения в Казахстане оппозиционных СМИ' [Statement on inadmissibility of destruction of opposition media in Kazakhstan], Adil Soz, 21 November 2012, http://www.adilsoz.kz/news/show/id/662/year/2012.

9   Joanna Lillis, 'Kazakhstan: Libel trial rekindles fears of media muzzling', *Eurasianet*, 1 July 2015, https://eurasianet.org/s/kazakhstan-libel-trial-rekindles-fears-of-media-muzzling.

10 Idem, 'Kazakhstan: Critical newspaper raided and banned', *Eurasianet*, 2 April 2014, https://eurasianet.org/s/kazakhstan-critical-newspaper-raided-and-banned.

11 Adam Klasfeld, 'Kazakh press safe from ban on leaked email', *Courthouse News Service*, 28 October 2015, www.courthousenews.com/CNSNEWS/Story/Index/83705.

12 Idem, 'Facebook can shield user info of Kazakh reporters', *Courthouse News Service*, 4 March 2016, https://www.courthousenews.com/facebook-can-shield-user-info-of-kazakh-reporters/.

13 'Заявление о недопустимости уничтожения в Казахстане оппозиционных СМИ'
    [Statement on inadmissibility of destroying opposition media in Kazakhstan], Adil
    Soz, 21 November 2012, http://www.adilsoz.kz/news/show/id/662/year/2012.

14 Exemption from the ban under the First Amendment: Eugene Volokh, 'Kazakhstan
    can't use U.S. courts to block Kazakh news site's publication of allegedly stolen
    Kazakh government documents', *Washington Post*, 29 October 2015, https://www.
    washingtonpost.com/news/volokh-conspiracy/wp/2015/10/29/kazakhstan-
    cant-use-u-s-courts-to-block-kazakh-news-sites-publication-of-allegedly-stolen-
    kazakh-government-documents/?utm_term=.c0324b93e474; failure to subpoena
    website and extract confidential information from Facebook: Klasfeld, 'Facebook
    can shield user info of Kazakh reporters'; New Zealand High Court order: Kate
    Newton, 'Mega ordered to hand over users' information', Radio New Zealand, 12
    May 2016, https://www.radionz.co.nz/news/national/303729/mega-told-to-hand-
    over-information.

15 Max Hunter, 'Operation Manul', Electronic Frontier Foundation, 4 August 2016,
    www.eff.org/wp/operation-manul.

16 Gabrielle Paluch, Kevin G. Hall and Ben Wieder, 'A Kazakh dirty-money suit threatens
    to reach Trump's business world', McClatchy DC, 30 May 2017 (updated 16 June
    2017), www.mcclatchydc.com/news/nationworld/national/article152934589.html.

17 David Greene and Karen Gullo, 'Kazakhstan's exploitation of flawed U.S. law to
    censor *Respublika* finally ends, in cautionary tale about CFAA abuse', Electronic
    Frontier Foundation, 19 January 2017, www.eff.org/deeplinks/2017/01/
    kazakhstans-exploitation-flawed-us-law-censor-respublika-finally-ends-cautionary.

18 Matthew Renda, 'Kazakhstan sues critic over email leak', *Courthouse News Service*,
    23 January 2017, https://www.courthousenews.com/kazakhstan-sues-critic-over-
    email-leak/.

19 Idem, 'California the wrong place for Kazakh hacking suit, judge says', *Courthouse
    News Service*, 22 December 2017, https://www.courthousenews.com/california-
    the-wrong-place-for-kazakh-hacking-suit-judge-says/.

20 User Irina Petrushova, 'Пора уходить' [Time to go], Facebook, 15 September 2016,
    www.facebook.com/ir.petrushova/posts/650810671766222.

21 Igor Savchenko, 'Казахстан: Преследования журналистов и блогеров'
    [Kazakhstan: prosecutions of journalists and bloggers], Open Dialog Foundation,
    22 January 2016, http://ru.odfoundation.eu/a/7229,kazahstan-presledovaniya-
    zhurnalistov-i-blogerov.

22 'European Parliament resolution on freedom of expression in Kazakhstan', 8
    March 2016, http://www.europarl.europa.eu/sides/getDoc.do?type=MOTION&
    reference=B8-2016-0337&language=EN.

23 Kazis Toguzbayev, 'Сообщается о смерти фигуранта дела "Казкома" Таира
    Калдыбаева' [Death of 'Kazkom' case defendant Tair Kaldybayev reported], Radio
    Azattyq, 5 July 2016, https://rus.azattyq.org/a/27840081.html.

24 'Казком вернёт 144 млн тенге семье бизнесмена Таира Калдыбаева, осуждённого
    на 4,5 года за распространение ложной информации' [Kazkom to return 144
    million tenge to family of businessman Tair Kaldybayev, sentenced to 4.5 years for
    dissemination of false information], *Informbyuro*, 7 July 2016, https://informburo.
    kz/novosti/kazkom-vernyot-seme-pogibshego-biznesmena-vsyu-vyplachennuyu-
    im-summu-materialnogo-ushcherba.html.

25 Kazis Toguzbayev, 'Гузяль Байдалинову выпустили из СИЗО' [Guzyal Baydalinova released from detention centre], Radio Azattyq, 12 July 2016, https://rus.azattyq. org/a/27854284.html.

6. Trials and Tribulations

1   'PR company proposed campaign against Sting', Bureau of Investigative Journalism, 1 December 2011, https://www.thebureauinvestigates.com/stories/2011-12-01/ pr-company-proposed-campaign-against-sting.

2   Deirdre Tynan, 'Kazakhstan: Top-notch PR firms help brighten Astana's image', Eurasianet, 18 January 2012, http://www.eurasianet.org/node/64860.

3   Alexei Trochev, 'Between convictions and reconciliations: Processing criminal cases in Kazakhstani courts', Cornell International Law Journal 50/1 (2017), https:// scholarship.law.cornell.edu/cgi/viewcontent.cgi?referer=&httpsredir=1&article= 1897&context=cilj.

4   Joshua Kucera, 'Kazakhstan: Obama–Nazarbayev meeting does not yield OSCE summit pledge', Eurasianet, 11 April 2010, https://eurasianet.org/s/kazakhstan-obama-nazarbayev-meeting-does-not-yield-osce-summit-pledge.

5   Michael Wines, 'Kazakhs reject appeal of editor who says he was framed for rape', New York Times, 13 March 2003, https://www.nytimes.com/2003/03/13/world/ kazakhs-reject-appeal-of-editor-who-says-he-was-framed-for-rape.html.

6   Batyrbek Agimbetov, 'Maksat Usenov guilty of another road accident in Almaty', Kazakhstanskaya Pravda, 15 November 2014, http://www.kazpravda.kz/en/news/ incidents/maksat-usenov-guilty-of--another--road-accident-in-almaty/.

7   Aktan Rysaliyev, 'Kazakhstan: Activist recantation demoralizes civil society', Eurasianet, 24 May 2017, http://www.eurasianet.org/node/83716.

7. Back to the USSR

1   'Kazakh journalist jailed for throwing manure at courthouse', Radio Free Europe/ Radio Liberty, 4 August 2010, https://www.rferl.org/a/Kazakh_Journalist_Jailed_ For_Throwing_Manure_At_Courthouse/2118677.html.

2   Joanna Lillis, 'Kazakhstan: Counting the costs of devaluation', Eurasianet, 27 February 2014, https://eurasianet.org/s/kazakhstan-counting-the-costs-of-devaluation.

3   Idem, 'Kazakhstan prevents protests as UN Rapporteur visits', Eurasianet, 24 January 2015, https://eurasianet.org/s/kazakhstan-prevents-protest-as-un-rapporteur-visits.

4   'Report of the Special Rapporteur on the rights to freedom of peaceful assembly and of association, Maina Kiai', 16 June 2015. Available for download at http:// freeassembly.net/reports/kazakhstan/.

5   Joanna Lillis, 'Kazakhstan: Arrest of children sparks one-woman protest', Eurasianet, 9 March 2014, http://www.eurasianet.org/node/68120.

6   'Kazakhstan's government squelches the least hint of dissent', The Economist, 26 April 2018, https://www.economist.com/asia/2018/04/26/kazakhstans-government-squelches-the-least-hint-of-dissent.

7   'Kazakhstan: Almaty notes, September 2–12, 2008', WikiLeaks, 16 September 2008, https://wikileaks.org/plusd/cables/08ASTANA1798_a.html.

8   'Н.Назарбаев: "Казахстан не отдаст ни йоту независимости кому бы то ни
    было"' [Kazakhstan will not cede an iota of independence to anyone], *Zakon.
    kz*, 25 March 2014, http://www.zakon.kz/4611637-n.nazarbaev-kazakhstan-ne-
    otdast-ni.html.

8. Stop the Presses

1   OSCE: 'Shutdown of independent magazine in Kazakhstan further endangers
    media pluralism, says OSCE Representative', OSCE Representative on Freedom
    of the Media, 26 November 2014, http://www.osce.org/fom/127436; Reporters
    Without Borders: 'Orchestrated throttling of Kazakh opposition weekly', Reporters
    Without Borders, 28 November 2014, https://rsf.org/en/news/orchestrated-
    throttling-kazakh-opposition-weekly.

2   Serikzhan Mauletbay, 'Тульжан Ергалиева продала "Свободу слова" за 2,5 млн
    долларов' [Gulzhan Yergaliyeva sold *Svoboda Slova* for $2.5 million], *Informbyuro*, 7
    October 2017, https://informburo.kz/novosti/gulzhan-ergalieva-prodala-svobodu-
    slova-za-25-mln-dollarov-13549.html.

3   'Report of the Special Rapporteur on the rights to freedom of peaceful assembly
    and of association, Maina Kiai', 16 June 2015. Available for download at http://
    freeassembly.net/reports/kazakhstan/.

4   Sultan-Khan Akkuly, 'Тульжан Ергалиева: "Эскадроны смерти" давно стали
    реальностью Казахстана' [Gulzhan Yergaliyeva: 'death squads' have long since
    become a reality of Kazakhstan], Radio Azattyq, 6 December 2008, https://rus.
    azattyq.org/a/Gulzhan_Ergalieva/1356642.html.

5   'Kazakhstan: Journal loses shutdown appeal', Human Rights Watch, 27 February
    2015, https://www.hrw.org/news/2015/02/27/kazakhstan-journal-loses-
    shutdown-appeal.

6   'Kazakh court bans broadcaster, suspends news website', Committee to Protect
    Journalists, 6 December 2012, https://cpj.org/2012/12/kazakh-court-bans-
    broadcaster-suspends-news-websit/.

7   Joanna Lillis, 'Kazakhstan: Court closes embattled magazine', *Eurasianet*, 22 October
    2015, https://eurasianet.org/s/kazakhstan-court-closes-embattled-magazine.

9. Bread and Circuses

1   Viktoriya Panfilova, 'Коррумпированной власти Назарбаева пора положить
    конец' [Time to put an end to Nazarbayev's corrupt rule], *Nezavisimaya Gazeta*,
    21 February 2005, http://www.ng.ru/courier/2005-02-21/11_tuiakbay.html.

2   'Kazakhstan: Presidential election roundup, November 8', WikiLeaks, 8 November
    2005, https://wikileaks.org/plusd/cables/05ALMATY4010_a.html.

3   Bagila Bukharbayeva, 'Kazakh opposition leader attacked for a second time in
    a month, party says', Associated Press, 3 May 2005. Available at http://www.
    pravdareport.com/news/world/ussr/03-05-2005/62609-0/.

4   Yekaterina Belyayeva, 'Дочь в могиле – брат в тюрьме' [Daughter in grave – brother
    in prison], *Vzglyad-Delovaya Gazeta*, 7 June 2008, http://vzglyad-kz.livejournal.
    com/4417.html.

5   'Kazakhstan: Opposition figure murdered at home', WikiLeaks, 22 November 2005,
    https://wikileaks.org/plusd/cables/05ALMATY4144_a.html.

6 'Kazakh opposition figure's death ruled suicide', Radio Free Europe/Radio Liberty, 29 November 2005, https://www.rferl.org/a/1063345.html.

7 'Republic of Kazakhstan presidential election 4 December 2005: OSCE/ODIHR election observation mission final report', OSCE Office for Democratic Institutions and Human Rights, 21 February 2006, http://www.osce.org/odihr/elections/kazakhstan/18153?download=true.

8 Joanna Lillis, 'Authorities in Kazakhstan tighten pressure on political opponents', *Eurasianet*, 5 June 2006, https://eurasianet.org/s/authorities-in-kazakhstan-tighten-pressure-on-political-opponents.

9 'Kazakhstan's post-Soviet political process, 1992–1997' (undated), Human Rights Watch, https://www.hrw.org/reports/1999/kazakhstan/Kaz1099b-02.htm.

10 Bruce Jacobs, 'Kazakhstan: Opposition group reappears under new name', Radio [Statement of Nazarbayev on resignation] Free Europe/Radio Liberty, 21 April 2005, https://www.rferl.org/a/1058594.html.

11 President's speech to parliament, 2 September 2007, http://www.parlam.kz/ru/presidend-speech/19.

12 Nazarbayev's speech at election victory rally on 4 April 2001. The full speech is available at the official site of the President of the Republic of Kazakhstan, http://www.akorda.kz/ru/events/segodnya-glava-gosudarstva-nursultan-nazarbaev-prinyal-uchastie-na-forume-pobeditelei-vpered-vmeste-s-liderom.

13 Joanna Lillis, 'Will there be a Central Asian Spring?', *Foreign Policy*, 24 January 2012, http://foreignpolicy.com/2012/01/24/will-there-be-a-central-asian-spring/.

14 Alexander Konstantinov, 'В случае внезапного ухода главы Казахстана именно Тимур Кулибаев сможет продолжить стратегический курс президента' [In case of sudden departure of Kazakhstan's leader, precisely Timur Kulibayev will be able to continue president's strategic course], *Kommersant*, 25 July 2011, https://www.kommersant.ru/doc/1685271.

15 Joanna Lillis, 'Democracy, Kazakh-style', *Eurasianet*, 5 July 2011, http://www.eurasianet.org/node/63797.

16 Idem, 'Kazakhstan: Is opposition politics officially dead?', *Eurasianet*, 19 September 2013, https://eurasianet.org/s/kazakhstan-is-opposition-politics-officially-dead.

17 'Kazakhstan court squeezes life out of Communists', *Eurasianet*, 17 August 2015, http://www.eurasianet.org/node/74711.

18 Joanna Lillis, 'Is Kazakhstan's political opposition creeping back?', *Eurasianet*, 24 May 2018, https://eurasianet.org/s/is-kazakhstans-political-opposition-creeping-back.

19 Idem, 'Kazakhstan: Election business settled before crisis worsens', *Eurasianet*, 7 March 2016, https://eurasianet.org/node/77691.

20 Asemgul Kasenova, 'Назарбаев подвел итоги выборов' [Nazarbayev sums up election results], *Tengri News*, 21 March 2016, https://tengrinews.kz/kazakhstan_news/nazarbaev-podvel-itogi-vyiborov-291213/.

21 'Elections in Kazakhstan', OSCE Office for Democratic Institutions and Human Rights, http://www.osce.org/odihr/elections/kazakhstan.

22 Vladimir Socor, Richard Weitz and Daniel Witt, 'Kazakhstan: Building democratic institutions for future generations', *Astana Times*, 19 March 2016, http://astanatimes.com/2016/03/kazakhstan-building-democratic-institutions-for-future-generations-by-vladimir-socor-richard-weitz-and-daniel-witt/.

23 'Назарбаев пригласил британских журналистов остаться в Казахстане и поговорить с людьми' [Nazarbayev invites British journalists to stay in Kazakhstan

and talk to people], *Tengri News*, 1 July 2013, https://tengrinews.kz/kazakhstan_news/nazarbaev-priglasil-britanskih-jurnalistov-ostatsya-237171/.

24   Ibid.

25   Yaroslav Krasiyenko, 'Женщины заставили Президента Назарбаева откровенничать' [Women force President Nazarbayev to be frank], KTK, 3 June 2015, http://www.ktk.kz/ru/news/video/2015/03/06/58114.

26   Interview with author, 13 April 2015.

27   'Nazarbayev. Live.' [video], KTK. Available on YouTube (recorded 4 July 2013, uploaded 5 July 2013), https://www.youtube.com/watch?v=2U2pz2iklFg.

28   Abdujalil Abdurasulov, 'Kazakhstan constitution: Will changes bring democracy?' BBC News, 6 March 2017, https://www.bbc.com/news/world-asia-39177708.

10. End of an Era

1   'Заявление Назарбаева об уходе в отставку' [Statement of Nazarbayev on resignation], Radio Azattyq, 19 March 2019, https://rus.azattyk.org/a/29830390.html.

2   'Названа численность казахстанцев после переписи населения' [Number of Kazakhstanis announced after population census], *Tengri News*, 8 December 2021, https://tengrinews.kz/kazakhstan_news/nazvana-chislennost-kazahstantsev-posle-perepisi-naseleniya-456004/.

3   User @champagne8th, Twitter, 19 March 2019, https://twitter.com/champagne8th/status/1107998503664533505.

4   User @iincognida, Twitter, 19 March 2019, https://twitter.com/iinkognida/status/1107999910736089088.

5   'Выступление Президента Республики Казахстан Касым-Жомарта Токаева на совместном заседании палат Парламента' [Speech of President of the Republic of Kazakhstan Qasym-Jomart Toqayev at joint session of chambers of Parliament], official site of the President of the Republic of Kazakhstan, 20 March 2019, http://www.akorda.kz/ru/speeches/internal_political_affairs/in_speeches_and_addresses/vystuplenie-prezidenta-respubliki-kazahstan-kasym-zhomarta-tokaeva-na-sovmestnom-zasedanii-palat-parlamenta.

6   User @myodium, Instagram, 22 March 2019, https://www.instagram.com/p/BvUJoDzgbpZ/?igshid=pdtqgn519g3q&fbclid=IwAR09zbXWJ9GvnooyrucsHYnSAFUm8SdWUGJhnrR3ipQJoqCeAAgj0QyO8PU.

7   Joanna Lillis, 'Kazakhstan: A president called Toqayev. A future called Nursultan', *Eurasianet*, 20 March 2019, https://eurasianet.org/kazakhstan-a-president-called-Toqayev-a-future-called-nursultan.

8   Joanna Lillis, 'Kazakhstan: Toqayev reign begins with arrests', *Eurasianet*, 22 March 2019, https://eurasianet.org/kazakhstan-Toqayev-reign-begins-with-arrests.

9   'Kazakhstan: Imprisoned for unfurling a banner', Amnesty International, 24 April 2019, https://www.amnesty.org/download/Documents/EUR5702602019ENGLISH.pdf.

10 'Kazakh activist jailed for people-power banner citing constitution', Radio Free Europe/Radio Liberty, 29 April 2019, https://www.rferl.org/a/kazakh-activist-jailed-for-people-power-banner-citing-constitution/29910764.html.

11 'Kazakh detained over empty placard vigil', BBC News, 7 May 2019, https://www.bbc.com/news/blogs-news-from-elsewhere-48187353.

12 Joanna Lillis, 'Kazakhstan: waking up to reform', *Eurasianet*, 11 June 2019, https://eurasianet.org/kazakhstan-waking-up-to-reform.

13 Almaz Kumenov, 'Kazakhstan: Government's exiled bête noire sentenced to life in jail', *Eurasianet*, 28 November 2018, https://eurasianet.org/kazakhstan-governments-exiled-bete-noire-sentenced-to-life-in-jail.

14 'Fugitive Kazakh opposition figure Ablyazov granted asylum in France', Radio Free Europe/Radio Liberty, 5 October 2020, https://www.rferl.org/a/fugitive-kazakh-opposition-figure-ablyazov-granted-asylum-france/30876695.html.

15 Joanna Lillis, 'Is Kazakhstan's political opposition creeping back?', *Eurasianet*, 24 May 2018, https://eurasianet.org/is-kazakhstans-political-opposition-creeping-back.

16 Interview with author, 20 November 2019.

17 'Republic of Kazakhstan early presidential election 9 June 2019: OSCE/ODIHR election observation mission final report', Office for Democratic Institutions and Human Rights, 4 October 2019, https://www.osce.org/odihr/elections/kazakhstan/434459?download=true.

18 'Kazakhstan updates tally of protest arrests to nearly 4,000' Associated Press, 18 June 2019. Available at https://www.voanews.com/south-central-asia/kazakhstan-updates-tally-protest-arrests-nearly-4000.

19 Interview with author, 19 November 2020.

20 Interview with author in presence of Shevchuk's lawyer, 20 November 2019.

21 Farangis Najibullah, 'Tragic fire in Astana gives Kazakh mothers' protests new momentum', Radio Free Europe/Radio Liberty, 12 February 2019, https://www.rferl.org/a/tragic-fire-in-astana-gives-kazakh-mothers-protests-new-momentum/29765930.html.

22 Interview with author in presence of Shevchuk's lawyer, 20 November 2019.

23 Joanna Lillis, 'Kazakhstan: Political Facebook posts land man with 4-year jail term', *Eurasianet*, 1 December 2018, https://eurasianet.org/kazakhstan-political-facebook-posts-land-man-with-4-year-jail-term.

24 'Kazakh family win Unexplained Wealth Order battle over London homes', BBC News, 8 April 2020, https://www.bbc.co.uk/news/uk-52216011.

25 Mike Eckel and Sarah Alikhan, 'Big houses, deep pockets', Radio Free Europe/Radio Liberty, 22 December 2020, https://www.rferl.org/a/kazakhstan-nazarbayev-family-wealth/31013097.html.

26 User Aisultan Jesus Rakhat, Facebook, 13 February 2020, https://www.facebook.com/aisultan.nazarbayev/posts/2817084081681396.

27 User Aisultan Jesus Rakhat, Facebook, 22 January 2020, https://www.facebook.com/aisultan.nazarbayev/posts/2772691279454010.

28 'Даурен Абаев прокомментировал посты Айсултана Рахата' [Dauren Abayev comments on Aisultan Rakhat's posts], *Tengri News*, 13 February 2020, https://tengrinews.kz/kazakhstan_news/dauren-abaev-prokommentiroval-postyi-aysultana-rahata-391515/.

29 Mike Eckel, 'British inquest says grandson of ex-Kazakh president Nazarbaev died of natural causes, cocaine addiction', Radio Free Europe/Radio Liberty, 24 March 2021, https://www.rferl.org/a/british-inquest-says-grandson-of-ex-kazakh-president-nazarbaev-died-of-natural-causes-cocaine-addiction/31167901.html.

30 Joanna Lillis, 'Who really is Kazakhstan's leader of the nation?', *Eurasianet*, 25 October 2019, https://eurasianet.org/who-really-is-kazakhstans-leader-of-the-nation.

31 'Заключение Конституционного Совета Республики Казахстан от 20 марта 2019 года № 2' [Conclusion of Constitutional Council of Republic of Kazakhstan of 20 March 2019 № 2], *Zakon.kz*, 20 March 2019, https://online.zakon.kz/document/?doc_id=39783395#pos=13;-35.

32 'Kazakhstan promises to allow public protests, just not yet', *The Economist*, 26 September 2019, https://www.economist.com/asia/2019/09/26/kazakhstan-promises-to-allow-public-protests-just-not-yet.

33 Saniyash Toyken, 'Активист Дулат Агадил заявил, что совершил побег из-за «необоснованного преследования»' [Activist Dulat Agadil says he carried out escape because of 'unfounded persecution'], Radio Azattyq, 19 November 2019, https://rus.azattyq.org/a/kazakh-activist-says-he-had-to-escape-custody-to-protest-his-arrest/30273463.html.

34 'В Талапкере похоронили Дулата Агадила. Прощание с активистом и призывы к властям' [Dulat Agadil buried in Talapker. Farewell to the activist and appeals to authorities], Radio Azattyq, 27 February 2020, https://rus.azattyq.org/a/kazakhstan-funeral-of-the-activist-dulat-agadil/30457335.html.

35 Tamara Vaal, 'Kazakh opposition activist dies in detention, sparking protest', Reuters, 25 February 2020, https://www.reuters.com/article/us-kazakhstan-activist/kazakh-opposition-activist-dies-in-detention-sparking-protest-idUSKCN20J0ZO.

36 «Дулат – жертва системы». Выступления после смерти активиста в СИЗО' ['Dulat is a victim of the system.' Speeches after death of activist in detention centre], Radio Azattyq, 1 March 2020, https://rus.azattyq.org/a/kazakhstan-protest-1-march/30462399.html placard.

37 Joanna Lillis, 'Kazakhstan: Grieving families count human cost of coronavirus', *Eurasianet*, 20 July 2020, https://eurasianet.org/kazakhstan-grieving-families-count-human-cost-of-coronavirus.

38 Tamara Vaal, 'Токаев о проблеме с доступом к лекарствам: «По отчетам чиновников проблем нет»' [Toqayev on problem of access to medicine: 'According to officials' reports there is no problem'], *Vlast.kz*, 26 January 2021, https://vlast.kz/novosti/43524-tokaev-o-probleme-s-dostupom-k-lekarstvam-po-otcetam-cinovnikov-problem-net.html.

39 Almaz Kumenov, 'Kazakhstan: Former health minister arrested', *Eurasianet*, 3 November 2020, https://eurasianet.org/kazakhstan-former-health-minister-arrested.

40 Interview over WhatsApp with author, 20 July 2020.

41 Almaz Kumenov, 'Kazakhstan: Nur-Sultan revelry sparks ire as coronavirus crisis escalates', *Eurasianet*, 7 July 2020, https://eurasianet.org/kazakhstan-nur-sultan-revelry-sparks-ire-as-coronavirus-crisis-escalates.

42 'Mystery pneumonia outbreak in Kazakhstan likely to be coronavirus: WHO', Deutsche Welle, 11 July 2020, https://www.dw.com/en/kazakhstan-pneumonia-coronavirus/a-54135982.

43 'Токаев вновь требует достоверной статистики по коронавирусу' [Toqayev again demands reliable statistics on coronavirus], *Vlast.kz*, 26 January 2021, https://vlast.kz/novosti/43519-tokaev-vnov-trebuet-dostovernoj-statistiki-po-koronavirusu.html.

44 David Trilling, 'Statistics show Central Asia underreporting COVID deaths', *Eurasianet*, 18 February 2021, https://eurasianet.org/statistics-show-central-asia-underreporting-covid-deaths.

45 'Kazakhstan rejects US researchers' estimation of COVID-19 mortality', Sputnik, 10 May 2021. Available at http://www.uniindia.com/news/world/health-kazakhstan-covid-fatality/2391535.html.

46 'Kazakhstan says spread of coronavirus has slowed', Reuters, 6 May 2020, https://www.usnews.com/news/world/articles/2020-05-06/kazakhstan-says-spread-of-coronavirus-has-slowed.

47 'Kazakhstan's economy to recover modestly in 2021, but COVID-19-induced poverty on the rise, says World Bank', World Bank, 29 January 2021, https://www.worldbank.org/en/news/press-release/2021/01/29/kazakhstan-economic-update-december-2020.

48 Medet Yesimkhanov, Pavel Bannikov and Asem Zhapisheva, 'Досье: Кто стоит за лоббированием отмены законов и распространением конспирологии в Казахстане' [Dossier: who is behind lobbying to change laws and spread of conspiracy theories in Kazakhstan?], Factcheck.kz, 24 February 2021, https://factcheck.kz/socium/dose-kto-stoit-za-lobbirovaniem-otmeny-zakonov-i-rasprostraneniem-konspirologii-v-kazaxstane/.

49 'Kazakhstan is awash in fake vaccination passports', The Economist, 24 July 2021, https://www.economist.com/asia/2021/07/24/kazakhstan-is-awash-in-fake-vaccination-passports.

50 Manshuk Asautay, '«Колотушка для нейтрализации». 405-я статья – инструмент против неугодных?' ['Mallet for neutralisation'. Article 405 – tool against the undesirable?], Radio Azattyq, 29 March 2021, https://rus.azattyq.org/a/kazakhstan-activists-criminal-prosecution-dck-koshe/31113140.html.

51 'Токаев: Логика конфронтации и идеология охлократии – путь в никуда' [Toqayev: Logic of confrontation and ideology of ochlocracy are road to nowhere], Informbyuro, 22 October 2020, https://informburo.kz/novosti/v-kazahstane-razrabotayut-socialnyy-kodeks-113005.html.

52 'All the parties in Kazakhstan's election support the government', The Economist, 7 January 2021, https://www.economist.com/asia/2021/01/09/all-the-parties-in-kazakhstans-election-support-the-government.

53 'Токаев: Со стороны властей сделано всё, чтобы обеспечить справедливость выборов' [Toqayev: On the part of the authorities everything was done to assure fairness of elections], Radio Azattyq, 10 January 2021, https://rus.azattyk.org/a/31040272.html.

54 'Lack of real competition and limitations to fundamental freedoms left voters without genuine choice in Kazakhstan's parliamentary elections, international observers say', Office for Democratic Institutions and Human Rights, 11 January 2021, https://www.osce.org/odihr/elections/kazakhstan/475544.

55 Aysulu Shaykulova, 'Оценка электорального поведения населения: участие и доверие' [Assessment of electoral behaviour of public: participation and trust], Strategiya Centre for Social and Political Studies, 2021 (undated), https://ofstrategy.kz/ru/research/politic-research/item/745-otsenka-elektoralnogo-povedeniya-naseleniya-uchastie-i-doverie.

56 Alena Shevtsova, 'Выбор или символический долг?' [Choice or symbolic duty?], Strategiya Centre for Social and Political Studies, 2021 (undated), https://ofstrategy.kz/ru/research/politic-research/item/742-vybor-ili-simvolicheskij-dolg.

57 Asylkhan Mamashuly, 'Протестный потенциал в Казахстане: сёла догоняют город' [Protest potential in Kazakhstan: villages outstrip city], Radio Azattyq, 13 April 2021, https://rus.azattyq.org/a/31191413.html.

58 'Majlis podcast: what's at stake in Kazakh elections?', Radio Azattyq, 27 December 2020, https://www.rferl.org/a/majlis-podcast-whats-at-stake-in-kazakh-elections/31021217.html.

59 Azamat Junisbai, 'Authoritarian learning: making sense of Kazakhstan's political transition', PONARS Eurasia, 9 July 2020, https://www.ponarseurasia.org/memo/authoritarian-learning-making-sense-kazakhstans-political-transition.

11. Kingdom of the Kazakhs

1 Asenov mentioned the number seven in comparison with *Game of Thrones*, referring with rhetorical flourish rather than precise historical accuracy to the various kingdoms that appeared in the centuries after the Golden Horde collapsed (although by some counts, depending on what historical time frame and geographical locations are included, there were seven in the wider region around present-day Kazakhstan). For more detail about entities that emerged from the collapse of the Golden Horde, see Charles Halperin, *Russia and the Golden Horde: The Mongol Impact on Medieval Russian History* (Bloomington, IN, 1987), p. 29. http://www.iupress.indiana.edu/product_info.php?products_id=21458.

2 'Всероссийский молодёжный форум "Селигер-2014"' [All-Russian youth forum 'Seliger-2014'], Presidential Press Office, 29 August 2014, http://kremlin.ru/events/president/news/46507#sel=140:1,148:15.

3 Almaz Kumenov, 'Russian nationalists again rile Kazakhstan by questioning its nationhood', *Eurasianet*, 15 December 2020, https://eurasianet.org/russian-nationalists-again-rile-kazakhstan-by-questioning-its-nationhood.

4 'Казахской государственности в 2015 году исполнится 550 лет – Назарбаев' [Kazakh statehood will turn 550 in 2015 – Nazarbayev], *Tengri News*, 22 October 2014, http://tengrinews.kz/kazakhstan_news/kazahskoy-gosudarstvennosti-2015-godu-ispolnitsya-550-let-263876/.

5 Interview with author, 15 February 2017.

12. Mother Russia

1 Entry on Kazakhstan, *Encyclopaedia Britannica*, https://www.britannica.com/place/Kazakhstan.

2 Rozaliya Kairbekova, Olga Pak and Dmitriy Ulyanov, *История Казахстана в таблицах и схемах* [*History of Kazakhstan in Tables and Charts*] (Almaty, 2015), p. 114.

3 Fariza A. Tolesh, 'The population history of Kazakhstan', paper presented to European Population Conference, Stockholm, 13–16 June 2012, http://epc2012.princeton.edu/papers/120586.

4 Bureau of National Statistics of the Agency for Strategic Planning and Reforms, https://stat.gov.kz/.

5 G. T. Alimbekova and E. A. Zaynalova, 'Миграция в Казахстане в постсоветский период' [Migration in Kazakhstan in the post-Soviet period] (undated), http://www.ciom.kz/upload/userfiles/files/Migratsiya_postsovetski_period.pdf.

6 Bureau of National Statistics of the Agency for Strategic Planning and Reforms, https://stat.gov.kz/.

7 Ibid. Statistics on the shares of Russians and Kazakhs in the national population are from preliminary results of a census in 2021, released in late 2021. Statistics on local ethnic breakdowns came from data released earlier in 2021, since local breakdowns from the census were not available at the time of going to press.

8 'Восстание в Жанаозене, успешно забытое ровно за 20 лет правления Назарбаева' [Uprising in Zhanaozen, successfully forgotten over precisely 20 years of Nazarbayev's rule], Radio Azattyq, 7 July 2009, http://rus.azattyq.org/a/sobytia_v_Zhanaozene/1770564.html.

9 Yerzhan Karabek, 'Уральские события 1991 года. Апогей конфликта' [Uralsk events of 1991. Peak of conflict], Radio Azattyq, 8 September 2011, http://rus.azattyq.org/a/uralskie_sobytia_1991_oral_okigasy_uralsk_events_kazakhstan_kazak/24320739.html.

10 Bruce Pannier, 'A tale of Russian separatism in Kazakhstan', Radio Free Europe/Radio Liberty, 3 August 2014, https://www.rferl.org/a/qishloq-ovozi-kazakhstan-russian-separatism/25479571.html.

11 Viktor Drobin, 'Аресты Русских в Казахстане' [Arrests of Russians in Kazakhstan], Zavtra, 29 November 1999, http://zavtra.ru/blogs/1999-11-3015.

12 Eduard Limonov, 'Идеальная Россия' [Ideal Russia], Russkaya Planeta, 8 April 2016, http://rusplt.ru/views/views_140.html.

13 Joanna Lillis, 'Kazakhstan: Man jailed over separatism sensitivities', Eurasianet, 19 November 2015, www.eurasianet.org/node/76166.

14 'В Крыму живут представители 175 национальностей – предварительные итоги переписи' [Representatives of 175 nationalities live in Crimea – preliminary results of census], Kryminform, 19 March 2015, http://www.c-inform.info/news/id/20417.

15 'Назарбаев не допустит дискриминации по языковому принципу' [Nazarbayev will not permit discrimination on basis of language], Total.kz, 3 April 2014, http://total.kz/politics/2014/04/03/nazarbaev_ne_dopustit_diskrimina/#begin_st.

13. Death to the Past

1 Mukhamet Shayakhmetov, The Silent Steppe (London, 2006), p. 3.

2 Ibid., pp. 3–4.

3 Ibid., p. 3.

4 Ibid., p. 51.

5 'The famine of 1932–33', Encyclopaedica Britannica, https://www.britannica.com/place/Ukraine/The-famine-of-1932-33#ref404577.

6 Interview with author, 14 February 2017.

7 Interview with author, 15 February 2017.

8 For a summary of estimates of the death toll from the Asharshylyk, see the memoirs of Nurziya Kazhibayeva, collated by her daughter, a historian: Nazira Nurtazina, 'Great famine of 1931–1933 in Kazakhstan: a contemporary's reminiscences', Acta Slavica Iaponica, 2011, http://src-h.slav.hokudai.ac.jp/publictn/acta/32/06Nurtazina.pdf.

9 http://asharshylyq.kz/?lang=ru.

10 Interviews with author, 29 March 2017.

11 Designation of 'act of genocide': 'Law of Ukraine No. 376-V "On Holodomor of 1932–33 in Ukraine", Embassy of Ukraine to Canada, http://canada.mfa.gov.ua/en/

ukraine-%D1%81%D0%B0/holodomor-remembrance/holodomor-remembrance-ukraine/holodomor-law-ukraine; definition of 'essential foundations of life': 'Analysis framework', Office of the UN Special Adviser on the Prevention of Genocide (OSAPG), http://www.un.org/ar/preventgenocide/adviser/pdf/osapg_analysis_framework. pdf; definition of 'intent to destroy': Gregory H. Stanton, 'What is genocide?', Genocide Watch, http://www.genocidewatch.org/genocide/whatisit.html; for Anne Applebaum quote, see Natalya Golitsina, 'Historian Anne Applebaum details Stalin's war against Ukraine: "I believe it was genocide"', Radio Free Europe/Radio Liberty, 25 September 2017, https://www.rferl.org/a/historican-anne-applebaum-interview-ukraine-holodomor-famine-stalin/28756181.html.

12   'Фото: Нурсултан Назарбаев открыл в Астане монумент памяти жертвам голодомора' [Photos: Nursultan Nazarbayev opens memorial in Astana to famine victims], *Tengri News*, 31 May 2012, https://tengrinews.kz/kazakhstan_news/foto-nursultan-nazarbaev-otkryil-astane-monument-pamyati-215083/.

14. The Gulag Archipelago

1   This figure is taken from Anne Applebaum's *Gulag: A History of the Soviet Camps* (London, 2004) and quoted in Steven Merritt Miner, 'The other killing machine', *New York Times*, 11 May 2003, https://www.nytimes.com/2003/05/11/books/the-other-killing-machine.html.

2   Meyrembek Baygarin, 'На территории Казахстана действовало 11 концлагерей' [11 concentration camps operated on Kazakhstan territory], *Kazinform*, 31 May 2015, www.inform.kz/ru/na-territorii-kazahstana-deystvovalo-11-konclagerey_a2781890.

3   'Киргизский (Казахский) край 1919–1920гг. [Kirgiz (Kazakh) Kray 1919–1920], Archive of the President of the Republic of Kazakhstan (undated), http://archive.president.kz/wp-content/uploads/A.-Kazahskij-kraj.pdf.

4   Rozaliya Kairbekova, Olga Pak and Dmitriy Ulyanov, *История Казахстана в таблицах и схемах* [*History of Kazakhstan in Tables and Charts*] (Almaty, 2015), p. 142.

5   *Kazakhstanskaya Pravda*, December 1994 [exact date not specified], http://e-history.kz/media/upload/4901/2015/07/31/8dbecef8e7f46237ofd1138eobf9c079.pdf.

6   Aleksandr Solzhenitsyn, *One Day in the Life of Ivan Denisovich* (London, 1963).

7   Michael Rywkin, *Moscow's Muslim Challenge: Soviet Central Asia* (Armonk, NY, 1990), p. 111.

8   'В Казахстане вспоминают жертв политических репрессий и массового голода' [Kazakhstan remembers victims of political repression and mass starvation], *Nur.kz*, 31 May 2015, https://www.nur.kz/772404-v-kazakhstane-vspominayut-zhertv-politi.html.

15. Exile of the Innocents

1   Sapiet Dakhshukaeva, 'Remembering Stalin's deportations', BBC News, 23 February 2004, http://news.bbc.co.uk/2/hi/europe/3509933.stm.

2   'May 18 – day of remembrance for the victims of Crimean Tatar genocide', Ministry of Foreign Affairs of Ukraine, 18 May 2016, https://mfa.gov.ua/en/news-feeds/foreign-offices-news/47611-18-travnyadeny-pamjati-zhertv-genocidu-krimsykotatarsykogo-narodu.

3   Sapiet Dakhshukaeva, 'Remembering Stalin's deportations'.

16. Sparks of Tension

1 'Report of the independent international commission of inquiry into the events in southern Kyrgyzstan in June 2010', Kyrgyzstan Inquiry Commission, 3 May 2011, https://reliefweb.int/sites/reliefweb.int/files/resources/Full_Report_490.pdf.

2 'Итоги Национальной переписи населения Республики Казахстан 2009 года' [Results of national population census of Republic of Kazakhstan of 2009], Bureau of National Statistics of the Agency for Strategic Planning and Reforms, www.stat. gov.kz/getImg?id=WC16200032648.

3 'Молодежь Казахстана должна обеспечить межнациональное согласие – Назарбаев' [Youth of Kazakhstan must ensure interethnic harmony – Nazarbayev], *Tengri News*, 11 November 2014, https://tengrinews.kz/kazakhstan_news/ molodej-kazahstana-doljna-obespechit-mejnatsionalnoe-265003/.

4 Naubet Bisenov, 'Ethnic clashes dent Kazakhstan's utopian image', *bne IntelliNews*, 13 February 2015, www.intellinews.com/ethnic-clashes-dent-kazakhstan-s-utopian-image-500444153/?archive=bne.

5 Joanna Lillis, 'Socio-economic tension threatens Kazakhstan's ethnic harmony', *Eurasianet*, 2 April 2007, https://eurasianet.org/s/socio-economic-tension-threatens-kazakhstans-ethnic-harmony.

6 Bureau of National Statistics of the Agency for Strategic Planning and Reforms, https://stat.gov.kz/.

7 Interviews with author, Masanchi, 9 February 2020.

8 'Осуждены отец и сын, избившие аксакала в Кордайском районе' [Father and son who beat up elder in Korday district convicted], *Tengri News*, 30 April 2020, https://tengrinews.kz/kazakhstan_news/osujdenyi-otets-syin-izbivshie-aksakala-kordayskom-rayone-400727/.

9 'Глава государства встретился с жителями села Каракемер' [Head of state meets with residents of village of Karakemer], official site of the President of the Republic of Kazakhstan, 1 March 2020, https://www.akorda.kz/ru/events/astana_kazakhstan/ working_trips/glava-gosudarstva-vstretilsya-s-zhitelyami-sela-karakemer.

10 Interview over WhatsApp with author, 27 April 2021.

11 Ibid.

12 Aksaule Abitay, 'Обвиняемые по делу о погромах в Кордайском районе заявляют о применении к ним пыток' [Accused in case of pogroms in Korday district declare torture used against them], Radio Azattyq, 19 January 2021, https://rus.azattyq. org/a/31052264.html.

13 Interview over WhatsApp with author, 27 April 2021.

14 Четверым участникам беспорядков в Кордайском районе смягчили приговор [Sentences reduced for four participants in unrest in Korday district], *Informbyuro*, 9 July 2021, https://informburo.kz/novosti/sud-smyagchil-nakazanie-chetverym-uchastnikam-besporyadkov-v-kordayskom-rayone.html; 'Суд смягчил наказание четверым участникам беспорядков в Кордайском районе' [Court reduces sentence of four participants in unrest in Korday district], *Informbyuro*, 19 November 2020, https://informburo.kz/novosti/sud-smyagchil-nakazanie-chetverym-uchastnikam-besporyadkov-v-kordayskom-rayone.html.

15 Letter from Yanduan Li, Chair of UN Committee on the Elimination of Racial Discrimination, to Permanent Representative of Kazakhstan, 7 August 2020, https:// tbinternet.ohchr.org/Treaties/CERD/Shared%20Documents/KAZ/INT_CERD_

ALE_KAZ_9240_E.pdf, https://kz.usembassy.gov/2020-country-reports-on-human-rights-practices-kazakhstan/.

16   Joanna Lillis, 'Kazakhstan: Trial over deadly ethnic violence leaves bitter taste for Dungans', *Eurasianet*, 28 April 2021, https://eurasianet.org/kazakhstan-trial-over-deadly-ethnic-violence-leaves-bitter-taste-for-dungans.

17. December of Discontent

1   First-hand memories of *Zheltoksan* were shared in interviews given to the author by: Talgat Ryskulbekov, 30 November 2011; Dos Kushim, 30 November 2011; Mukhtar Shakhanov, 21 March 2016; Gulbakhram Zhunis, 16 December 2016.

2   'Итоги Национальной переписи населения Республики Казахстан 2009 года' [Results of national population census of Republic of Kazakhstan of 2009], Bureau of National Statistics of the Agency for Strategic Planning and Reforms, www.stat.gov.kz/getImg?id=WC16200032648. Statistics from a census conducted in 2021 were not available at the time of going to press.

3   Bureau of National Statistics of the Agency for Strategic Planning and Reforms, https://stat.gov.kz/.

4   'Сообщение сопредседателя комиссии, члена Верховного Совета СССР, народного депутата СССР Шаханова М. О ходе работы Комиссии по дополнительному выяснению обстоятельств, связанных с декабрьскими событиям 1986 г.' [Report of co-chairman of commission, member of Supreme Soviet of USSR, people's deputy of USSR M. Shakhanov. On progress of work of Commission on further investigation into circumstances linked to December 1986 events], 4 November 1989, http://www.lib.knigi-x.ru/23istoriya/226829-1-muhtar-shahanov-osnove-privedennih-knige-podlinnih-dokumentov-chitatelyu-predostavlyaetsya-vozmozhnost-samostoyat.php.

5   'Желтоксан, ты в памяти нашей!' [Zheltoksan, you are in our memory!], *Kazakhstanskaya Pravda*, 12 December 2006, http://www.nomad.su/?a=15-200612130224.

6   'Kazakh riots widespread, premier says', Associated Press, 19 February 1987, http://articles.latimes.com/1987-02-19/news/mn-4491_1_riots.

7   Galina Skripnik, 'Герои независимости: "Иной судьбы не стану я просить" - участник декабрьских событий 1986 года Кайрат Рыскулбеков в своих стихах и воспоминаниях современников' [Heroes of Independence: 'I will not ask for a different fate' – Kayrat Ryskulbekov, participant in December 1986 events, in his own poems and reminiscences of contemporaries], *Kazinform*, 17 December 2011, http://www.inform.kz/kz/geroi-nezavisimosti-inoy-sud-by-ne-stanu-ya-prosit-uchastnik-dekabr-skih-sobytiy-1986-goda-kayrat-ryskulbekov-v-svoih-stihah-i-vospominaniyah-sovremennikov_a2427035.

8   'Документы КГБ Казахской ССР по уголовному делу, возбужденному по статье 60 УК КазССР' [Documents of KGB of Kazakh SSR on criminal case opened under Article 60 of Criminal Code of Kazakh SSR] (undated). Available at https://qamba.info/site/book/online/qazaq-ult-azattyq-qzghalysy-hx-kitap/content/content_10.xhtml/.

9   Ibid.

10   Talgat Dyuysenbek, 'История фотоснимка из зала суда над участниками Декабрьских событий' [History of courtroom photograph from trial of participants

in December events], Radio Azattyq, 15 December 2009, https://rus.azattyq.org/a/kazakh_activists_demonstration_court_photo/1903507.html.

11 Nurbek Tusivkhan, Aynur Alimova, Tokmolda Kusainov and Rinat Fazilbayev, 'Уцелевшие кадры Декабрьских событий' [Surviving clips of December events], Radio Azattyq, 18 December 2016, https://rus.azattyq.org/a/kazakhstan-zheltoksan-86-utselevshaya-videozapis/28175911.html.

12 Bolat Abilov, Oraz Zhandosov, Tulegen Zhukeyev, Berik Abdygaliyev, Nurlan Zhumakhan, Bolatbek Korpebayuly and Aydos Sarym, *Желтоксан-86: Статьи и публикации за 1986–1995* [*Zheltoksan-86: Articles and Publications 1986–1995*], p. 289.

13 Ibid., p. 104.

14 Skripnik, 'Герои независимости'.

15 'Мұхтар Шаханов 1989 жыл Кремльде сөйлеген сөзі' [Mukhtar Shakhanov's 1989 speech in Kremlin] [video]. Available on YouTube (recorded 6 June 1989, uploaded 3 March 2015), https://www.youtube.com/watch?v=tx_ogWhonjc.

16 Nazarbayev's claims originally appeared in an article in the newspaper *Ekspress-khronika* in December 1990 (exact date unknown), which is quoted in 'Назарбаев и Желтоксан. Первая большая тайна Нурсултана' [Nazarbayev and *Zheltoksan*. Nursultan's first big secret], Radio Azattyq, 24 June 2009, https://rus.azattyq.org/a/nazarbaev_v_dekabre_1986_goda/1759919.html.

17 Nursultan Nazarbayev, *Без Правых и Левых* [Without right and left] (Moscow, 1991). Also available online at the official site of the President of the Republic of Kazakhstan, p. 180, http://personal.akorda.kz/images/file/f1a45bf03d51ef2252 40cco6bdf1b3b1.pdf.

18 Bagila Bukharbayeva, 'Kazakhs remembering uprising of 1986', Associated Press, 16 December 2006, http://www.washingtonpost.com/wp-dyn/content/article/2006/12/16/AR2006121600465_pf.html.

19 Skripnik, 'Герои независимости'.

18. Lure of the Land

1 'Kazakh security forces crack down on land code protests', Radio Free Europe/Radio Liberty, 21 May 2016, https://www.rferl.org/a/almaty-kazakhstan-protests-arrests/27749024.html.

2 'Китайские компании производят более 25% нефти в Казахстане - Т. Кулибаев' [Chinese companies produce over 25 per cent of oil in Kazakhstan – T. Kulibayev], *Kazinform*, 30 September 2015, http://www.inform.kz/ru/kitayskie-kompanii-proizvodyat-bolee-25-nefti-v-kazahstane-t-kulibaev_a2823461.

3 'Митинг в Атырау, все события за три минуты' [Rally in Atyrau, all events in three minutes] [video]. Available on YouTube (recorded 24 April 2016, uploaded 25 April 2016), https://www.youtube.com/watch?v=3qDsBhPKUXA.

4 Alex Marshall, *Republic or Death! Travels in Search of National Anthems* (London, 2015), p. 141.

5 Joanna Lillis, 'Kazakhstan: China looking to lease land for agricultural purposes', *Eurasianet*, 3 February 2010, https://eurasianet.org/s/kazakhstan-china-looking-to-lease-land-for-agricultural-purposes.

6   'Назарбаев не позволит превратить Казахстан во вторую Украину' [Nazarbayev will not allow Kazakhstan to be turned into another Ukraine], *Ukraina.ru*, 6 May 2016, https://ukraina.ru/news/20160506/1016300686.html.

7   Interview with author after news conference, Almaty National Press Club, 23 May 2016.

8   Ibid.

9   Aina Shormanbayeva, 'Kazakhstan: A showcase for shrinking civic space', openDemocracy, 7 June 2017, https://www.opendemocracy.net/od-russia/aina-shormanbayeva/kazakhstan-showcase-for-shrinking-civic-space.

10 Interview with author after news conference, Almaty National Press Club, 23 May 2016.

11 'Пресс-релиз' [Press release], General Prosecutor's Office, 27 May 2016, http://prokuror.gov.kz/rus/novosti/press-releasy/press-reliz-192.

12 Kseniya Voronina, 'Несанкционированных митингов в Казахстане не было – МВД РК' [There were no unsanctioned rallies in Kazakhstan – RK Ministry of Internal Affairs], *Kazakhstanskaya Pravda*, 21 May 2016, http://www.kazpravda.kz/news/proisshestviya/nesanktsionirovannih-mitingov-v-kazahstane-ne-bilo--mvd-rk/.

13 News conference, Almaty National Press Club, 23 May 2016.

14 'Портрет недели' [Portrait of the week], KTK, 22 May 2016, www.ktk.kz/ru/programs/portret_nedeli/69533.

15 Broadcast on First Channel Eurasia, 13 May 2016, https://1tv.kz/404/. Former link no longer working, but the report is embedded in '"Первый канал Казахстана" показал видео раздачи денег на "земельных митингах"' [Kazakhstan's First Channel shows video of distribution of money at 'land rallies'], https://www.nur.kz/1127920-kazakhstanskiy-telekanal-pokazal-vid.html.

16 'Кто владеет средствами массовой информации Казахстана?' [Who owns media in Kazakhstan?], *Fergana News*, 15 May 2017, http://www.fergananews.com/article.php?id=9412.

17 'Пресс-релиз' [Press release], General Prosecutor's Office, 27 May 2016, http://prokuror.gov.kz/rus/novosti/press-releasy/press-reliz-191.

18 'Версия с Тулешовым выглядит фантастической' [Version involving Tuleshov looks fanciful], *Ashyk Alan/Tribuna*, 28 June 2016, http://tribunakz.com/interview/453-versiya-s-tuleshovym-vyglyadit-fantasticheskoy.html. Link no longer working.

19 'Kazakhstan: Security services lay out coup plot account', *Eurasianet*, 11 July 2016, https://eurasianet.org/node/79596.

20 'Тулешов задолжал 200 миллионов долларов, в этот период возникла идея переворота – КНБ' [Tuleshov ran up debts of $200 million, in that period coup idea arose – KNB], *Tengri News*, 6 July 2016, https://tengrinews.kz/kazakhstan_news/tuleshov-zadoljal-200-millionov-dollarov-etot-period-298384/.

21 Aygerim Abilmazhitova, 'Тулешов прокомментировал в суде земельные митинги' [Tuleshov comments in court on land rallies], *Tengri News*, 16 October 2016, https://tengrinews.kz/kazakhstan_news/tuleshov-prokommentiroval-v-sude-zemelnyie-mitingi-304290/.

22 'Революционный взрыв застает врасплох всех' [Revolutionary outburst catches everyone unawares], *Ashyk Alan/Tribuna*, 18 August 2016, http://tribunakz.com/

politics/495-dosym-satpaev-revolyucionnyy-vzryv-zastaet-vrasploh-vseh.html. Link no longer working.

23 Joanna Lillis, 'Kazakhstan: Campaigners urge legal reform to protect free speech', *Eurasianet*, 19 January 2016, http://www.eurasianet.org/node/76876.

24 Jailing of opposition activists for discussing book: idem, 'Kazakhstan: Authorities jail two more activists', *Eurasianet*, 22 January 2017, http://www.eurasianet.org/node/76946; comments on Facebook: Andrey Sviridov, 'Политические узники социальных сетей' [Political prisoners of social networks], Kazakhstan International Bureau for Human Rights and Rule of Law, 6 December 2016, https://bureau.kz/novosti/sobstvennaya_informaciya/politicheskie_uzniki_socialnykh_setei/; sentencing: 'В Актобе на 3 года посадили известного общественника за критику Путина' [In Aktobe well-known public activist jailed for three years for criticism of Putin'], *Nur.kz*, https://www.nur.kz/1359991-v-aktobe-na-3-goda-posadili-izvestnogo-o.html.

25 Lillis, 'Kazakhstan: Campaigners urge legal reform to protect free speech'.

26 'На земельной комиссии в Атырау требовали освободить двух активистов. О сотнях допрашиваемых так и не узнали' [Land commission in Atyrau hears demands to free two activists. They still did not find out about hundreds interrogated], *Ak Zhayyk*, 23 July 2016, http://azh.kz/ru/news/view/37995.

27 'Kazakhstan: Activists face jail for planning peaceful rally: Maks Bokaev, Talgat Ayan and Zhanat Esentaev', Amnesty International, 10 June 2016, https://www.amnesty.org/en/documents/eur57/4220/2016/en/.

28 Yerlan Kaliyev, 'Суд над Аяном и Бокаевым: последнее слово еще не последнее' [Trial of Ayan and Bokayev: last word is not the last one], Kazakhstan International Bureau for Human Rights and Rule of Law, 22 November 2016, https://bureau.kz/novosti/sobstvennaya_informaciya/poslednee_slovo_eshe_ne_poslednee/.

29 Aynash Ondiris, 'Активиста Талгата Аяна освободили из колонии' [Activist Talgat Ayan released from colony], *Tengri News*, 16 April 2018, https://tengrinews.kz/kazakhstan_news/aktivista-talgata-ayana-osvobodili-iz-kolonii-342190/.

30 'Kazakhstan: Land rights activists on trial', Human Rights Watch, 10 October 2016, https://www.hrw.org/news/2016/10/10/kazakhstan-land-rights-activists-trial.

31 Watchdog's verdict: 'Kazakhstan: 2 activists sentenced to 5 years', Human Rights Watch, 28 November 2016 (updated 23 January 2017), https://www.hrw.org/news/2016/11/28/kazakhstan-2-activists-sentenced-5-years; EU quote: 'Statement by the Spokesperson on the sentencing of Max Bokayev and Talgat Ayan in Kazakhstan', European Union External Action Service, 30 November 2016, https://eeas.europa.eu/headquarters/headquarters-homepage/16135/statement-by-the-spokesperson-on-the-sentencing-of-max-bokayev-and-talgat-ayan-in-kazakhstan_en.

32 Interviews over WhatsApp with author, 9-10 February 2021.

33 'Kazakhstan bans land sales to foreigners to head off protests', AFP, 13 May 2021, https://www.barrons.com/news/kazakhstan-bans-land-sales-to-foreigners-to-head-off-protests-01620893413.

19. Homeward Bound

1 Yerbolat Uatkhanov, 'One and a half million ethnic Kazakhs live in China', *Astana Times*, 30 September 2016, http://astanatimes.com/2016/09/one-and-a-half-million-ethnic-kazakhs-live-in-china/.

2   Bureau of National Statistics of the Agency for Strategic Planning and Reforms, https://stat.gov.kz/.

3   Aysultan Kulshmanov, 'Фонд поддержки казахов "Отандастар" поручил создать Назарбаев' [Nazarbayev orders creation of 'Compatriots' foundation to support Kazakhs], *Tengri News*, 23 June 2017, https://tengrinews.kz/kazakhstan_news/fond-podderjki-kazahov-otandastar-poruchil-sozdat-nazarbaev-320920/.

4   Darkhan Umirbekov, 'Kazakhstan: Words mean everything in ethnic Kazakh debate', *Eurasianet*, 10 October 2019, https://eurasianet.org/kazakhstan-words-mean-everything-in-ethnic-kazakh-debate.

5   Bureau of National Statistics of the Agency for Strategic Planning and Reforms, https://stat.gov.kz/.

6   Vyacheslav Baturin, 'Почти миллион оралманов прибыло в Казахстан за 25 лет' [Almost a million oralmans arrive in Kazakhstan in 25 years], *Kapital*, 9 February 2016, https://kapital.kz/gosudarstvo/47713/pochti-million-oralmanov-pribylov-kazahstan-za-25-let.html.

7   Bureau of National Statistics of the Agency for Strategic Planning and Reforms, https://stat.gov.kz/. Statistics on the shares of Russians and Kazakhs in the national population are from preliminary results of a census in 2021, released in late 2021. Statistics on local ethnic breakdowns came from data released earlier in 2021, since local breakdowns from the census were not available at the time of going to press.

8   Ibid.

9   Interview with author, 23 June 2014.

10   Anna Genina, 'Claiming ancestral homelands: Mongolian Kazakh migration in Inner Asia', PhD thesis, University of Michigan, 2015, https://deepblue.lib.umich.edu/bitstream/handle/2027.42/111536/anngen_1.pdf?sequence=1&isAllowed=y.

20. Behind the Red Wall

1   '"Eradicating ideological viruses". China's campaign of repression against Xinjiang's Muslims', Human Rights Watch, 9 September 2018, https://www.hrw.org/report/2018/09/09/eradicating-ideological-viruses/chinas-campaign-repression-against-xinjiangs.

2   Eradicating ideological viruses.

3   Nurtay Lakhanuli, 'Кто эти женщины у консульства Китая? История Халиды Акытхан' [Who are these women outside the consulate of China? The story of Khalida Akytkhan], Radio Azattyq, 29 July 2021, https://rus.azattyq.org/a/khalida-akhytkhan-shyngzhang/31383174.html.

4   Eradicating ideological viruses.

5   Vicky Xiuzhong Xu, Danielle Cave, James Leibold, Kelsey Munro and Nathan Ruser, 'Uighurs for sale', Australian Strategic Policy Institute, 1 March 2020, https://www.aspi.org.au/report/uighurs-sale.

6   Victor Ordonez, 'China's persecuted Muslims find haven in the US', ABC News, 20 May 2021, https://abcnews.go.com/International/chinas-persecuted-muslims-find-haven-us/story?id=77789396.

7   'Vocational education and training in Xinjiang', *China Daily*, 17 August 2019, http://www.chinadaily.com.cn/a/201908/17/WS5d574e53a310cf3e355664b1.html.

8   'Full transcript: Interview with Xinjiang government chief on counterterrorism, vocational education and training in Xinjiang', Xinhua, 16 October 2018, http:// www.xinhuanet.com/english/2018-10/16/c_137535821.htm.

9   'China claims all Xinjiang detainees have 'graduated,' drawing skepticism from experts, exile groups', Radio Free Asia, 9 December 2019, https://www.rfa.org/ english/news/uyghur/graduation-12092019154443.html.

10 Eradicating ideological viruses.

11 'China launches "strike hard" crackdown in restive west', Reuters, 3 November 2009, https://www.reuters.com/article/us-china-xinjiang-idUSTRE5A20C220091103.

12 'Xinjiang's population increases 18.5 pct over past decade', Xinhua, 14 June 2021, http://www.xinhuanet.com/english/2021-06/14/c_1310006836.htm.

13 China launches "strike hard" crackdown in restive west.

14 '"East Turkistan" terrorist forces cannot get away with impunity', Information Office of the State Council, 21 January 2002. Available at https://www.fmprc.gov.cn/ce/ cetur/eng/xwdt/t160708.htm.

15 'Why is there tension between China and the Uighurs?', BBC News, 26 September 2014, https://www.bbc.com/news/world-asia-china-26414014.

16 China Claims All Xinjiang Detainees Have 'Graduated'.

17 Eradicating ideological viruses.

18 'China cuts Uighur births with IUDs, abortion, sterilization', Associated Press, 29 June 2020, https://apnews.com/article/ap-top-news-international-news-weekend-reads-china-health-269b3de1af34e17c1941a514f78d764c.

19 '37 countries defend China over Xinjiang in UN letter', AFP, 12 July 2019. Available at https://www.france24.com/en/20190712-37-countries-defend-china-over-xinjiang-un-letter.

20 '"Outrageous lies": China dismisses US accusations its treatment of Uighurs amounts to "genocide"', SBS News, 20 January 2021, https://www.sbs.com.au/ news/outrageous-lies-china-dismisses-us-accusations-its-treatment-of-uighurs-amounts-to-genocide/43d26b32-2ffa-48c5-b885-4b9d5779e852.

21 'West sanctions China over Xinjiang abuses, Beijing hits back at EU', Reuters, 23 March 2021, https://www.reuters.com/article/uk-usa-china-eu-sanctions/west-sanctions-china-over-xinjiang-abuses-beijing-hits-back-at-eu-idUSKBN2BE2LF.

22 Irwin Cotler and Yonah Diamond, 'China's Uyghur genocide is undeniable', Project Syndicate, 3 June 2021, https://www.project-syndicate.org/commentary/evidence-of-china-uyghur-genocide-by-irwin-cotler-and-yonah-diamond-2021-06.

23 Stephanie Nebehay, 'China rejects genocide charge in Xinjiang, says door open to UN', Reuters, 22 February 2021, https://www.reuters.com/article/us-china-rights-idUSKBN2AM1UX.

24 Almaz Kumenov, 'Kazakhstan: Xinjiang Kazakh finds haven in Europe', Eurasianet, 3 June 2019, https://eurasianet.org/kazakhstan-xinjiang-kazakh-finds-haven-in-europe.

25 'Xinjiang activist freed in Kazakh court after agreeing to stop campaigning', AFP, 17 August 2019. Available at https://www.theguardian.com/world/2019/aug/17/ xinjiang-activist-freed-in-kazakh-court-after-agreeing-to-stop-campaigning.

26 'Kazakh China rights advocate detained on hate speech charges – activists', Reuters, 10 March 2019, https://www.reuters.com/article/uk-kazakhstan-china-activist-idUKKBN1QR0M3.

27 User Хидаят Хидаятович [Khidayat Khidayatovich], Facebook, 8 February 2019, https://www.facebook.com/hidayat.biz/videos/605562183230469/?hc_location=ufi.

28 'Opinions adopted by the Working Group on Arbitrary Detention at its eighty-eighth session, 24-28 August 2020', Human Rights Council Working Group on Arbitrary Detention, 14 December 2020, https://undocs.org/en/A/HRC/WGAD/2020/43.

29 Bruce Pannier, 'Activist defending ethnic Kazakhs in China explains why he had to flee Kazakhstan', Radio Free Europe/Radio Liberty, 18 January 2021, https://www.rferl.org/a/31051495.html.

30 Chris Rickleton, 'After tentative start, Kazakhstan is obliterating Xinjiang activism', *Eurasianet*, 22 February 2021, https://eurasianet.org/after-tentative-start-kazakhstan-is-obliterating-xinjiang-activism.

31 Miles Kenyon, 'WeChat surveillance explained', Citizen Lab, University of Toronto, 7 May 2020, https://citizenlab.ca/2020/05/wechat-surveillance-explained/.

32 Xinjiang Victims Database, https://shahit.biz/eng/#home.

33 Gene Bunin, 'From camps to prisons: Xinjiang's next great human rights catastrophe', Art of Life in Chinese Central Asia, 5 October 2019, https://livingotherwise.com/2019/10/05/from-camps-to-prisons-xinjiangs-next-great-human-rights-catastrophe-by-gene-a-bunin/.

22. *Opium of the People*

1 UN Human Rights Council, 'United Nations Human Rights Council: 28th Session', 19 March 2015, https://humanism.org.uk/wp-content/uploads/2015-03-19-v1-AC-hrc28-item6Kazakhstan-UPR.pdf; European Parliament, 'European Parliament resolution on the human rights situation in Kazakhstan', 16 April 2013, http://www.europarl.europa.eu/sides/getDoc.do?type=MOTION&reference=B7-2013-0177&language=GA; US government commission: 'USCIRF urges the Kazakh government to release two activists', United States Commission on International Religious Freedom, 25 July 2013, www.uscirf.gov/news-room/press-releases/uscirf-urges-the-kazakh-government-release-two-activists.

2 'Выступление Президента Республики Казахстан Нурсултана Назарбаева на открытии IV Съезда лидеров мировых и традиционных религий' [Speech of President of Republic of Kazakhstan Nursultan Nazarbayev at opening of IV Congress of Leaders of World and Traditional Religions], official site of the President of the Republic of Kazakhstan, 13 May 2012, http://www.akorda.kz/ru/speeches/external_political_affairs/ext_speeches_and_addresses/vystuplenie-prezidenta-respubliki-kazakhstan-nursultana-nazarbaeva-na-otkrytii-iv-sezda-liderov-mir_1341999186.

3 'Итоги Национальной переписи населения Республики Казахстан 2009 года' [Results of national population census of Republic of Kazakhstan of 2009], Bureau of National Statistics of the Agency for Strategic Planning and Reforms, www.stat.gov.kz/getImg?id=WC16200032648.

4 'Kazakhstan: Taraz city attack kills seven', BBC News, 12 November 2011, http://www.bbc.co.uk/news/world-asia-15705308.

5 Maria Gordeyeva, 'Suicide bomber attacks security police in Kazakh city', Reuters, 17 May 2011, https://www.reuters.com/article/us-kazakhstan-blast/suicide-bomber-attacks-security-police-in-kazakh-city-idUSTRE74G3QV20110517.

6   'Kazakhstan says all gunmen behind attacks arrested', AFP, 13 June 2016. Available at http://www.qatar-tribune.com/news-details/id/7074.

7   Aigerim Toleukhanova, 'Kazakhstan: Almaty shooting spree trial comes to a close', *Eurasianet*, 28 October 2016, https://eurasianet.org/s/kazakhstan-almaty-shooting-spree-trial-comes-to-a-close.

8   'Надо разобраться с вопросом религиозного экстремизма – Назарбаев' [Nazarbayev: It is necessary to deal with question of religious extremism], *Tengri News*, 6 March 2017, https://tengrinews.kz/kazakhstan_news/razobratsya-voprosom-religioznogo-ekstremizma-nazarbaev-313611/.

9   Felix Corley, 'Kazakhstan: five years jail, three year ban', Forum 18, 3 May 2017, www.forum18.org/archive.php?article_id=2277.

10 'USCIRF urges the Kazakh government to release two activists', United States Commission on International Religious Freedom, 25 July 2013, www.uscirf.gov/news-room/press-releases/uscirf-urges-the-kazakh-government-release-two-activists.

11 Ibid.

12 'Kazakhstan escalates harassment of media, confines blogger to clinic', Reporters Without Borders, 4 April 2018, https://rsf.org/en/news/kazakhstan-escalates-harassment-media-confines-blogger-clinic.

13 Mushfig Bayram, 'Kazakhstan: criminal investigation, "hallucinogenic" communion wine, "extremist" books?', Forum 18, 19 October 2012, www.forum18.org/archive.php?article_id=1756.

14 Felix Corley, 'Kazakhstan: criminal conviction, large "moral damages" – and new criminal case?' Forum 18, 17 February 2014, www.forum18.org/archive.php?article_id=1929.

15 Bureau of National Statistics of the Agency for Strategic Planning and Reforms, https://stat.gov.kz/.

16 Kazis Toguzbayev, 'Прекращено первое дело правозащитника из Риддера Харламова' [First case of Ridder human rights defender Kharlamov closed], Radio Azattyq, 5 May 2018, https://rus.azattyq.org/a/29209799.html.

17 More information about the opening of the case can be found in Felix Corley, 'Kazakhstan: Atheist writer faces more criminal charges', Forum 18, 17 February 2017, http://www.forum18.org/archive.php?article_id=2258&layout_type=mobile; more detail about the closure of the case can be found idem., 'Kazakhstan: 22nd known 2017 criminal conviction', Forum 18, http://www.forum18.org/archive.php?article_id=2311k.

23. *Culture Wars*

1   'Рекламщики изобразили поцелуй Курмангазы и Пушкина' [Advertisers portray kiss of Kurmangazy and Pushkin], *Tengri News*, 25 August 2014, https://tengrinews.kz/strange_news/reklamschiki-izobrazili-potseluy-kurmangazyi-i-pushkina-260689/.

2   'Преступлением назвал министр культуры выпуск постера с поцелуем Курмангазы и Пушкина' [Minister of culture calls release of poster with Kurmangazy and Pushkin kiss a crime], *Tengri News*, 27 August 2014, https:/tengrinews.kz/picture_art/prestupleniem-nazval-ministr-kulturyi-vyipusk-postera-260867/.

3   'Постер с поцелуем Курмангазы и Пушкина возмутил российскую партию
      "Родина"' [Poster with Kurmangazy and Pushkin kiss angers Russian party
      'Rodina'], *Tengri News*, 26 August 2014, https://tengrinews.kz/strange_news/
      poster-potseluem-kurmangazyi-pushkina-vozmutil-rossiyskuyu-260787/.

4   'Kazakhstan: Lawsuits over same-sex kiss on poster', Human Rights Watch, 1 October
      2014, https://www.hrw.org/news/2014/10/01/kazakhstan-lawsuits-over-same-
      sex-kiss-poster.

5   Asel Asanova, 'Казахстанским геям хотят запретить работать в госаппарате
      и служить в армии' [They want to ban Kazakhstani gays from working in civil
      service and serving in army], *Zakon.kz*, 11 September 2014, https://www.zakon.
      kz/4652542-kazakhstanskim-gejam-khotjat-zapretit.html.

6   'В Казахстане депутаты предложили принять закон против гомосексуализма'
      [In Kazakhstan, deputies propose adopting law against homosexuality], *Kazakhstan
      Today*, 22 May 2013, http://www.kt.kz/rus/society/v_kazahstane_deputati_
      predlozhili_prinjatj_zakon_protiv_gomoseksualizma_1153572508.html.

7   'Противодействовать однополым бракам предложил казахстанский депутат'
      [Kazakhstani deputy proposes counteracting same-sex marriages], *Tengri News*,
      17 May 2013, https://tengrinews.kz/kazakhstan_news/protivodeystvovat-
      odnopolyim-brakam-predlojil-kazahstanskiy-234272/.

8   Legislation to 'root out homosexual relations': 'Законопроект против
      гомосексуальных отношений предложил разработать мажилисмен'
      [Parliamentarian proposes drafting bill against homosexual relations], *Tengri News*,
      2 October 2013, https://tengrinews.kz/kazakhstan_news/zakonoproekt-protiv-
      gomoseksualnyih-otnosheniy-predlojil-242764/; other quotes from Smagul: Joanna
      Lillis, 'Kazakhstan's parliament hears another call for anti-gay law', *Eurasianet*, 2
      October 2013, https://eurasianet.org/node/67576.

9   Idem, 'Kazakhstan says no to gays in military', *Eurasianet*, 13 June 2012, http://
      www.eurasianet.org/node/65533.

10   Will Kohler, 'Call Borat! – Kazakhstan considering copying Russia's anti-gay laws',
      Back2Stonewall, 20 August 2013, www.back2stonewall.com/2013/08/call-borat-
      kazakhstan-copying-russias-anti-gay-laws.html.

11   'Запрет пропаганды гомосексуализма среди детей поддержали казахстанские
      сенаторы' [Kazakhstani senators support ban on propaganda of homosexuality
      among children], *Tengri News*, 19 February 2015, https://tengrinews.kz/
      kazakhstan_news/zapret-propagandyi-gomoseksualizma-sredi-detey-podderjali-
      270361/.

12   For more on Kazakhstan's efforts to promote its image abroad, see: Paul Bartlett,
      'Kazakhstan going into soft power overdrive', *Eurasianet*, 6 February 2017, https://
      eurasianet.org/s/kazakhstan-going-into-soft-power-overdrive.

13   Joanna Lillis, 'Kazakhstan strikes down "gay propaganda" law after Olympics outcry',
      Eurasianet, 27 May 2015, https://eurasianet.org/s/kazakhstan-strikes-down-gay-
      propaganda-law-after-olympics-outcry.

14   Vitaliy Portnikov, 'Постер "Курмангазы–Пушкин" обернулся эмиграцией'
      [Kurmangazy–Pushkin poster ends in emigration], Radio Azattyq, 13 July 2015,
      https://rus.azattyq.org/a/darija-hamitzhanova-emigratsiya-potselui-kurmangazy-
      pushkin/27123305.html.

24. *The Curse of Corruption*

1   Ilan Greenberg, 'Doctors, and a medical procedure, on trial in Kazakhstan', *New York Times*, 20 March 2007, http://www.nytimes.com/2007/03/20/world/asia/20kazakhstan.html?module=ArrowsNav&contentCollection=Asia%20Pacific&action=keypress&region=FixedLeft&pgtype=article.

2   Maria Golovnina, 'Health workers jailed in Kazakh baby AIDS death case', Reuters, 27 June 2007, https://www.reuters.com/article/idUSL27767557.

3   Joanna Lillis, 'HIV trial spotlights fight against AIDS', IRIN, 6 March 2007, http://www.irinnews.org/printreport.aspx?reportid=70532.

4   'Назарбаев о борьбе с коррупцией: "Крыши" здесь не будет' [Nazarbayev on fight against corruption: There will be no 'protection' here], *Tengri News*, 1 July 2015, https://tengrinews.kz/kazakhstan_news/nazarbaev-o-borbe-s-korruptsiey-kryishi-zdes-ne-budet-277103/.

5   'Национальный доклад о противодействии коррупции' [National report on combating corruption], Agency of the Republic of Kazakhstan for Civil Service Affairs and Anti-Corruption, 27 April 2017, http://kyzmet.gov.kz/ru/pages/nacionalnyy-doklad-o-protivodeystvii-korrupcii.

6   'Не менее 1 млн тенге взятки получили госслужащие РК' [At least 1 million tenge in bribes received by civil servants of Republic of Kazakhstan], *Kazinform*, 20 July 2017, http://www.inform.kz/ru/ne-menee-1-mln-tenge-vzyatki-poluchili-gossluzhaschie-rk_a3047142.

7   'За чистоту власти' [For purity of government], *Izvestiya*, 6 May 2002, https://iz.ru/news/261575.

8   'Осужден бывший председатель Туркестанского городского суда' [Former chairman of Turkestan town court convicted], *Tengri News*, 15 January 2018, https://tengrinews.kz/crime/osujden-byivshiy-predsedatel-turkestanskogo-gorodskogo-suda-335418/.

9   Miranda Patrucic, Vlad Lavrov and Ilya Lozovsky, 'Kazakhstan's secret billionaires', Organized Crime and Corruption Reporting Project, 5 November 2017, https://www.occrp.org/en/paradisepapers/kazakhstans-secret-billionaires.

10 Amirzhan Kosanov, 'Kazakhstan's thin red line', openDemocracy, 12 December 2016, www.opendemocracy.net/od-russia/amirzhan-kosanov/kazakhstan-s-thin-red-line.

11 Ron Stodghill, 'Oil, cash and corruption', *New York Times*, 5 November 2006, www.nytimes.com/2006/11/05/business/yourmoney/05giffen.html.

12 'Kazakhstan economic and energy update, April 29–May 12, 2007', WikiLeaks, 28 May 2007, https://wikileaks.org/plusd/cables/07ASTANA1430_a.html.

13 Colby Pacheco and Swathi Balasubramanian, 'Achieving development impact with an inclusive asset-return model', IREX, 2015, https://www.irex.org/sites/default/files/node/resource/bota-case-study-executive-summary.pdf.

14 Eurocopter Group bung: see Yann Philippin, 'Les 12 millions d'euros d'Airbus pour le Premier Ministre Kazakh' [Airbus's 12 million euros for Kazakh prime minister], *Mediapart*, 31 May 2016, www.mediapart.fr/journal/france/310516/les-12-millions-d-euros-d-airbus-pour-le-premier-ministre-kazakh?onglet=full, and Sara Ghibaudo, 'Le patron d'Airbus plonge dans la tempête judiciaire', [Airbus boss plunges into legal storm], France Inter, 23 November 2017, https://www.franceinter.fr/emissions/le-zoom-de-la-redaction/le-zoom-de-la-redaction-23-novembre-2017; investigation ongoing in mid-2021: '"Kazakhgate": un ex-cadre d'Airbus et un intermédiaire mis en

examen' ['Kazakhgate': a former Airbus executive and an intermediary placed under formal investigation], *Paris Normandie*, 7 July 2021, https://www.paris-normandie.fr/id210577/article/2021-07-07/kazakhgate-un-ex-cadre-dairbus-et-un-intermediaire-mis-en-examen. Rolls Royce bribes for deals: Sarah N. Lynch, 'U.S. Justice Department unseals charges in Rolls-Royce Holdings foreign bribery case', Reuters, 7 November 2017, https://www.reuters.com/article/us-rolls-royce-hldg-corruption/u-s-justice-department-unseals-charges-in-rolls-royce-holdings-foreign-bribery-case-idUSKBN1D7345.

15 'Kazakhstan's former prime minister released from prison early', Radio Free Europe/Radio Liberty, 21 September 2017, https://www.rferl.org/a/kazakhstan-akhmetov-released-from-prison-early-/28748592.html.

16 Asel Satayeva, 'Талгат Ермегияев осужден на 14 лет' [Talgat Yermegiyayev sentenced to 14 years], *Tengri News*, 9 June 2016, https://tengrinews.kz/kazakhstan_news/talgat-ermegiyaev-osujden-na-14-let-296150/.

17 Dana Kruglova, '"Чёрного генерала" Амирхана Аманбаева приговорили к 14 годам лишения свободы' ['Black General' Amirkhan Amanbayev sentenced to 14 years in prison], *Informbyuro*, 22 February 2017, https://informburo.kz/novosti/chyornogo-generala-amirhana-amanbaeva-prigovorili-k-14-godam-lisheniya-svobody.html.

18 Anna Babinets, 'State weapons exporter caught in cross-border bribery scandal', Organized Crime and Corruption Reporting Project, 13 December 2013, https://www.occrp.org/en/daily/28-ccwatch/cc-watch-indepth/2261-state-weapons-exporter-caught-in-cross-border-bribery-scandal.

19 Aynur Kaipova, 'Досрочное освобождение генерала-коррупционера: адвокаты ищут логику в происходящем' [Corrupt general's early release: lawyers seek logic in what happened], *Informbyuro*, 7 September 2016, https://informburo.kz/novosti/dosrochnoe-osvobozhdenie-generala-korrupcionera-advokaty-ishchut-logiku-v-proishodyashchem-.html.

20 Matt Reynolds, '9th circuit revives Kazakh city's fraud case against ex-mayor', *Courthouse News Service*, 31 March 2017, www.courthousenews.com/9th-circuit-revives-kazakh-citys-fraud-case-ex-mayor/.

21 Nancy Trejos, 'Trump name comes off New York hotel', *USA Today*, 21 December 2017 (updated 22 December 2017), https://www.usatoday.com/story/travel/roadwarriorvoices/2017/12/21/trump-name-comes-off-new-york-hotel/974010001/.

22 Gabrielle Paluch, Kevin G. Hall and Ben Wieder, 'A Kazakh dirty-money suit threatens to reach Trump's business world', McClatchy DC, 30 May 2017 (updated 16 June 2017), www.mcclatchydc.com/news/nationworld/national/article152934589.html

23 'Kazakhstan: New cabinet to maintain policy course', WikiLeaks, 16 January 2007, https://wikileaks.org/plusd/cables/07ASTANA125_a.html.

24 Manshuk Asautay, 'Виктора Храпунова заочно приговорили к 17 годам тюрьмы' [Viktor Khrapunov sentenced *in absentia* to 17 years in prison], Radio Azattyq, 8 October 2018, https://rus.azattyq.org/a/kazakhstan-almaty-former-mayor-khapunov-sentence/29532219.html

25 'Kazakh political exile Khrapunov gets asylum in Switzerland', *Swissinfo.ch*, 7 January 2021, https://www.swissinfo.ch/eng/kazakh-political-exile-khrapunov-gets-asylum-in-switzerland/46268342.

26 Cristina Maza, 'Kazakh who allegedly laundered money through Trump Tower ordered to pay bank back', *Newsweek*, 23 August 2018, https://www.

newsweek.com/british-high-court-backs-banks-case-against-kazakhs-who-allegedlylaundered-1088665.

27 'Назарбаев об оффшорах' [Nazarbayev on offshore accounts] [video], Tengri TV. Available on YouTube (uploaded 25 April 2013), https://www.youtube.com/watch?v=1i2wBeLzR3A.

28 Nurali Aliyev assets: Vlad Lavrov and Irene Velska, 'Kazakhstan: President's grandson hid assets offshore', Organized Crime and Corruption Reporting Project, 4 April 2016, www.occrp.org/en/panamapapers/kazakh-presidents-grandson-offshores/; Dariga Nazarbayeva assets: Ryan Chittum and Will Fitzgibbon, 'New Panama Papers leak reveals fresh financial secrets', Organized Crime and Corruption Reporting Project, 20 June 2018, https://www.occrp.org/en/panamapapers/new-panama-papers-leak-reveals-fresh-financial-secrets.

29 'Kazakh family win Unexplained Wealth Order battle over London homes', BBC News, 8 April 2020, https://www.bbc.co.uk/news/uk-52216011.

30 Dinara and Timur Kulibayev shared wealth: 'The world's billionaires', Forbes, https://www.forbes.com/billionaires/list/4/#version:static; Dariga Nazarbayeva fortune: '50 богатейших людей Казахстана – 2012' [50 richest people in Kazakhstan – 2012], Forbes Kazakhstan, May 2012, https://forbes.kz/ranking/50_bogateyshih_lyudey_kazahstana_-_2012; out-of-court settlement between Bolat and ex-wife: Chava Gourarie, 'Kazakh tycoon lists Plaza apartment for $18m', The Real Deal, 14 October 2016, https://therealdeal.com/2016/10/14/kazakh-tycoon-lists-plaza-apartment-for-18m/.

31 'OIG investigation in Kazakhstan', Global Fund, 28 January 2015, www.theglobalfund.org/en/oig/updates/2015-01-28-oig-investigation-in-kazakhstan/.

32 Email to the author from the communications department of the Global Fund, 6 March 2017.

33 Almaz Kumenov, 'Kazakhstan: Former health minister arrested', Eurasianet, 3 November 2020, https://eurasianet.org/kazakhstan-former-health-minister-arrested.

34 'Kazakhstan is awash in fake vaccination passports', The Economist, 24 July 2021, https://www.economist.com/asia/2021/07/24/kazakhstan-is-awash-in-fake-vaccination-passports.

25. The Shrinking Sea

1 Figures quoted in this paragraph are combined from three different sources: Phillip Whish-Wilson, 'The Aral Sea environmental health crisis', Journal of Rural and Remote Environmental Health i/2 (2002), pp. 29–34, http://jrtph.jcu.edu.au/vol/vo1whish.pdf; Behzod Gaybullaev, Su-Chin Chen and Yi-Ming Kuo, 'Water volume and salinity forecasts of the Small Aral Sea for the years 2025', Journal of Chinese Soil and Water Conservation xliv/3 (2013), pp. 265–70, http://www.cswcs.org.tw/AllDataPos/JournalPos/VOL44/NO3/jcswc44(3)265_270_08.pdf; and 'The Kazakh miracle: Recovery of the North Aral Sea', Environment News Service, 1 August 2008, http://www.ens-newswire.com/ens/aug2008/2008-08-01-01.html.

2 Vladimir Lenin, 'Письмо В.И.Ленина Рыбакам Аральского Моря' [Letter from V. I. Lenin to fishermen of Aral Sea], 7 October 1921. The letter can be read at http://aralsk-6.narod.ru/Lenin-s-letter.htm.

3 'Contaminated water devastates health across the Aral Sea region', Food and Agriculture Organization of the United Nations, 17 January 1997, www.fao.org/News/1997/970104-e.htm.

4 'Implementation status & results, Kazakhstan, Syr Darya Control & Northern Aral Sea Phase I Project (P046045)', World Bank. Available at http://documents.worldbank.org/curated/en/303701468753338067/pdf/P046045oISRoDio22020101292883938609.pdf.

5 'Рыбу из Аральского моря начали поставлять в Брюссель' [Fish from Aral Sea started being supplied to Brussels], *Tengri News*, 25 December 2015, https://tengrinews.kz/kazakhstan_news/ryibu-iz-aralskogo-morya-nachali-postavlyat-v-bryussel-286327/.

6 'Аральское море или Аралкум? Что происходит с озером сегодня' [Aral Sea or Aral desert? What is happening with the lake today], *Tengri News*, 9 August 2019, https://tengrinews.kz/kazakhstan_news/aralskoe-more-ili-aralkum-chto-proishodit-s-ozerom-segodnya-375780/.

7 'Implementation status & results, Kazakhstan'.

8 Stephen M. Bland, 'Kazakhstan: Measuring the Northern Aral's comeback', *Eurasianet*, 27 January 2015, https://eurasianet.org/s/kazakhstan-measuring-the-northern-arals-comeback.

9 'Рыбу из Аральского моря начали поставлять в Брюссель'.

10 Behzod Gaybullaev, Su-Chin Chen and Yi-Ming Kuo, 'Water volume and salinity forecasts of the Small Aral Sea for the years 2025', *Journal of Chinese Soil and Water Conservation* xliv/3 (2013), pp. 265–70.

26. The Wasteland

1 'Глава государства выступил на торжественном мероприятии в честь 20-летия прекращения испытаний на Семипалатинском ядерном полигоне' [Head of state speaks at ceremonial event in honour of 20th anniversary of end to tests at Semipalatinsk nuclear test site], *Zakon.kz*, 18 June 2009, https://www.zakon.kz/141107-glava-gosudarstva-vystupil-na.html.

2 'International Day Against Nuclear Tests', United Nations (undated), http://www.un.org/en/events/againstnucleartestsday/history.shtml.

3 Reid Standish, 'Meet the Central Asian nation trying to benefit from the Iran nuclear deal', *Foreign Policy*, 1 April 2016, http://foreignpolicy.com/2016/04/01/meet-the-central-asian-nation-trying-to-benefit-from-the-iran-nuclear-deal-kazakhstan-russia/.

4 Rustam Qobil, 'Soviet-era nuclear testing is still making people sick in Kazakhstan', Public Radio International, 13 March 2017, www.pri.org/stories/2017-03-13/soviet-era-nuclear-testing-still-making-people-sick-kazakhstan.

5 Skype interview with author, 3 August 2016.

6 A. Akanov, S. Yamashita, S. Merimanov, A. Indershyiev and A. Musakhanova, *Nuclear Explosions and Public Health Development* (Nagasaki-Almaty, 2008), quoted by Togzhan Kassenova in 'The lasting toll of Semipalatinsk's nuclear testing', *Bulletin of the Atomic Scientists*, 28 September 2009, http://thebulletin.org/lasting-toll-semipalatinsks-nuclear-testing.

7 Email to author, 23 March 2016.

8 'Еще несколько поколений казахстанцев будут ощущать на себе последствия ядерных испытаний – Назарбаев' [Several more generations of Kazakhstanis will feel the consequences of nuclear tests – Nazarbayev], *Tengri News*, 29 August 2016, https://tengrinews.kz/kazakhstan_news/neskolko-pokoleniy-kazahstantsev-budut-oschuschat-sebe-301199/.

9 'Глава государства выступил на торжественном мероприятии в честь 20-летия прекращения испытаний на Семипалатинском ядерном полигоне' [Head of state speaks at ceremonial event in honour of 20th anniversary of end to tests at Semipalatinsk nuclear test site].

10 Anastasiya Mikhaylova, 'Осторожно, плутоний: Более 20 тыс лет потребуется для полного распада химэлемента на полигоне Семея' [Careful, plutonium: more than 20,000 years needed for the total decay of chemical elements at Semey *polygon*], *New Times*, 28 June 2021, https://newtimes.kz/eksklyuziv/132025-ostorozhno-plutonii-bolee-20-tys-let-potrebuetsia-dlia-polnogo-raspada-khimelimenta-na-poligone-semeia.

11 'The Semipalatinsk test site, Kazakhstan', International Atomic Energy Agency, updated 9 December 2014, www-ns.iaea.org/appraisals/semipalatinsk.asp.

12 Joanna Lillis, 'Kazakhstan: Astana takes the lead in lobbying for nuclear-free world', *Eurasianet*, 14 July 2009, https://eurasianet.org/s/kazakhstan-astana-takes-the-lead-in-lobbying-for-nuclear-free-world.

13 Joanna Lillis, 'Kazakhstan: Grieving families count human cost of coronavirus', *Eurasianet*, 20 July 2020, https://eurasianet.org/kazakhstan-grieving-families-count-human-cost-of-coronavirus.

14 Interview over WhatsApp with author, 9 July 2020.

28. The Slumbering Steppe

1 Joanna Lillis, 'Kazakhstan: The slumbering steppe', *Eurasianet*, 12 March 2015, https://eurasianet.org/s/kazakhstan-the-slumbering-steppe.

2 Petr Trotsenko, 'Доброе утро, Калачи: как живет село после «сонной болезни»' [Good morning, Kalachi: how the village is living after the 'sleeping sickness'], Radio Azattyq, 21 September 2020, https://rus.azattyq.org/a/kazakhstan-akmola-regoin-kalachi-reportage/30845602.html.

3 'Тайна раскрыта: почему жители поселка Калачи в Казахстане впадают в спячку' [Secret uncovered: why inhabitants of village of Kalachi in Kazakhstan fall into slumber], *Novosti OON*, 21 June 2016, https://news.un.org/ru/audio/2016/06/1034511#.WT-10OuGNow.

29. The Collective Farm

1 Tulegen Darbasov, 'Срубленная лоза' [Felled vine], *Forbes Kazakhstan*, April 2014, https://forbes.kz/finances/markets/srublennaya_loza.

2 'Министр государственных доходов Казахстана признался, что скрывал свои доходы от налогов' [Kazakhstan's minister of state revenues admits he concealed his revenue from taxes], Radio Svoboda, 6 July 2001, www.svoboda.org/a/24123959.html.

3   'Blocking of news website and detention of journalists in Kazakhstan of grave concern, says OSCE Representative on Freedom of the Media', Organisation for Security and Co-operation in Europe, 5 April 2018, https://www.osce.org/representative-on-freedom-of-media/376966.

4   'Дело «Какимжанов против СМИ»: журналисты дошли до ООН' ["Kakimzhanov against media" case: journalists go to UN], *Forbes Kazakhstan*, 8 January 2019, https://forbes.kz/massmedia/delo_kakimjanov_protiv_smi_jurnalistyi_doshli_do_oon/?utm_source=forbes&utm_medium=themes.

Bibliography

Abilov, Bolat, Oraz Zhandosov, Tulegen Zhukeyev, Berik Abdygaliyev, Nurlan Zhuma-khan, Bolatbek Korpebayuly and Aydos Sarym, *Желтоксан-86: Статьи и публикации за 1986–1995* [*Zheltoksan-86: Articles and publications 1986–1995*] (Almaty, 2006).

Aitken, Jonathan, *Nazarbayev and the Making of Kazakhstan* (London/New York, 2009).

Applebaum, Anne, *Gulag: A History of the Soviet Camps* (London, 2004).

——— *Red Famine: Stalin's War on Ukraine* (London, 2017).

Auezov, Mukhtar, *Путь Абая* [*The Way of Abay*] (Almaty, 2013).

Cooley, Alexander and John Heathershaw, *Dictators Without Borders: Power and Money in Central Asia* (New Haven, CT and London, 2017).

Dave, Bhavna, *Kazakhstan: Ethnicity, Language and Power* (London, 2007).

Frankopan, Peter, *The Silk Roads: A New History of the World* (London, 2015).

Halperin, Charles, *Russia and the Golden Horde: The Mongol Impact on Medieval Russian History* (Bloomington, IN, 1987).

Hopkirk, Peter, *Setting the East Ablaze: On Secret Service in Bolshevik Asia* (Oxford, 1984).

——— *The Great Game: On Secret Service in High Asia* (Oxford 1990).

Kairbekova, Rozaliya, Olga Pak and Dmitriy Ulyanov, *История Казахстана в таблицах и схемах* [*History of Kazakhstan in Tables and Charts*] (Almaty, 2015).

LeVine, Steve, *The Oil and the Glory: The Pursuit of Empire and Fortune on the Caspian Sea* (London, 2007).

Maclean, Fitzroy, *Eastern Approaches* (London, 1949).

Marshall, Alex, *Republic or Death! Travels in Search of National Anthems* (London, 2015).

Meyer, Karl E. and Shareen Blair Brysac, *Tournament of Shadows: The Great Game and the Race for Empire in Asia* (London, 2001).

Murray, Craig, *Murder in Samarkand* (Edinburgh, 2006).

Nazarbayev, Nursultan, *Без Правых и Левых* [*Without Right and Left*] (Moscow, 1991).

Nurtazina, Nazira, 'Great Famine of 1931–1933 in Kazakhstan: A contemporary's reminiscences', *Acta Slavica Iaponica* 32 (2012), pp. 105–21.

Rappaport, Helen, *Ekaterinburg: The Last Days of the Romanovs* (London, 2008).

Roy, Olivier, *The New Central Asia: The Creation of Nations* (London, 2000).

Rywkin, Michael, *Moscow's Muslim Challenge: Soviet Central Asia* (London, 1990).

Satpayev, Dosym and Yerbol Zhumagulov, *Легенда о «Nomenclatura»* [*Legend about the 'Nomenclatura'*] (Almaty, 2009).

Satpayev, Dosym, Tolganay Umbetaliyeva, Andrey Chebotaryov, Rasul Zhumaly, Rustem Kadyrzhanov, Zamir Karazhanov, Aydos Sarym and Ayman Zhusupova,

«*Сумеречная зона*» *или* «*ловушки*» *переходного периода* [*The 'Twilight Zone' or the 'Pitfalls' of the Transition Period*] (Almaty, 2013).

Schatz, Edward, *Modern Clan Politics: The Power of 'Blood' in Kazakhstan and Beyond* (Seattle, 2004).

Shayakhmetov, Mukhamet, *The Silent Steppe* (London, 2006).

Solzhenitsyn, Aleksandr, *One Day in the Life of Ivan Denisovich* (London, 1963).

—— *The First Circle* (London, 1968).

—— *The Gulag Archipelago, 1918–1956: An Experiment in Literary Investigation* (New York, 1974).

Soucek, Svat, *A History of Inner Asia* (Cambridge, 2000).

Teissier, Beatrice, *Russian Frontiers: Eighteenth-Century British Travellers in the Caspian, Caucasus and Central Asia* (Oxford, 2011).

Yelubay, Smagul, *Lonely Yurt* (New York, 2016).

Yesenberlin, Ilyas, *Кочевники* [*Nomads*] (Almaty, 2005).

Acknowledgements

First and foremost, I would like to thank the people of Kazakhstan who have so generously shared with me the stories that make up this book. They are too numerous to thank individually, but I am especially grateful to those who told me their emotionally heart-rending life stories: Mayra and Zhannur Zhumageldina and Berik Syzdykov and his mother Zina Syzdykova, who live every day of their lives with the devastating consequences of Soviet nuclear testing; Nurziya Kazhibayeva, who survived the 1930s famine, and her daughter Nazira Nurtazina; Polina Ibrayeva, a deportee from Chechnya, and her son Ansar Ibrayev; Svetlana Tynybekova, whose grandparents were victims of Stalin's Terror; Talgat Ryskulbekov, Gulbakhram Zhunis and all the others who recounted their memories of the *Zheltoksan* protests of 1986; the oil workers of Zhanaozen; and the families of HIV-infected children in southern Kazakhstan. My thanks go to all other interviewees and all the people who have informed my reporting on Kazakhstan over the last 17 years by sharing insights and expertise. Any mistakes in the book are my own.

I thank Tomasz Hoskins, commissioning editor, for proposing the idea of this book and encouraging it through to completion, and the rest of the team at I.B. Tauris and Bloomsbury for their hard work to bring *Dark Shadows* to publication, especially David Campbell and Sara Magness, the production editors, Alex Billington, the project manager, Nayiri Kendir, assistant editor, Sophie Campbell, production manager, and Sarah Terry, the eagle-eyed copy-editor, who introduced numerous improvements into the text. Thanks also go to Viswasirasini Govindarajan and the team at Integra Software Services for stewarding the paperback to publication.

I would like to thank the Ministry of Foreign Affairs of the Republic of Kazakhstan and its Press Service for their cooperation and support over the years that I have been accredited to work as a journalist in the country.

Some of the reporting in this book would not have been possible without the *Eurasianet* website, an invaluable news outlet with a profound commitment to publishing in-depth reporting on the under-reported region of Central Asia. *Eurasianet* has not only published stories that would otherwise never have reached an audience, it has also funded trips to far-flung places that resulted in on-the-ground reporting for this book. I would like to extend my thanks to my editors Justin Burke, David Trilling and Peter Leonard. I would also like to thank Open Society Foundations, whose support for independent media in parts of the world where it is embattled allows important stories to reach the public eye.

I would like to thank Shaun Greaves, Lara Greaves and Sandy Forrester for reading chapters and providing invaluable feedback and suggestions. I would like to thank my mother, Arline Gaskell, for driving me and my sisters to France in her blue Mini for holidays when we were children and sparking my fascination with travel and languages; my father, Kevin Lillis, for exotic trips; and my mother and father for teaching me the value of a good education and always supporting my choices. Thanks to my sister Sandy for constant pep talks during the writing of this book, and my sister Cathy for her offers of proofreading.

I would like to thank Naubet Bisenov, my (voluntary) research assistant, who has done more than I have space to list: interpreting, translating and transliterating; researching enigmatic facts and sharing insightful ideas; casting a hypercritical eye over reams of copy and correcting my mistakes (in no uncertain terms); and sharing laughs and escapades on travels around Kazakhstan, China and Mongolia. He has given unstintingly of his time and encyclopaedic knowledge and I am grateful for his expertise, his generosity and especially his friendship. I would like to thank all friends in Kazakhstan and Uzbekistan for fun times and firm friendships that have withstood difficult tests.

Finally, I thank Paul Bartlett, who has shared with me the experiences recounted in this book and many more adventures in our years living in Kazakhstan, Uzbekistan and Russia. He has been the most enthusiastic and energetic champion of *Dark Shadows* from the outset, and an unflinching rock of support when the going got tough. Paul spent many hours teasing out the themes and coaxing out the content – sometimes word by word. Without his indefatigable encouragement, this book would never have seen the light of day. As well as providing extensive assistance with research and ideas, he read many drafts and offered shrewd suggestions, judicious changes of emphasis and incisive interpretations of the improbable, incredible and sometimes perplexing events that have unfolded around us in Kazakhstan over the years. When events have cast dark shadows over a country that I love, Paul's unflagging support and pungent sense of the ridiculous have lifted my mood.

Index